INTERPRETING AND ANALYZING

FINANCIAL STATEMENTS

A PROJECT-BASED APPROACH

SIXTH EDITION

KAREN P. SCHOENEBECK

MARK P. HOLTZMAN

Editor in Chief: Donna Battista
Director, Product Development: Ashley Santora
Editorial Project Manager: Christina Rumbaugh
Editorial Assistant: Jane Avery and Lauren Zanedis
Director of Marketing: Maggie Moylan Leen
Marketing Manager: Alison Haskins
Production Project Manager: Clara Bartunek
Cover Designer: Suzanne Behnke
Cover Image: FikMik / Fotolia.com
Printer/Binder: LSC Communications
Cover Printer: LSC Communications

Credits and acknowledgments borrowed from other sources and reproduced, with permission, in this textbook appear on appropriate page within text.

Many of the designations by manufacturers and seller to distinguish their products are claimed as trademarks. Where those designations appear in this book, and the publisher was aware of a trademark claim, the designations have been printed in initial caps or all caps.

Library of Congress Cataloging-in-Publication Data is available.

28 17

www.pearsonhighered.com

ISBN 10: 0-13-274624-7
ISBN 13: 978-0-13-274624-3

TABLE OF CONTENTS

CHAPTER 1—INTRODUCTION

Nike, Under Armour, Adidas

CHAPTER 2—BALANCE SHEET

The Walt Disney Company, News Corp, Time Warner

CHAPTER 3—INCOME STATEMENT

Amazon.com, Sears Holdings, eBay, Starbucks

CHAPTER 4—STATEMENT OF STOCKHOLDERS' EQUITY

Freeport-McMoRan Copper & Gold

CHAPTER 5—STATEMENT OF CASH FLOWS

Cedar Fair, L.P.

CHAPTER 6—SPECIFIC ACCOUNTS

Research in Motion Limited, Motorola Mobility, Inc.

CHAPTER 7—THE ACCOUNTING CYCLE

CHAPTER 8—COMPREHENSIVE REVIEW

CHAPTER 9—CAPSTONE PROJECT

PREFACE

This book introduces a financial statement analysis approach to the first course in accounting. As we developed this new approach, we identified two fundamental skills that students should learn in the first accounting course. **First, business students should be able to analyze a company's annual report and conclude as to its profitability, efficiency, liquidity, and solvency. Second, students should be able to record basic debit–credit journal entries and prepare simple financial statements.** The traditional first course in financial accounting emphasizes building students' knowledge of different kinds of transactions and accounts. While retaining the course content that has been collectively developed by the Academy over many decades, we shifted the emphasis of the course toward building students' skills first in financial statement analysis, as analysis takes time to develop, and second in transaction analysis. As such, the redesigned course that we present in this book appeals to the needs and interests of today's students, fits beautifully into the standard curriculum, and is a joy for the experienced instructor to teach.

INCREASED STUDENT MOTIVATION

After we redesigned the first course in accounting with these goals in mind, teacher-course evaluations improved. Students appreciated acquiring skills needed in the real business world. They enjoyed analyzing real companies' financial statements, thinking about whether or not these companies would make good investments. And at the end of the course, they had less trouble learning the accounting cycle, with debits and credits. Our students enjoy the redesigned course, it arouses their curiosity, and it helps motivate them to learn more. **Accounting majors go into Intermediate Accounting with a firm foundation in understanding the financial statements, their uses, and the debit–credit system.** Other business majors finish the course understanding how to read and analyze the "language" of accounting.

In the first part of the course, students learn the contents of the four financial statements and how to analyze them for profitability, efficiency, liquidity, and solvency. **As they learn these skills, using the financial statements of real companies that they might already be familiar with, students can immediately grasp the importance of the lessons, and their applicability to the real world.** The emphasis is on building students' analytical skills, rather than rote calculations, so that students can begin to understand the appropriate ranges for different financial analysis ratios.

THE CURRICULUM

We have taught this course with many of the innovative methods developed over the past 20 years. We found that what became known as the "user approach" was still transaction-based. Whether students used debits and credits in journal entries, or inventive new charts, the focus of the course was still on teaching students how transactions affect accounts. Furthermore, under a transaction-based approach, students get little exposure to analyzing profitability, efficiency, liquidity, and solvency. These fundamental concepts should be understood by all business students, in all majors.

With the fundamental goals of the course redesigned, building a firm foundation in the accounting cycle, with debits and credits, builds up students' skills for intermediate accounting and what follows.

Furthermore, accounting students understand how to analyze financial statements, a powerful conceptual base for future professionals. Non-accounting majors also have the skills to understand how to read and analyze financial statements. They can better understand how to speak in the "language of business." This helps them in other business courses. Our finance faculty have remarked how, after our course redesign, students seem better prepared for finance classes.

We also took this opportunity to fully integrate International Financial Reporting Standards (IFRS) into the course. As examples, we use many international companies that are based outside the United States, such as Adidas, Anheuser-Busch InBev, Lenovo Group, and Research in Motion. Furthermore, the chapters explain where U.S. GAAP and IFRS differ.

ENJOYABLE TO TEACH

We love teaching accounting this way. We get great satisfaction from helping students learn to improve their analytical skills. We like to challenge them to think about difficult problems that have no clear solution. We also feel that we can draw on our full depth of knowledge about accounting, our creativity, and our experience to develop compelling and enjoyable classroom sessions. Most importantly, we feel confident that our approach is comprehensive. It's not watered-down. It includes almost all of the topics included in the traditional first course in accounting. The few topics we omitted, such as bond amortization and special journals, are generally better learned in intermediate and bookkeeping courses.

We found that debits and credits are much easier for students to learn at the end of the course, after they are already familiar with asset, liability, equity, revenue, and expense accounts. At this point in the course, it is almost a trivial exercise for most students to learn to prepare financial statements. This cuts out much of the rote memorization that students must otherwise go through at the beginning of the course to learn how to record journal entries and prepare financial statements.

THE CHAPTERS

NEW in this Edition … crossword puzzles that reinforce accounting concepts and vocabulary. The common-size Statement of Cash Flows is now introduced in Chapter 5. Another comprehensive problem is added to Chapter 8 … Chipotle Mexican Grill. The Capstone Project is streamlined into only two activites, a written report and a presentation. Throughout the text, financial statements have been updated to the most current amounts available on December 31, 2011.

In Chapter 1, students immediately learn about the basic financial statements. At once they learn four basic financial analysis ratios, common-size analysis, and trend analysis. They will use these tools throughout the course. Chapters 2 through 5 cover the basic financial statements, with full chapters dedicated to the statement of cash flows and the statement of stockholders' equity. **Chapter 6 deals with topics that are traditionally covered in the first accounting course, such as inventory and property, plant, and equipment.** In Chapter 7, students learn the accounting cycle, with the debit–credit system, adjusting, and closing journal entries. Chapter 8 offers a comprehensive review of all topics covered in previous chapters. Activities walk students through financial analyses of real companies, working with more than one financial statement and combining issues in profitability, efficiency, liquidity, and solvency. Chapter 9 provides a project for each student to research, analyze, and prepare a comprehensive written report and presentation on the public corporation of their choice. To complete the project, each student obtains a copy of the corporate financial statements and utilizes a variety of resources. Because the company is the student's choice, interest is high and a quality product results. This project has several parts, which can be assigned throughout the semester or as a capstone project at the end.

The text and activities format allow the instructor to use this book as a stand-alone text for the first accounting course. The text sections are engaging to read but also provide students with a useful reference tool. The activity sections encourage students to learn accounting through real-life examples, to interact with the companies studied. Activities can be assigned for homework, given for small-group discussion, reviewed in lecture sessions, or a combination of the three. We like to assign them for home or in-class preparation, then have students compare answers, and then review the answers in class. Review exercises titled "Test Your Understanding" provide thorough comprehensive reviews that will build students' confidence.

One of the most powerful aspects of our course design is that it includes most of the classic elements of the traditional accounting course, while reordering the topics to emphasize financial statement analysis and decision making. We cover the financial statements, debits and credits, specific areas in the financial statements, such as inventory and depreciation of noncurrent assets, and financial statement analysis, including ratios, trend analysis, and common-size statements. We'd approximate that 90% of the curriculum in the typical first financial accounting course is right here in this book.

When implementing this text, faculty have many options. We recommend that faculty always include Chapters 1 (Introduction), 2 (Balance Sheet), and 3 (Income Statement). These form the fundamental core of the book. From here, faculty can choose to emphasize:

- The financial statements in Chapter 4 (Statement of Stockholders' Equity) and Chapter 5 (Statement of Cash Flow); Chapter 4 provides additional focus on stock and investment issues, while Chapter 5 helps students to understand concepts of cash flow and interactions among operating, investing, and financing activities.
- Accounting for different kinds of transactions in Chapter 6. This chapter covers cash, investments, receivables, inventory, noncurrent assets, liabilities, and stockholders' equity. Faculty can cover the entire chapter or specific sections.
- The accounting cycle in Chapter 7. Students learn the complete accounting cycle with debits and credits, journal entries, adjusting journal entries, financial statements, and closing entries.
- The comprehensive review in Chapter 8 ties together topics in all chapters.
- The capstone project in Chapter 9 is designed to help students integrate all of the topics learned in the course, using real companies of their choice. Each student prepares a financial statement analysis and ratio analysis of their company, researches news, stock market activity, prepares a written report, and delivers a presentation. Students can begin parts of the written activity after completing Chapter 1, completing more and more parts as the course progresses.

Have fun with this course! Integrate real-world numbers and actual companies into the classroom! Challenge your students to use accounting information to make decisions! Our students enjoy the redesigned course, and we hope that yours do too.

Please visit www.pearsonhighered.com to download the Solutions Manual that accompanies this text. Feel free to contact us with comments and questions. Our e-mail addresses are kaliforniakaren@gmail.com and mark.holtzman@shu.edu.

Karen P. Schoenebeck and Mark P. Holtzman, authors

ABOUT THE AUTHORS

Karen P. Schoenebeck, MBA, CPA, is a professor, consultant, practitioner, and author.

Karen is a licensed CPA with over 20 years of academic experience, undergraduate and graduate, national and international, and has been cited for outstanding teaching. She received her MBA from the University of Minnesota and is currently a Senior University Lecturer at New Jersey Institute of Technology.

She is president and founder of Two-Paved Roads, a consulting firm, served as Director of the MBA program at Southwestern College in Kansas, and is currently serving on the national board of directors for the Educational Foundation for Women in Accounting. As a Master Presenter for the Leadership Training Series and the Institute of Management Accountants (IMA) Leadership Academy she is a regular presenter at national and regional conferences.

Karen is a leader in curriculum redesign. Using her practical experience as a consultant, she brings real-world relevance into the accounting classroom for all business majors. Financial Statement Analysis is used to introduce financial accounting and decision making is the focus of managerial accounting.

In addition, Karen is an avid traveler, leading educational tours to Europe, Southeast Asia, and Egypt. She can be reached at kaliforniakaren@gmail.com.

Mark P. Holtzman, PhD, CPA is Associate Professor of Accounting and Chair of the Department of Accounting and Taxation at the Stillman School of Business, Seton Hall University, South Orange, New Jersey. After receiving a bachelor's degree in business administration at Hofstra University, he began his accounting career in the New York office of Deloitte & Touche. He later earned a PhD in accounting from The University of Texas at Austin. Dr. Holtzman has published articles in *Journal of Accountancy, CPA Journal, Research in Accounting Regulation, Advances in Accounting, Strategic Finance*, and *Accounting Historian's Journal*. He is a member of the American Accounting Association, the American Institute of Certified Public Accountants, and Financial Executives Institute. In his spare time, he enjoys blogging, studying Talmud, and hiking with his family. He can be reached at mark.holtzman@shu.edu. His blogs can be found at www.accountinator.com and www.freakingaccountant.com. His twitter handles are @accountinator and @freakingcpa.

DEDICATIONS

To Casey and Grant and my friends who encourage me to take chances.

—Karen P. Schoenebeck

To Rikki, Dovid, Aharon Yehuda, Levi Shalom, and Esther Chaya.

—Mark P. Holtzman

ACKNOWLEDGMENTS

WE WOULD LIKE TO THANK ...

The Pearson staff including Christina Rumbaugh and Deborah Hoffman who discovered Karen's materials and encouraged her to submit them for publishing.

To Karen Boroff, Reed Easton, David Gelb, Brian Greenstein, Theresa Henry, David Mest, Susan Pinto, Elven Riley, Jonathan Stout, Riad Twal, and Renee Weiss, who helped develop and implement the redesigned course, providing invaluable ideas and feedback.

Our students who provide continued opportunities for us to learn and are always ready to give honest and helpful feedback. Especially to Rachel Rasmussen, Michael Lelescu, Shalu Oza, Christie Deskiewicz, Chris Ives, Andrew Jurkiewicz, Scott King, Simin Ma, Michael Massood, Jacqueline Munguia, Brian Nelson, Michael Ojo, Mark Scimeca, and Drew Tomafsky for their help in preparing this text.

Our friends and family who continue to support our writing and encourage us to explore new endeavors.

Karen P. Schoenebeck and Mark P. Holtzman, authors

CHAPTER 1

INTRODUCTION

LEARNING OBJECTIVES

1. Understand what accounting is and why it is important.
2. Identify the four financial statements.
3. Explain the basic information provided by each financial statement.
4. Identify the elements of the financial statements.
5. Understand that accountants use Generally Accepted Accounting Principles (GAAP) when preparing financial statements and apply the historical cost principle.
6. Understand that U.S. companies may soon be required to use International Financial Reporting Standards (IFRS).
7. Compute and interpret basic financial statement ratios.
8. Prepare and interpret ratio, trend, and common-size analysis.

WHAT IS ACCOUNTING?

Look forward a few years. As you build a career you will accumulate savings to invest. After much research, suppose that you invest $100,000 of your savings in a new convenience store. You give the entrepreneur starting this business a $100,000 investment of equity, and she gives you stock certificates representing a 50% share in the business. After a year, you visit this entrepreneur and ask, "How's it going?"

What kind of answer would you expect? You would want facts and figures. How much money did the business receive this year? How much did it pay for expenses? How valuable are the assets that it owns? How much money does it owe? How much profit did it earn? How much salary did the entrepreneur receive? Are there any lawsuits?

You would need to converse in the language of accounting. **Accounting** is the system of recording, classifying, and reporting financial information. More importantly, it is the language for conducting business. Business people speak about revenues, expenses, net income, assets, liabilities, equity, and cash flow: all accounting terms. Learning accounting helps you learn the language of business, so that, if you invest in a business, you can understand how it presents its operations and financial position. If you are an entrepreneur, accounting gives you a language with which to present your performance to investors and creditors. If you are a manager, accounting allows you to measure the performance of your business and to make important decisions for it, such as purchasing machinery and compensating employees. Perhaps most importantly, investors rely on accounting information to make investment decisions. Based on financial statements, downloaded off the Internet, investors choose among a dizzying array of investments. Other investors read analyst reports, which are also based on financial statements.

This book will help you to learn how to interpret and analyze financial statements, allowing you to read almost any company's annual report in order to decide whether to invest in that company.

Companies present four basic financial statements:

1. Balance Sheet
2. Income Statement
3. Statement of Stockholders' Equity
4. Statement of Cash Flows

Each statement provides information about a different perspective of the company's finances.

What does the company own and who has claims against the company? The **BALANCE SHEET** provides a snapshot of a company's financial position as of a certain date. It reports **assets,** items of value such as inventory and equipment, and whether the assets are financed with **liabilities** (debts) or **stockholders' equity** (owners' shares).

BALANCE SHEET	
Assets	Liabilities
	Stockholders' equity

How profitable is the company? The **INCOME STATEMENT** reports the company's profitability during an accounting period. It reports **revenues,** amounts received from customers for products sold or services provided, and **expenses,** the costs incurred to produce revenues. Their difference is **net income** (also called **earnings**).

INCOME STATEMENT
Revenues
(Expenses)
Net income

Who owns the company? The **STATEMENT OF STOCKHOLDERS' EQUITY** reports if the **earnings** (net income) of this accounting period are distributed as **dividends** or retained in the business as **retained earnings.** It also reports amounts paid (contributed) to the company by stockholders to purchase common stock and preferred stock.

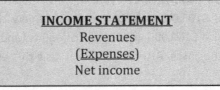

STATEMENT OF STOCKHOLDERS' EQUITY	
Retained earnings, beginning	Contributed capital, beginning
+ Net income	+ Issuance of shares
(Dividends)	(Repurchase to retire shares)
Retained earnings, ending	Contributed capital, ending

Does the company generate cash flow? The **STATEMENT OF CASH FLOWS** reports cash inflows and cash outflows during an accounting period.

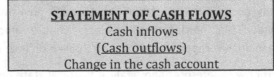

STATEMENT OF CASH FLOWS
Cash inflows
(Cash outflows)
Change in the cash account

Together, these four financial statements help investors understand a company's finances.

The Balance Sheet reports assets and the amount of assets financed with liabilities and stockholders' equity as of a certain date. It is based on the **accounting equation:**

$$\text{Assets} = \text{Liabilities} + \text{Stockholders' Equity}$$

In this chapter, we explore the financial statements of Nike, Inc.:

> *Nike is the largest seller of athletic footwear and athletic apparel in the world, selling in over 170 countries. Focus is on innovation and high-quality construction. It also markets apparel with licensed college team, professional team, and league logos. Almost all of Nike's products are manufactured by independent contractors and virtually all footwear and apparel products are produced outside the United States.*

Nike also sells products under the Cole Haan, Converse, Chuck Taylor, All Star, One Star, Jack Purcell, Hurley, and Umbro brands.

Here is Nike's May 31, 2011 Balance Sheet:

Nike (NKE) May 31, 2011 BALANCE SHEET ($ in millions)			
ASSETS		**LIABILITIES**	
Cash and cash equivalents	$ 1,955	Notes payable	$ 187
Short-term investments	2,583	Accounts payable	1,469
Accounts receivable, net	3,138	Other current liabilities	2,302
Inventories	2,715	Long-term debt	276
Other current assets	906	Other noncurrent liabilities	921
Property, plant, and equipment, net	2,115	Total liabilities	5,155
Goodwill and other intangibles	692	**STOCKHOLDERS' EQUITY**	
Other noncurrent assets	894	Contributed capital	3,947
		Retained earnings	5,801
		Other stockholders' equity	95
		Total SE	9,843
Total Assets	**$ 14,998**	**Total L & SE**	**$ 14,998**

ASSETS are items of value that a corporation has a right to use. Typical asset accounts include cash, accounts receivable, inventory, equipment, buildings, and land. **Accounts receivable** are amounts to be *received* in the future from customers.

Notice that Nike's largest reported asset is "accounts receivable, net" of $3,138 million. These are moneys that customers owe to Nike for items purchased. The second largest asset item is inventory, items held for sale to retailers, of $2,715 million. Nike had $1,955 million in cash on May 31, 2011.

Nike had $2,115 of property, plant, and equipment, which consist of land, buildings, vehicles, and other equipment. Because almost all of Nike's products are manufactured by independent contractors, it has not had to invest in factories to manufacture its own goods. Therefore, property, plant, and equipment is relatively low.

LIABILITIES are amounts owed to creditors; the amount of debt owed to third parties. Typical liability accounts include accounts payable, wages payable, notes payable, and bonds payable. The key word found in many liability accounts is *payable*. **Accounts Payable** are amounts that the corporation must pay to suppliers in the future. Accounts payable of $1,469 million was Nike's second-largest liability. The company's largest liability item was "other current liabilities" of $2,302 million.

STOCKHOLDERS' EQUITY is the portion of assets the owners own free and clear of any liabilities. Stockholders' equity may also be referred to as shareholders' equity or owners' equity.

Typical stockholders' equity accounts include:

> **Contributed Capital**—amounts paid-in (contributed) to the company by stockholders to purchase common stock and preferred stock.

> **Retained Earnings**—net income earned by the company since its incorporation and not yet distributed as dividends.

Since Nike opened in 1968, it received $3,947 million in investments from stockholders. The retained earnings account indicates that, over these years, Nike has earned $5,801 million in net income that has not yet been distributed to stockholders as dividends.

Based on the accounting equation, assets can be financed either with liabilities or with stockholders' equity. For example, Nike's $14,998 million in assets were financed with $5,155 million worth of liabilities (debt) and $9,843 million in stockholders' equity. To use the accounting equation:

Assets	=	Liabilities	+	Stockholders' Equity
$14,998 million	=	$5,155 million	+	$9,843 million

The income statement reports a company's profitability during an accounting period.

Nike (NKE) 2011 INCOME STATEMENT ($ in millions)	
Revenues	$ 20,862
Cost of sales	11,354
Gross profit	9,508
Selling and administrative expense	6,693
Interest (income) expense, net	4
Other (income) expense, net	(33)
Income before income tax	2,844
Provision for income tax	711
Net income	$ 2,133

REVENUES are amounts received from customers for products sold and services provided. **Sales Revenue** and **Service Revenue** are amounts earned engaging in the primary business activity.

Nike sold $20,862 million worth of footwear, apparel, equipment, and accessories.

EXPENSES are the costs incurred to produce revenues. Obviously, it would only make sense for companies to incur expenses that will generate revenue and increase profits. The largest expense item for manufacturers and retailers is usually **cost of sales** expense (also referred to as **cost of goods sold**), which reports the wholesale costs of inventory sold to customers during the accounting period.

Nike's largest expense is "Cost of sales" of $11,354 million. It also incurred $6,694 in selling and administrative expense and $4 million in interest expense. Related income taxes were $711 million.

NET INCOME is the difference between revenues and expenses. Net income is also referred to as profit (loss), earnings, or the bottom line.

> **Revenues – Expenses = Net Income**

Nike was profitable. It earned $2,133 million, or approximately $2.1 billion in profits for the year ending May 31, 2011.

STATEMENT OF STOCKHOLDERS' EQUITY

The Statement of Stockholders' Equity reports changes in the contributed capital and retained earnings accounts during an accounting period.

Nike (NKE) 2011 STATEMENT OF STOCKHOLDERS' EQUITY ($ in millions)				
	Contributed Capital	Retained Earnings	Other Equity	Total SE
Beginning balance	$ 3,444	$ 6,095	$ 215	$ 9,754
Issuance of shares	503			503
Net income		2,133		2,133
Dividends		(569)		(569)
Other transactions		(1,858)	(120)	(1,978)
Ending balance	**$ 3,947**	**$ 5,801**	**$ 95**	**$ 9,843**

Retained earnings, earnings not distributed as dividends, is increased by net income (earnings) of the accounting period and decreased when earnings are distributed as dividends to the stockholders. **Contributed capital** is increased when the company receives new investments from investors in exchange for newly issued stock. It is decreased when the company buys back and retires stock.

Nike received $503 million in investments from owners, which increased contributed capital to $3,947 million. It issued new stock certificates in exchange for these investments. Nike's retained earnings increased by $2,133 million in net income the company earned, but decreased by the $569 million paid as dividends to stockholders, resulting in ending retained earnings of $5,801 million.

STATEMENT OF CASH FLOWS

The Statement of Cash Flows reports cash inflows and outflows during an accounting period.

Nike (NKE) 2008 STATEMENT OF CASH FLOWS ($ in millions)	
Net cash received from *operating* activities (NCOA)	$ 1,812
Net cash paid for *investing* activities (NCIA)	(1,021)
Net cash paid for *financing* activities (NCFA)	(1,972)
Effect of exchange rate changes	57
Change in cash	$ (1,124)
+ Cash, beginning of the period	3,079
= Cash, end of the period	$ 1,955

Business activity can be divided into three distinct areas: operating, investing, and financing. **OPERATING ACTIVITIES** relate to a company's main business: selling products or services to earn net income. **INVESTING ACTIVITIES** relate to the need for investing in property, plant, and equipment or expanding by making investments in other companies. **FINANCING ACTIVITIES** relate to how a company finances its assets—with debt or stockholders' equity. The Statement of Cash Flows describes a company's cash inflows and outflows for each of these three areas.

Nike's sales generated $1,812 million in cash flow after paying the company's expenses. Nike paid $1,021 for new investing activities. The company paid $1,972 for financing activities. Most of these payments went to repurchase stock and to pay dividends.

GENERALLY ACCEPTED ACCOUNTING PRINCIPLES (GAAP)

Accountants and the federal government have created a system of setting rules and auditing companies to verify that they follow those rules.

GAAP (Generally Accepted Accounting Principles) are the rules that companies must follow when preparing financial statements available to investors. Currently, most accounting reporting standards that formulate GAAP are set by the seven full-time voting members of the **FASB (Financial Accounting Standards Board)**.

Audits attest to whether a company's financial statements comply with the GAAP rules. Only **CPAs (Certified Public Accountants)**, licensed by the states, can conduct these audits. Ethical behavior is defined by the **AICPA (American Institute of CPA)** Code of Professional Conduct. This code holds CPAs accountable for serving the public interest.

The five full-time members of the **Public Company Accounting Oversight Board (PCAOB)** establish auditing standards and conduct inspections of the public accounting firms that perform audits.

The **SEC (Securities and Exchange Commission)** has legislative authority to set the reporting rules for accounting information of publicly held corporations. With few exceptions, it has designated GAAP, as written by the FASB, to be the official rules. The SEC oversees the Financial Accounting Standards Board (FASB) and the Public Company Accounting Oversight Board (PCAOB).

HISTORICAL COST PRINCIPLE

The **Historical Cost Principle** states that companies should record assets and services at their acquisition cost, the amount paid for them, because this is the most reliable information.

Suppose that Nike purchased land for $1 million in 2002. Assume that in 2012 the land is appraised to be worth $1.2 million. The land would appear on Nike's 2012 balance sheet at $1 million, not the appraised value, because different appraisers would suggest different estimates of the land's current market value. Market value is difficult to verify and could easily change. Therefore, GAAP requires financial statements to use historical cost.

Many have criticized the Historical Cost Principle, saying that some assets' historical costs mislead investors because they are outdated or insignificant in comparison with their market value. For example, suppose that Nike acquired prime real estate in 1968 for $1 million and today the market value is $30 million. On Nike's balance sheet, this real estate will appear as a $1 million dollar asset, giving investors with no clue that the property is now worth more.

INTERNATIONAL FINANCIAL REPORTING STANDARDS (IFRS)

We are a global economy, and it is expected that soon U.S. companies will be permitted to or required to use **International Financial Reporting Standards (IFRS)**, rather than U.S. GAAP. In 1973, the **International Accounting Standards Committee (IASC)** was formed to develop a single set of global accounting standards. In 2001, this committee was reorganized to become the **International Accounting Standards Board (IASB)** with the objectives (1) *to develop a single set of high quality, understandable and enforceable global accounting standards that lead to transparent and comparable information in general purpose financial statements, and* (2) *to cooperate with national accounting standard-setters to achieve convergence in accounting standards across the world*. This is no small task, as each country had its own unique set of accounting principles. In essence, there was British GAAP, German GAAP, Egyptian GAAP, U.S. GAAP, and so on. Now more than 100 jurisdictions, including China, Hong Kong, Australia, and all of the countries in the European Union (EU), either require or permit IFRS in some form.

In 2002, the FASB and IASB signed the Norwalk Agreement, formalizing their commitment to converging U.S. GAAP and IFRS. As of early 2012, the United States has not fully adopted IFRS, but progress continues to be made. Throughout the text we point out important differences that still remain between U.S. GAAP and IFRS.

Why should the United States adopt IFRS? Differences among the accounting standards of different countries make it difficult for global investors to compare companies and for multinational corporations to comply with multiple accounting standards.

RATIO ANALYSIS

Ratio analysis can reveal valuable information about a company's financial attributes, such as profitability, efficiency in managing assets, and whether the company has too much debt. When computing ratios, analysts often compare a company's ratios with prior periods, competitors, or industry averages.

We will compute certain financial ratios for Nike (NKE), and compare them with those of two competitors, Under Armour (UA) and Adidas (ADDYY). The financial statements of the three companies appear on the following page.

DEBT RATIO

The **Debt Ratio** reveals the proportion of assets financed with debt.

$$\text{Debt Ratio} = \text{Total Liabilities} / \text{Total Assets}$$

Companies owing too much debt might not be able to make regular payments of interest or the full amount due at maturity. If a company cannot pay its debts on time it could lose assets to creditors or even go bankrupt.

Although Adidas Group's financial statements are denominated in euros, the three companies' ratios can still be compared.

($ and € in millions)	Date	Total Assets	Total Liabilities	Debt Ratio
Nike (NKE)	May 31, 2011	$ 14,998	$ 5,155	34%
Under Armour (UA)	Dec 31, 2010	$ 676	$ 178	26%
Adidas (ADDYY)	Dec 31, 2010	€ 10,618	€ 5,995	56%

Whereas Nike and Adidas both have more than $10 billion in assets (€10,618 million equals approximately $13,700 million), Under Armour is significantly smaller with only 5% of the assets of Nike. Under Armour's $178 million in debt looks much smaller than the other two companies'. However, Under Armour's liabilities are still 26% of assets. Nike's liabilities are 34% of assets (0.34 in decimal form) and Adidas has significantly more debt—56% of assets.

Consolidated Balance Sheets			
($ and € in millions)	Nike (NKE) May 31, 2011	Under Armour (UA) December 31, 2010	Adidas (ADDYY) December 31, 2010
ASSETS			
Current assets	$ 11,297	$ 556	€ 5,880
PPE, net	2,115	76	855
Goodwill and intangibles	692	4	3,128
Other assets	894	40	755
Total Assets	$ 14,998	$ 676	€ 10,618
LIABILITIES			
Current liabilities	$ 3,958	$ 149	€ 3,908
Noncurrent liabilities	1,197	29	2,087
Total liabilities	$ 5,155	$ 178	€ 5,995
STOCKHOLDERS' EQUITY			
Contributed capital	$ 3,947	$ 225	€ 0
Retained earnings	5,801	270	4,616
Other SE	95	2	7
Total equity	$ 9,843	$ 497	€ 4,623

Consolidated Income Statements			
($ and € in millions)	Nike (NKE) May 31, 2011	Under Armour (UA) December 31, 2010	Adidas (ADDYY) December 31, 2010
Sales revenue	$ 20,862	$ 1,064	€ 11,990
Cost of goods sold	11,354	533	6,260
Gross profit	9,508	531	5,730
Operating expenses	6,693	418	4,836
Nonoperating (rev) exp	(29)	4	88
Income B4 income tax	2,844	109	806
Provision for income tax	711	40	238
Net income	$ 2,133	$ 69	€ 568

ASSET TURNOVER RATIO

Asset Turnover, computed by dividing total revenues by total assets, measures how efficiently the company uses assets to generate revenue.

> ### Asset Turnover = Sales Revenue / Total Assets

How well does a company produce revenues from its assets? The more assets a company has, the higher its revenues should be. For example, one would expect Under Armour to have lower revenues than Nike because it is smaller. Under Armour has fewer assets available to produce revenues than Nike.

($ and € in millions)	Year Ended	Sales Revenue	Total Assets	Asset Turnover
Nike (NKE)	May 31, 2011	$ 20,862	$ 14,998	1.39
Under Armour (UA)	Dec 31, 2010	$ 1,064	$ 676	1.57
Adidas (ADDYY)	Dec 31, 2010	€ 11,990	€ 10,618	1.13

However, even though Nike is larger than Under Armour, the asset turnover ratios indicate that Under Armour is more efficient. Nike has an asset turnover of 1.39, whereas Under Armour's is 1.57. Adidas was much less efficient at using its assets to produce revenues, delivering an asset turnover ratio of just 1.13.

RETURN ON SALES (ROS) RATIO

The **Return on Sales (ROS)** ratio, (also referred to as Net Profit Margin), measures the profitability of each dollar of revenue.

> ### Return on Sales = Net Income / Sales Revenue

How well does a company control expenses? A high ROS ratio depends on controlling expenses to keep net income high.

($ and € in millions)	Year Ended	Net Income	Sales Revenue	ROS
Nike (NKE)	May 31, 2011	$ 2,133	$ 20,862	10.2%
Under Armour (UA)	Dec 31, 2010	$ 69	$ 1,064	6.5%
Adidas (ADDYY)	Dec 31, 2010	€ 568	€ 11,990	4.7%

Nike's ROS is 10.2% (0.102 in decimal form), nearly twice that of Under Armour's 6.5%, indicating that Nike earns, on average, more than 10 cents of profit for each dollar of revenue, compared to Under Armour's average earnings of 6.5 cents of profit per revenue dollar. Another way of looking at this is that it takes Nike approximately 89.8 cents of expense to generate a dollar of revenue, whereas Under Armour uses 93.5 cents of expense to generate a dollar of revenue. Either way, Nike is better at controlling expenses than both Under Armour and Adidas, resulting in higher profits.

RETURN ON ASSETS (ROA) RATIO

The **Return on Asset (ROA)** ratio reveals how efficiently assets are used to generate profit (net income).

> ### Return on Assets = Net Income / Total Assets

A high ROA ratio depends on managing asset investments and controlling expenses to keep net income high. Return on Assets is the broadest measure of profitability.

($ and € in millions)	Year Ended	Net Income	Total Assets	ROA
Nike (NKE)	May 31, 2011	$ 2,133	$ 14,998	14.2%
Under Armour (UA)	Dec 31, 2010	$ 69	$ 676	10.2%
Adidas (ADDYY)	Dec 31, 2010	€ 568	€ 10,618	5.3%

With Return on Assets of 14.2% (0.142 in decimal form), Nike outperforms its competitors. Under Armour is second, with an ROA of 10.2%, whereas Adidas Group comes in third with 5.3%.

Return on Assets can also be computed by multiplying the two components, Return on Sales by Asset Turnover:

$$\textbf{Return on Sales} \times \textbf{Asset Turnover} = \textbf{Return on Assets}$$
$$\frac{\text{Net income}}{\text{Sales revenue}} \times \frac{\text{Sales revenue}}{\text{Total assets}} = \frac{\text{Net income}}{\text{Total assets}}$$

Analyzing the two components of Return on Assets will help describe corporate strategy. Some companies focus on return on sales, relying on product differentiation to boost profits. Others focus on asset turnover, using high volume to gain strong net income.

($ and € in millions)	Year Ended	ROS	Asset Turnover	ROA
Nike (NKE)	May 31, 2011	10.2%	1.39	14.2%
Under Armour (UA)	Dec 31, 2010	6.5%	1.57	10.2%
Adidas (ADDYY)	Dec 31, 2010	4.7%	1.13	5.3%

Even though Under Armour has about 5% of the assets of Nike, it generated higher asset turnover. However, Nike showed its ability to control costs with its strong return on sales of 10.2%, resulting in return of assets almost 50% higher than that of Under Armour. This indicates that Nike is able to follow the business strategy of product differentiation. Customers are willing to pay more for Nike's strong brand names.

Adidas, on the other hand, is not faring as well. The company is less profitable than the other two, earning its investors a weak 5.3% return on assets, comprised of a meager return on sales of 4.7%, and a less efficient asset turnover of 1.13.

TREND ANALYSIS

Trend Analysis compares amounts of a more recent year to a base year, the earliest year being studied. The analysis measures the percentage of change from the base year and indicates growth trends for a company. To compute the trend index, divide the amount reported for each account by the amount reported for the base year and multiply by 100.

> **Trend Index = Current amount / Base year amount x 100**

For example, consider this trend analysis for Nike from 2008 to 2011:

NIKE ($ in millions)	2011		2010		2009		2008 Base Year	
Sales revenue	$ 20,862	112	$ 19,014	102	$ 19,176	103	$ 18,627	100
Total expenses	18,729	112	17,107	102	17,689	106	16,744	100
Net income	$ 2,133	113	$ 1,907	101	$ 1,487	79	$ 1,883	100

Note that the most recent year (2011) is shown on the left. This is because users in the world of accounting ask "What have you done for me lately?" They are more interested in the most recent year's result.

Let's examine the computations of the trend index using Nike's sales revenue. For 2008, divide $18,627 of sales revenue by the amount of sales revenue reported for the base year $18,627 and multiply by 100. Because a number divided by itself is always 100%, likewise, the trend index will always be 100 for the base year. The trend index for 2009 of 103 is the result of dividing 2009 sales revenue of $19,176 by the sales revenue of the base year of $18,627 and multiplying by 100. For 2010, $19,014 / $18,627 x 100 results in a trend index of 102. And for 2011, $20,862 / $18,627 x 100 results in a trend index of 112.

From 2008 to 2009, sales had increased 3% (trend index of 103 less 100) and expenses increased 6%, resulting in a 21% decrease in net income (100 - 79). By 2011, sales had increased by 12% since the base year of 2008, expenses increased 12%, and net income increased 13%.

A similar trend analysis can be constructed for Nike's balance sheet:

NIKE ($ in millions)	2011		2010		2009		2008 Base Year	
Assets	$ 14,998	121	$ 14,419	116	$ 13,249	106	$ 12,443	100
Liabilities	5,155	112	4,665	101	4,556	99	$ 4,617	100
Stockholders' Equity	$ 9,843	126	$ 9,754	125	$ 8,693	111	$ 7,826	100

From 2008 to 2011, assets increased 21%, liabilities increased 12%, and stockholders' equity increased 26%. Although asset growth was financed with both liabilities and stockholders' equity, Nike relied more heavily on stockholders' equity.

The **Common-Size Income Statement** compares all amounts within one year to revenue of that same year. The analysis measures each income statement as a percentage of revenue, making it easier to compare income statements for different years and different-size companies. Here are common-size income statements for Nike:

NIKE ($ in millions)	2011	%	2010	%	2009	%	2008 Base Year	%
Sales revenue	$ 20,862	100	$ 19,014	100	$ 19,176	100	$ 18,627	100
Total expenses	18,729	90	17,107	90	17,689	92	16,744	90
Net income	$ 2,133	10	$ 1,907	10	$ 1,487	8	$ 1,883	10

Even though Nike's sales have grown by 12% from 2008 to 2011 (per the trend analysis), total expenses are always about 90% of sales revenue and net income about 10% of sales revenue.

The **Common-Size Balance Sheet** compares all amounts within one year to total assets of that same year. The analysis measures each balance sheet amount as a percentage of total assets. Here are four years of common-size balance sheets for Nike:

NIKE Dec. 31, ($ in millions)	2011	%	2010	%	2009	%	2008 Base Year	%
Assets	$ 14,998	100	$ 14,419	100	$ 13,249	100	$ 12,443	100
Liabilities	5,155	34	4,665	32	4,556	34	4,617	37
Stockholders' Equity	$ 9,843	66	$ 9,754	68	$ 8,693	66	$ 7,826	63

Even though total liabilities increased from $4,617 in 2008 to $5,155 in 2011, liabilities have actually decreased 3% as a percentage of assets, keeping the company in a stable financial position.

SUMMARY

Accounting provides a system for recording, classifying, and reporting transactions. Entrepreneurs, managers, investors, and creditors use accounting information as a language for conducting business. The purpose of this book is to help you learn to interpret and analyze financial statements in order to make investment decisions.

In their financial statements, companies present four basic financial statements: (1) the balance sheet, (2) the income statement, (3) the statement of stockholders' equity, and (4) the statement of cash flows. The balance sheet reports assets and the amount of assets financed with liabilities and stockholders' equity as of a certain date. The income statement reports a company's profitability during an accounting period. The statement of stockholders' equity reports changes in retained earnings and contributed capital during an accounting period. The statement of cash flows reports cash inflows and outflows during an accounting period.

Companies prepare financial statements in accordance with Generally Accepted Accounting Principles (GAAP), a system of rules formulated by the Financial Accounting Standards Board (FASB). One principle behind GAAP is the Historical Cost Principle, which states that assets and services provided should be reported at the cost of acquisition, the amount paid for them.

In 2002, the FASB and the International Accounting Standards Board (IASB) signed the Norwalk Agreement, formalizing a commitment to the convergence of U.S. GAAP and International Financial Reporting Standards (IFRS). As U.S. GAAP and IFRS are still in the process of converging, throughout the text we point out important differences that still remain between the two sets of accounting standards.

Financial statement ratios reveal valuable information about a company's finances, such as profitability, efficiency in managing assets, and whether the company has too much debt. The debt ratio (total liabilities divided by total assets) indicates the proportion of assets financed with debt. Asset turnover (revenue divided by total assets) indicates how efficiently a company uses assets to generate revenue. Return on sales (net income divided by revenue) measures a company's ability to control expenses. Return on assets (net income divided by total assets), the most comprehensive profitability ratio, indicates how efficiently assets are used to generate profits. To prepare a trend analysis on the balance sheet or income statement, divide all amounts by the corresponding amounts for a base year and multiply by 100. This reveals information about a company's growth. To prepare a common-size analysis on the balance sheet, divide all amounts by total assets. To prepare a common-size analysis on the income statement, divide all amounts by net revenues. Common-size analysis permits easy comparison of financial statements for different years and different companies in the same industry.

RATIO	ROS x	ASSET TURNOVER	= ROA	DEBT RATIO
Type	*Profitability*	*Efficiency*	*Profitability*	*Solvency*
Formula	NI / Sales Revenue	Sales Revenue / Total Assets	NI / Total Assets	Total Liabilities / Total Assets
Nike (NKE)	10.2%	1.39	14.2%	34.4%
Under Armour (UA)	6.5%	1.57	10.2%	26.3%
Adidas (ADDYY)	4.7%	1.13	5.3%	56.5%
* **Industry	13.1%	1.6	19.8%	33.3%
**S&P 500	10.0%	1.0	10.0%	60.0%

*   Industry: Textile—Apparel Footwear and Accessories *Industry and S&P 500 ratio averages from moneycentral.msn.com*

**   There are no official rules governing how these ratios are calculated. Therefore, the ratio formulas used may differ from the formulas in the text.

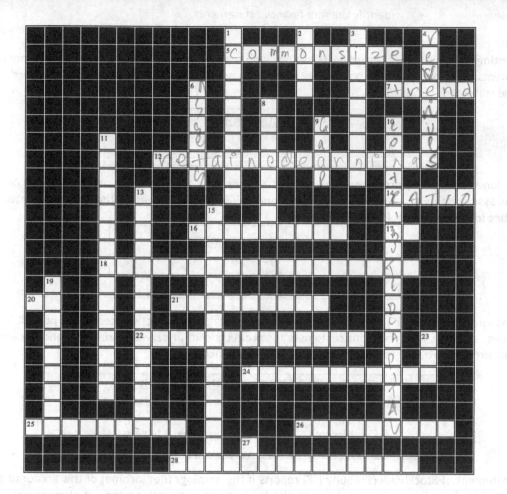

Across

5. Statement reporting all amounts as percentages (2 Words)
7. Analysis used to compare revenues over a 5-year period
12. Net income earned, but not yet distributed to stockholders (2 Words) *Retained E.*
14. Analysis revealing relationships among two or more accounts *Ratio*
16. Activity including cash transactions involving long-term assets *Investing*
17. Statement reporting assets and how they are financed (abbreviation) *BS*
18. Statement reporting changes in contributed capital and retained earnings (2 Words) *Stockho E.*
20. Assets = Liabilities + *SE* (abbreviation)
21. Activity including cash transactions from a company's central business *Operating*
22. Measures how efficiently assets are used to generate revenue (2 Words) *Debt Ratio Asset turn*
24. Amounts owed *Liabilities*
25. Proportion of assets financed by debt (2 Words) *debt ratio*
26. Statement reporting changes in cash (2 Words) *cash flow*
28. Reveals how efficiently assets generate profits (3 Words) *ROA*

Down

1. System for recording, classifying, and summarizing financial information *Accounting*
2. Wholesale costs of inventory sold (abbreviation) *COGS.*
3. Activity including cash transactions that involve stockholders and creditors *SE*
4. Amounts earned selling to or servicing customers *Net Income*
6. Items of value *Assets.*
8. Costs incurred to produce revenues *Expenses*
9. Rules for preparing the financial statements (abbreviation) *GAAP*
10. Amounts paid-in by stockholders to purchase stock (2 Words)
11. Amounts to be paid to suppliers (2 Words) *a/c payable*
13. Principle that requires assets be recorded at the amount paid for them (2 Words)
15. Statement reporting profitability (2 Words) *Income st*
19. Profit (loss), earnings, or the bottom line (2 Words) *Net Income*
23. Proportion of profit from revenue (abbreviation) *Return on sale*
27. Amounts to be received from customers (abbreviation) *A.R.*

Purpose:
- Identify the four financial statements.
- Understand the basic information provided by each financial statement.

Accounting is the system of recording, classifying, and reporting financial information. Four financial statements report this information: balance sheet, income statement, statement of stockholders' equity, and the statement of cash flows.

> **BALANCE SHEET**
> | Assets | Liabilities |
> |---|---|
> | | Stockholders' equity |

The Balance Sheet (BS) provides a snapshot of a company's financial position as of a certain date. It reports **assets,** items of value such as inventory and equipment, and whether the assets are financed with **liabilities** (debt) or **stockholders' equity** (equity).

> **INCOME STATEMENT**
> Revenues
> (Expenses)
> Net income

The Income Statement (IS) reports the company's profitability during an accounting period. It reports **revenues,** amounts received from customers for products sold or services provided, and **expenses,** the costs incurred to produce revenues. The difference is **net income.**

> **STATEMENT OF STOCKHOLDERS' EQUITY**
> | Retained earnings, beginning | Contributed capital, beginning |
> |---|---|
> | + Net income | + Issuance of shares |
> | (Dividends) | (Repurchase to retire shares) |
> | Retained earnings, ending | Contributed capital, ending |

The Statement of Stockholders' Equity (SE) reports if the **earnings** (net income) of this accounting period are distributed as **dividends** or retained in the business as **retained earnings**. It also reports amounts paid-in (contributed) by stockholders to purchase common stock and preferred stock.

> **STATEMENT OF CASH FLOWS**
> Cash inflows
> (Cash outflows)
> Change in the cash account

The Statement of Cash Flows (CF) reports cash inflows and cash outflows during an accounting period.

Q1   Which financial statement reports:

a.   whether assets are primarily financed with debt or equity?   (**BS** / IS / SE / CF)

b.   whether the company was profitable or not?   (BS / **IS** / SE / CF)

c.   cash received from customers during the accounting period?   (BS / IS / SE / **CF**)

d.   dividends declared by the board of directors for shareholders?   (BS / IS / **SE** / CF)

e.   retained earnings at the beginning of the accounting period?   (BS / IS / **SE** / CF)

f.   the expenses of a corporation?   (BS / **IS** / SE / CF)

g.   the assets of a corporation?   (**BS** / IS / SE / CF)

Purpose:
- Understand the information provided by the balance sheet.
- Identify asset, liability, and stockholders' equity accounts reported on the balance sheet.
- Understand the accounting equation.

PEPSICO (PEP*) 12/25/2010 BALANCE SHEET ($ in millions)			
ASSETS		**LIABILITIES**	
Cash and cash equivalents	$ 5,943	Accounts payable	$ 3,865
Short-term investments	426	Short-term debt	4,898
Accounts receivable, net	6,323	Other current liabilities	7,129
Inventories	3,372	Long-term debt	19,999
Other current assets	1,505	Other noncurrent liabilities	11,098
Property, plant, and equipment, net	19,058		
Goodwill	14,661	**STOCKHOLDERS' EQUITY**	
Other intangible assets	13,808	Contributed capital	4,449
Long-term investments	1,368	Retained earnings	37,090
Other noncurrent assets	1,689	Treasury stock and other equity	(20,375)
Total Assets	**$68,153**	**Total L & SE**	**$68,153**

— Net income

The balance sheet reports assets and the amount of financing from liabilities and stockholders' equity as of a certain date. This relationship is summarized by the **accounting equation** which is:

> **Assets = Liabilities + Stockholders' Equity**

Assets are items of value that a corporation owns or has a right to use. Typical asset accounts include cash, accounts receivable, inventory, equipment, buildings, and land. Accounts *receivable* are amounts to be *received* in the future from customers.

Liabilities are amounts owed to creditors; the amount of debt owed to third parties. Typical liability accounts include accounts payable, wages payable, notes payable, and bonds payable. The key word found in many liability accounts is *payable*. Accounts *payable* are amounts to be *paid* in the future to suppliers.

Stockholders' Equity is the portion of assets the owners own free and clear. Stockholders' equity may also be referred to as shareholders' equity or owners' equity. Typical stockholders' equity accounts include:

> *Contributed Capital*—Amounts paid-in (contributed) by stockholders to purchase common stock and preferred stock.

> *Retained Earnings*—Net income earned by the company since its incorporation and not yet distributed as dividends.

Q1   Identify the accounting equation amounts for PepsiCo Corporation using the information above.

Assets $ __68153__ million = Liabilities $ __46989__ million + Stockholders' Equity $ __21 164__ million

Q2   Assets can either be financed with __debt/liabilities__ or __stockholder's equity__.

Q3   Will the accounting equation hold true for every corporation? (**Yes** / No / Can't tell)

Why? __Because every company has assets, liabilities, and equity.__
__the balance sheet must always tie.__

* Stock market symbols are shown in parentheses.

Q4   PepsiCo is primarily financed with (**liabilities** / stockholders' equity). How can you tell?

there is more money on the liabilities side

Q5   Circle whether the account is classified as an (A)sset, (L)iability, or part of Stockholders' Equity (SE) on the balance sheet.

a.   Cash   (**A** / L / SE)

b.   Accounts *payable*   (A / **L** / SE)

c.   Accounts *receivable*   (**A** / L / SE)

d.   Land   (**A** / L / SE)

e.   Common stock   (A / L / **SE**)

f.   Equipment   (**A** / L / SE)

g.   Notes payable   (A / **L** / SE)

h.   Building   (**A** / L / SE)

i.   Retained earnings   (A / L / **SE**)

j.   Inventory   (**A** / L / SE)

k.   Mortgage payable   (A / **L** / SE)

l.   Bonds payable   (A / **L** / SE)

Q6   Use PepsiCo's balance sheet on the previous page to answer the following questions:

a.   What amount of cash does this company expect to receive from customers within the next few months? $ _6,323_ million

b.   The largest asset account is _PPE_ reporting $ _19,058_ million.

       What types of asset costs are included in this account?

       Office buildings
       Factory Equipment
       Accum. Depre.

c.   How much does this company currently owe suppliers? $ _3,865_ million

d.   Since the company started business, what is the total amount shareholders have paid for their shares of stock? $ _4,449_ million

e.   Since the company started business, how much net income was earned and not yet distributed as dividends? $ _37,090_ million

Purpose:
- Understand the information reported on the income statement.
- Identify revenue and expense accounts reported on the income statement.

PEPSICO (PEP) 2010 INCOME STATEMENT ($ in millions)	
Sales revenue	$ 57,838
Cost of goods sold	26,575
Gross profit	31,263
Selling, general and administrative (SGA) expense	22,326
Research and development expense	488
Other operating expenses	217
Income before income tax	8,232
Provision for income tax	1,912
Net income	$ 6,320

(handwritten: revenue; 5; 300; 3; w; — profit)

The income statement reports the company's profitability during an accounting period.

Revenues are amounts received from customers for products sold and services provided. *Sales revenue* and *service revenue* are amounts earned engaging in the primary business activity.

Expenses are the costs incurred to produce revenues. Expenses are recorded in the accounting period they benefit (if a cause and effect relationship exists) or are incurred (if there is no cause and effect relationship). *Cost of goods sold* expense reports the wholesale costs of inventory sold to customers during the accounting period.

Net income is the difference between revenues and expenses. Net income is also referred to as *profit (loss)*, *earnings*, or the *bottom line*.

> **Revenues – Expenses = Net income**

Q1   Circle whether the account is classified as a (Rev)enue, (Exp)ense, or (Not) reported on the income statement.

   a.   Wage expense   **(Rev /(Exp)/ Not)**   d.   Service revenue   **((Rev)/ Exp / Not)**

   b.   Inventory   **(Rev / Exp /(Not))**   e.   Rent expense   **(Rev /(Exp)/ Not)**

   c.   Cost of goods sold   **(Rev /(Exp)/ Not)**   f.   Building   **(Rev / Exp /(Not))**

Q2   Review PepsiCo's 2010 income statement above and answer the following questions:

   a.   This company reports **((1)/ 2 / 3 / 4)** revenue account(s) and **(2 / 3 / 4 /(5))** expense accounts.

   b.   Beverages and snacks were sold to customers for $ _57,838_ million that cost the company $ _26,575_ million to produce.

   c.   The title of the largest expense account is ___COGS___ reporting $ _26,575_ million, which is typically the largest expense account for a company within the **((retail)/ service)** industry.

     (handwritten: shipping) What specific types of costs would be included in this account for PepsiCo? _____ *(handwritten: – Direct materials / Direct labor / Factory overhead)*

   d.   Was PepsiCo profitable? **((Yes)/ No)** How much profit was reported? $ _6320_ million

Q3   Net income can also be referred to as **(revenues / expenses / common stock /(earnings))**

Purpose:
- Understand information provided by the Statement of Stockholders' Equity.
- Understand changes within contributed capital and retained earnings.
- Identify relationships among the IS, RE, and the BS.

PEPSICO (PEP) 2010 STATEMENT OF STOCKHOLDERS' EQUITY ($ in millions)				
	Contributed Capital	Retained Earnings	Other Equity	Total Stockholders Equity
Beginning balance	$ 176	$ 33,805	$ (17,177)	$ 16,804
Issuance of shares	4,273			4,273
Net income		6,320		6,320
Dividends		(3,041)		(3,041)
Other transactions		6	(3,198)	(3,192)
Ending balance	**$ 4,449**	**$ 37,090**	**$(20,375)**	**$ 21,164**

The statement of stockholders' equity reports changes within the contributed capital, retained earnings, and other equity accounts during an accounting period. **Contributed capital** (CC) is increased when additional shares of stock are issued and decreased when those shares are retired. **Retained earnings** (RE) is increased by **net income** (earnings) of the accounting period and decreased when earnings are distributed as **dividends** to the stockholders. Earnings not distributed as dividends are reported as retained earnings.

Q1 Earnings is another word for (**revenue / receivables /** ~~net income~~).
Earnings of a corporation belong to the (**managers /** ~~stockholders~~).
Earnings can either be distributed to the stockholders as (~~dividends~~ **/ expenses / retained earnings**) or kept in the business as (**dividends / expenses /** ~~retained earnings~~).

Q2 Income statement: Revenues - Expenses = ___net income___ or ___
Balance sheet: Assets = ___liab___ + ___stock eq___
Stockholders' Equity = Contributed capital + ___Retained___ + Other Equity
Statement of SE: Beg Retained Earnings + ___net income___ - Dividends = ___Ending retain___

Q3 Net income is computed on the (~~IS~~ **/ SE / BS**) and then transferred to the Statement of Stockholders' Equity to increase (**CC /** ~~RE~~ **/ Other SE**). Ending retained earnings is reported on the Statement of Stockholders' Equity and then transferred to the (**IS / SE /** ~~BS~~).

Q4 Circle whether the account is reported on the Income Statement (IS), Statement of Stockholders' Equity (SE), or the Balance Sheet (BS). Note: *Three amounts are reported on two statements.*

a.	Contributed capital	(IS / ~~SE~~ / BS)	e.	Sales revenue	(~~IS~~ / SE / BS)
b.	Net income	(~~IS~~ / SE / BS)	f.	Accounts receivable	(IS / SE / ~~BS~~)
c.	Dividends	(IS / ~~SE~~ / BS)	g.	Wage expense	(~~IS~~ / SE / BS)
d.	Retained earnings	(IS / ~~SE~~ / BS)	h.	Bonds payable	(IS / SE / ~~BS~~)

Q5 Use PepsiCo's 2010 statement of stockholders' equity above to answer the following questions:
a. Contributed capital reported at the end of the accounting period is $__4449__ million, which is the amount shareholders paid for (**net income / dividends /** ~~issued shares~~).

b. Retained earnings increased by (~~net income~~ **/ dividends / issued shares**) of $__6320__ million and decreased by (**net income /** ~~dividends~~ **/ issued shares**) of $__3041__ million.

c. When the company issues shares of stock, total stockholders' equity (~~increases~~ **/ decreases**). When the company buys back shares of stock, total stockholders' equity (**increases /** ~~decreases~~).

Purpose:
- Understand information provided by the Statement of Cash Flows.
- Understand that cash flows are organized as operating, investing, and financing activities.

The statement of cash flows organizes cash inflows and cash outflows as operating activities, investing activities, and financing activities.

PEPSICO (PEP) 2010 STATEMENT OF CASH FLOWS ($ in millions)	
Net cash received from *operating* activities (NCOA)	$ 8,448
Net cash paid for *investing* activities (NCIA)	(7,668)
Net cash received from *financing* activities (NCFA)	1,386
Effect of exchange rate changes	(166)
Change in cash	2,000
+ Cash, beginning of the period	3,943
= Cash, end of the period	$ 5,943

Business activities can be classified into three distinct categories: *operating*, *investing*, and *financing*. **Operating Activities** relate to a company's main business of selling products or services to earn net income. **Investing Activities** relate to the need for investing in property, plant, and equipment or expanding by making investments in other companies. **Financing Activities** relate to how a company finances its assets—with debt or stockholders' equity. The Statement of Cash Flows describes a company's cash inflows and outflows for each of these three areas.

Q1   Use PepsiCo's 2010 statement of cash flows above to answer the following questions:

a.   PepsiCo's operating activities generated cash inflows of $ _8 448_ million.

b.   PepsiCo purchased property, plant, and equipment, which resulted in a cash (**inflow / outflow**) of $ _7 668_ million from (**operating / investing / financing**) activities.

c.   PepsiCo borrowed money, which resulted in a cash (**inflow / outflow**) of $ _1386_ million from (**operating / investing / financing**) activities.

d.   At the beginning of 2010, cash was $ _3943_ million. During the year, cash (**increased / decreased**) by $ _2600_ million, resulting in an ending cash balance of $ _5943_ million.

e.   Cash at the end of 2010 is the (**same as / different than**) cash at the beginning of 2011.

Q2   Circle whether the account is reported on the Income Statement (IS), the Balance Sheet (BS), or the Statement of Cash Flows (CF).

a.	Retained earnings	(**IS / BS / CF**)	e.	Cash from issuing common stock	(**IS / BS / CF**)
b.	Rent expense	(**IS / BS / CF**)	f.	Sales revenue	(**IS / BS / CF**)
c.	Rent payable	(**IS / BS / CF**)	g.	Accounts receivable	(**IS / BS / CF**)
d.	Cash paid for rent	(**IS / BS / CF**)	h.	Cash received from customers	(**IS / BS / CF**)

Purpose:
- Understand that GAAP (Generally Accepted Accounting Principles) are the rules of financial accounting.
- Apply the historical cost principle.

GAAP (Generally Accepted Accounting Principles) are the rules that companies must follow when preparing financial statements.

- The **SEC (Securities and Exchange Commission)** has legislative authority to set the reporting rules for accounting information of the publicly held corporations it regulates. It has designated GAAP to be the official rules. The SEC provides oversight and enforcement authority over the Financial Accounting Standards Board (FASB) and the Public Company Accounting Oversight Board (PCAOB).
- The seven full-time voting members of the **FASB (Financial Accounting Standards Board)** set accounting reporting standards and formulate GAAP.
- **Audits** attest to whether a company's financial statements comply with GAAP. Only **CPAs (Certified Public Accountants)**, licensed by the state, can conduct the audits.
- **Ethical behavior** is defined by the **AICPA's (American Institute of CPA's)** Code of Professional Conduct. This code holds CPAs accountable for serving the public interest.
- The five full-time members of the **PCAOB (Public Company Accounting Oversight Board)** establish auditing standards and conduct inspections of the public accounting firms that perform audits.

Q1 (FASB / SEC / ~~GAAP~~ / AICPA) are the rules that must be followed when preparing the financial statements for external use.

Q2 **GAAP** stands for ___Generally Accepted Acco~~~ Principle___.

Q3 (~~CPAs~~ / Management / Corporate accountants) conduct audits that attest to whether a company's financial statements comply with GAAP.

HISTORICAL COST PRINCIPLE

GAAP #1: The Historical Cost Principle states that assets and services should be recorded at their acquisition cost, thus using *verifiable* information that is the most *reliable* information.

Q4 An auto has a sticker price of $20,000. A company purchases the auto, but negotiates with the sales person and pays a price of only $18,000. On the balance sheet, (**$18,000** / $20,000) will be reported for the auto. Thirty years ago, land was purchased for $2,000, which now has a current market value of $100,000. On the balance sheet, (**$2,000** / $100,000) will be reported for the land.

Q5 When the financial statements are prepared according to GAAP, assets and services are reported at their (**acquisition cost** / current market value).

Q6 THINK ABOUT IT: Is knowledge of an asset's current market value ever useful?   (**Yes** / No)
    If so, when? _selling / buying_

INTERNATIONAL FINANCIAL REPORTING STANDARDS (IFRS)

Q7 There (**are** / are not) differences among the accounting standards of different countries. IFRS are global accounting standards that U.S. GAAP is (**converging toward** / in full compliance with).

Purpose:
- Understand that analysis reveals relationships.
- Explore the relationships among assets, liabilities, revenues, and net income.
- Examine the debt ratio, ROS (return-on-sales) ratio, asset-turnover ratio, and the ROA (return-on-asset) ratio.

The *three types of analysis* are Ratio Analysis, Trend Analysis (horizontal analysis), and Common-Size Statements (vertical analysis). *Analysis reveals relationships* by comparing amounts to:

(1)   other amounts for the same period (ratios and common-size statements),

(2)   the same information from a prior period (trend analysis),

(3)   competitor information, and industry norms.

RATIOS

Tiffany & Co (TIF), **Wal-Mart Stores** (WMT), and **Ford Motor Company** (F) are well-known companies, but how much do you really know about them?

Q1   *FINANCIAL TRIVIA*   For the fiscal years ending below, put a large circle in the box of the company that you *guess* has …

a.   the greatest amount of *assets*. (This one is completed for you.)

b.   the greatest amount of *liabilities*.

c.   the greatest amount of *revenue*.

d.   the greatest amount of *net income*.

($ in millions)	TIF Jan 31, 2011	WMT Jan 31, 2011	F Dec 31, 2010
ASSETS	$	$	$ (164,687)
LIABILITIES	$	$	$ (150,000)
REVENUE	$	$ (400,000)	$
NET INCOME	$	$ (15,000)	$

Q2   *FINANCIAL TRIVIA*   In each large circle, place the **amount** that you **guess** for …

a.   the greatest amount of *assets*. (This is completed for you.)

b.   the greatest amount of *liabilities*.

c.   the greatest amount of *revenue*.

d.   the greatest amount of *net income*.

Now turn to page 25 and see how well you guessed.

Q3 a. Compute the debt ratio for each company listed below. The debt ratio reveals the proportion of assets financed with debt. **Debt ratio = Total liabilities / Total assets**

($ in millions)	Year Ended	Total Assets	Total Liabilities	Debt Ratio
Tiffany & Co (TIF)	1/31/2011	$ 3,736	$ 1,558	41.70%
Wal-Mart Stores (WMT)	1/31/2011	$ 180,663	$ 112,121	62.06%
Ford Motor Company (F)	12/31/2010	$ 164,687	$ 165,360	100.41 %

b. Wal-Mart is primarily financed with ((debt) / **equity**), resulting in a debt ratio that is (**less** / (more)) than 50.00%, whereas a company primarily financed with equity will have a debt ratio that is ((less) / **more**) than 50.00%. Ford has a debt ratio greater than (**50%** / (100%)), indicating its liabilities are ((greater) / **less**) than its assets.

Q4 a. Compute Return on Sales (ROS) for each company listed below. ROS reveals the portion of each revenue dollar that results in profit. **ROS = Net income / Sales revenue**

($ in millions)	Year Ended	Revenue	Net income	ROS
TIF	1/31/2011	$ 3,085	$ 368	11.93%
WMT	1/31/2011	$ 421,849	$ 16,389	3.89%
F	12/31/2010	$ 128,954	$ 6,561	5.09%

b. Wal-Mart has ((greater) / **less**) revenue than Tiffany & Co, but Tiffany & Co has a ((higher) / **lower**) ROS ratio than Wal-Mart. The ROS ratio for Tiffany & Co indicates __11.93__ % of every revenue dollar resulted in profit (net income), but for Wal-Mart only __3.89__ % of every revenue dollar resulted in profit.

c. For Wal-Mart, __96.11__ cents of each revenue dollar went to pay for all of the costs of running the business, leaving __3.89__ cents of each revenue dollar for profit.

d. The corporation with the strongest ROS ratio is ((TIF) / **WMT** / **F**).
   How can a company increase its ROS ratio?
   higher Net Income, lower the cost

e. Does a low ROS ratio indicate a weak corporation? (**Yes** / (No)) Why?
   They just need more control of expenses. And the industry.

Q5 a. Compute Asset Turnover for each company listed below. Asset Turnover reveals how efficiently assets are used to generate revenue. **Asset Turnover = Sales Revenue / Total Assets**

($ in millions)	Year Ended	Revenue	Total Assets	Asset Turnover
TIF	1/31/2011	$ 3,085	$ 3,736	0.8257
WMT	1/31/2011	$ 421,849	$ 180,663	2.3350
F	12/31/2010	$ 128,954	$ 164,687	0.7830

b. The asset turnover ratios computed above are in the range ((less than 3) / **3 or more**).

c. (**TIF** / (WMT) / **F**) has the strongest asset turnover, indicating the company makes profits by generating a large volume of revenue using relatively few assets. Wal-Mart generates $ __2.34__ in revenue for every $1 invested in assets.

Q6 a. Compute Return on Assets (ROA) for each company listed below. ROA reveals how efficiently a company uses its assets to generate profit (net income). A high ROA ratio depends on managing asset investments and controlling expenses to keep net income high. Analyze the components, ROS and Asset Turnover, to better understand corporate strategy (product-differentiation vs. low-cost strategies). ROA is the broadest measure of profitability. **ROA = Net Income / Total Assets**

($ in millions)	Year Ended	Net Income	Total Assets	ROA
TIF	1/31/2011	$ 368	$ 3,736	9.85%
WMT	1/31/2011	$ 16,389	$ 180,663	9.07 %
F	12/31/2010	$ 6,561	$ 167,687	3.91 %

b. For each company below, compute ROA by multiplying the two components, Return on Sales and Asset Turnover (previously computed). **ROA = ROS x Asset T/O**

($ in millions)	Year Ended	ROS x	Asset Turnover	= ROA
TIF	1/31/2011	11.93%	0.8257	9.85%
WMT	1/31/2011	3.89 %	2.3350	9.083 %
F	12/31/2010	5.09 %	0.7830	3.985 %

c. The corporation with the strongest overall measure of profitability is (**TIF**/ **WMT** / **F**) with an ROA of __9.85__ %, indicating that for each dollar invested in assets, the company generates, on average, __9.85__ cents in profits.

The corporation with the weakest ROA is (**TIF** / **WMT** / **F**).

d. Wal-Mart has a (**high** / **low**) ROS and a (**high** / **low**) Asset Turnover, indicating that a (**low-cost** / **product-differentiation**) strategy is used, whereas Tiffany & Co has a (**high** / **low**) ROS and a (**high** / **low**) Asset Turnover, indicating that a (**low-cost** / **product-differentiation**) strategy is used. Ford Motor Company has (**high** / **low**) ROS and (**high** / **low**) Asset Turnover, indicating that it is (**doing well** / **still recovering**).

Q7 a. The ratio that measures the ability to translate revenue into profit is the (**Debt** / **ROS** / **Asset Turnover** / **ROA**) ratio.

b. The ratio that measures the proportion of debt used to finance assets is the (**Debt** / **ROS** / **Asset Turnover** / **ROA**) ratio.

c. The broadest measure of profitability that can be broken down into components to better understand corporate strategy is the (**Debt** / **ROS** / **Asset Turnover** / **ROA**) ratio.

d. A high (**Debt** / **ROS** / **Asset Turnover** / **ROA**) ratio indicates a high-volume strategy

Solutions to *FINANCIAL TRIVIA* Q1 and Q2.

($ in millions)	TIF Jan 31, 2011	WMT Jan 31, 2011	F Dec 31, 2010
ASSETS	$ 3,736	$ 180,663	$ 164,687
LIABILITIES	1,558	112,121	**165,360**
STOCKHOLDERS' EQUITY	2,178	**68,542**	(673)
REVENUE	3,085	**421,849**	128,954
NET INCOME	$ 368	$ 16,389	$ 6,561

Purpose: •   Prepare a trend analysis and understand the information provided.

A **trend analysis** compares amounts of a more recent year to a base year. The base year is the earliest year being studied. The analysis measures the percentage of change from the base year.

Q1   Complete the trend indexes for *Total expenses* and *Net income* using the amounts listed below. To compute, divide each amount by the amount of the base year and multiply by 100. Record the resulting *trend index* in the shaded area below. Use 2007 as the base year.

PEPSICO ($ in millions)	2010		2009		2008		Base Year 2007	
Sales revenue	$57,838	147	$43,232	110	$43,251	110	$39,474	100
Total expenses	51,518	152	37,286	110	38,109	115	33,794	100
Net income	$ 6,320	111	$ 5,946	105	$ 5,142	90	$ 5,682	100

Q2   From 2007 to 2010 sales growth for PepsiCo was 47%. During the same period, total expenses increased ____52____%. When net sales increase, expenses would be expected to (**increase** / **stay the same / decrease**). It is favorable when sales increase by 47% and expenses increase at a (**greater / lesser**) rate than 47%. From 2007 to 2010 (**revenues / expenses**) of PepsiCo increased at a greater rate, which is (**favorable / unfavorable**), resulting in a (**small / large**) increase in net income.

Q3   Assume PepsiCo had a goal of increasing profits by 5% each year. This goal was (**met / not met**).

Q4   The best year financially for PepsiCo was (**2010** / **2009 / 2008**). *Why?*

The worst year financially for PepsiCo was (**2010 / 2009 / 2008**). *Why?*

Q5   Complete the trend indexes for *Liabilities* and *Stockholders' Equity* using the amounts listed below. To compute, divide each amount by the amount for the base year and multiply by 100. Record the resulting *trend index* in the shaded area below. Use 2007 as the base year.

PEPSICO ($ in millions)	12/25/2010		12/26/2009		12/27/2008		Base Year 12/29/2007	
Assets	$68,153	197	$39,848	115	$35,994	104	$34,628	100
Liabilities	46,989	270	23,044	132	23,888		17,394	100
SEquity	$21,164		$16,804		$12,106		$17,234	100

Q6   The assets of PepsiCo increased by 97% from 12/29/2007 to 12/25/2010, indicating PepsiCo is (**growing / shrinking**). From 12/29/2007 to 12/25/2010, (**assets / liabilities**) increased at a greater rate, indicating the corporation is relying (**more / less**) on debt to finance assets.

Q7   Stockholders' equity amounts are greater than the base year on (**12/25/2010 / 12/26/2009 / 12/27/2008**) when the trend index is (**greater / less**) than 100. Stockholders' equity amounts are less than the base year on (**12/25/2010 / 12/26/2009 / 12/27/2008**) when the trend index is (**greater / less**) than 100.

Q8   It is easier to analyze PepsiCo (**before / after**) preparing the trend analysis.

Purpose: •   Prepare common-size statements and understand the information provided.

The **COMMON-SIZE INCOME STATEMENT** compares all amounts within one year to revenue of that same year. The analysis measures each income statement amount as a percentage of revenue.

Q1   Prepare the common-size statements for the Coca-Cola (KO) and the Starbucks (SBUX) companies listed below. To compute, divide each amount on the income statement by sales revenue. Record the resulting *common-size percent* in the shaded area provided.

2010	PEPSICO (PEP)		COCA-COLA (KO)		STARBUCKS (SBUX)	
($ in millions)	Amount	%	Amount	%	Amount	%
Sales revenue	$57,838	100	$35,119	100	$10,707	100
Total expenses	51,518	89	23,310	66	9,761	91
Net income	$ 6,320	11	$11,809	34%	$ 946	9 .

Q2   (**PEP** / **KO** / **SBUX**) is the largest company above, reporting sales revenue of approximately $57.8 (**trillion / billion / million / thousand**). ROS for PepsiCo is _____% or ___._____ in decimal form, which indicates _____ cents of every dollar of sales revenue resulted in profit.

     ROS = NI / Revenue

Q3   On the common-size income statement, every amount is compared to or divided by total (**assets / liabilities / sales revenue / net income**).

Q4   Common-size statements are helpful when comparing companies of different size. (**True** / **False**)

Q5   Based only on the information provided above, which company would be your choice of investment? (**PEP** / **KO** / **SBUX**)

     Why?   ROS is 34%

The **COMMON-SIZE BALANCE SHEET** compares all amounts within one year to total assets of that same year. The analysis measures each balance sheet amount as a percentage of total assets.

Q6   Prepare the common-size statements for the Coca-Cola (KO) and Starbucks (SBUX) companies listed below. To compute, divide each amount on the balance sheet by total assets. Record the resulting *common-size percent* in the shaded area provided.

2010	PEPSICO (PEP)		COCA-COLA (KO)		STARBUCKS (SBUX)	
($ in millions)	Amount	%	Amount	%	Amount	%
Assets	$68,153	100	$72,921		$6,386	
Liabilities	46,989	69	41,918		2,712	
SEquity	$21,164	31	$31,003		$3,674	

Q7   Starbucks primarily finances assets with (**liabilities / stockholders' equity**). The debt ratio for Starbucks is _____%, which indicates debt (liabilities) is used to finance _____% of assets and equity (stockholders' equity) is used to finance _____% of assets. On the common-size balance sheet, every amount is compared to or divided by total (**assets / liabilities**).
     Debt Ratio = Liabilities / Assets

COCA-COLA (KO*) 12/31/2010 BALANCE SHEET ($ in millions)

ASSETS		LIABILITIES	
Cash and cash equivalents	$ 8,517	Accounts payable	$ 1,887
Short-term investments	2,820	Short-term debt	8,100
Accounts receivable, net	4,430	Other current liabilities	8,521
Inventories	2,650	Long-term debt	14,041
Other current assets	3,162	Other non-current liabilities	9,369
Property, plant, and equipment, net	14,727		
Goodwill	11,665	**STOCKHOLDERS' EQUITY**	
Other intangibles	15,244	Contributed capital	10,937
Long-term investments	7,585	Retained earnings	49,278
Other non-current assets	2,121	Other stockholders' equity	(29,212)
TOTAL ASSETS	**$ 72,921**	**TOTAL L & SE**	**$ 72,921**

COCA-COLA (KO) 2010 INCOME STATEMENT ($ in millions)

Sales revenue	$ 35,119
Cost of goods sold	12,693
Gross profit	22,426
Selling, general, and administrative expense	7,199
Other operating expenses	6,778
Nonoperating (revenues) and expenses	(5,794)
Income before income tax	14,243
Provision for income tax	2,434
Net income	$ 11,809

COCA-COLA (KO) 2010 STATEMENT OF STOCKHOLDERS' EQUITY ($ in millions)

	Contributed Capital	Retained Earnings	Other Equity	TOTAL S/E
Beginning balance	$ 9,417	$ 41,537	$ (26,155)	$ 24,799
Issuance of shares	1,520			1,520
Net income		11,809		11,809
Dividends		(4,068)		(4,068)
Other transactions			(3,057)	(3,057)
Ending balance	$ 10,937	$ 49,278	$(29,212)	$ 31,003

COCA-COLA (KO) 2010 STATEMENT OF CASH FLOWS ($ in millions)

Net cash received from operating activities (NCOA)	$ 9,532
Net cash paid from investing activities (NCIA)	(4,405)
Net cash paid from financing activities (NCFA)	(3,465)
Effect of exchange rate changes	(166)
Change in cash	1,496
+ Cash, beginning of the period	7,021
= Cash, end of the period	$ 8,517

Purpose:
- Review the four financial statements.
- Compute net income.
- Prepare and evaluate trend analyses, common-size statements, and ratios.

Q1　Make the following statements true by correcting the false information.

Note: There may be more than one way to correct the false information.

a.　The four financial statements include the revenue statement, statement of contributed capital, asset sheet, and the statement of cash flows.

b.　The statement of cash flows reports the assets of the business and how those assets are financed.

c.　Assets are financed either by liabilities or expenses.

d.　Retained earnings is an asset account, accounts receivable is a liability account, and accounts payable is a stockholders' equity account.

e.　Accounts receivable are amounts to be paid later to suppliers by the corporation.

f.　The income statement reports cash inflows and cash outflows.

g.　Cash is the amount earned engaging in the primary business activity.

h.　Earnings is another term for revenue.

i.　Net income distributed to shareholders is referred to as contributed capital.

j.　Dividends are reported as an expense on the income statement.

Q2　Circle the income statement amounts and cross out amounts not reported on the income statement. Then compute net income.

Supply expense	$ 8,000	Sales revenue	$100,000
Notes payable	30,000	Common stock	50,000
Cost of goods sold	70,000	Dividends	2,000
Net income totals $			

Q3　Suppose that during the first year of business $100,000 of wage costs were incurred; $90,000 were paid in cash to employees; and the remaining wages will be paid to employees on January 3 of the coming year, the next payday. What account title and amount will be reported on the following year-end financial statements?

a.　Income Statement account title:　　Wages (**expense** / payable / paid) of $_____

b.　Balance Sheet account title:　　　Wages (expense / **payable** / paid) of $_____

c.　Statement of Cash Flows account title:　Wages (expense / payable / **paid**) of $_____

Q4 Review the 2010 Financial Statements of the Coca-Cola Company on page 28 to answer the following questions:

a. Assets $___72,912___ million = Liabilities $___41,918___ million + SE $___31,003___ million

Is the accounting equation in balance? (**Yes** / **No**)

b. Net Income of $___11,809___ million is reported on the Income Statement. It is also reported on the (**Statement of Stockholders' Equity** / **Balance Sheet** / **Statement of Cash Flows**).

c. The ending balance of retained earnings on the Statement of Stockholders' Equity is $___49,278___ million. It is also reported on the (**Income Statement** / **Balance Sheet** / **Statement of Cash Flows**).

d. Cash reported on the Balance Sheet is $___8,517___ million. It is also reported on the (**Income Statement** / **Statement of Stockholders' Equity** / **Statement of Cash Flows**).

e. Total Assets of $___72,912___ million helped to generate Sales Revenue of $___35,119___ million, which results in an Asset Turnover ratio of 0. ___48.2___. $\frac{35119}{72912}$

f. Sales Revenue of $___35,119___ million helped to generate Net Income of $___11,809___ million, which results in a ROS ratio of ___33.6___ %. $ROS = \frac{11809}{35119}$

g. Total Assets of $___72,912___ million helped to generate Net Income of $___11,809___ million, which results in a ROA ratio of ___16.2___ %. $\frac{11809}{72912}$

h. The most comprehensive measure of profitability is (**Asset Turnover** / **ROS** / **ROA**). For Coca-Cola, ROA of ___16.2___ % = Asset Turnover of 0. ___48.2___ x ROS of ___33.6___ %, indicating that a (**low-cost** / **product-differentiation**) strategy is used.

Q5 Complete Coca-Cola's trend indexes for *Total expenses* and *Net income* using the amounts listed below. Record the resulting *trend index* in the shaded area. Use 2007 as the base year.

Coca-Cola (KO) ($ in millions)	2010		2009		2008		Base Year 2007	
Sales revenue	$35,119	122	$30,990	107	$31,994	111	$28,857	100
Total expenses	23,310	102	24,166	106	26,187	114	22,876	100
Net income	$11,809	197	$ 6,824	114	$ 5,807	97	$ 5,981	100

From 2007 to 2010 sales revenue of Coca-Cola increased by ___22___ %, while expenses increased by ___2___ %, resulting in an increase in net income of ___97___ %. Coca-Cola has (**kept** / **not kept**) spending under control, resulting in a (**small** / **large**) increase in net income that is (**greater** / **less**) than the increase in sales revenue over the same time period.

Q6 Complete Coca-Cola's common-size statements for 12/31/2008, 12/31/2009, and 12/31/2010 using the amounts listed below. Record the resulting *common-size percent* in the shaded area provided.

Coca-Cola (KO) ($ in millions)	Dec 31, 2010	%	Dec 31, 2009	%	Dec 31, 2008	%	Dec 31, 2007	%
Assets	$72,921	100	$48,671	100	$40,519	100	$43,269	100
Liabilities	41,918	57	23,872	59	20,047	49	21,525	50
SEquity	$31,003	43	$24,799	51	$20,472	51	$21,744	50

On 12/31/2007, __50__ % of assets were financed with liabilities and on 12/31/2010 assets were primarily financed with **(liabilities / stockholders' equity)**, indicating that on 12/31/2010 this company is relying **(more / less)** on debt to finance assets.

In the common-size *balance sheet*, every amount is compared to or divided by ___total asset___.

In the common-size *income statement*, every amount is compared to or divided by ___Revenue___.

Q7 To answer the following questions, use the chart below that presents financial information for PepsiCo, Coca-Cola, and ratio averages for the beverage industry.

($ in millions)	PEP 12/25/2010	KO 12/31/2010	Beverage Industry Average
Assets	$ 68,153	$ 72,921	NA
Liabilities	46,989	41,918	NA
Stockholders' Equity	21,164	31,003	NA
Revenue	57,838	35,119	NA
Net Income	$ 6,320	$ 11,809	NA
ROS	10.93%	33.63%	19%
Asset Turnover	0.8486	0.4816	0.80
ROA	9.27%	16.19%	15%
Debt Ratio	68.95%	57.48%	74%

a. **(PEP / KO)** has a stronger ROS, indicating it generates more **(expense / profit)** from each dollar of revenue.

b. **(PEP / KO)** reports the greatest volume of sales as indicated by the **(ROS / Asset Turnover / ROA)** ratio.

c. The most comprehensive measure of profitability, the **(ROS / Asset Turnover / ROA)** ratio, indicates **(PEP / KO)** is the more profitable company.

d. **(PEP / KO / both / neither)** are at greater financial risk than average for the beverage industry, which is indicated by the **(ROS / Asset Turnover / ROA / Debt)** ratio.

Q8 Are Generally Accepted Accounting Principles (GAAP) necessary? **(Yes / No)** Why or why not?

to understand

BALANCE SHEET

1. Understand how the balance sheet is organized.
2. Identify individual components of the balance sheet.
3. Understand similarities and differences between U.S. GAAP and IFRS among asset items.
4. Explain how debt and equity affect financial risk.
5. Compute and interpret liquidity and solvency ratios.
6. Prepare and interpret trend and common-size balance sheets.

INTRODUCTION

How would you assess your personal finances? One approach is to consider your net worth. First of all, add up everything you own: cash in the bank account, your car, books, and gadgets. These are your assets. Then add up everything you owe: credit card bills, student loans, and perhaps personal debts. These are your liabilities. Subtracting your liabilities from your assets will give you "net worth," the value of your assets after all liabilities have been paid.

> *For example, suppose that Kirsten, a college student, has $1,000 in the bank and an auto she recently purchased for $4,000 in cash. That makes $5,000 in assets. She also owes $700 on a credit card. That's $700 in liabilities. Kirsten has net worth of $4,300 ($5,000 - 700). Kirsten has financed her assets primarily with her own net worth.*
>
> *Mike also has $1,000 in the bank and a car recently purchased for $4,000 in cash; $5,000 in assets. He owes $700 on a credit card, just like Kirsten, but also owes $20,000 in student loans. Mike has liabilities of $20,700 and net worth of negative $15,700 ($5,000 - 20,700). Mike has financed his assets with liabilities.*

The **Balance Sheet** provides a snapshot of a company's financial position as of a certain date. It reports assets and whether those assets are financed with liabilities or stockholders' equity. The Balance Sheet is also referred to as the **Statement of Financial Position**.

> *Both Kirstin and Mike have the same amount of cash in the bank, $1,000. However, learning about their net worth helps us understand how easily they can pay off debt. In the long term, Mike will need to obtain more assets than Kirsten to pay off his student loan liabilities. If he can't obtain those assets, he will not be able to pay the liabilities. Kirsten, on the other hand, will not have this problem. However, because student loans won't begin to come due until a year after graduation, both Kirsten and Mike should have the same ability to pay off their liabilities in the next year.*

The Balance Sheet is important because investors use it to understand a company's liquidity and solvency. **Liquidity** describes a company's ability to pay liabilities as they come due *in the next year*. **Solvency** describes a company's ability to pay liabilities *for many years into the future*. To survive, companies must have strong liquidity and healthy solvency.

In this chapter, we learn to understand and interpret amounts reported on the balance sheet in order to evaluate the liquidity and solvency of The Walt Disney Company. The following are Walt Disney's consolidated balance sheets (**Consolidated** means that this financial statement combines the results of all Walt Disney subsidiaries).

The Walt Disney Company (DIS)	BALANCE SHEET	($ in millions)
ASSETS	**10/2/2010**	**10/3/2009**
Current assets:		
Cash and cash equivalents	$ 2,722	$ 3,417
Receivables	5,784	4,854
Inventories	1,442	1,271
Television costs	678	631
Deferred income taxes	1,018	1,140
Other current assets	581	576
Total current assets	12,225	11,889
Film and television costs	4,773	5,125
Investments	2,513	2,554
Parks, resorts, and other property, at cost:		
Attractions, buildings, and equipment	$32,875	$32,475
Accumulated depreciation	(18,373)	(17,395)
	14,502	15,080
Projects in progress	2,180	1,350
Land	1,124	1,167
	17,806	17,597
Intangible assets, net	5,081	2,247
Goodwill	24,100	21,683
Other assets	2,708	2,022
TOTAL ASSETS	$ 69,206	$ 63,117
LIABILITIES		
Current liabilities:		
Accounts payable and other accrued liabilities	$ 6,109	$ 5,616
Current portion of borrowings	2,350	1,206
Unearned royalties and other advances	2,541	2,112
Total current liabilities	11,000	8,934
Borrowings	10,130	11,495
Deferred income taxes	2,630	1,819
Other long-term liabilities	6,104	5,444
Commitments and contingencies	--	--
SHAREHOLDERS' EQUITY		
Preferred stock, $.01 par value Authorized—100 million shares, Issued—none	--	--
Common stock, $.01 par value Authorized—4.6 billion shares at 10/2/2010 and 3.6 billion shares at 10/3/2009, Issued—2.7 billion shares at 10/2/2010 and 2.6 billion shares at 10/3/2009	28,736	27,038
Retained earnings	34,327	31,033
Accumulated other comprehensive loss	(1,881)	(1,644)
Treasury stock, at cost, 803.1 million shares at 10/2/2010 and 781.7 million shares at 10/3/2009	(23,663)	(22,693)
Noncontrolling Interests	1,823	1,691
	39,342	35,425

TOTAL L & SE		$ 69,206	$ 63,117

UNDERSTANDING THE WALT DISNEY COMPANY'S BALANCE SHEET

This financial statement is called the "balance sheet" because assets are "equal to" or "balance" with the sum of liabilities and stockholders' equity. It is based on the accounting equation:

Assets = Liabilities + Stockholders' Equity

Recall that **Assets** are items of value that a corporation has a right to use. **Liabilities** are amounts owed to creditors, the amount of debt owed to third parties. **Stockholders' Equity** is the portion of assets the owners own free and clear of the liabilities. Stockholders' Equity is also referred to as **Shareholders' Equity**, as on Disney's Balance Sheet:

October 2, 2010

Assets	$ 69,206	Liabilities	$ 29,864
		Stockholders' Equity (SE)	39,342
Total assets	**$ 69,206**	**Total liabilities and SE**	**$ 69,206**

Above, Disney owns $69,206 million in assets. It also owes $29,864 million in liabilities to its creditors (6,109+ 2,350 + 2,541 + 10,130 + 2,630 + 6,104). This leaves $39,342 million of assets that are financed by stockholders. Disney is accountable to the creditors to pay back loans received from them, with interest. Similarly, Disney managers are accountable to the stockholders, to take good care of their company and earn a healthy return on investment.

From 2009 to 2010, Disney's assets have increased from $63,117 to $69,206, or 9.6%. This indicates that Disney's assets are growing relatively quickly. By comparison, the trend analysis in Chapter 1 revealed that Nike's assets grew 21% over the past three years, or about 7% per year.

The Balance Sheet lists assets and liabilities in the order of **liquidity,** the ease with which each account can be converted into cash. The most liquid asset, cash, always appears first. The least liquid asset, often goodwill, is listed last. Similarly, liabilities are listed in the order of payment, so that the most liquid liability, that which is due earliest, is listed at the top. Usually this is accounts payable. The least liquid liabilities are usually long-term debt.

Along these lines, assets and liabilities are both split into "current" and "noncurrent" portions. **Current assets** are expected to be converted into cash, sold, or consumed within the next twelve months. **Noncurrent assets** are all assets not listed as current. **Current liabilities** are liabilities due within 12 months. **Noncurrent liabilities** are due after 12 months. As we will see later in this chapter, these distinctions help financial statement users assess a company's liquidity and solvency.

In the next sections, we discuss current and noncurrent assets, and current and noncurrent liabilities. Stockholders' Equity is discussed in Chapter 4.

Current assets are those assets that are expected to be converted into cash, sold, or consumed within 12 months. These assets are highly liquid items that the company can readily use to pay for its operations.

The Walt Disney Company (DIS) BALANCE SHEET ($ in millions)		
ASSETS	**10/2/2010**	**10/3/2009**
Current assets:		
Cash and cash equivalents	$ 2,722	$ 3,417
Receivables	5,784	4,854
Inventories	1,442	1,271
Television costs	678	631
Deferred income taxes	1,018	1,140
Other current assets	581	576
Total current assets	**$ 12,225**	**$ 11,889**

The balance sheet always begins with **cash and cash equivalents,** which are actual currency, bank accounts, and investments that can be liquidated immediately. Cash flow is extremely important to operating a business. After all, banks don't take net income, they take cash. To pay banks, suppliers, and employees, a company must use cash. The Statement of Cash Flows is designed to help investors understand the nature of a company's cash flows and will be discussed in Chapter 5.

Receivables are monies to be received by the company from customers. Companies typically conduct business by extending credit to one another rather than demanding cash immediately. For example, if you owned a video store and sold a *Muppets* DVD, you would most likely collect payment in cash. However, if Disney sold Target Stores a truckload of *Muppets* DVDs, it would most likely extend credit to Target Stores and then collect payment weeks later. It would not demand payment from the loading dock workers before unloading the truck. Accounts Receivable and bad debts are discussed in Chapter 6.

Inventories are merchandise held for sale to customers. For Disney, inventories would include DVDs for resale and licensed merchandise sold by the Disney Stores and at their Parks and Resorts. Retail companies typically own a great deal of merchandise, which they sell to earn net income. On the other hand, service companies own little or no inventory. They sell services which do not require inventory, such as theme park experiences or cable television shows. Because the sale of consumer products is a relatively small portion of Disney's operations, inventory is only 2% of Disney's total assets. Inventory is explained in greater depth in Chapter 6.

Television costs are the cost of television programs that will be aired during the next year. To film new television shows, such as the *Suite Life of Zack and Cody*, Disney must pay costs such as actors' salaries and set design. The costs of these new shows are considered assets because Disney will use them to earn revenues from advertising.

Noncurrent assets are all assets not listed as current. Companies use noncurrent assets in their operations, but do not plan to sell them anytime soon.

The first noncurrent asset listed is **Film and television costs**. These are the costs of films and television shows that the company plans to air long into the future. For example, in 2010 Disney released *Toy Story 3* and *Alice in Wonderland*. Film and television costs may include the cost of this film and other successful films that have become part of Disney's archive. In order to generate advertising and other revenues, the company can regularly broadcast these films and television shows, and sell DVDs.

Parks, resorts, and other property, also known as **Property, plant, and equipment** or **Fixed Assets,** summarize attractions, buildings, equipment, and land. These are long-term assets that are expected to benefit future years. For Disney, these costs include theme parks, such as Disneyland, Disney World, Euro Disney, Hong Kong Disneyland, and even ships in Disney's own cruise line.

Depreciation expense is the cost allocated to each year of the asset's life. For example, if a new Disney attraction cost $1 million and had an expected life of 20 years, the company would record $50,000 of depreciation expense each year. **Accumulated depreciation** is the total amount of depreciation expensed since the assets' date of purchase. Here, Disney's attractions, buildings, and equipment originally cost $32,875 million. However, the company has recorded $18,373 million worth of depreciation, leaving Disney with $14,502 in **Book Value**. This is the cost that Disney can still depreciate—expense on the income statement.

The Walt Disney Company (DIS) BALANCE SHEET ($ in millions)		
	10/2/2010	**10/3/2009**
Film and television costs	$ 4,773	$ 5,125
Investments	2,513	2,554
Parks, resorts, and other property, at cost:		
Attractions, buildings, and equipment	$32,875	$32,475
Accumulated depreciation	(18,373)	(17,395)
[Book value]	14,502	15,080
Projects in progress	2,180	1,350
Land	1,124	1,167
[Total parks, resorts, and other property, net]	17,806	17,597
Intangible assets, net	5,081	2,247
Goodwill	24,100	21,683
Other assets	2,708	2,022
Total noncurrent assets	**$ 56,981**	**$ 51,228**

Disney has also recorded **Projects in progress**. These are fixed assets that are being constructed, such as new theme park attractions and resort hotels. **Land** is a separate category for all land held by the company. Because land is not depreciated, accountants keep the cost of land separate from the cost of buildings. Property, plant, and equipment and depreciation expense are discussed in greater depth in Chapter 6.

Intangible assets include patents, trademarks, and copyrights that have value but not any physical presence. Disney has a rich portfolio of intangibles: Mickey Mouse, Goofy, Winnie the Pooh, Muppets, and many classic films and television programs. **Goodwill** is extra value that is recorded when buying another company. For example, on December 31, 2010, Disney acquired Marvel. Disney paid $4,200 million, even though Marvel had only $2,000 million in stockholders' equity (assets minus liabilities). The difference of $2,200 million was goodwill, extra value that Disney paid when making this acquisition. Companies can record goodwill only when buying other companies. They cannot include goodwill that comes from their own good business practices.

CURRENT LIABILITIES

The Walt Disney Company (DIS) BALANCE SHEET ($ in millions)		
LIABILITIES	**10/2/2010**	**10/3/2009**
Current liabilities:		
Accounts payable and other accrued liabilities	$ 6,109	$ 5,616
Current portion of borrowings	2,350	1,206
Unearned royalties and other advances	2,541	2,112
Total current liabilities	**$ 11,000**	**$ 8,934**

Current liabilities are liabilities due within 12 months. These are bills that are usually paid from a company's current assets, usually cash.

Accounts payable are amounts owed to suppliers in the future. Accounts payable are the mirror image of accounts receivable, in the sense that Disney's accounts payable are, to its suppliers, accounts receivable.

Current portion of borrowings is the portion of long-term debt due within the next 12 months. For example, if Disney has an installment loan payable, which requires the company to make a monthly payment, the next 12 months' payments would be classified as current, whereas any later payments would be classified as noncurrent.

Unearned royalties and other advances include prepaid amounts from advertising subscribers and advance theme park ticket sales. *Rf paid in advance* [handwritten annotation]

NONCURRENT LIABILITIES

The Walt Disney Company (DIS) BALANCE SHEET ($ in millions)		
	10/2/2010	**10/3/2009**
Borrowings	$ 10,130	$ 11,495
Deferred income taxes	2,630	1,819
Other long-term liabilities	6,104	5,444
Commitments and contingencies	--	--

Noncurrent liabilities are amounts due after 12 months.

Borrowings are loans or other payables due over the long term. **Deferred income tax liabilities** usually come from tax rules that allow companies to earn income now but pay taxes later. Following the expression that "there are only two certainties in life: death and taxes," companies must record these as liabilities. As companies earn income, they must record liabilities for income taxes even if the taxes might not come due for many years.

Most companies place a line item for **commitments and contingencies** on their balance sheets. This line reminds investors that lawsuits and other events could create new liabilities for the company. For example, Mr. Stephen Slesinger sued Disney, claiming that the company owed him royalties for the use of Winnie the Pooh. More information is provided about these items in the notes to the financial statements.

Stockholders' Equity is discussed in Chapter 4. Current and Long-term Liabilities are discussed in greater depth in Chapter 6.

Here are 10 years' selected data from Disney's balance sheets with reported amounts in millions of dollars.

Fiscal year ended in	2001	2002	2003	2004	2005	2006	2007	2008	2009	2010
Current assets	7,029	7,849	8,314	9,369	8,845	9,562	11,314	11,666	11,889	12,225
Total assets	43,810	50,045	49,988	53,902	53,158	59,998	60,928	62,497	63,117	69,206
Current liabilities	6,219	7,819	8,669	11,059	9,168	10,210	11,391	11,591	8,934	11,000
Total liabilities	21,138	26,600	26,197	27,821	26,948	28,178	30,175	30,174	27,692	29,864
Stockholders' equity	22,672	23,445	23,791	26,081	26,210	31,820	30,753	32,323	35,425	39,342

Disney's total assets have increased from $43,810 million in 2001 to $69,206 million in 2010.

INTERNATIONAL FINANCIAL REPORTING STANDARDS (IFRS)

The joint "financial statement presentation" project of the FASB (Financial Accounting Standards Board of the United States) and the IASB (International Accounting Standards Board) will dramatically change the format of all financial statements, including the balance sheet. They are working toward a common format, organized into operating, investing, and financing activities.

IFRS and U.S. GAAP treatment of cash and receivables are essentially the same. However, IFRS allows a company to revalue property, plant, and equipment (PPE) to fair value, rather than keeping it at historical cost as required by U.S. GAAP. Also, the FASB and the IASB are working together to develop a common conceptual framework, which could alter the way liabilities are reported.

DEBT VERSUS EQUITY

Companies finance their assets with a mix of debt and equity. Large amounts of debt are usually issued in the form of bonds. The borrowing corporation records bonds payable and is referred to as the **debtor.** The entity loaning the money records an asset—bond receivable—and is referred to as the **creditor.** The debtor must pay back the amount borrowed plus interest to the creditor. The interest paid by the borrowing corporation is an expense that reduces taxable income. Because creditors are not owners of the corporation, they have no ownership rights. Bonds are discussed in Chapter 6.

Equity refers to the issuance of stock, which may be common stock or preferred stock. Entities owning shares of stock are the owners of the corporation and are referred to as **stockholders** or **shareholders.** Stockholders' primary ownership rights include a right to vote at annual meetings and a right to a portion of the profits (net income). Dividends are the distribution of profits to stockholders. The corporate board of directors decides whether to pay dividends or not and has no obligation to purchase the shares of stock back from the stockholders. If stockholders sell their shares of stock, they usually sell to another investor using a stockbroker, who in turn executes the trade on a stock exchange such as the New York Stock Exchange or NASDAQ. Stockholders earn a return on their investment by receiving dividends or selling the stock for a greater amount than the purchase price.

The balance sheet helps both creditors and stockholders to assess a corporation's financial risk. In general, the more a corporation relies on debt to finance assets, the greater the corporation's financial risk.

ANALYZING THE BALANCE SHEET

LIQUIDITY: CURRENT RATIO

The **current ratio,** current assets divided by current liabilities, measures the ability to pay current liabilities as they come due. It is a measure of short-term **liquidity,** a company's ability to pay amounts due in the next 12 months.

$$\text{Current Ratio} = \frac{\text{Current Assets}}{\text{Current Liabilities}}$$

Here are current ratios for Disney, compared with two similar companies: News Corporation and Time Warner. News Corp owns Fox Broadcasting and many newspapers. Time Warner owns AOL, Warner Brothers films, HBO and many other cable channels, and magazines such as *Time* and *Sports Illustrated*.

2010 ($ in millions)	Disney (DIS)	News Corp (NWS)	Time Warner (TWX)
Current assets	$12,225	$18,024	$ 13,138
Current liabilities	$11,000	$ 8,862	$ 8,643
Current ratio	1.11	2.03	1.52

A healthy current ratio is generally considered to be around one, indicating that current assets are at least equal to current liabilities. In 2010, Disney reported a current ratio of 1.11, which is low compared to News Corp (2.03) and Time Warner (1.52). All three companies seem to have healthy current ratios, and do not appear to have liquidity problems.

SOLVENCY: DEBT RATIO

The **debt ratio,** total liabilities divided by total assets, indicates the percentage of the company financed with debt (liabilities). It is used to measure **solvency,** a company's ability to pay back long-term debt when due. When the debt ratio is lower, there is less financial risk and stronger solvency. High debt ratios, which could sometimes exceed 100%, indicate that a company might have too much debt. If it cannot pay back principal plus interest on its long-term debt, the creditors could claim collateral owned by the company or even force it into bankruptcy.

> *The difference between the current ratio and the debt ratio, between liquidity and solvency, is that the current ratio, measuring liquidity, addresses the company's ability to pay amounts due in the next 12 months. The debt ratio, measuring solvency, addresses the company's ability to pay amounts owed over a longer term.*

$$\text{Debt Ratio} \quad = \quad \frac{\text{Total Liabilities}}{\text{Total Assets}}$$

Here are debt ratios for Disney and our two comparison companies:

2010 ($ in millions)	Disney (DIS)	News Corp (NWS)	Time Warner (TWX)
Total liabilities	$ 29,864	$ 28,843	$ 33,579
Total assets	$ 69,206	$ 54,384	$ 66,524
Debt ratio	43.2%	53.0%	50.5%

Disney's debt ratio is approximately 43%. This means that 43% of assets are financed with debt, whereas 57% (1 - 43%) of assets are financed with equity. News Corp., has a 53% debt ratio, indicating that 53% of its assets are financed by debt, and therefore, 47% by stockholders' equity. This indicates News Corp. has more financial risk than Disney. Time Warner's 2010 debt ratio was 51%, slightly lower than News Corp.

Trend analysis helps to compare amounts of a more recent year to an older base year. The base year is the earliest year being studied. This analysis measures the percentage of change from the base year to shed light on growth trends in the company's financial position.

DISNEY	2010		2009		2008		2007	
($ in millions)	$	Trend	$	Trend	$	Trend	$	Trend
Current assets	12,225	108	11,889	105	11,666	103	11,314	100
PPE, net	17,806	102	17,597	101	17,532	101	17,433	100
Goodwill + intangibles	29,181	119	23,930	97	24,579	100	24,579	100
Other assets	9,994	131	9,701	128	8,720	115	7,602	100
Total assets	**69,206**	**114**	**63,117**	**104**	**62,497**	**103**	**60,928**	**100**
Current liabilities	11,000	97	8,934	78	11,591	102	11,391	100
NC liabilities	18,864	100	18,758	100	18,583	99	18,784	100
Common stock	28,736	119	27,038	112	26,546	110	24,207	100
R/Earnings	34,327	138	31,033	125	28,413	115	24,805	100
Other SE	(23,721)	130	(22,646)	124	(22,636)	124	(18,259)	100
Total L and SE	**69,206**	**114**	**63,117**	**104**	**62,497**	**103**	**60,928**	**100**

[handwritten margin notes: "they are expanding, buying out", "treasury stock", "Typ J buying back shares"]

In the above table, we assign 2007, the base year, trend indexes of 100. For each subsequent year, we compute the trend index as:

> **Trend Index = Current amount / Base year amount x 100**

Increases from the base year are above 100, while decreases are below 100. For example, current assets increased from $11,314 million in 2007 to $12,225 million in 2011, reflected in the trend index of 108, an 8% (108 - 100) increase from 2007. All trend indexes reflect changes from the base year rather than the previous year.

Analyzing this table from 2007 to 2011, we see total assets increased by 14% (trend figure of 114), whereas noncurrent liabilities barely changed (trend index in 2011 is 100). Common stock has increased by 19% and retained earnings by 38%, an increase greater than the increase in assets, indicating asset growth was primarily financed by equity, not liabilities.

Based on this analysis, we see that Disney's assets have grown slowly, at an average rate of approximately 4.7% (= 14%/3 years) per year.

COMMON-SIZE BALANCE SHEET

The **common-size balance sheet** measures each balance sheet item as a percentage of total assets. Divide each balance sheet figure by total assets of that year. The percentages should add up to 100% for assets, and also, for liabilities plus stockholders' equity.

It is difficult to directly compare different companies' balance sheets because each company is a different size. Consider our comparison of Nike with Under Armour in the prior chapter. Under Armour is just 4% the size of Nike—how could you compare them? By standardizing each balance sheet on a 100 percentage point scale, common-size analysis simplifies these comparisons. See the common-size balance sheet for Disney, compared with News Corp and Time Warner.

2010	Disney (DIS)		News Corp (NWS)		Time Warner (TWX)	
($ in millions)	$	%	$	%	$	%
Current assets	12,225	18%	18,024	33%	13,138	20%
PPE, net	17,806	26%	5,980	11%	3,874	6%
Goodwill + intangibles	29,181	42%	22,055	41%	40,313	60%
Other assets	9,994	14%	8,325	15%	9,199	14%
Total assets	**69,206**	**100%**	**54,384**	**100%**	**66,524**	**100%**
Current liabilities	11,000	16%	8,862	16%	8,643	13%
NC liabilities	18,864	27%	19,981	37%	24,936	38%
Common stock	28,736	41%	17,434	32%	157,162	236%
Retained earnings	34,327	50%	7,679	14%	(94,557)	-142%
Other SE	(23,721)	-34%	428	1%	(29,660)	-45%
Total L and SE	**69,206**	**100%**	**54,384**	**100%**	**66,524**	**100%**

For all three companies, the greatest proportion of assets is in goodwill and other Intangibles, indicating that these companies primarily expand through the acquisition of other companies.

PPE (property, plant, and equipment), net is 26% of Disney's assets, compared with only 11% for News Corp, and 6% for Time Warner. This is because Disney invests in theme parks such as Disneyland and Walt Disney World. Current assets and other assets are of lower proportions and, therefore, of lesser significance for all three companies.

Disney reports using about the same percentage of current liabilities (16%) as News Corp (16%) and Time Warner (13%). Disney reports a lower percentage of noncurrent liabilities (27%) when compared with News Corp (37%) and Time Warner (38%).

Also of interest is that Disney uses approximately equal parts of liabilities (43%), common stock (41%), and retained earnings (50%) to finance assets, whereas Time Warner primarily finances assets with common stock. Time Warner also has a huge negative retained earnings (also referred to as an accumulated deficit) of $94,557 million. AOL and Time Warner merged on January 11, 2001, when the market price of technology stocks was at an all time high. Soon after the merger, the tech bubble burst, and the high price of tech stocks fell. Therefore, the original amount reported for goodwill as a result of the merger had to be written down, as that intangible value no longer existed. The impairment of goodwill was reflected in a $97,217 loss reported in 2002, which continues to be reflected in retained earnings today.

In summary, we learn from this analysis that Disney has a substantial investment in goodwill as a result of acquiring other companies, and in PPE, due to its investment in theme parks. From the current ratio, we learned that the company has sufficient liquidity, the ability to pay debts that come due over the next 12 months, and adequate solvency, the ability to pay off debts in the long term. In short, the company's financial condition appears to be relatively safe. But is it a good investment?

To understand whether a company might be a good investment, you must delve into the income statement to understand its profitability, the next chapter's topic.

SUMMARY

The balance sheet reports assets and the amount of assets financed with liabilities and stockholders' equity as of a certain date. It is prepared based on the formula, Assets = Liabilities + Stockholders' Equity. Assets are items of value that a company has the right to use. Liabilities are amounts owed to creditors. Stockholders' Equity is the portion of assets that owners own free and clear, after subtracting all liabilities.

The balance sheet lists assets and liabilities in the order of liquidity, how easily each asset can be converted into cash, and when each liability is expected to be paid. The most liquid assets and liabilities appear first, while the least liquid assets and liabilities appear last. Current assets are expected to be converted into cash, sold, or consumed within the next 12 months. All assets not listed as current are classified as noncurrent. Similarly, current liabilities are due within 12 months, whereas noncurrent assets are due later.

Receivables are monies expected to be received from customers. Inventories are merchandise held for sale to customers. Property, plant, and equipment are long-term assets expected to benefit future years. Depreciation expense is recorded for property, plant, and equipment, allocating its historical cost to each year of an asset's life. Accumulated depreciation is the total amount of depreciation expensed since the date an asset was purchased. Intangible assets include goodwill, patents, trademarks, and copyrights that have value but no physical presence.

Accounts payable are amounts owed to suppliers. Current portion of borrowings is the portion of long-term debt due within the next 12 months. Borrowings, or long-term debt, are due more than 12 months from the balance sheet date. Most companies place a line item on the balance sheet for commitments and contingencies to remind investors that lawsuits and other events could create new liabilities for the company.

IFRS and U.S. GAAP treatment of cash and receivables are essentially the same. One difference is that IFRS allows revaluation of property, plant, and equipment (PPE) to fair value.

Liquidity measures a company's ability to pay debts due in the next 12 months. The current ratio (current assets divided by current liabilities) is used to measure liquidity. Solvency addresses the company's ability to pay amounts owed over the long term. The debt ratio (total liabilities divided by total assets) is one measure of solvency.

Trend analysis can help users to compare different years' balance sheets. Common-size analysis can help users to compare the balance sheets of different companies in the same industry.

RATIO	ROS x	ASSET TURNOVER	= ROA	CURRENT RATIO	DEBT RATIO
Type	Profitability	Efficiency	Profitability	Liquidity	Solvency
Formula	NI / Revenue	Revenue / Total Assets	NI / Total Assets	Current Assets / Current Liabilities	Total Liabilities / Total Assets
Disney (DIS)	10.4%	0.550	5.7%	1.11	43.2%
News Corp (NWS)	8.1%	0.602	4.9%	2.03	53.0%
Time Warner (TWX)	9.6%	0.404	3.9%	1.52	50.5%
* **Industry	10.8%	0.600	6.0%	1.50	32.4%
**S&P 500	10.0%	1.0	10.0%	1.40	60.0%

*   Industry: *Entertainment—Diversified   Industry and S&P 500 ratio averages from money.msn.com*

**   There are no official rules governing how these ratios are calculated. Therefore, the ratio formulas used may differ from the formulas in the text.

Across
5. Lends money
6. Extra value recorded when buying another company
8. Reports assets, liabilities, and stockholders' equity (2 words)
9. Investments available for quick liquidation (2 words)
12. Patents, copyrights, and brand names
13. Accounts payable is a _____ account
16. Buildings, equipment, and land (abbreviation)
17. Cost allocation _depreciation_
20. Acquisition Cost less Accumulated Depreciation (2 words)
22. Owners of a corporation
23. Income tax amounts to be paid later
24. Money in the bank
25. Ratio that measures the ability to pay current liabilities with current assets _current ratio_
26. Total liabilities divided by total assets (2 words) _debt ratio_

Down
1. Amounts owed to suppliers (2 words) _a/c payable_
2. Distribution of earnings _dividends_
3. Merchandise held for sale _inventory_
4. Borrows money _Debtor_
7. Ratios that measure the ability to pay liabilities as they come due
9. Lawsuits and other events that could create new liabilities for the company _contigencies_
10. Inventory is an _____ account
11. Total amount of depreciation expensed since the assets' date of purchase
14. Monies to be received from customers
15. Equipment is a _____ asset account, which is used for more than one year _non-current_
18. Ratios that measure the ability to pay liabilities for many years _solvency ratio_
19. Balance Sheet reporting all amounts as a percentage of total assets (2 words)
21. Liabilities due within 12 months

Purpose: • Identify account classifications typically used on the balance sheet.

STARBUCKS (SBUX) 10/02/2011 BALANCE SHEET ($ in millions)			
ASSETS		**LIABILITIES**	
Cash and cash equivalents	$ 1,148.1	Accounts payable	$ 540.0
Short-term investments	902.6	Short-term debt	0.0
Accounts receivable	385.6	Other current liabilities	1,535.8
Inventories	965.8	Long-term debt	549.5
Other current assets	392.8	Other noncurrent liabilities	350.2
PPE, net	2,355.0	**STOCKHOLDERS' EQUITY**	
Goodwill and intangibles	433.5	Contributed capital	41.2
Long-term investments	479.3	Retained earnings	4,297.4
Other noncurrent assets	297.7	Other stockholders' equity	46.3
TOTAL ASSETS	**$7,360.4**	**TOTAL L & SE**	**$7,360.4**

Handwritten annotations in left margin: CA, CA, CA, CA, CA next to asset rows; OA, OA next to lower asset rows.

A classified balance sheet breaks the three major account types (assets, liabilities, and stockholders' equity) into smaller classifications to help decision makers better understand the information presented. Typical classifications and a brief description follow.

- **Current assets** (CA) are those assets expected to be converted into cash, sold, or consumed within 12 months.
- **Property, plant, and equipment** (PPE) summarize amounts for equipment, buildings, and land. These are long-term assets that are expected to benefit more than one accounting period. **Depreciation expense** is the cost allocated to each year of an asset's long-term useful life. **Accumulated depreciation** is the total amount of depreciation expensed since the asset's date of purchase. Acquisition cost − accumulated depreciation = the **book value** of PPE, which is the amount added to compute total assets on the balance sheet. Land is not depreciated.
- **Goodwill** is created when acquiring a company for an amount greater than its net assets; amounts paid for the value of its management team, customer base, and overall reputation. **Other intangible assets** include amounts paid for patents, copyrights, and brand names.
- **Other assets** are noncurrent asset (NCA) accounts such as long-term investments, which are not included in any other asset classification.
- **Current liabilities** (CL) are amounts owed to creditors that are expected to be repaid within 12 months. Examples include accounts payable and short-term debt.
- **Noncurrent liabilities** (NCL) are amounts owed to creditors that are expected to be repaid in more than 12 months. Examples include bonds payable and long-term debt.
- **Contributed capital** (CC) are amounts paid-in (contributed) by stockholders to purchase common stock and preferred stock. Accounts include capital stock and additional-paid-in capital (APIC).
- **Retained earnings** (RE) is net income earned by the company since its incorporation and not yet distributed as dividends.
- **Other stockholders' equity** includes treasury stock and adjustments to stockholders' equity such as the change in value of long-term investments.

To answer the following questions refer to the balance sheet presented above.

Q1   How many accounts listed are Current Assets? (1 / 3 / 5) Property, Plant, and Equipment? (1 / 3 / 5)
       Goodwill and Intangibles? (1 / 3 / 5)   Other Assets? (1 / 2 / 5)

Q2   What is the total amount reported for Current Liabilities? $ 2,075.8 million 4,384.9
       Noncurrent Liabilities? $ 899.7 million   Total Stockholders' Equity? $ 4,98.9 million

Purpose: •   Identify the value at which amounts are reported on the balance sheet.

Use Starbucks' balance sheet dated 10/02/2011 (on the opposite page) to answer the following questions.

a. How much do customers owe this company? $___385.6___ million

b. For *inventories*, $965.8 million is the (**acquisition cost** / **current market value** / **can't tell**) ✗ *Notes needed*

c. For *property, plant, and equipment, net*, $2,355.0 million is the (**acquisition cost** / **current market value** / **book value** / **can't tell**).

d. What amount of investments does this company intend to hold for more than a year? $___479.3___ million

e. (**PPE** / **Goodwill** / **Long-term Investments**) is created when a company is acquired.

f. How much does this company owe to suppliers? $___540___ million   *a/c payable*

g. Current assets total $___3794.9___ million and current liabilities total $___2075.8___ million. Current assets are used to pay off (**current** / **noncurrent**) liabilities. This company has (**sufficient** / **insufficient**) current assets to pay off its current liabilities.

h. Noncurrent assets total $___3565.5___ million and noncurrent liabilities total $___899.7___ million. Noncurrent liabilities are used to finance (**current** / **noncurrent**) assets.

i. Contributed capital represents (**amounts borrowed** / **amounts paid-in by shareholders** / **net income earned by the company**).

j. This company is relying primarily on (**long-term debt** / **contributed capital** / **retained earnings**) to finance assets, which is an (**external** / **internal**) source of financing.   → *Income Statement*

k. The balance sheet reports a company's financial position (**as of a certain date** / **over a period of time**).

l. Assets and liabilities are recorded on the balance sheet in order of (**magnitude** / **alphabetically** / **liquidity**), which means that (**PPE** / **cash**) will always be reported before (**PPE** / **cash**).

m. U.S. GAAP and IFRS treat (**cash** / **PPE**) essentially the same. However, for (**cash** / **PPE**), IFRS allows valuation at fair value, whereas U.S. GAAP requires (**historical cost** / **fair value**).

Purpose:
- Identify the value at which amounts are reported on the balance sheet.
- Understand what an increase or a decrease in an account indicates.
- Develop strategies for analyzing the balance sheet.

STARBUCKS (SBUX) BALANCE SHEET ($ in millions)				
ASSETS	**10/02/2011**	**10/03/2010**	**9/27/2009**	**9/28/2008**
Cash and cash equivalents	$ 1,148.1	$ 1,164.0	$ 599.8	$ 269.8
Short-term investments	902.6	285.7	66.3	52.5
Accounts receivable	385.6	302.7	271.0	329.5
Inventories	965.8	543.3	664.9	692.8
Other current assets	392.8	460.7	433.8	403.4
Property, plant, and equipment	6,163.1	5,888.7	5,700.9	5,717.3
Accumulated depreciation	(3,808.1)	(3,472.2)	(3,164.5)	(2,760.9)
PPE, net	2,355.0	2,416.5	2,536.4	2,956.4
Goodwill and other intangibles	433.5	333.2	327.3	333.1
Long-term investments	479.3	533.3	423.5	374.0
Other noncurrent assets	297.7	346.5	253.8	(L)
TOTAL ASSETS	**$ 7,360.4**	**$ 6,385.9**	**$ 5,576.8**	**$ 5,672.6**
LIABILITIES				
Accounts payable	$ 540.0	$ 282.6	$ 267.1	$ 324.9
Short-term debt	0.0	0.0	0.0	713.0
Other current liabilities	1,535.8	1,496.5	1,313.9	1,151.8
Long-term debt	549.5	549.4	549.3	549.6
Other noncurrent liabilities	350.2	382.7	400.8	442.4
STOCKHOLDERS' EQUITY				
Contributed capital	41.2	146.3	187.1	40.1
Retained earnings	4,297.4	3,471.2	2,793.2	2,402.4
Other stockholders' equity	46.3	57.2	65.4	48.4
TOTAL L & SE	**$ 7,360.4**	**$ 6,385.9**	**$ 5,576.8**	**$ (Z)**

Q1   Calculate the amounts that should be reported for (L) and (Z) on the 9/28/2008 balance sheet:
    (L) = $ _261.1_ million   (Z) = $ _5,672.6_ million

Q2   What was the beginning balance of the inventories account for the fiscal year ended on
    10/02/2011? $_543.3_ million   10/03/2010? $_664.9_ million   9/27/2009? $_692.8_ million

Q3   What amount of property, plant, and equipment was purchased (assuming no PPE was sold) during
    fiscal year ended   10/02/2011? $ _244.4_ million   10/03/2010? $_____ million

Q4   From 9/28/2008 to 10/02/2011 accounts payable (increased / decreased), indicating
    (more / less) financial risk. This company paid off accounts payable during fiscal years ended in
    (2011 / 2010 / 2009). As of 10/02/2011 this company owes $_540_ million to its suppliers.

Q5 Total Assets are (**increasing** / **decreasing**), indicating that this company is (**expanding** / **shrinking**).

Q6 Compute total liabilities for the fiscal year ended on:

10/02/2011? $ 2,975.5 million   9/28/2008? $ 3,181.7 million

Now compute the debt ratio for the fiscal year ended on:

10/02/2011? 40 %   9/28/2008? 56 %

Discuss the change in the company's use of debt over this 4-year period.

2075.8/3794.9   1779.1/2756.4

Q7 From 9/28/2008 to 9/27/2009, Contributed Capital (**increased** / **decreased**), indicating the company (**issued more stock** / **purchased more assets** / **reported net income**) during this accounting period.

Q8 Retained Earnings is (**increasing** / **decreasing**), indicating the company (**issued more stock** / **purchased more assets** / **reported net income**) during this accounting period. Assuming no dividends were issued, how much net income (loss) was reported for the fiscal year ended on:

10/02/2011? $ 826.2 million   10/03/2010? $ 678 million   9/27/2009? $ 340.8 million

The most profitable year was fiscal year ended (**2011** / **2010** / **2009**).

Q9 Develop a strategy to analyze the balance sheet. Which line would you look at first? Second? Third? *Why?* First would look at the Assets, second would be liabilities, then stockholder's equity. Check the debt ratios and figure out net income/loss.

Q10 Review the series of balance sheets. This company appears to report a (**strong** / **weak**) financial position. *Why?* Support your response with at least two observations. They earn more income every year. Their debt ratio lowers each year as well.

Purpose:
- Identify the characteristics of debt and equity.
- Assess financial risk.

Corporations externally finance the purchase of assets with debt (liabilities) or equity (common stock).

> **Assets = Liabilities + Stockholders' Equity**

Large amounts of **debt** are usually issued in the form of bonds. The borrowing corporation records a bond payable and is referred to as the *debtor,* while the entity loaning the money records a bond receivable and is referred to as the *creditor*. The debtor must pay back the amount borrowed plus interest to the creditor. The interest paid by the borrowing corporation is an expense that reduces taxable income. The return to creditors is the interest received. Creditors are not owners of the corporation and, therefore, have no ownership rights.

Equity refers to the issuance of stock, which may be common stock or preferred stock. Entities owning shares of stock are the owners of the corporation and are referred to as *stockholders* or shareholders. Stockholders' primary ownership rights include a right to vote at annual meetings and a right to a portion of the profits (net income). *Dividends* are the distribution of profits to stockholders. The corporate board of directors decides whether to pay dividends or not and has no obligation to purchase the shares of stock back from the stockholders. If stockholders sell their shares of stock, they usually sell to another investor using a stockbroker, who in turn executes the trade on a stock exchange such as the New York Stock Exchange or NASDAQ. Stockholders earn a return on their investment by receiving dividends or selling the stock for a greater amount than the purchase price.

The balance sheet helps investors, both creditors and stockholders, assess the degree of financial risk a corporation is assuming. In general, the more a corporation relies on debt to finance assets, the greater the financial risk of the corporation.

($ in millions)	Google (GOOG) 12/31/2011	General Mills (GIS) 5/29/2011
Assets	$ 72,574	$ (Y) *18675*
Liabilities	$ 14,429	$ 12,309
Stockholders' equity	*58145* $ (B)	$ 6,366
Debt ratio	*19.88* %	*65.9* %

Q1 Compute the values for (B) and (Y) in the above chart. Compute the **Debt Ratio** and record in the above chart. (*Debt ratio = Liabilities / Assets*)   This ratio quantifies the proportion of assets financed with debt. (**Google / GIS**) is financing assets primarily with debt; therefore, (**Google / GIS**) is assuming the greater financial risk. Based only on the information presented above, which company would you choose as an investment? (**Google / GIS**) *Why*?

Q2 For each item circle the correct response when comparing the issuance of debt and equity.

a. The corporation (**does / does not**) have to pay interest to creditors, but (**does / does not**) have to pay dividends to shareholders.

b. The corporation (**must / never has to**) repay amounts borrowed from creditors, but (**must / never has to**) repay amounts invested by shareholders, thus the title, "contributed" capital.

c. The interest expense of debt (**reduces / does not reduce**) taxable income, but dividends paid to shareholders (**reduce / do not reduce**) taxable income.

d. Issuing additional debt (**does / does not**) dilute current shareholders' ownership, but issuing additional shares of common stock (**does / does not**) dilute current shareholders' ownership.

e. If you were the CFO of a company, how would you recommend financing assets? Primarily with (**debt / equity**). *Why*?

Purpose:　　　　• 　　Understand the information provided by the current ratio and the debt ratio.

Liquidity and Solvency Ratios measure the ability to meet financial obligations and the level of financial risk.

The **Current Ratio** measures the ability to pay current payables as they come due by comparing current assets to current liabilities. It is a measure of short-term liquidity. A higher ratio indicates a stronger ability to pay current debts.

$$\text{Current Ratio} = \frac{\text{Current assets}}{\text{Current liabilities}}$$

The **Debt Ratio** measures the proportion of assets financed by debt by comparing total liabilities to total assets. It is a measure of long-term solvency. A higher ratio indicates greater financial risk.

$$\text{Debt Ratio} = \frac{\text{Total liabilities}}{\text{Total assets}}$$

For the year 2010	Industry Average for Restaurants	DineEquity (DIN)	Darden Restaurants (DRI)	Nathan's Famous (NATH)
Current Ratio	1.1	1.32	0.54	6.12
Debt Ratio	52%	97%	64%	17%
Debt-to-Equity Ratio*	1.10	33.17	1.77	0.20

Use the chart above to answer the following questions. Stock symbols are shown in parentheses.

Q1　　Of the above three restaurant chains, which is your favorite? (**DIN / DRI / NATH**)

　　　• _DIN_ operates Applebee's Neighborhood Grill & Bar and IHOP.

　　　• (_DRI_) operates Red Lobster, Olive Garden, Bahama Breeze, and Smokey Bones Barbeque and Grill.

　　　• _NATH_ operates Nathan's Famous.

Q2　　(**DIN** / **DRI** / **NATH**) have sufficient current assets to pay off current liabilities and, therefore, have a current ratio (**greater** / less) than 1.0. A current ratio that is (**lower** / higher) than the industry average may indicate a lack of short-term liquidity, which includes (**DIN** / **DRI** / **NATH**). Does this indicate that this corporation is insolvent or unable to pay its bills? (**Yes** / **No**) *Explain.*

Q3　　(**DIN** / **DRI** / **NATH**) are relying more on debt to finance assets and have a debt ratio (**greater** / less) than 50%. Darden Restaurants is financing ___64___ % of assets with debt. For a company wanting to be lower risk and less dependent on debt, a(n) (**increasing** / **decreasing**) trend in the debt ratio is considered favorable. A company that has higher financial risk will, in general, be required to pay (**higher** / **lower**) interest rates when borrowing money.

Q4　　*Why* does a company with a higher debt ratio tend to have greater financial risk?

　　　Because they are borrowing more than their potential earnings.

Q5　　Does a high debt ratio indicate a weak corporation? (**Yes** / **No**) *Explain* your answer.

　　　A company could have a high amount of borrowings but still has potential to pay it off.

*　　*Instead of reporting the Debt Ratio, some financial sources report the Debt-to-Equity ratio, computed as liabilities divided by stockholders' equity. To convert: Debt ratio = [Debt-to-equity ratio/(1 + Debt-to-equity ratio)]. For DineEquity 0.97 = 33.17 / 34.17*

Purpose: •   Prepare a trend analysis and understand the information provided.

A **Trend Analysis** compares amounts of a more recent year to a base year. The base year is the earliest year being studied. The analysis measures the percentage of change from the base year.

Q1   For Starbucks, use the amounts listed below to compute the trend indexes for noncurrent (NC) liabilities, common stock, and retained earnings by the amount for the base year. Record the resulting *trend index* in the shaded area. Use 9/28/2008 as the base year.

STARBUCKS	10/02/2011		10/03/2010		9/27/2009		9/28/2008	
($ in millions)	$	Trend	$	Trend	$	Trend	BASE YEAR	
Current assets	3,794.9	217	2,756.4	158	2,035.8	116	1,748.0	100
PPE, net	2,355.0	80	2,416.5	82	2,536.4	86	2,956.4	100
Goodwill + Intang.	433.5	130	333.2	100	327.3	98	333.1	100
Other assets	777.0	122	879.8	139	677.3	107	635.1	100
TOTAL ASSETS	**7,360.4**	**130**	**6,385.9**	**113**	**5,576.8**	**98**	**5,672.6**	**100**
Current liabilities	2,075.8	95	1,779.1	81	1,581.0	72	2,189.7	100
NC liabilities	899.7	*91*	932.1	*94*	950.1	*96*	992.0	
Common stock	41.2	*103*	146.3	*365*	187.1	*467*	40.1	
Retained earnings	4,297.4	*179*	3,471.2	*144*	2,793.2	*116*	2,402.4	
Other SE	46.3	96	57.2	118	65.4	135	48.4	100
TOTAL L and SE	**7,360.4**	**130**	**6,385.9**	**113**	**5,576.8**	**98**	**5,672.6**	**100**

Refer to the series of balance sheets and the trend analysis above to answer the following questions.

Q2   A trend index of 130 (total assets) indicates that the dollar amount is (**greater / less**) than the (**previous / base**) year, whereas a trend index of 80 (PPE, net) indicates the dollar amount is (**greater / less**) than the (**previous / base**) year. For *total assets*, the trend index of 130 is computed by dividing $7,360.4 (total assets on 10/02/2011) by $___*136.0*___ million (total assets of the base year). A trend index of 130 indicates *total assets* (**increased / decreased**) by _____% (from an index of 100 to 130) from 9/28/2008 to 10/02/2011.

Q3   From 9/28/2008 to 10/02/2011, which of the following accounts increased at a greater rate than total assets? (**Noncurrent liabilities / Common stock / Retained earnings**). The assets of this company are primarily financed with (**liabilities / contributed capital / retained earnings**). This is referred to as (**internal / external**) financing because these funds are generated by operations. Issuing stocks and bonds are forms of (**internal / external**) financing because these funds come from investors outside of the firm.

Q4   The annual total asset growth rate can be compared between companies.
       Assume less than 5% is low, 5 to 15% is moderate, and more than 15% is high.
       The three-year average total asset growth rate of this company is considered (**low / moderate / high**).

Q5   Examine the financial information reported above and *comment* on at least two items of significance that the trend analysis helps to reveal.

assets ↑, retained earnings, common stock

trend index @ 130 ÷ base year @ by 30 ÷ 1.7 15% growth

ACTIVITY 19 — ANALYSIS: COMMON-SIZE STATEMENTS

Purpose: • Prepare common-size statements and understand the information provided.

The **Common-Size Balance Sheet** compares all amounts to total assets of that same year. The analysis measures each item as a percentage of total assets.

Q1   For DineEquity and Chipotle Mexican Grill listed below, complete the common-size statements by dividing each item on the balance sheet by the amount of total assets. Record the resulting common-size percentage in the shaded area provided.

(*Hint*: Percentages for CA + PPE, net + Goodwill + Other = 100% and CL + LTD + Other NCL + CS + RE + Other = 100 %.)

2010	DineEquity (DIN)		Darden Restaurants (DRI)		Nathan's Famous (NATH)	
($ in millions)	$	CS%	$	CS%	$	CS%
Current assets	351.0	12.3 %	678.5	12.9%	43.82	82.11 %
PPE, net	612.2	21.43%	3,403.7	64.9%	5.47	10.25%
Goodwill + intangibles	1533.4	53.0 %	994.9	19.0%	1.44	2.70 %
Other assets	360.0	12.60%	170.3	3.2%	2.63	4.93 %
TOTAL ASSETS	**2,856.6**	100 %	**5,247.4**	**100.0%**	**53.37**	100 %
Current liabilities	265.1	9.28%	1,254.6	23.9%	7.16	13.42%
Long-term debt	2,013.0	70.47%	1,466.3	27.9%	0.0	0.00 %
Other NC liabilities	494.7	17.32%	632.5	12.1%	1.91	2.58 %
Contributed capital	234.5	8.21 %	2,297.9	43.8%	52.1	97.62%
Retained earnings	124.3	4.35 %	2,621.9	50.0%	16.8	31.48 %
Other SE	(275.0)	(9.63)%	(3,025.8)	(57.7)%	(24.6)	(46.09)%
TOTAL L and SE	**2,856.6**	100 %*	**5,247.4**	**100.0%**	**53.37**	100 %

   * Note: The percentages may not sum to 100% due to rounding error.

Refer to the information above to answer the following questions.

Q2   The debt ratio (Total liabilities / Total assets) for Darden Restaurants is __63.90__ % or ___._____ (decimal form).

Q3   Which company finances assets primarily with amounts *borrowed long term*? (**DIN** / DRI / NATH)

Q4   Which company finances assets primarily with amounts *invested by shareholders*? (DIN / DRI / **NATH**)

Q5   Which company finances assets primarily with *past profits*?   (DIN / **DRI** / NATH)

Q6   Review the balance sheet information presented above for the three restaurant chains and comment on at least two items of significance that the common-size statements help to reveal.

Q7   These companies were easier to compare (**before / after**) you prepared the common-size statements. *Why?*

Purpose: •   Understand and interpret amounts reported on the balance sheet.

YUM! BRANDS (YUM)   BALANCE SHEET   ($ in millions)

ASSETS	12/25/2010	12/26/2009	12/27/2008	12/29/2007
Cash and cash equivalents	$ 1,426	$ 353	$ 216	$ 789
Accounts receivable	256	239	229	225
Inventories	189	122	143	128
Other current assets	442	494	363	339
Property, plant, and equipment	7,103	7,247	6,897	7,132
Accumulated depreciation	(3,273)	(3,348)	(3,187)	(3,283)
PPE, net	3,830	3,899	3,710	3,849
Goodwill and other intangibles	1,134	1,102	940	1,026
Long-term investments	154	144	65	153
Other noncurrent assets	885	795	861	679
TOTAL ASSETS	**$8,316**	**$7,148**	**$6,527**	**$7,188**
LIABILITIES				
Accounts payable	$ 540	$ 499	$ 508	$ 519
Short-term debt	673	59	25	288
Other current liabilities	1,235	1,095	1,189	1,255
Long-term debt	2,915	3,207	3,564	2,924
Other noncurrent liabilities	1,377	1,263	1,349	1,063
STOCKHOLDERS' EQUITY				
Contributed capital (CC)	86	253	7	0
Retained earnings (RE)	1,717	996	303	1,119
Other stockholders' equity (SE)	(227)	(224)	(418)	20
TOTAL L & SE	**$8,316**	**$7,148**	**$6,527**	**$7,188**

YUM! BRANDS (YUM)   Classified Balance Sheet / Common-Size Statements   ($ in millions)

	12/25/2010		12/26/2009		12/27/2008		12/29/2007	
	$	CS%	$	CS%	$	CS%	$	CS%
Current assets	2313	27.8%	1208	16.9%	951	14.6%	1,481	20.6%
PPE, net	3830	46.1%	3899	54.0%	3,710	56.8%	3,849	53.5%
Goodwill + Intang.	1134	13.6%	1102	15.4%	940	14.4%	1,026	14.3%
Other assets	1039	12.5%	939	13.1%	926	14.2%	832	11.6%
TOTAL ASSETS	8316	100 %	7148	100%	6,527	100.0%	7,188	100.0%
C liabilities	2448	29.4%	1653	23.1%	1,722	26.4%	2,062	28.7%
NC liabilities	4292	51.6%	4470	62.0%	4,913	75.3%	3,987	55.5%
TOTAL LIAB	6740	81.0%	6123	85.7%	6,635	101.7%	6,049	84.2%
CCapital	86	1.0%	253	3.5%	7	0.0%	0	0.0%
REarnings	1717	20.7%	996	13.9%	303	4.7%	1,119	15.5%
Other SE	(227)	(2.7)%	(224)	-3.1%	(418)	(6.4)%	20	0.3%
TOTAL SE	1576	19.6%	1025	14.3%	(108)	(1.7)%	1,139	15.8%

Common size
CA / TA , Non CA / TA

CL / TA , Non CL / TA

SE / TA , SE / TA

YUM! BRANDS (YUM) RATIOS					
	Industry Norm	12/25/2010	12/26/2009	12/27/2008	12/29/2007
Current ratio	*1.10*			0.55	0.72
Debt ratio	*52%*			102%	84%

Refer to the series of balance sheets for Yum! Brands (on the previous page) to answer the following questions.

Q1   YUM! Brands is the largest restaurant chain (larger than McDonald's) when measured by (**sales / # of units**) and operates more than 36,000 restaurants in more than 110 countries. (*Hint: Refer to company descriptions in Appendix A—Featured Corporations*).

Which is your favorite YUM! Brands restaurant? (**KFC / Pizza Hut / Taco Bell / Long John Silver's / A&W**)

Q2   *Total Assets* increased by $ 11128 million since 12/29/2007, an increase of 16 %, which is the result of (**purchasing additional assets / issuing more common stock / increasing net income**). This company has a major investment in (**inventories / PPE / goodwill**), which (**is** / **is not**) expected.

Q3   On 12/29/2007, the retained earnings account reports a (**positive / negative**) amount, which is most likely the result of previously (**selling assets / purchasing treasury stock / reporting net income**). *beginning RE + NI-less dividends = RE*

Q4   This company distributed dividends and other amounts to shareholders of $322 million in 2008, $362 million in 2009, and $412 million in 2010. Use this information to compute net income for:

2010 $ 1133 million;   2009 $ 1055 million;   2008 $ 494 million

Q5   For 12/26/2009 and 12/25/2010 complete the classified balance sheet by adding the items within each classification. Record your results in the area provided on the previous page. Classified balance sheets for 12/29/2007 and 12/27/2008 have already been completed.

(*Remember* CA + PPE, net + Goodwill + Other = Total Assets and CL + NCL + CS + RE + Other = Total L + SE)

Q6   For 12/26/2009 and 12/25/2010 complete the common-size statements by dividing each item on the classified balance sheet by the amount of total assets for the same year. Record your results in the area provided on the previous page. Common-size statements for 12/29/2007 and 12/27/2008 have already been completed. **Comment** on the trends in Total Liabilities and Total Stockholders' Equity and what this indicates. *assets have increased while liabilities have stayed the same SE- after net loss in 2008 profit has returned*

Q7   For 12/26/2009 and 12/25/2010 compute the current ratio and the debt ratio. Record your results in the area provided above. Ratios for 12/29/2007 and 12/27/2008 have already been computed. **Comment** on the results. *current ratio = $\frac{2313}{2448}$ = .945   2010   2009 = .731   current liability is more than assets   increased liquidity*

Q8   If you had $10,000, would you consider investing in this company? (**Yes / No**) *Why?* Support your response with at least three good reasons. *debt ratio = 81.049%   2010   86%   2009   increased   debt financing*

Purpose: • Understand and interpret amounts reported on the balance sheet.

McDONALD's (MCD) BALANCE SHEET ($ in millions)				
ASSETS	12/31/2010	12/31/2009	12/31/2008	12/31/2007
Cash and cash equivalents	$ 2,387.0	$ 1,796.0	$ 2,063.4	$ 1,981.3
Accounts receivable	1,179.1	1,060.4	931.2	1,053.8
Inventories	109.9	106.2	111.5	125.3
Other current assets	692.5	453.7	411.5	421.5
Property, plant, and equipmt	$34,482.4	$33,440.5	$31,152.4	$32,203.7
Accumulated depreciation	(12,421.8)	(11,909.0)	(10,897.9)	(11,219.0)
PPE, net	22,060.6	21,531.5	20,254.5	20,984.7
Goodwill	2,586.1	2,425.2	2,237.4	2,301.3
Long-term investments	1,335.3	1,212.7	1,222.3	1,156.4
Other noncurrent assets	1,624.7	1,639.2	1,229.7	1,367.4
TOTAL ASSETS	$31,975.2	$30,224.9	$28,461.5	$29,391.7
LIABILITIES				
Accounts payable	$ 943.9	$ 636.0	$ 620.4	$ 624.1
Short-term debt	0.0	0.0	0.0	1,126.6
Other current liabilities	1,980.8	2,352.7	1,917.5	2,747.8
Long-term debt	11,497.0	10,560.3	10,186.0	7,310.0
Other noncurrent liabilities	2,919.3	2,642.0	2,355.0	2,303.4
STOCKHOLDERS' EQUITY				
Common stock, par	16.6	16.6	16.6	16.6
Additional paid-in capital	5,196.4	4,853.9	4,600.2	4,226.7
Retained earnings	33,811.7	31,270.8	28,953.9	26,461.5
Treasury stock	(25,143.4)	(22,854.8)	(20,289.4)	(16,762.4)
Other stockholders' equity	752.9	747.4	101.3	1,337.4
TOTAL L & SE	$31,975.2	$30,224.9	$28,461.5	$29,391.7

McDONALD's Classified Balance Sheet / Trend Analysis ($ in millions)							
	12/31/2010		12/31/2009		12/31/2008		12/31/2007
	$	Trend	$	Trend	$	Trend	BASE YEAR
Current assets	4,368.50	122	3,416.30	95	3,517.6	98	3,581.9	100
PPE, net	22,060.60	105	21,531.50	103	20,254.5	97	20,984.7	100
Goodwill	2,586.10	112	2,425.20	105	2,237.4	97	2,301.3	100
Other assets	2,960.	117	2,851.90	113	2,452.0	97	2,523.8	100
TOTAL Assets	31,975	109	30,224.90	103	28,461.5	97	29,391.7	100
Current liabilities	2,924.70	65	2,988.70	66	2,537.9	56	4,498.5	100
NC Liabilities	14,416.80	150	13,202.30	137	12,541.0	130	9,613.4	100
TOTAL Liab	17,341.	123	16,191	115	15,078.9	107	14,111.9	100
Contributed capital	5,213	123	4,870.50	115	4,616.8	109	4,243.3	100
Retained earnings	33,811.70	128	31,270.80	118	28,953.9	109	26,461.5	100
Other SE	(24,390.50)	158	(22,109.40)	143	(20,188.1)	131	(15,425.0)	100
TOTAL SE	14,634.20	96	14,033.90	92	13,382.6	88	15,279.8	100

McDONALD's (MCD) RATIOS					
	Industry Norm	12/31/2010	12/31/2009	12/31/2008	12/31/2007
Current ratio	*1.10*	*1.49*	*1.14*	1.39	0.80
Debt ratio	*52%*	*54.23*	*53.57*	53%	48%

Refer to McDonald's balance sheets on the previous page to answer the following questions.

Q1   McDonald's is the world's (**#1** / **#2**) restaurant chain when measured by (**sales** / **# of units**) and has more than 32,000 restaurants in more than 120 countries.
Hint: Refer to company descriptions in Appendix A—Featured Corporations.

Q2   In regard to assets, this company has a major investment in (**inventories** / **PPE** / **goodwill**). On average, the PPE has been used for (**more** / **less**) than half of its useful life.

Q3   *Long-term debt* was borrowed during (**2010** / **2009** / **2008**).

Q4   This company was able to attract new shareholders during (**2010** / **2009** / **2008**). As of 12/31/2010 shareholders have contributed a total of $ _5813_ million to this corporation.

Q5   This company distributed dividends of $1,823.4 million in 2008, $2,235.5 million in 2009, and $2,408.1 million in 2010. Use this information to compute net income for:

    2010 $ _4949_ million;   2009 $ _4552.4_ million;   2008 $ _4315.8_ million

Q6   Treasury stock results from (**selling assets** / **refinancing debt** / **repurchasing common stock**). Additional *treasury stock* was acquired during (**2010** / **2009** / **2008**).

Q7   For 12/31/2009 and 12/31/2010 complete the classified balance sheet by adding the accounts within each classification. Record your results in the area provided on the previous page. Classified balance sheets for 12/31/2007 and 12/31/2008 have already been completed.

    (*Remember* CA + PPE, net + Goodwill + Other = Total Assets and CL + NCL + CS + RE + Other = Total L + SE)

Q8   *Refer to the Classified Balance Sheet.* The assets of this company are primarily financed with (**liabilities** / **contributed capital** / **retained earnings**), which is (**internal** / **external**) financing.

Q9   For 12/31/2009 and 12/31/2010 complete the trend analysis by dividing each amount by the amount for the base year of 12/31/2007, and then multiply by 100. Record the resulting *trend index* in the area provided on the previous page. For 12/31/2007 and 12/31/2008 the trend indexes have already been computed.

Q10   *Refer to the trend index.* At the end of 2008, assets were (**above** / **below**) base year levels, an indication of a (**recovering** / **poor**) economy, while at the end of 2010 assets were (**above** / **below**) base year levels, an indication of a (**recovering** / **poor**) economy.
    Since the base year, total assets (**increased** / **decreased**) by _91_ %, total liabilities (**increased** / **decreased**) by _83_ %, while total stockholders' equity (**increased** / **decreased**) by _96_ %, indicating a greater reliance on (**debt** / **equity**) financing.
    Current liabilities (**increased** / **decreased**) by _(4)_ %, while noncurrent liabilities (**increased** / **decreased**) by _50_ %, indicating (**greater** / **lesser**) reliance on long-term financing.
    Retained earnings (**increased** / **decreased**) by _28_ %, which is the result of (**purchasing additional assets** / **acquiring other companies** / **reporting net income**). _128 - 100   28_

Q11   For 12/31/2009 and 12/31/2010 compute the current ratio and the debt ratio. Record your results in the area provided above. Ratios for 12/31/2007 and 12/31/2008 have already been computed.

Q12   Review the financial information of this company and ***comment*** on
    a.   signs of financial strength. _RE ↑, Assets ↑ expanding_
    b.   warning signs or signs of financial weakness. _Non current ↑, debt ratio ↑._

Q13   If you had $10,000, would you consider investing in this company? (**Yes** / **No**) *Why or why not?*

Purpose: • Understand and interpret amounts reported on the balance sheet.

BALANCE SHEETS ($ in millions)				
ASSETS	**CORP A** 6/30/2010	**CORP B** 5/31/2010	**CORP C** 12/31/2010	**CORP D** 12/31/2010
Cash and cash equivalents	$ 344.6	$ 3,079.1	$ 1,526.4	$ 27,972
Short-term investments	0.0	2,066.8	1,357.7	1,044,590
Accounts receivable	45.1	2,649.8	1,028.9	608,139
Inventories	26.7	2,040.8	0.0	0
Other current assets	84.6	1,122.7	432.6	0
Property, plant, and equipment	2,099.3	4,389.8	2,551.2	0.0
Accumulated depreciation	(970.3)	(2,457.9)	(897.8)	0.0
PPE, net	1,129.0	1,931.9	1,653.4	0
Goodwill + Intangibles	124.1	654.6	3,937.5	38,210
Long-term investments	0.0	0.0	4,803.0	0
Other noncurrent assets	98.0	873.6	188.6	194,991
TOTAL ASSETS	**$1,852.1**	**$14,419.3**	**$14,928.1**	**$1,913,902**
LIABILITIES				
Accounts payable	$ 112.8	$ 1,254.5	$ 162.4	$ 51,749
Short-term debt	0.0	138.6	0.0	258,348
Other current liabilities	337.1	1,971.1	1,463.5	873,168
Long-term debt	524.5	445.8	142.8	362,983
Other noncurrent liabilities	149.0	855.3	601.3	204,186
STOCKHOLDERS' EQUITY				
Contributed capital	483.4	3,443.4	10,111.2	101,628
Retained earnings	1,923.6	6,095.5	1,942.7	79,559
Other stockholders' equity	(1,678.3)	215.1	504.2	(17,719)
TOTAL L & SE	**$1,852.1**	**$14,419.3**	**$14,928.1**	**$1,913,902**

Classified Balance Sheets / Common-Size Statements ($ in millions)								
	A 6/30/2010		**B** 5/31/2010		**C** 12/31/2010		**D** 12/31/2010	
	$	CS%	$	CS%	$	CS%	$	CS%
Current assets	501.0	27.0	10,959.2	76.0	4,345.6	29.1	1,680,701	87.8
PPE, net	1,129.0	61.0	1,931.9	13.4	1,653.4	11.1	-0-	0.0
Goodwill+	124.1	6.7	654.6	4.5	3,937.5	26.4	38,210	2.0
Other assets	98.0	5.3	873.6	6.1	4,991.6	33.4	194,991	10.2
TTL Assets	**1,852.1**	**100.0**	**14,419.3**	**100.0**	**14,928.1**	**100.0**	**1,913,902**	**100.0**
C Liabilities	449.9	24.3	3,364.2	23.3	1,625.9	10.9	1,183,265	61.8
NC Liabilities	673.5	36.4	1,301.1	9.0	744.1	5.0	567,169	29.7
TTL Liab	**1,123.4**	**60.7**	**4,665.3**	**32.3**	**2,370.0**	**15.9**	**1,750,434**	**91.5**
Cont capital	483.4	26.1	3,443.4	23.9	10,111.2	67.7	101,628	5.3
R/Earnings	1,923.6	103.9	6,095.5	42.3	1,942.7	13.0	79,559	4.2
Other SE	(1,678.3)	(90.7)	215.1	1.5	504.2	3.4	(17,719)	(1.0)
TTL SE	**728.7**	**39.3**	**9,754.0**	**67.7**	**12,558.1**	**84.1**	**163,468**	**8.5**

RATIOS	CORP A 6/25/2010	CORP B 5/31/2010	CORP C 12/31/2010	CORP D 12/31/2010
Current ratio	1.11	3.26	2.67	1.42
Debt ratio	61%	32%	16%	91%

Q1   Analyze the financial attributes of the four corporations on the previous page by placing an X in the box when the company has the characteristics noted below.

Which corporation ...	CORP A	CORP B	CORP C	CORP D
Has significant cash, ST or LT investments?		X	X	X
Has significant receivables and inventory?		X		
Has no inventories?			X	X
Has significant property, plant, and equipment?	X	X	X	
Finances assets primarily with...				
liabilities?				
contributed capital?				
retained earnings?				
Is the smallest company?				
Is the largest company?				

Q2   Use the descriptions below to match each corporation with its corresponding financial information. Then comment on why you selected the match.

BRINKER INTERNATIONAL (EAT) owns, develops, operates, and franchises the Chili's Grill & Bar (Chili's), On The Border Mexican Grill & Cantina (On The Border), Maggiano's Little Italy (Maggiano's), and Romano's Macaroni Grill (Macaroni Grill) restaurant brands.

Brinker International must be Corporation   (**A / B / C / D**).   *Why?*

CITIGROUP (C) is a diversified global financial services holding company whose businesses provide a range of financial services to consumer and corporate customers. The company operates in five business segments: Global Cards, Consumer Banking, Institutional Clients Group, Global Wealth Management, and Other.

Citigroup must be Corporation   (**A / B / C / D**).   *Why?*

NIKE (NKE) is engaged in the design, development, and worldwide marketing of athletic footwear, apparel, equipment, and accessory products. It sells its products to retail accounts, through NIKE-owned retail, including stores and Internet sales, and through a mix of independent distributors and licensees, in more than 180 countries around the world.

Nike must be Corporation   (**A / B / C / D**).   *Why?*

YAHOO! (YHOO) is a global Internet brand. The Company's offerings to users fall into six categories: Front Doors, Communities, Search, Communications, Audience, and Connected Life. Yahoo! generates revenues by providing marketing services to advertisers across a majority of Yahoo! Properties and Affiliate sites. The majority of its offerings are available in more than 30 languages.

Yahoo! must be Corporation   (**A / B / C / D**).   *Why?*

CHAPTER 3

INCOME STATEMENT

1. Understand how the multi-step income statement is organized.
2. Interpret trends in income statement revenues, expenses, subtotals, and totals.
3. Understand the accrual basis for accounting, revenue recognition, and the matching principle.
4. Compute and interpret profitability ratios.
5. Prepare and interpret trend and common-size income statements.

INTRODUCTION

The **Income Statement** reports a company's profitability by adding revenues and subtracting expenses. This statement is also called the **Statement of Income, Statement of Earnings, Statement of Operations,** or **Statement of Profit and Loss (P&L).**

The Income Statement is important because investors use it to understand the results of a company's operations. By comparing income statement amounts to prior periods, investors can understand whether a company's sales, expenses, and net income are increasing. Investors can compare a company's performance to competitors by comparing income statement amounts to other companies in the same industry. In fact, net income is probably the most commonly used number when evaluating a company's performance.

In this chapter, we will evaluate the profitability of Amazon.com, interpret amounts reported on its income statement, introduce the concepts used to prepare the statement, and analyze this statement using simple financial analysis tools.

UNDERSTANDING AMAZON.COM'S INCOME STATEMENT

Some companies use a **single-step income statement** that combines all revenues and gains at the top of the income statement and then subtracts all expenses and losses below.

> **(Revenues and Gains) – (Expenses and Losses) = Net Income**

On the other hand, the **multi-step income statement** lists items in order of importance. Revenues and Cost of Sales, which are deemed most important, are listed at the top. These are followed by Operating Expenses, Nonoperating Items, the Provision for Income Tax, and Nonrecurring Items.

Amazon.com, Inc. CONSOLIDATED STATEMENTS OF OPERATIONS (In millions, except per share data)			
	Year Ended December 31,		
	2010	2009	2008
Step One — Net sales	$34,204	$24,509	$19,166
Cost of sales	26,561	18,978	14,896
Gross profit	7,643	5,531	4,270
Step Two — Operating expenses:			
Fulfillment	2,898	2,052	1,658
Marketing	1,029	680	482
Technology and content	1,734	1,240	1,033
General and administrative	470	328	279
Other operating expense (income)	106	102	-24
Total operating expenses	6,237	4,402	3,428
Income from operations	1,406	1,129	842
Step Three — Interest income	51	37	83
Interest expense	(39)	(34)	(71)
Other income (expense), net	79	29	47
Remeasurements and other	0	0	0
Total nonoperating expense	91	32	59
Income before income tax	1,497	1,161	901
Step Four — Provision (benefit) for income tax	(352)	(253)	(247)
Equity-movement investment activity, net of tax	7	(6)	(9)
Income before nonrecurring items	1,152	902	645
Step Five — Nonrecurring items	-	-	-
Net income	$ 1,152	$ 908	$ 645
Basic earnings per share	$2.58	$2.08	$1.52
Diluted earnings per share	$2.53	$2.04	$1.49
Weighted average shares used in computation of earnings per share:			
Basic	447	433	423
Diluted	456	442	432

See accompanying notes to consolidated financial statements.

Amazon.com, Inc. CONSOLIDATED STATEMENTS OF OPERATIONS ($ in millions)			
	Year Ended December 31,		
(Excerpts)	2010	2009	2008
Net sales	$34,204	$24,509	$19,166
Cost of sales	26,561	18,978	14,896
Gross profit	$ 7,643	$ 5,531	$ 4,270

REVENUES AND REVENUE RECOGNITION

Revenues are inflows from a company's primary operations. **Sales** typically refer to revenues from the sale of merchandise. **Net Sales** indicate that returns or discounts were subtracted from total sales. Amazon.com reports one revenue item, Net Sales of $34,204 in 2010. Amazon.com's Net Sales includes a wide range of products.

> *In its retail division, Amazon.com sells books, music, DVD's, VHS tapes, magazines and newspapers, video games, software, electronics, audio and video equipment, camera and photo equipment, cell phones and service, computers and PC hardware, office products, musical instruments, outlet merchandise, home and garden, bed and bath, furniture and décor, gourmet food, kitchen and housewares, outdoor living, pet supplies, automotive, tools and hardware, industrial and scientific, apparel and accessories, shoes, jewelry and watches, groceries, beauty aids, health and personal care products, sports and outdoors products, toys and games, and baby merchandise. Amazon.com also works with third-party sellers, earning a commission for each sale (similar to eBay). It offers e-commerce services to retailers such as Target and Web services to program developers.*

Since Amazon.com's initial public offering (IPO) in 1997, the company's wide range of products has generated phenomenal growth in Net Sales. According to the Notes to the Financial Statements, almost half of the Company's sales were outside North America ($15,497 or 45% of total Net Sales).

Accountants record revenue according to the **Revenue Recognition Principle**. This means revenues are recorded in the period **earned**, not necessarily in the period that the company collects the money. Revenues are typically earned when merchandise is delivered or when services are provided. For example, suppose that a customer orders a book in January, Amazon.com delivers it in February, and the company collects payment in March. The company must record the revenue in its February income statement because that was when the company earned the revenue by delivering the merchandise.

Exceptions to the Revenue Recognition Principle occur when the company is uncertain whether it will be able to collect payment from customers or when the price has not been set. This may occur with customers who have poor credit history or who are likely to return merchandise. In these cases a company cannot record revenue until collection takes place or at least until collection is more certain. For example, consider a software company that allows customers to try software for 30 days before purchasing it. This company will not record a sale on its income statement when the user downloads the software. Rather, the company must wait until the user actually pays for the software. Similarly, rent-to-own companies that rent inexpensive furniture and appliances to college students typically do not record revenue until they collect payment.

Currently, IFRS and U.S. GAAP provide similar guidance regarding revenue recognition. However, the FASB and the IASB have undertaken a major project that is reconsidering the timing and measurement of revenue.

EXPENSES AND THE MATCHING PRINCIPLE

Expenses are the costs incurred to produce revenues. Most companies' largest expense is **Cost of Sales**, the cost of purchasing or manufacturing the actual products sold. Cost of sales is also known as **Cost of Goods Sold (COGS)**. Suppose that Amazon.com were to purchase a book for $100 and resell it for $120. It would report Net Sales of $120 and Cost of Sales of $100. For retail companies, Cost of Sales includes the cost of purchasing merchandise that was sold during the year plus delivery costs. For manufacturing companies, Cost of Sales includes materials, labor, and factory costs associated with producing the merchandise sold during the year. Service companies, which do not sell merchandise, typically do not report Cost of Sales but may report Cost of Services.

Since we define expenses as the cost of bringing in revenues, we record expenses in the period they help to generate revenues. For example, suppose that Amazon.com purchased a DVD for $10 in June, paid for it in July, delivered it in August, and then collected payment in September. According to the Revenue Recognition Principle discussed above, Amazon.com would record the revenue in August, when it earned the revenue. Cost of Sales would *also* be recorded in August, matching expenses to revenues. This is called the **Matching Principle**.

The Revenue Recognition and Matching Principles form the basis for **Accrual Accounting**, the idea that accountants usually record transactions when they occur, not necessarily when cash is received or paid. Don't confuse accrual accounting with **Cash-basis Accounting**, which records transactions when cash is received or paid. Now compare the results under accrual accounting from Amazon.com's Income Statement with cash-basis accounting from the Statement of Cash Flows:

Amazon.com, Inc. ($ in millions)			
Year Ended December 31,	2008	2007	2006
Income from Operations (*from the Income Statement*)	$1,406	$1,129	$ 842
Net Cash Provided by Operating Activities (*from the Statement of Cash Flows*)	$3,495	$3,293	$1,697

Amazon.com's Income from Operations, prepared under accrual principles, is significantly lower than related cash flows. This difference could be caused by noncash expenses, such as depreciation expense, which are recorded under the accrual method but don't actually cost the company any cash. The difference could also be caused by collecting accounts receivable more quickly or paying accounts payable more slowly. Both of these strategies would improve a company's cash flows but not affect net income under accrual accounting.

Under accrual accounting, Cost of Sales equals the actual cost of purchasing the merchandise that was sold during the year. It does not include the cost of merchandise sold in *other* years. The year that the company actually paid for the merchandise is irrelevant.

Concluding the first step of the multi-step income statement, **Gross Profit** equals the difference between Revenues and Cost of Sales. It represents the profit left over after covering the cost of producing or manufacturing the merchandise. Many investors use gross profit to measure a company's profitability. Amazon.com reported Gross Profit of $7,643 in 2010. This means that after deducting the cost of merchandise sold, the company's sales generated $7,643 (Net Sales $34,204 − Cost of Sales $26,561 = Gross Profit $7,643). With gross profit increasing from just $29 million in 1997 to $7,643 million in 2010, Amazon has benefited from the Internet explosion. As can be seen in the following graph, Amazon.com's Gross Profit has increased dramatically:

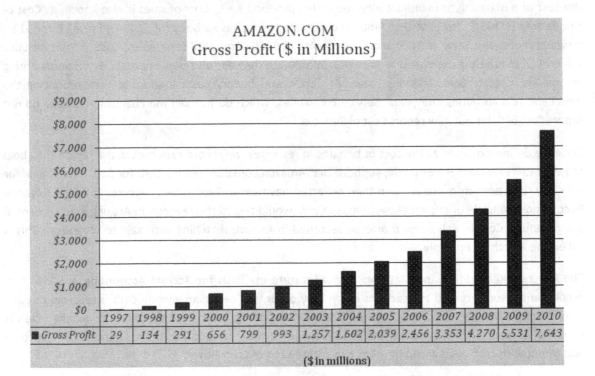

AMAZON.COM
Gross Profit ($ in Millions)

	1997	1998	1999	2000	2001	2002	2003	2004	2005	2006	2007	2008	2009	2010
Gross Profit	29	134	291	656	799	993	1,257	1,602	2,039	2,456	3,353	4,270	5,531	7,643

($ in millions)

Amazon.com, Inc. CONSOLIDATED STATEMENTS OF OPERATIONS ($ in millions)			
	Year Ended December 31,		
(Excerpts)	2010	2009	2008
Gross profit	$7,643	$5,531	$4,270
Operating expenses:			
Fulfillment	2,898	2,052	1,658
Marketing	1,029	680	482
Technology and content	1,734	1,240	1,033
General and administrative	470	328	279
Other operating expense (income)	106	102	(24)
Total operating expenses	6,237	4,402	3,428
Income from operations	$1,406	$1,129	$ 842

Operating Expenses include all costs of generating sales besides Cost of Sales. Companies set up different categories of operating expenses based on their operations. Amazon.com reports five categories of Operating Expenses, according to the Notes to the Financial Statements:

1. *Fulfillment Expenses* for Amazon.com include the costs of operating and staffing the fulfillment and customer services centers that warehouse and distribute inventories to customers. They also include costs of handling customer payments and inquiries.

2. *Marketing Costs* consist of online advertising, commissions, public relations, and other related costs.

3. *Technology and Content Costs* include the cost of paying Web developers, website editors, computer systems managers, and employees who select and buy merchandise.

4. *General and Administrative Expenses* include the cost of paying employees in corporate functions such as accounting, finance, tax, legal, and human resources.

5. *Other Operating Expense.*

Operating expenses of other companies typically include Depreciation Expense, which is the cost of using buildings and equipment owned by the company, and Research and Development Expense.

After subtracting operating expenses from gross profit, we arrive at **Operating Income**, also referred to as **Income from Operations**, a company's profit from its primary operations. Operating Income excludes items not central to a company's operations, such as investing costs, financing costs, and income tax transactions. Therefore, this income statement amount is suitable for comparing different companies' operating income.

The following chart indicates that Amazon.com's Operating Income rose dramatically from an $864 million Operating Loss in 2000 to an all-time high of $1406 million in 2010.

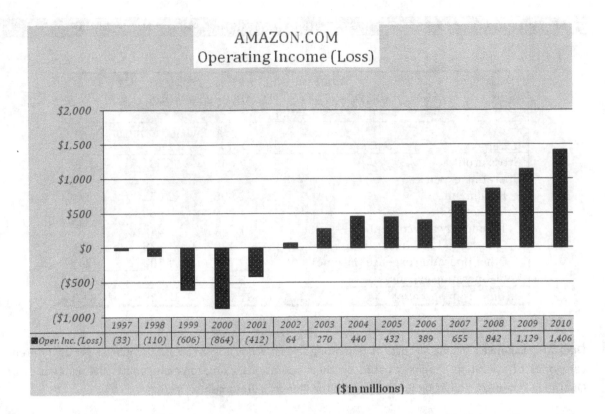

AMAZON.COM
Operating Income (Loss)

	1997	1998	1999	2000	2001	2002	2003	2004	2005	2006	2007	2008	2009	2010
■ Oper. Inc. (Loss)	(33)	(110)	(606)	(864)	(412)	64	270	440	432	389	655	842	1,129	1,406

($ in millions)

STEP THREE: OPERATING INCOME +/- NONOPERATING REVENUES AND EXPENSES = INCOME BEFORE INCOME TAX

Amazon.com, Inc. CONSOLIDATED STATEMENTS OF OPERATIONS ($ in millions)			
	Year Ended December 31,		
(Excerpts)	2010	2009	2008
Income from operations	$1,406	$1129	$842
Interest income	51	37	83
Interest expense	(39)	(34)	(71)
Other income (expense), net	79	29	47
Total nonoperating expense	91	32	59
Income before income tax	$1,497	$1,161	$901

The third section of the multi-step income statement reports items that affect income but have little relevance to operations. For example, in this section Amazon.com reported interest income and expense. If Amazon.com were a bank, it would include interest as part of operations.

Also found in this section are **Gains and Losses**. Gains and losses arise from the sale of long-lived assets or investments. They are computed as the difference between the selling price and the book value of any asset sold. For example, if Amazon.com purchased shares of IBM stock for $2,000,000, and later sold them for $2,500,000, it would report a $500,000 gain on this transaction. Similarly, if Amazon.com sold land for $4 million that had originally cost $5 million, it would record a $1 million loss. Note that gains and losses are only recorded for items that are outside a company's primary operations. If Amazon.com were an investment firm, it would include revenues from sales of IBM stock in operations. Similarly, if it were a real estate developer, it would include revenues from sales of land in operations.

After adding or subtracting this miscellaneous category of items, the company will arrive at **Income Before Income Tax**, sometimes reported as **Income from Continuing Operations before Income Tax**.

STEP FOUR: INCOME BEFORE INCOME TAX – PROVISION FOR INCOME TAX = INCOME FROM CONTINUING OPERATIONS

	Year Ended December 31,		
Amazon.com, Inc. CONSOLIDATED STATEMENTS OF OPERATIONS ($ in millions)			
(Excerpts)	2010	2009	2008
Income before income tax	$1497	$1161	$ 901
Provision (benefit) for income tax	(352)	(253)	(247)
Equity-movement investment activity, net of tax	7	(6)	(9)
Income before nonrecurring items	$1152	$ 902	$ 645

Corporations pay income taxes to the federal government, state governments, and foreign governments. **Provision for Income Tax,** also known as **Income Tax Provision** or **Income Tax Expense,** typically ranges from 25% to 45% of a company's income before income tax.

Corporations reporting a taxable loss can actually report an **Income Tax Benefit**. This benefit, reducing the company's loss, is the result of federal, state, or foreign governments issuing tax refunds to the company. Think of it this way: The government is your "partner." When you earn profits, your "partner" takes its share. However, when you incur losses, your "partner" must also share the loss. Typically, when recording a loss, companies can get money back from the government, claiming refunds of prior years' taxes paid or taking credits that offset future years' taxes.

> *In 2004, Amazon.com added a $233 million Income Tax Benefit to $355 million in Income before Income Tax. This tax windfall resulted from over $2,000 million of net losses accumulated during Amazon.com's first nine years.*

After subtracting provision for income tax, accountants arrive at **Income from Continuing Operations**.

Amazon.com, Inc. CONSOLIDATED STATEMENTS OF OPERATIONS ($ in millions)			
(Excerpts)	**Year Ended December 31,**		
	2010	**2009**	**2008**
Income before nonrecurring items	$1,152	$902	$645
Nonrecurring items	-	-	-
Net income	$1,152	$902	$645

Nonrecurring Items, which accountants deem unusual and infrequent, may appear in the bottom section of a company's income statement. These include:

- **Discontinued Operations**. These are recorded when a company closes down or sells part of its business. For example, if Amazon.com sold its Developer Services Division to Google, the gain or loss would be recorded here.

- **Extraordinary Items**. These are highly unusual transactions that are considered unusual in nature and infrequent in occurrence. Losses from Hurricane Katrina? Not extraordinary. Tornados? No. Acts of terror on September 11? Not extraordinary. In the past, only a few rare transactions related to government regulation or changes in accounting rules have qualified as extraordinary.

Amazon.com had no nonrecurring items for the three years shown.

After adding or subtracting these items, we arrive at **net income**, which equals all revenues and gains less all expenses and losses from operating, nonoperating, and nonrecurring items. It is also referred to as earnings, the bottom line, or profit (loss).

In the future, the Income Statement (like the other financial statements) will use a common format (specified by the FASB and the IASB) that organizes the financial information into operating, investing, and financing activities.

The definition of **Discontinued Operations** differs considerably between IFRS and U.S. GAAP. IFRS restricts the discontinued component of the entity to either a major line of business or a geographical area of operations, whereas U.S. GAAP uses a much broader definition. IFRS does not allow the reporting of extraordinary items due to the difficulty of defining extraordinary across cultures.

When reading an income statement, your goal is to interpret and understand a company's profitability. Three comparisons will help:

- Compare income statement amounts to other amounts in the company's financial statements of the same year (ratios and common-size statements),

- Compare income statement amounts to prior years (trend analysis),

- Compare income statement amounts to competitors and industry norms.

By analyzing the Income Statement and understanding a company's profitability, you can better predict a company's future profits and dividends, the ultimate reward for careful investors.

Most income statement ratios are premised on the idea that companies should generate as much revenue and squeeze as much profit as they can from the limited resources available. For example, compare a doctor's office with a hospital. Both are in the business of helping people to get well. The doctor's office might have a single physician, a physician's assistant, and a receptionist to treat patients during 30-minute appointments. However, the hospital might have dozens of physicians, nurses, expensive equipment, operating rooms, and beds for overnight stays. Because of its limited resources, the doctor's office could not be expected to perform open-heart surgery in an examination room. On the other hand, a hospital's resources would be completely wasted if it treated only one patient at a time for short visits.

Similarly, when looking at a company's performance, we can't expect Google-class performance from a new Internet start-up, nor should we expect Internet-startup performance from Google. The more assets a company has, the higher our expectations should be.

Furthermore, it is important to understand the concept of **Productivity**. Productivity measures how efficiently you can generate desired outputs from given inputs. For example, consider a common measure of automotive productivity: gas mileage. To measure gas mileage, we typically compute "Miles per Gallon" by dividing the miles driven (output) by the number of gallons used (input):

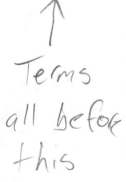

$$\textbf{Miles per Gallon} \quad = \quad \frac{\textbf{Miles Driven (output)}}{\textbf{Number of Gallons Used (input)}}$$

> *After filling the tank of my car, I looked at the trip odometer, which indicated that I drove 275 miles. Then, I looked at the gas pump, which revealed that the tank needed 9.0 gallons to fill. 275/9.0 = 30.6 MPG. Then I zeroed-out the trip odometer for the next tank of gas.*

Similarly, in accounting, profitability ratios divide output by input. In the next sections, we'll measure how productively a company uses its resources to generate profits.

Ideally, profits increase smoothly at an increasing rate. Microsoft, for example, has historically produced a strong record of profitability:

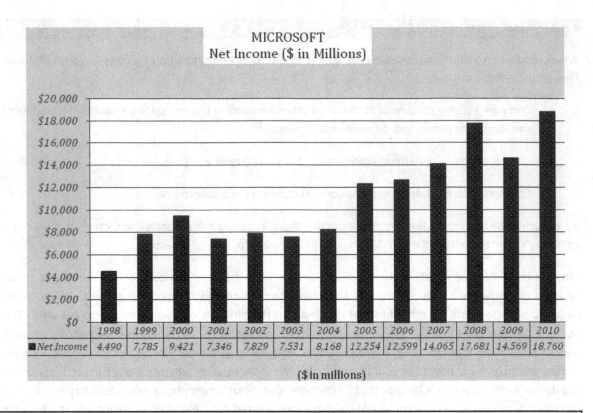

MICROSOFT
Net Income ($ in Millions)

	1998	1999	2000	2001	2002	2003	2004	2005	2006	2007	2008	2009	2010
■Net Income	4,490	7,785	9,421	7,346	7,829	7,531	8,168	12,254	12,599	14,065	17,681	14,569	18,760

($ in millions)

RETURN ON SALES

Return on Sales (ROS), also known as **Net Profit Margin,** measures the profitability from each dollar of revenue. It expresses net income as a percentage of revenue:

Net Profit Margin

Return on Sales	**=**	**Net Income**
		Sales Revenue

This is a key test of how effectively a company can squeeze net income from net sales. How well can a company control expenses to maximize the amount of net income it earns for each dollar of revenue?

> *It's easy to remember ratio formulas because their names typically explain their computation. For example, take the ratio "Return on Sales" literally. "Return" indicates profitability, or net income, computed "on" or over, "Sales." ROS = Net Income / Sales Revenue*

To help analyze financial statement ratios, it is useful to make comparisons with other companies and previous periods. Comparing results to similar companies will help you to understand the nature of competition within an industry. Comparing results to prior periods will help you to understand whether the company's performance is improving or deteriorating.

The analysis in this chapter will compare Amazon.com to Sears Holdings and online retailer eBay. Like Amazon.com, Sears Holdings sells a wide array of products. However, most of its sales are made through its 4,038 bricks-and-mortar stores.   eBay is an online auction website that earned $9,156 million in revenues in 2010 from fees on sales that it brokered, plus other transactions.

Companies try to maximize net income, as well as return on sales, squeezing as much net income as they can out of each sales dollar. Following is a comparison of the three companies' Return on Sales.

Return on Sales										
($ in millions)	Amazon.com			Sears Holdings			eBay			
	2010	**2009**	**2008**	**2010**	**2009**	**2008**	**2010**	**2009**	**2008**	
Net income	1,152	902	645	150	297	99	1,801	2,389	1,779	A
Sales revenue	34,204	24,509	19,166	43,326	44,043	46,770	9,156	8,727	8,541	B
Return on sales	**3.4%**	**3.7%**	**3.4%**	**0.3%**	**0.7%**	**0.2%**	**19.7%**	**27.4%**	**20.8%**	A/B

Return on Sales indicates that Amazon.com's performance remains steady, between 3.4% and 3.7%. Sears Holdings' ROS is very low: less than 1%. eBay's ROS increased from 20.8% in 2008 to 27.4% in 2009, then dropping to 19.7% in 2010.

It sometimes pays to investigate the financial statement amounts that underlie the ratios. When an unusual item appears, consider recalculating the ratios to exclude the unusual item from the financial statements. Suppose that a hurricane destroyed one of a company's factories. To better understand the rest of the company's operations, recalculate the ratios excluding that hurricane loss. When computing ratios like ROS, analysts commonly exclude research and development expense. They do not consider research and development a real expense, but rather, an investment that will generate future revenues. Therefore, they exclude it from expenses when calculating certain ratios.

ASSET TURNOVER RATIO

The **Asset Turnover ratio** measures how efficiently a company uses its assets to produce revenue. It is computed by dividing Revenue by Assets:

$$\textbf{Asset Turnover} \ = \ \frac{\textbf{Sales Revenue}}{\textbf{Total Assets}}$$

Company assets are necessary for generating revenues and profits. For example, a pharmaceutical company needs to invest in research laboratories and factories in order to develop, produce, and sell pharmaceuticals. Asset turnover measures how efficiently a company uses its limited assets (input) to generate revenue (output). Following are asset turnover ratios for Amazon.com, Barnes & Noble, and eBay:

Asset Turnover										
($ in millions)	Amazon.com			Sears Holdings			eBay			
	2010	**2009**	**2008**	**2010**	**2009**	**2008**	**2010**	**2009**	**2008**	
Sales revenue	34,204	24,509	19,166	43,326	44,043	46,770	9,156	8,727	8,541	A
Total assets	18,797	13,813	8,314	24,268	24,808	25,342	22,004	18,408	15,592	B
Asset turnover	1.8	1.8	2.3	1.8	1.8	1.8	0.4	0.5	0.5	A/B

In 2010 for every $1 in assets, Amazon.com generated $1.8 in sales revenue. The decrease from 2008 to 2009 and 2010 indicates that Amazon.com used its assets less productively to generate revenues in 2009 and 2010. Because productive use of assets is a worthwhile objective, investors should look for high asset turnovers that increase.

RETURN ON ASSETS

Return on Assets (ROA) measures how productively a company uses its assets to generate profits. This ratio can be compared among other companies, industries, and investments. Like Asset Turnover, ROA compares an income statement amount to total assets:

$$\text{Return on Assets} = \frac{\text{Net Income}}{\text{Total Assets}}$$

Given the amount of assets they have, managers try to maximize the amount of net income they generate.

($ in millions)	Amazon.com			Sears Holdings			eBay			
	2010	2009	2008	2010	2009	2008	2010	2009	2008	
Net income	1,152	902	645	150	297	99	1,801	2,389	1,779	A
Total assets	18,797	13,813	8,314	24,268	24,808	25,342	22,004	18,408	15,592	B
Return on assets	6.1%	6.5%	7.8%	0.6%	1.2%	0.4%	8.2%	13.0%	11.4%	A/B

The above chart summarizes the three companies' ROA. Amazon.com's net income and ROA decreased during the three years. Sears Holdings stagnated between just 0.4% and 1.2%. eBay's ROA increased from 11.4% in 2008 to 13.0% in 2009, and then decreased to 8.2% in 2010.

Recall from Chapter 1 that Return on Assets can be broken down into elements of profitability and productivity (efficiency), multiplying Return on Sales by Asset Turnover to arrive at Return on Assets:

$$\text{Return on Assets} = \text{Return on Sales x Asset Turnover} = \frac{\text{Net Income}}{\text{Total Assets}}$$

Do not put ROS in decimal form.

2010	Return on Sales Profitability	x	Asset Turnover Productivity (Efficiency)	=	Return on Assets Profitability
Amazon.com	3.37%		1.820		6.1%
Sears Holdings	0.35%		1.785		0.6%
eBay	19.67%		0.416		8.2%

Companies' strategies can focus on high profitability that comes from high prices and strong product differentiation, or they can focus on high turnover that comes from efficient use of assets. This table clearly distinguishes the three companies' strategies. Amazon.com focuses on productivity, reporting low profit margin (ROS) and high turnover, as does Sears Holdings. On the other hand, eBay has very strong product differentiation. The resulting high profit margin (ROS), in spite of low asset turnover, returns the highest ROA shown. It appears that because eBay earned the highest ROS, it also produced the highest ROA.

Gross Profit Margin (GP%), also known as **Gross Margin,** compares gross profit to revenue, expressing gross profit as a percentage of net revenue. It measures how successfully a company buys and sells merchandise at a profit.

$$\text{Gross Profit Margin} \quad = \quad \frac{\text{Gross Profit}}{\text{Sales Revenue}}$$

How much does it cost to brew a cup of coffee? Suppose that you purchased a latte at Starbucks this morning for $4.00. Here is an excerpt from Starbucks' Income Statement:

Starbucks , Gross Profit Margin			
($ in millions)	FYE October 3, 2010		Cup of Coffee
Sales revenues	$10,707	100.0%	$4.00
Cost of sales	4,459	41.6%	1.67
Gross profit	$ 6,248	58.4%	$2.33

Starbucks' gross profit margin = 6,248/10,707 = 58.4%. Therefore, one could estimate that a $4.00 cup of coffee creates $2.33 of gross profit for Starbucks, on average. This gross profit would be used to cover other expenses of the company. According to Starbucks' own financial statements, that cup of coffee cost the company $1.67 ($4.00 - $2.33) to make.

Investors can use this information to compare Starbucks' operations with other companies within the industry.

Gross profit is an especially important measure for companies in the retail and manufacturing industries, such as discount retailers and department stores. Tiny improvements in gross profit can have a tremendous impact on net income.

Gross Profit Margin										
	Amazon.com			Sears Holdings			eBay			
($ in millions)	2010	2009	2008	2010	2009	2008	2010	2009	2008	
Gross Profit	7,643	5,531	4,270	11,878	12,219	12,652	6,592	6,248	6,313	A
Sales Revenue	34,204	24,509	19,166	43,326	44,043	46,770	9,156	8,727	8,541	B
Gross Profit Margin	22.3%	22.6%	22.3%	27.4%	27.7%	27.1%	72.0%	71.6%	73.9%	A/B

In terms of Gross Profit, eBay earns much more than Amazon.com or Sears Holdings. This is because eBay sells a service while the other companies sell merchandise. eBay sells access to its website so that some customers (buyers) can purchase products from other customers (vendors). It simply collects a fee for each sale. However, Amazon.com and Sears Holdings offer a wide variety of physical products. These two companies must deduct the cost of these products as part of Cost of Sales, reporting a lower Gross Profit Margin. Therefore, comparing eBay with the other two companies is like comparing apples and oranges.

Comparing Amazon.com to Sears Holdings, we learn that, while both companies' ratios decrease from 2009 to 2010, Sears Holdings consistently outperforms Amazon.com in Gross Profit Margin.

Trend analysis indicates how different accounts on the income statement are changing. To prepare a trend analysis of the income statement, set the earliest year as a "base year." Then divide each line item amount by the base year and multiply by 100. Here is the trend analysis for Amazon.com:

Amazon.com, Inc. Income Statement Trend Analysis			
Year Ended December 31,	2010	2009	2008
Net sales	178	128	100
Cost of sales	178	127	100
Gross profit	179	130	100
Operating expenses:			
Fulfillment	175	124	100
Marketing	213	141	100
Technology and content	168	120	100
General and administrative	168	118	100
Other operating expense (income)	442	425	100
Total operating expenses	179	128	100
Income from operations	179	128	100
Interest income	167	134	100
Interest expense	61	45	100
Other income (expense), net	55	48	100
Remeasurements and other	NA	NA	NA
Total nonoperating expense	154	54	100
Income before income tax	166	129	100
Provision (benefit) for income tax	-143	102	100
Equity-movement investment activity, net of tax	NA	NA	NA
Income before nonrecurring items	179	140	100
Nonrecurring items	NA	NA	NA
Net income	179	140	100

First of all, the trend analysis indicates that Amazon.com's Net Sales increased 78% (178 - 100), Gross Profit increased 79% (179 - 100), and Net Income increased by 79% (179-100), all dramatic increases over two years. For comparison, consider Sears Holdings and eBay:

Income Statement Trend Analysis								
	Amazon.com, Inc.			Sears Holdings			eBay		
(Excerpts)	2010	2009	2008	2010	2009	2008	2010	2009	2008
Revenue	178	128	100	94	97	100	104	99	100
Gross profit	179	130	100	93	94	100	107	102	100
Net income	179	140	100	152	300	100	101	134	100

Amazon is showing amazing growth: 79% in two years. While Sears reduced Revenues by 6%, the company managed to increase its Net Income by 52%. However, eBay's results seem to be stagnating over these three years.

By reducing financial statements to a 100-point scale, common-size analysis allows comparisons among different years and even among companies of different size. To prepare a common-size income statement, divide all amounts by sales revenue or net sales for that year.

Amazon.com, Inc. Common-Size Income Statement			
	Year Ended December 31,		
	2010	2009	2008
Net sales	100.0%	100.0%	100.0%
Cost of sales	77.7%	77.4%	77.7%
Gross profit	22.3%	22.6%	22.3%
Operating expenses:			
Fulfillment	8.5%	8.4%	8.7%
Marketing	3.0%	2.8%	2.5%
Technology and content	5.1%	5.1%	5.4%
General and administrative	1.4%	1.3%	1.5%
Other operating expense (income)	0.3%	0.4%	(0.1%)
Total operating expenses	95.9%	95.4%	95.6%
Income from operations	4.1%	4.6%	4.4%
Interest income	0.1%	0.2%	0.4%
Interest expense	(0.1%)	(0.1%)	(0.4%)
Other income (expense), net	0.2%	0.1%	0.2%
Total nonoperating expense	0.3%	0.1%	0.3%
Income before income tax	4.4%	4.7%	4.7%
Provision (benefit) for income tax	1.0%	1.0%	1.3%
Equity-movement investment activity, net of tax	0.0%	0.0%	0.0%
Net income	3.4%	3.7%	3.4%

The common-size income statement helps to explain Amazon.com's increase in net income. In 2010, most expenses, as a percentage of net sales, changed very little. For example, Fullfillment Expense, as a percentage of Net Sales, equaled between 8% and 9% every year. However, Income before Income Tax, as a percentage of Net Sales, decreased from 4.7% to 4.4%. Accordingly, we attribute most of the increase in Net Income to the 78% increase in Net Sales over two years (see Trend Analysis).

SUMMARY

The Income Statement provides information about a company's profitability by adding revenues and gains and subtracting expenses and losses. It is based on accrual accounting, which recognizes revenues when earned and records expenses when the company benefits from those expenses. Accrual accounting is different from cash-basis accounting, which records cash inflows when received and cash outflows when paid. The multi-step income statement is organized according to the importance of each item to the company's operations. Revenues, Cost of Sales, and Gross Profit are reported at the top of the multi-step income statement. These are followed by Operating Expenses, Nonoperating Revenues and Expenses, the Provision for Income Tax, and Nonrecurring Items.

Profitability ratios measure how well a company uses resources to generate profits. These ratios can be compared to prior years and to other companies in the same industry. The Asset Turnover Ratio measures how productively a company uses its assets to produce revenue. Return on Sales measures the profits earned from each dollar of revenue. Return on Assets measures how efficiently the company uses available assets to generate profits. Gross Profit Margin measures how much Gross Profit the company generates from Sales Revenues.

Trend analysis describes how individual items on the income statement "grow" with the rest of the company. Common-size analysis helps the user to compare different years' income statements and understand how a company's cost structure is changing.

RATIO	ROS x	ASSET TURNOVER	= ROA	GROSS PROFIT MARGIN
Type	*Profitability*	*Efficiency*	*Profitability*	*Profitability*
Formula	NI / Sales Revenue	Sales Revenue / Total Assets	NI / Total Assets	Gross Profit / Sales Revenue
Amazon.com (AMZN)	3.4%	1.8	6.1%	22.3%
Sears Holdings (SHLD)	0.3%	1.8	0.6%	27.4%
eBay (EBAY)	19.7%	0.4	8.2%	72.0%
* **Industry	9.9%	1.8	7.3%	38.7%
**S&P 500	10.0%	1.0	10.0%	40.0%

*   Industry: *Catalog and Mail Order Houses*   *Industry and S&P 500 ratio averages from moneycentral.msn.com*

**   There are no official rules governing how these ratios are calculated. Therefore, the ratio formulas used may differ from the formulas in the text.

Across

2. Statement of profit and loss or the P&L (2 words) *Income Statement*
5. Income from _____ Operations is the profit resulting from operating and non-operating activities, including the impact of income tax *continuing*
7. Costs of generating sales besides COGS (2 words) *operating exp*
9. ROS times Asset Turnover (abbreviation) *ROA*
10. Accounting method following the Revenue Recognition and Matching Principles *Accrual*
11. Cost of purchasing or manufacturing products sold (4 words) *COGS*
12. Principle requiring expenses be recorded in the period they help to generate revenues *Matching*
17. Principle stating revenues are recorded in the period earned, not necessarily in the period money is collected (2 words) *revenue recognition*
18. (Revenues and Gains) minus (Expenses and Losses) (2 words) *Net Income*
20. Net profit margin (3 words) *Return on Sales*
21. Amounts earned from a company's primary operations *revenues*
22. Difference between Revenues and Cost of Sales (2 words) *Gross profit*

Down

1. A high ratio indicates a low-cost, high-volume business strategy (2 words) *Asset turnover*
2. Subtotal reporting profitability from both operating and nonoperating activities (4 words) *Income before income tax*
3. Gross Profit _____ expresses gross profit as a percentage of revenue
4. _____ revenues and expenses affect net income, but have little relevance to operations *Nonoperating*
6. Results when the selling price is less than the book value *Loss*
8. Accrual-based vs. _____ (2 words) *Cash based*
13. Subtotal equaling gross profit less all operating expenses (2 words) *operating income / income from operati*
14. Unusual and infrequent items, including Discontinued Operations and Extraordinary Items *no recurring*
15. Ratios measuring the ability to generate income *profitability common size*
16. Income Statement reporting all amounts as a percentage of revenue (2 words) *common size*
19. _____ for Income Tax is based on the amount reported for income before income tax *Provisi*

Purpose:
- Identify the types of accounts presented on the income statement.
- Understand the organization of the multi-step income statement.

When amounts are requested, refer to the income statement of Apple, Inc. on the next page.

Revenues are inflows from a company's primary operations. **Expenses** are the costs of bringing in revenues. **Cost of Goods Sold (COGS),** also referred to as Cost of Sales, is the cost of purchasing or manufacturing the actual products sold. It is an operating expense.

Q1 *Sales revenue* earned from the sale of Mac computers, iPods, iPhones, iPads, iTunes, and other related products and services totals (**$ 65225** **million / can't tell**) and the *cost of* those products totals (**$ 39541 million / can't tell**).

Operating expenses include all costs of generating sales besides COGS. **Nonoperating revenues and expenses** affect income, but have little relevance to operations. These typically include financing expenses, investment income, and gains and losses on the sale of assets other than inventory.

Q2 Apple's income statement lists (**2 / 3 / 4**) *operating expense* accounts (other than COGS) that total $ **7299** million. (**COGS / operating expenses**) is(are) greater (**by far / by a little bit**), which is (**expected / unexpected**) for a manufacturing firm.

Q3 *Nonoperating revenues and expenses* refer to (**operating / investing / financing**) revenues and expenses. *Interest expense* reflects the firm's cost of borrowing and is a(n) (**operating / investing / financing**) cost that is classified on the income statement as a(n) (**operating / nonoperating**) expense. *Investment income* (**does / does not**) result from Apple's primary business activity, and therefore, should be classified as (**operating / nonoperating**) revenue. When retailers and manufactures sell inventory (**revenue / a gain (loss)**) is reported, and when they sell property, plant, and equipment (**revenue / a gain (loss)**) is reported. For Apple, *nonoperating revenues and expenses* total $ **155** million.

Provision for income tax is income tax expense based on the amount reported for *income before income tax*. **Nonrecurring items** are gains and losses which accountants deem unusual and infrequent. They include (**D**)iscontinued operations, and (**E**)xtraordinary items.

Q4 Apple's *average income tax rate* was (**7% / 18% / 24%**).

Q5 *Nonrecurring items* are items that occur (**once / twice / continuously**) within the life of a company. Identify each of the following as either a (**D**)iscontinued or (**E**)xtraordinary type of nonrecurring item.

    (**D / E**)   PepsiCo sells off Pizza Hut, Taco Bell, and KFC.

    (**D / E**)   Due to global warming the tundra melts in Barrow, Alaska, resulting in flooding an entire factory and closing it indefinitely.

IFRS does not allow (**D / E**) items and has a narrower definition of (**D / E**) items.

Q6 The income statement reports the results of operations (**as of a certain date / over a period of time**).

Q7 Income statement accounts are listed in (**alphabetical order / order of relationship to the primary business activity / no particular order**). Therefore, (**operating revenues / nonrecurring items**) are reported at the top and (**operating revenues / nonrecurring items**) are reported at the bottom of the income statement.

Apple Computer (AAPL) INCOME STATEMENT ($ in millions)		
Fiscal year ended (FYE)		**9/25/2010**
Sales revenue		$ 65,225
Cost of goods sold (COGS)		39,541
Gross profit		25,684
Research and development expense (R&D)	$ 1,782	
Selling, general, administrative expense (SGA)	5,517	
Depreciation and amortization expense	0	
Other operating expenses	0	
Total operating expenses		7,299
Operating Income		18,385
Interest income (expense)	0	
Investment income (expense)	0	
Gains (losses) on the sale of assets	0	
Other revenues (expenses)	155	
Total nonoperating revenues and expenses		+ 155
Income before income tax		18,540
Provision for income tax		4,527
Income from continuing operations		14,013
Nonrecurring items		0
Net income		$ 14,013

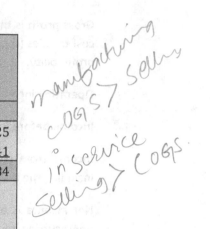

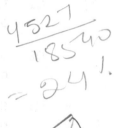

Purpose:
- Identify subtotals and totals on the multi-step income statement and how they are computed.
- Understand the information presented by each multi-step subtotal and total.

Gross profit is the difference between sales revenue (inflows from a company's primary operations) and cost of sales (the cost of purchasing or manufacturing the actual products sold). It is the first indication of profitability.

Operating income is gross profit less all operating expenses. It indicates how well a firm is managed.

Income before income tax indicates profitability from both operating and nonoperating activities.

Income from continuing operations indicates profitability from operating and nonoperating activities including the impact of income tax.

Net income is all revenues and gains less all expenses and losses from operating, nonoperating, and nonrecurring items. It is also referred to as earnings, the bottom line, or profit (loss).

When amounts are requested, refer to the income statement of Apple Computer for the fiscal year ended on 9/25/2010 on the previous page.

Q1   Sales Revenue minus (**operating expenses / nonoperating revenues and expenses / COGS**) equals *Gross Profit* that totals $ 25684 million.

Q2   Gross profit minus (**provision for income tax / operating expenses (other than COGS) / nonoperating revenues and expenses**) equal *Operating Income* that totals $ 18385 million.

Q3   Operating income plus or minus (**provision for income tax / operating expenses / nonoperating revenues and expenses**) equal *Income before Income Tax* that totals $ 18540 million.

Q4   Income before income tax minus (**provision for income tax / nonoperating revenues and expenses / COGS**) equals *Income from Continuing Operations* that totals $ 14013 million.

Q5   Income from continuing operations plus or minus (**provision for income tax / nonrecurring items / nonoperating revenues and expenses**) equal *Net Income* that totals $ 14013 million.

Q6   Net income can either be distributed to stockholders as (**dividends / gross profit / retained earnings**) or be retained in the business as (**dividends / gross profit / retained earnings**).

Q7   On the multi-step income statement, (**3 / 4 / 5 / 6**) different subtotals and totals provide helpful information for decision makers.

Q8   When comparing companies within the same industry, it is best to compare (**Operating Income / Income from Continuing Operations / Net Income**). *Why?*

includes all the information.
exp, margins, revenues.

Q9 In this accounting period BLOOMIN' FLOWERS, a florist shop, purchased flowers from a wholesaler costing $24,000 and sold them to customers for $32,000. Wages and other operating expenses total $3,000. Back in the year 2003, the company purchased land for $2,000 (that was never utilized) and sold it during this accounting period for $6,000. Using these events, prepare the income statement for Bloomin' Flowers below.

Bloomin' Flowers INCOME STATEMENT	
Sales revenue	$ 32000
Cost of sales	$ 24000
Gross profit	$ 8000
Operating expenses	$ 3000
Operating income	$ 5000
+ Nonoperating revenues and expenses	$ +4000 (6000 - 2000)
Income before income tax	$ 9000.

Q10 What is the difference between revenue, a gain, and net income? — *only primary business actv. — generated by adding all rev.*
any sales

Q11 The FASB and the IASB are working to establish a common format, organizing information into operating, investing, and financing activities for the (**balance sheet / income statement / statement of cash flows**).

Purpose:
- Understand accrual accounting and how it differs from cash accounting.
- Apply the Realization Concept and the Matching Concept.

GAAP requires companies to use *accrual accounting* to report revenues and expenses, which means that companies must comply with the Revenue Recognition and Matching Principles described below.

GAAP #2:	Accountants record revenue according to the **Revenue Recognition Principle.** This means revenues are recorded in the period **earned,** not necessarily in the period that the company collects the money. Revenues are typically earned when merchandise is delivered or when services are provided.

Q1   On December 1, Year 1 RETAIL STORE sells a $1,500 computer. Customer Nancy pays $500 in cash and signs an installment agreement for the remaining $1,000 to be paid the following year, Year 2. On the income statement of RETAIL STORE, how much revenue should be recognized?
   a.   In Year 1 $ _1500_
   b.   In Year 2 $ _—_

GAAP #3:	The **Matching Principle** requires accountants to record expenses in the period they help to generate revenues. Therefore: 1) If there is an associated cause and effect, report the expense in the same period as the revenues it helped to generate. Examples include cost of goods sold and commissions. 2) If no association can be found, then expense immediately. Examples include advertising, utility, and administrative expenses. 3) If neither (1) nor (2) apply, then use a systematic and rational allocation method if you can. Examples include depreciation and amortization.

Q2   In this accounting period, CYCLES GALORE purchased 10 bicycles for $200 each at wholesale and sold 6 bicycles for $500 each to customers. On the income statement of CYCLES GALORE, how much will be reported for:
   a.   Sales revenue? $ _3000_   6×500
   b.   Cost of goods sold? $ _1200_   6×200
   c.   Gross profit? $ _1800_
   d.   The cost of the four unsold bicycles will remain part of (**inventory** / COGS / retained earnings) reported on the (**BS** / IS / RE / CF). What amount will be reported? $ _800_
        Asset   4×200

Q3   Kiger Kayaking, a sporting goods retailer, began operations on August 1 with the following transactions during the first month of operation. Compute August net income (using accrual-based accounting) and the August 31 cash balance.

Accrual	Cash		
$ (4000)	$ (4000)	Aug 1	Paid August office rent of $4,000.
$	$ (32000)	Aug 5	Purchased and paid $32,000 for merchandise inventory.
$ 54,000 (20000)	$ 54,000	Aug 16	Sold merchandise for $54,000 to customers at retail that cost $20,000 wholesale. Received cash from customers.
$ (500)	$ (1,500)	Aug 17	Received and paid a $1,500 advertising bill for August, September, and October.
$ 4000	$ (4000)	Aug 30	Paid September office rent of $4,000.
XXXXXXX	$ 12,500	Aug 31	Change in cash balance
$ 29500	XXXXXXX	Aug 31	August net income

gained 34000
Assets
prepaid
exp $1000

A SERIES OF MULTI-STEP INCOME STATEMENTS

Purpose:

- Understand the relationship between the trend of revenue and the trends of other income statement accounts.
- Interpret the meaning of increases and decreases in the various income statement accounts.
- Identify the meaning of parentheses reported on financial statements.
- Develop strategies for analyzing the income statement.

APPLE (AAPL) INCOME STATEMENT   ($ in millions)

Fiscal year ended (FYE)	9/25/2010	09/26/2009	09/27/2008	09/29/2007
Sales revenue	$ 65,225	$ 42,905	$ 37,491	$ 24,006
Cost of goods sold (COGS)	39,541	25,683	24,294	15,852
Gross profit	25,684	17,222	13,197	8,154
Selling, general, admin expense (SGA)	$ 5,517	$ 4,149	$ 3,761	$ 2,963
Research and development expense (R&D)	1,782	1,333	1,109	782
Depreciation/amortization expense	0	0	0	0
Other operating expenses	0	0	0	0
Total operating expenses	7,299	5,482	4,870	3,745
Operating Income	18,385	11,740	8,327	4,409
Interest income (expense)	0	0	0	0
Other revenues (expenses)	155	326	620	599
Total nonoperating revenues and expenses	+ 155	+ 326	+ 620	+ 599
Income before income tax	18,540	12,066	8,947	5,008
Provision for income tax	4,527	3,831	2,828	1,512
Income from continuing operations	14,013	8,235	6,119	3,496
Nonrecurring items	0	0	0	0
Net income	$ 14,013	$ 8,235	$ 6,119	$ 3,496

Not cons.

When amounts are requested, refer to the series of income statements of Apple Computer presented on the previous page.

Q1   From 9/29/2007 to 9/25/2010 *sales revenues* (**increased** / **decreased**), indicating the company is (**competitive within its industry** / **successful at controlling costs** / **well managed**).

Q2   *Cost of goods sold* (COGS) is a(n) (**revenue** / **expense** / **asset** / **liability**) account that *totaled* what amount for fiscal year ended …
      9/25/2008? $ _24,294_ million   9/26/2009? $_25683_ million   9/27/2010? $ _39541_ million

      The *beginning* balance of COGS was what amount for fiscal year ended …
      9/25/2008? $ _0_ million   9/26/2009? $ _0_ million   9/27/2010? $ _0_ million

Q3   What is the greatest expense for this company? (**COGS** / **SGA expense** / **provision for income tax**). What typical costs might be included in this expense?
      material, labor, F. Ohead.

Q4   Let's compare some trends in the data:

      a.   From 9/29/2007 to 9/25/2010, *Sales Revenue* (**decreased** / **more than doubled** / **tripled**).

      b.   From 9/29/2007 to 9/25/2010, *COGS* (**decreased** / **more than doubled** / **tripled**). This amount of increase is (**expected** / **unexpected**). *Why?*

      c.   From 9/29/2007 to 9/25/2010, *R&D* (**decreased** / **more than doubled** / **tripled**). What does this indicate?
            innovation is necessary trying to plan for future

      d.   From 9/29/2007 to 9/25/2010, *provision for income tax* (**decreased** / **doubled** / **tripled**). This amount of increase is (**expected** / **unexpected**). *Why?*

      e.   From 9/29/2007 to 9/25/2010, *net income* (**decreased** / **more than tripled** / **more than quadrupled**), which is an extremely (**favorable** / **unfavorable**) trend, indicating the company is (**selling more merchandise** / **collecting amounts due from customers** / **increasingly earning more revenues and gains than incurring expenses and losses**).

Q5   When preparing financial statements, use the following rules for placing parentheses.

      o   Accounts that are *typically* <u>added</u> or that can <u>either</u> be added or subtracted to compute net income … use no parentheses when added and parentheses when subtracted.

      o   Accounts that are *typically* <u>subtracted</u> to compute net income … use no parentheses when subtracted and parentheses when added. A minus sign may be used instead of parentheses.

      Parentheses indicate to (**subtract** / **add** / **do the opposite of typical**).

      For example, COGS is typically (**added** / **subtracted**) to arrive at net income, and therefore, no parentheses indicate to (**add** / **subtract**) the amount.

Q6   Develop a strategy to evaluate the income statement.
      Which line of the income statement would you look at first? Second? Third? *Why?*
      operating section

Purpose:
- Understand the information provided by profitability ratios.
- Understand that an increasing trend is preferred for profitability ratios.
- Understand that the expected range of ratios varies by industry.
- Understand that comparing a ratio to industry norms enhances meaning.
- Understand that reviewing a number of ratios helps to provide an overall impression of profitability.

The **three types of analysis** are Ratio Analysis, Trend Analysis (horizontal analysis), and Common-Size Statement Analysis (vertical analysis). **Analysis reveals relationships** by comparing amounts to:

    (a)   Other amounts for the same period (ratios and common-size statements),
    (b)   The same information from a prior period (trend analysis),
    (c)   Competitor information, and industry norms.

RATIOS

Profitability Ratios measure the ability to generate profits; the overall performance of a firm. A higher ratio indicates greater profitability. *See Appendix B—Ratios for additional profitability ratios.*

Return on Sales (ROS) measures the profitability from each dollar of revenue. It expresses net income as a percentage of revenue. This ratio is also referred to as *Net Profit Margin*.

$$ROS = \frac{Net\ income}{Sales\ revenue}$$

[handwritten: revenue per dollar]

Asset Turnover (A T/O) measures how efficiently a company uses its assets to produce revenue. It is computed by dividing Revenue by Assets. It is a measure of asset management efficiency and of profitability.

$$Asset\ Turnover = \frac{Sales\ revenue}{Total\ assets}$$

[handwritten: Sales volume]

Return on Assets (ROA) measures how productively a company uses its assets to generate profits. A high ROA ratio depends on managing asset investments to produce the greatest amount of revenue and controlling expenses to keep net income high. ROA is the most comprehensive measure of profitability because it takes into account both the profitability of each dollar of revenue (ROS) and sales volume (Asset T/O). ROS x Asset T/O = ROA

$$ROA = \frac{Net\ income}{Total\ assets}$$

[handwritten: best!!]

Gross Profit Margin (GP%), also known as **Gross Margin**, compares gross profit to revenue, expressing gross profit as a percentage of net revenue. It measures how successfully a company buys and sells merchandise at a profit.

$$GP\% = \frac{Gross\ profit}{Sales\ revenue}$$

Q1 Use the information below for J.C. Penney and Intel to answer the following questions.

FYE 2010 ($ in millions)	J.C. Penney Corp (JCP)		Intel (INTC)	
Sales revenue	$	17,759	$	(X)
Expense		(A)	32,159	
Net income	$	389	$	11,464
ROS		2 %	26 %	

Handwritten: 17,370 (A); 43,623; NI/SR

a. Calculate the values for (A) and (X). Revenue for INTC is more than (**2 times** / **10 times**) greater than revenue for JCP, whereas net income for INTC is approximately (**2 times** / **10 times** / **30 times**) greater than net income for JCP.

b. Examine the relationship between Sales Revenue and Net Income.

1. (**JCP** / **INTC**) corporation is generating the most net income from each dollar of revenue.

2. This relationship is measured by the (**ROS** / **Asset Turnover** / **ROA**) ratio.

3. Calculate ROS and record in the space provided above.

4. ROS of (**JCP** / **INTC**) is clearly much higher, revealing that (**JCP** / **INTC**) has a greater ability to translate revenue into profits; keep expenses under control. But does the higher ROS mean that one company is better than the other company? (**Yes** / **No**), because these companies are from different industries, and ROS averages (**are the same** / **differ**) among industries.

Handwritten margin note: ROA is more comparable

Q2 Let's examine three companies within the Personal Computer Systems industry. Use the chart below to answer the following questions. Stock symbols are shown in parentheses.

Personal Computer Systems Industry FYE 2011	Industry Average	Apple Computer (AAPL)	DELL (DELL)	Hewlett Packard (HPQ)
Return on Sales (ROS)	12.1%	29.54%	5.67%	7.61%
Asset Turnover (Asset TO)	1.00	0.87	1.60	1.03
Return on Assets (ROA)	24.2%	25.75%	9.07%	7.84%
Gross Profit Margin (GP%)	37.3%	39.30%	18.84%	22.3%

a. For AAPL, profits were __29.54__ cents of each revenue dollar, while __70.5__ cents of each revenue dollar were used to pay for the costs of running the business. *(handwritten: 100−29.)*

b. One measure of sales volume is the (**ROS** / **Asset Turnover** / **ROA**) ratio.

Handwritten margin: SR/TA

c. Companies invest in assets to generate additional revenue, to increase net income. AAPL earned __25.8__ cent(s) in profit from each dollar invested in assets. Is a company with a greater ROA ratio using assets more efficiently to generate profits than a company with a lower ROA ratio? (**Yes** / **No** / **Can't tell**), because ROA (**is** / **is not**) comparable among industries.

Handwritten margin: ROA NI/TA

d. It was shown in Activity 8 that Wal-Mart makes profits by generating a large volume of sales on items with low profitability. ROS for Wal-Mart is relatively (**low** / **high**), whereas Asset Turnover is relatively (**low** / **high** / **can't tell**). ROS x Asset T/O = (**ROA** / **GP%** / **debt ratio**), which is considered the (**least** / **most**) comprehensive measure of profitability.

60.70

e. During 2010, it cost AAPL _39.30_ cents of each revenue dollar to produce Mac computers, iPods, iPhones, iPads, iTunes, and other related products and services leaving _60.70_ _39.30_ cents of each revenue dollar to cover all remaining operating expenses, nonoperating expenses, and profits. The Gross Profit Margin (GP%) is the (**first** / **second** / **last**) indication of profitability shown on the income statement. The information for both the numerator and denominator of the GP% ratio come from the (**balance sheet** / **income statement** / **statement of cash flows**).

f. For profitability ratios a (**high** / **low**) ratio indicates greater profitability and an increasing trend is considered (**favorable** / **unfavorable**).

On the previous page, for each ratio, circle the strongest among the three companies in the Personal Computer Systems industry.

g. Meaning is added to a ratio by comparing that ratio to industry norms because success may vary by industry. On the previous page, cross out each ratio that is weaker than the Personal Computer Systems industry average.

h. Review the ratios that were circled as the strongest and those ratios that were crossed out for being lower than the industry average to answer the following questions.

1. Which company has the greatest markup on products sold?   (**AAPL** / **DELL** / **HPQ**)
    Which ratio reveals this information?   (**ROS** / **Asset TO** / **ROA** / **GP%**)

2. Which company appears to sell at a low markup to generate a greater volume of sales?
    (**AAPL** / **DELL** / **HPQ**)
    Which two ratios reveal this information?   (**ROS** / **Asset TO** / **ROA** / **GP%**)

wish to with low margin

Asset turn- volume

3. According to the most comprehensive measure of profitability, which company is the most profitable?   (**AAPL** / **DELL** / **HPQ**)
    Which ratio reveals this information?   (**ROS** / **Asset TO** / **ROA** / **GP%**)

4. Which company has the lowest product costs compared to sales revenue?
    (**AAPL** / **DELL** / **HPQ**)
    Which ratio reveals this information? _big markup_   (**ROS** / **Asset TO** / **ROA** / **GP%**)

5. Which company has the *strongest* profitability? (**AAPL** / **DELL** / **HPQ**) *Why*?

    Apple; highest ROS, GP% & ROA

6. Which company has the *weakest* profitability? (**AAPL** / **DELL** / **HPQ**) *Why*?   → ROA

    Lowest GP% & ROS

ACTIVITY 29　　　ANALYSIS: TREND

Purpose:

- Prepare a trend analysis and understand the information provided.

The **TREND ANALYSIS** compares amounts of a more recent year to a base year. The base year is the earliest year being studied. The analysis measures the percentage of change from the base year.

Q1　For Apple Computer, use amounts listed below to complete the trend indexes for *Income before income tax* and the lines below. Divide each amount by the amount for the base year. Record the resulting *trend index* in the shaded area. Use FYE 9/29/2007 as the base year.

Apple Computer (AAPL)　($ in millions)

Fiscal year ended (FYE)	9/25/2010		9/26/2009		9/27/2008		9/29/2007	
	Amount	Trend Index	Amount	Trend Index	Amount	Trend Index	BASE YEAR	Trend Index
Sales revenue	$ 65,225	272	$ 42,905	179	$ 37,491	156	$ 24,006	100
Cost of goods sold	39,541	249	25,683	162	24,294	153	15,852	100
Gross profit	25,684	315	17,222	211	13,197	162	8,154	100
Operating expenses	7,299	195	5,482	146	4,870	130	3,745	100
Operating Income	18,385	417	11,740	266	8,327	189	4,409	100
Nonoperating revenues (expenses)	155	26	326	54	620	104	599	100
Income before income tax	18,540	370	12,066	241	8,947	179	5,008	100
Provision for income tax	4,527	299	3,831	253	2,828	187	1,512	100
Income from continuing operations	14,013	401	8,235	236	6,119	175	3,496	100
Nonrecurring items	0	NA	0	NA	0	NA	0	NA
Net income	$ 14,013	401	$ 8,235	236	$ 6,119	175	$ 3,496	100

Amounts with opposite signs cannot be accurately compared.

Refer to the series of income statements and the trend analysis on the previous page to answer the following questions.

Q2   Sales growth was 172% (272–100) from FYE 9-29-2007 to FYE 9-25-2010 with the greatest increase during FYE (**9-25-10** / **9-26-09** / **9-27-08** / **9-29-07**). When sales revenue increases, expenses would be expected to (**increase** / **stay the same** / **decrease**). It is favorable when sales revenue increases by 172% and expenses increase at a (**higher** / **lower**) rate than 172%. If an expense account increases at a rate greater than sales revenue, this indicates costs (**were kept under control** / **got out of control**).

Q3   From FYE 9-29-2007 to FYE 9-25-2010, which of the following expenses increased at a greater rate than sales revenue? (**COGS** / **Operating expenses** / **Provision for income tax**). For Apple, the most important cost to keep under control is (**COGS** / **operating expenses** / **provision for income tax**). Overall, it appears that Apple costs (**were kept under control** / **got out of control**).

Q4   The FYE 9-25-2010 trend index for *Sales Revenue* of 272 is (**greater** / **less**) than 100, indicating the amount for that year is (**about the same as** / **almost double** / **almost triple**) the (**base year** / **previous year**) amount. The FYE 9-25-2010 trend index for *Net Income* of 401 is (**greater** / **less**) than 100, indicating the amount for that year is (**about the same as** / **double** / **quadrupled**) the (**base year** / **previous year**) amount. (**Sales revenue** / **Net Income**) increased at a greater rate, indicating (**revenues** / **expenses**) increased at a greater rate from FYE 9-29-2007 to FYE 9-25-2010, which is (**favorable** / **unfavorable**).

Q5   The annual revenue growth rate can be compared between companies.

Assume less than 5% is low, 5 to 15% is moderate, and more than 15% is high.

The three-year average revenue growth rate is (**low** / **moderate** / **high**).

Q6   Compute *gross profit margin* (Gross profit / Sales revenue) for fiscal years ended:
9-25-2010 _39.38_%;   9-26-2009 _40.14_ %;   9-27-2008 _35.20_%;   9-29-2007 **33.97%**
During this time period the *gross profit margin* (**increased** / **decreased**), which is a(n) (**favorable** / **unfavorable**) trend. *What does this trend indicate?*

The sales/profit is steady throughout the years.

Q7   Compute the *Return on Sales* (Net income / Sales revenue) for fiscal years ended:
9-25-2010 _21.48_ %;   9-26-2009 _19.14_ %;   9-27-2008 _16.32_ %;   9/29/2007 **14.56%**
During this time period ROS (**increased** / **decreased**), which is a(n) (**favorable** / **unfavorable**) trend. *What* does this trend indicate?

Spending this dollars to increase/generate more profit revenue.

Q8   Operationally, the best year was FYE (**9-25-10** / **9-26-09** / **9-27-08** / **9-29-07**). *Why?*
List as many items as you can to support your response.

higher sales revenue, higher gross profit, net income, + sales, were cont
expense were more controlled, NJ rev, +

Q9   Operationally, the worst year was FYE (**9-25-10** / **9-26-09** / **9-27-08** / **9-29-07**). *Why?*
List as many items as you can to support your response.

Return on sales was the lowest.

Q10   It is easier to analyze Apple (**before** / **after**) preparing the trend analysis. *Why?*

You can see where the company started and if it is doing better or worse as years go on.

Purpose: • Prepare common-size statements and understand the information provided.

The **common-size income statement** compares all amounts to revenues. The analysis measures each item as a percentage of revenue.

Q1   For Lenovo and Hewlett Packard companies listed below, complete the common-size statements by dividing each item on the income statement by sales revenue. Record the resulting common-size percentage in the shaded area provided.

Fiscal year ended ($ in millions)	Lenovo (LNVGY) 3/31/2010		DELL (DELL) 1/30/2011		Hewlett Packard (HPQ) 10/31/2010	
	Amount	CS%	Amount	CS%	Amount	CS%
Sales revenue	$ 16,605	100 %	$ 61,494	100.0%	$ 126,033	100 %
Cost of goods sold (COGS)	14,815	89.20%	50,098	81.5%	96,089	76.20%
Gross profit	1,790	10.80%	11,396	18.5%	29,944	23.80%
Selling, Gen , Adm expenses	1,406	8.50%	7,234	11.9%	12,585	10 %
Research and development	214	1.30%	657	1.0%	2,959	2.30%
Other expenses	34	0.20%	0	--%	2,921	2.30%
Operating income	136	80%	3,505	5.5%	11,479	9.10%
Nonoperating rev (exp)	+ 41	0.20%	(155)	--%	(505)	-0.40%
Income before income tax	177	1.10%	3,350	5.5%	10,974	8.70%
Provision for income tax	47	0.30%	715	1.2%	2,213	1.80%
Income from continuing operations	130	0.80%	2,635	4.3%	8,761	7.00%
Nonrecurring items	0	0.00%	0	0.0%	0	0.00%
Net income	$ 130	0.80%	$ 2,635	4.3%	$ 8,761	7.00%

COGS
Sales
cf / Sales

₂1078   ₂1853   9 2376

Refer to the information above to answer the following questions.

Q2   The greatest amount of *sales revenue* was reported by (**LNVGY/ DELL / HPQ**) and the greatest *net income* was reported by (**LNVGF / DELL / HPQ**), which would be (**expected / unexpected**).

Q3   The company that reported the *highest* ratio for:
       a.   Gross profit margin?   (**LNVGY / DELL / HPQ**)
       b.   Operating income as a percentage of sales?   (**LNVGY / DELL / HPQ**)
       c.   ROS?   (**LNVGY / DELL / HPQ**)
       d.   A (**higher / lower**) profitability ratio is preferred.

Q4   The company that reported the *greatest* percentage of expense for:
       a.   COGS   (**LNVGY/ DELL / HPQ**), which is considered (**favorable / unfavorable**). *Why?*

       b.   SGA   (**LNVGY/ DELL / HPQ**), which is considered (**favorable / unfavorable**). *Why?*

       c.   R&D   (**LNVGY/ DELL / HPQ**), which is considered (**favorable / unfavorable**). *Why?*

Q5   During 2010, (**LNVGF / DELL / HPQ**) remained the #1 direct-sale computer vendor.
       (*Hint: Refer to company descriptions in Appendix A—Featured Corporations*)

Purpose: • Understand and interpret amounts reported on the income statement

Hewlett-Packard (HPQ) INCOME STATEMENTS ($ in millions)				
Fiscal years ended October 31,	2010	2009	2008	2007
Sales revenue	$ 126,033	$ 114,552	$ 118,364	$ 104,286
Cost of goods sold (COGS)	96,089	87,524	90,069	78,887
Gross profit	29,944	27,028	28,295	25,399
Selling, general, and admin expense (SGA)	12,585	11,613	13,326	12,226
Research and development expense (R&D)	2,959	2,819	3,543	3,611
Restructuring changes	1,144	640	311	387
Other operating expenses	1,777	1,820	642	456
Total operating expenses	18,465	16,892	17,822	16,680
Operating income	11,479	10,136	10,473	8,719
Interest income (expense) and other	(505)	(721)	0	+458
Total nonoperating revenue (expense)	(505)	(721)	0	+458
Income before income tax	10,974	9,415	10,473	9,177
Provision for income tax	2,213	1,755	2,144	1,913
Income from continuing operations	8,761	7,660	8,329	7,264
Nonrecurring items / Minority interest	0	0	0	0
Net income	$ 8,761	$ 7,660	$ 8,329	$ 7,264

Refer to the series of income statements presented above to answer the following questions.

Q1   Since 10/31/2007, sales revenue growth was $ _21,747_ million, which is a _20.85_ % change in sales revenue. The annual revenue growth rate can be compared between companies.
        Assume less than 5% is low, 5 to 15% is moderate, and more than 15% is high
        The three-year average revenue growth rate is considered (**low / moderate /(high)**).

Q2   Using 10/31/2007 as the base year, compute the trend index on 10/31/2010 for:
        a.   Sales revenue   _121_   trend index
        b.   Cost of goods sold   _122_   trend index
        c.   Gross profit   _118_   trend index
        d.   From 10/31/2007 to 10/31/2010, *COGS* increased at a (**greater**/ **lesser**) rate than sales revenue, which is considered (**favorable** /**unfavorable**). As a result, gross profit margin will also (**increase** /**decrease**).

Q3   Compute ROS (Net income / Sales revenue) for fiscal years ended on:
        10/31/2010 _6.95_ %;   10/31/2009 _6.69_ %   10/31/2008 _7.04_% 10/31/2007 _6.97_%
        The trend is (**increasing / decreasing /(steady)**) which is (**favorable / unfavorable /(neutral)**).

Q4   Review all of the information presented above. If you had $10,000, would you consider investing in this company? (**Yes /(No)**) *Why?*

        Even though the company has a steady trend I would rather invest in a more favorable company.

Purpose: • Understand and interpret amounts reported on the income statement.

LENOVO GROUP (LNVGY) INCOME STATEMENTS ($ in millions)				
For fiscal year ended March 31,	**2010**	**2009**	**2008**	**2007**
Sales revenue	$ 16,605	$ 14,901	$ 16,352	$ 13,978
Cost of sales (COGS)	14,815	13,104	13,902	12,091
Gross profit	1,790	1,797	2,450	1,887
Selling, general, and distribution exp (SGA)	1,406	1,566	1,700	1,521
Research and development expense (R&D)	214	220	230	196
Other operating expenses	(49)	203	21	9
Total operating expenses	1,571	1,989	1,951	1,726
Operating income	219	(192)	499	161
Interest Expense	63	38	38	35
Other nonoperating income	21	42	52	29
Total nonoperating revenue (expense)	(42)	4	14	(6)
Income before income tax	177	(188)	513	155
Provision for income tax	47	38	48	27
Income from continuing operations	130	(226)	465	128
Nonrecurring items	0	0	+19	+33
Net income	$ 130	$ (226)	$ 484	$ 161

Refer to the series of income statements presented above to answer the following questions.

Q1   Prepare a trend analysis of Sales Revenue for all four years:

Fiscal year ended March 31	2010	2009	2008	2007
Sales revenue				

The greatest increase took place in (**2010 / 2009 / 2008**). What are some likely reasons for this increase?

Q2   The greatest expense is (**COGS / SGA / R&D**) followed by (**COGS / SGA / R&D**). Lenovo is a (**manufacturing / retail / service**) company so COGS is (**expected / not expected**) to be the largest expense.

Q3   Compute common-size percentages during 2010 and 2008 for the amounts below.

	2010	2008
Sales revenue	%	%
COGS	%	%
Gross profit	%	%
Operating expenses	%	%
Operating income	%	%

Q4   Review all of the information presented above. Lenovo Group appears to report a (**strengthening / steady / weakening**) operating position.
Why? Support your response with at least two observations.

Purpose: • Understand and interpret amounts reported on the income statement.

(in millions of $ or €)	CORP A 04/30/2011		CORP B 12/31/2011		CORP C 12/31/2011	
	Amount	CS%	Amount	CS%	Amount	CS%
Sales revenue	6,998.6	100.0%	53,999	100.0%	39,046	100.0%
Cost of goods sold (COGS)	5,205.7	-74.4%	20,242	-37.5%	16,634	-42.6%
Gross profit	*1792.9*	*25.6%*	*33757*	*62.5%*	*22412*	*57.4%*
SGA expense	1,629.4	-23.3%	7,670	-14.2%	10,499	-26.9%
R&D	0.0	0.0%	8,350	-15.5%	0	0.0%
Depreciation/amortization	228.7	-3.3%	260	-0.5%	0	0.0%
Other operating expenses	0.5	-0.0%	132	-0.2%	0	0.0%
Interest expense (income)	57.4	-0.8%	(192)	+0.4%	*(469)*	-1.2%
Investment expense (income)	0.0	0.0%	(112)	+0.2%	0	0.0%
Other expenses (revenues)	0.0	0.0%	(135)	+0.2%	1,619	-4.2%
Provision for income tax	(48.5)	+0.7%	4,839	-9.0%	1,856	-4.8%
Minority interest	0.0	0.0%	0	0%	2,104	-5.4%
Net income	$/€ *-74*	*-1.1*%	$/€ *12945* *25.9* %		$/€ *5865* *15%* %	

Q1   Compute gross profit, gross profit margin, net income, and the return on sales ratio for each corporation. Record the amounts in the appropriate space above.

Q2   Analyze the financial attributes of the three corporations by circling the corporation with...
  a.   the lowest GP%   CORP (**A** / B / C)
  b.   significant R&D expense   CORP (A / **B** / C)
  c.   significant interest expense   CORP (A / B / **C**)
  d.   the lowest ROS   CORP (**A** / B / C)

Q3   *Use the descriptions below to identify each corporation using their financial information.*
ANHEUSER-BUSCH INBEV (BUD) is a publicly-traded company based in Leuven, Belgium. It is the leading global brewer and one of the world's top five consumer products companies. A true consumer-centric, sales-driven company, Anheuser-Busch InBev manages a portfolio of nearly 300 brands that includes global flagship brands Budweiser®, Stella Artois®, and Beck's®. Anheuser-Busch InBev's dedication to heritage and quality is rooted in brewing traditions that originate from the Den Hoorn brewery in Leuven, Belgium, dating back to 1366 and the pioneering spirit of the Anheuser & Co. brewery, established in 1860 in St. Louis, USA. Anheuser-Busch InBev has significant debt financing.
Anheuser-Busch InBev must be Corporation   (A / B / **C**)   Why? *highest interest exp.*

INTEL CORPORATION (INTC) is the largest producer of semiconductors in the world, currently possessing 80% of the market share. Intel's most notable products include its Pentium and Celeron microprocessors. Intel also makes flash memories and is #1 globally in this market. Dell is the company's largest customer.
Intel must be Corporation   (A / **B** / C).   Why? *R&D*   *Research & Dev. Apple & Intel.*

BARNES & NOBLE (BKS) operates in the highly competitive retail industry of selling books, magazines, newspapers, and other content through its multi-channel distribution platform.
Barnes & Noble must be Corporation   (**A** / B / C).   Why? *low GP. high volume*

CHAPTER 4

STATEMENT OF STOCKHOLDERS' EQUITY

LEARNING OBJECTIVES

1. Understand how the statement of stockholders' equity is organized.
2. Identify and explain common and preferred stock.
3. Understand par value and additional paid-in capital.
4. Understand typical items that affect retained earnings.
5. Understand treasury stock.
6. Understand accumulated other comprehensive income.
7. Compute ratios and use ratio analysis to evaluate solvency, profitability, and investment performance.

INTRODUCTION

More than a hundred years ago, gold prospectors Harry and Sam put their life savings into a plot of Nevada land. They invested $100 each. They suspected that the land contained gold. Agreeing to share any profits half-and-half, they became equal partners. They dug a mine, to no avail, finding nothing. Then they hired prospector Tex, a self-professed expert in finding gold ore. Having no money, they offered Tex a 1/3 share in the mine in exchange for his hard work, thereby reducing their own shares in any profits to 1/3 each.

With Tex now a full partner, Harry and Sam reduced their shares in any profits. Before Tex came along, $15,000 in gold could be split 50–50, $7,500 each. Now, with Tex, each partner would have to be content with $5,000.

How a company divvies up ownership shares is important. Some companies offer more than one type of ownership shares, some more valuable than others. Others offer employees stock at a discount, thereby diluting existing stockholders' shares, reducing their value.

Investors ignore this information at their peril. They may not realize that their own shares are not entitled to dividends until after dividends on "higher priority" shares are paid, and they may not realize how stock options and other transactions reduce the value of their ownership in the company.

The **Statement of Stockholders' Equity** provides information about changes in a company's stockholders' equity, including contributed capital and retained earnings. It helps investors understand the structure of a company's ownership. In this chapter, we evaluate the stockholders' equity of Freeport-McMoRan Copper & Gold, Inc. (FCX), an operator of copper and gold mines. We will review the different components of FCX's Statement of Stockholders' Equity and analyze how it distributes its dividends.

Corporations divide their ownership into shares of **stock.** For example, if a corporation issues 1,000 shares of stock, then each share of stock represents 1/1,000 of the total ownership of the corporation. An investor purchasing 100 shares of this stock would own 10% (100/1,000) of the corporation. Many corporations are **publicly traded,** meaning that their shares are bought and sold on stock exchanges such as the New York Stock Exchange. Investors can easily buy and sell shares by calling a stockbroker or through a broker's website. As shares of stock are traded, their prices change with supply and demand.

Corporations must file a charter with a state, such as Delaware. This filing will determine the total number of stock shares **authorized.** This will be the maximum number of shares that a corporation is permitted to print. Then, the corporation will **issue** shares, selling them to investors in exchange for assets, usually cash. This issuance can occur as part of an **Initial Public Offering (IPO),** when a company sells stock to the public for the first time as a publicly traded corporation. Corporations can also buy back shares of stock from investors. Such stock is called **Treasury Stock.** The number of **Shares Outstanding** is the total number of shares actually held by investors at a given time, which equals the number of shares issued less the number of shares of treasury stock that were bought back by the company.

> **Shares outstanding = Shares issued – Treasury shares**

When analyzing stockholders' equity, it's important to understand the concept of **Par Value.** This is a legal value assigned to each share of stock. Par value is usually less than the actual amount of money that the company received when it originally issued the stock. For example, suppose that a company issues $1.00 par stock for $5.00. It would record the stock on its balance sheet for $1.00 per share. The amount received in excess of par, $4.00, is recorded in a separate account on the balance sheet, titled **Additional Paid-in Capital** or **Capital in Excess of Par.**

As we previously stated, companies must choose a mix of liabilities and equity to finance their assets. To pay for assets some companies borrow more (liabilities), whereas others issue more stock (equity). Recall that the debt ratio (total liabilities / total assets) measures solvency. Companies with high debt ratios have high liabilities and low stockholders' equity in relation to total assets. Because liabilities and the related interest must be paid back, companies with poor solvency might not be able to pay their liabilities, thereby defaulting on their debts. Default can result in giving up valuable assets to creditors or even bankruptcy. On the other hand, companies with a low debt ratio have strong solvency, and can more easily pay their debts. These companies finance most of their operations with stockholders' equity.

Some companies issue more than one type of stock; some offer two types of stock—preferred stock and common stock. **Preferred stock** is "preferred" over common in two ways. First, when the Board of Directors declares a dividend, preferred stock dividends take precedence over **Common Stock** dividends. Preferred stock usually carries a dividend rate, which must be paid to preferred stockholders before any dividends can be paid to common stockholders. Second, in the event of bankruptcy liquidation, preferred stockholders receive a return of their investments before the common stockholders receive anything.

> *Suppose that a company with both preferred and common stock declared $1,000,000 in dividends. If the preferred stock carried a dividend rate of 7% on $20,000,000 of par value ($20,000,000 x 7% = $1,400,000 million in annual dividends), then preferred stockholders would receive the entire dividend and common stockholders would receive nothing. If the company declared $2,000,000 in dividends, then everyone—preferred and common—would receive payments—$1,400,000 for preferred and the remaining $600,000 for common shareholders. The Board of Directors also has the right to declare no dividends, in which case **no** stockholders—preferred or common—would receive anything.*

Here's a description of FCX:

> *FCX is an international mining company with one of the largest reserves of copper, gold, and molybdenum in the world. Its portfolio of assets include the Grasberg minerals district in Indonesia (that contains the largest single recoverable copper reserve and the largest single gold reserve of any mine in the world), the Tenke Fungurume minerals district in the Democratic Republic of Congo (DRC), and significant mining operations in North and South America. It also operates Atlantic Copper, a wholly owned copper smelting and refining unit in Spain. Headquarters are located in Phoenix, Arizona.*

We can get a quick introduction to FCX's stockholders' equity by looking at the stockholders' equity section of its Consolidated Balance Sheet:

Freeport McMoRan Copper & Gold, Inc. **Consolidated Balance Sheets (Excerpts)** (In millions)		
December 31,	**2010**	**2009**
Stockholders' equity:		
6 ¾% Mandatory Convertible Preferred Stock, 29 shares issued and outstanding at December 31, 2009	$ 0	$ 2875
Common stock, par value $0.10, 1067 shares and 981 shares issued, respectively	107	98
Capital in excess of par value	18,751	15,637
Retained earnings (Accumulated Deficit)	(2,590)	(5,805)
Accumulated other comprehensive income (loss)	(323)	(273)
Common stock held in treasury—122 shares, at cost	(3,441)	(3,413)
Total stockholders' equity	**$12,504**	**$9,119**

The Balance Sheet indicates that Stockholders' Equity increased from $9,119 million in 2009 to $12,504 million in 2010. This appears to be caused by a huge decrease in the accumulated deficit, from negative $5,805 million in 2009 up to negative $2,590 in 2010. Later on we'll explore the reasons for this.

According to the Consolidated Balance Sheet, FCX has offered two classes of stock:
- Mandatorily convertible preferred stock
- Common stock

The 6¾% Mandatory Convertible Preferred Stock automatically converted into common stock, as explained in the Notes to the Financial Statements:

> *On March 28, 2007, FCX sold 28.75 million shares of 6¾% Mandatory Convertible Preferred Stock, with a liquidation preference of $100 per share, for net proceeds of $2.8 billion. The 6¾% Mandatory Convertible Preferred Stock will automatically convert on May 1, 2010, into between approximately 39 million and 47 million shares of FCX common stock at a conversion rate that will be determined based on FCX's common stock price or other certain events.*

How do these different classes of stock affect investors? Like our gold prospectors Harry and Sam, who admit Tex as a new partner, FCX will issue new common stock shares to the preferred stockholders, possibly diluting existing common stockholders' own portion of the profits.

Note how the Balance Sheet discloses Common Stock, presenting the number of shares issued:

($ in millions) December 31,	2010	2009
Common stock, par value $0.10, 1,067 shares and 981 shares issued, respectively	$ 107	$ 98
Capital in excess of par value	18,751	15,637

FCX has 1,067,000,000 shares of common stock issued, with a par value of $0.10. The total par value is $107 million, computed as 1,067,000,000 shares x $0.10 each, rounded. The capital in excess of par value represents amounts investors paid FCX for stock issued, above and beyond par value. The total amount of capital common stockholders paid into the company equals $18,858 million ($107 million + $18,751 million). On average, common stock investors paid $17.67 ($18,858 million / 1,067 million) per share when purchasing stock from the company.

It is interesting to note that IFRS classifies preferred stock as debt, not as equity, on the balance sheet and reports dividends on preferred stock as interest expense on the income statement.

STATEMENT OF STOCKHOLDERS' EQUITY

The **Statement of Stockholders' Equity** provides information about changes in a company's stockholders' equity, including contributed capital and retained earnings. This helps us understand changes in stockholders' equity from one year's balance sheet to the next. It emphasizes stockholders' equity transactions that affect different classes of stockholders.

Analyzing the Statement of Stockholders' Equity reveals many important issues. For the following discussion, refer to FCX's Statement of Stockholders' Equity on the next page.

Freeport McMoRan Copper & Gold, Inc.—Consolidated Statements of Stockholders' Equity (Excerpts) (In Millions)

	Mandatory Convertible Preferred Stock		Common Stock		Capital in Excess of Par Value	Retained Earnings	Accumulated Other Comprehensive Income (Loss)	Common Stock Held in Treasury		Total Stockholders' Equity
	Number of Shares	At Par Value	Number of Shares	At Par Value				Number of Shares	At Cost	
Balance at December 31, 2009	29	$2,875	981	98	15,637	(5,805)	(273)	122	(3,413)	9119
Conversions of 6 3/4% Mandatory Convertible Preferred Stock	(29)	(2875)	79	8	2,867	-	-	-	-	-
Conversions of 7% Convertible Senior Notes	-	-	-	-	1	-	-	-	-	1
Exercised and issued stock-based awards	-	-	7	1	109	-	-	-	-	110
Stock-based compensation costs	-	-	-	-	129	-	-	-	-	129
Tax benefit for stock-based awards	-	-	-	-	8	-	-	-	-	8
Tender of shares for stock-based awards	-	-	-	-	-	-	-	-	(28)	(28)
Dividends on common stock	-	-	-	-	-	(1058)	-	-	-	(1,058)
Dividends on preferred stock	-	-	-	-	-	(63)	-	-	-	(63)
Comprehensive income (loss):										
Net income	-	-	-	-	-	4336	-	-	-	4,336
Other comprehensive income (loss), net of taxes:										
Unrealized gain on securities	-	-	-	-	-	-	2	-	-	2
Defined benefit pension plans:										
Net loss during period, net of taxes of $19 million	-	-	-	-	-	-	(67)	-	-	(67)
Amortization of unrecognized Amounts	-	-	-	-	-	-	15	-	-	15
Other comprehensive loss	-	-	-	-	-	-	(50)	-	-	(50)
Total comprehensive loss										4286
Balance at December 31, 2010	-	-	1067	107	18,751	(2,590)	(323)	122	(3,441)	12,504

FCX distributed $110 million in stock-based awards to employees. Many executives receive a portion of their compensation in stock, or in stock options, which permit them to buy shares of stock at a discount. It is generally believed that this type of compensation encourages executives to think like shareholders, and to act in their best interest. Executives will personally benefit from stock price increases if they work to maximize the value of stock. However, as we previously discussed, stock-based awards can dilute other stockholders' proportion of net income. (As I heard one investment manager put it, "Why would you give the company away for free to the help?")

Because of the danger of dilution, companies make many disclosures about stock-based awards in the **Notes to the Financial Statements,** detailed disclosures after the financial statements in the annual report. In this Statement of Stockholders' Equity, FCX presents three separate figures. The first, $110 million, is the amount of money received from executives to exercise their stock options and purchase stock at a discounted price from FCX. The second, $129 million, is the estimated cost benefit of the discount to the employees exercising their stock options; this is compensation to the employee. The third, $8 million, is the tax savings from providing this type of compensation.

This, of course, begs a question: Where does the stock sold to executives come from? Does the company issue new shares? Not usually. Instead, companies usually buy the shares back from other stockholders. This stock is called Treasury Stock.

TREASURY STOCK

Treasury Stock is stock bought back from investors. One reason for this, just discussed, is to issue the stock to executives as stock-based compensation. Another reason is to increase earnings per share (EPS). By reducing the number of shares outstanding, the profits per shareholder, EPS, will increase. Therefore, buying back treasury stock has the effect of increasing shareholder wealth. Managers often buy treasury stock when they believe that the company's stock price will increase. Buying stock at a low price, and later selling it back to shareholders at a higher price, creates cash flow for the company.

The accounting treatment of treasury stock is important to understand. Treasury stock, stock bought back from investors, reduces stockholders' equity on the balance sheet. It's negative stockholders' equity. **It is not recorded as an asset because it is impossible for a company to own itself.** Furthermore, if a company buys treasury stock at a low price, and then resells it at a higher price, the difference between the selling price and cost is not recorded as a gain, but rather as an increase in Additional Paid-in Capital. Likewise, a lower selling price would not be recorded as a loss, but rather as a decrease to Additional Paid-in Capital.

In its Consolidated Statement of Stockholders' Equity, the $28 million "Tender of shares for stock-based awards," was for the purchase of treasury stock in order to resell the stock to executives for stock-based compensation.

RETAINED EARNINGS

Recall that **Retained Earnings** is net income earned by the company since its incorporation and not yet distributed as dividends. Accordingly, net income increases retained earnings and dividends decrease retained earnings. A net loss would be treated as negative net income, reducing Retained Earnings.

FCX paid dividends to common and preferred stockholders. As shown in the Statement of Stockholders' Equity, the company paid $1,058 million in dividends on common stock, and $63 million in dividends on preferred stock, both reducing retained earnings.

FCX earned $4,336 million in Net Income in 2010, increasing retained earnings. However, in 2008, the company experienced a loss of $11,067 million, which reduced retained earnings. That year, the company recorded something called a "goodwill impairment" for $5,987 million and "long-lived asset impairments and other charges" totaling $10,978 million. Together, these items reduced operating income by a whopping $16,965 million.

What happened? Copper prices dropped from an average price of $3.61 per pound during the first nine months of 2008 to just $1.32 per pound on December 31, 2008. Another ore, molybdenum, dropped in price from $33 per pound for the first nine months of 2008 to just $9.50 per pound on December 31, 2008. This dramatically reduced the value of FCX's copper and molybdenum mines and reserves. Furthermore, it dramatically reduced the value of goodwill that FCX paid when it bought another company two years earlier. In effect, these price decreases caused a $17 billion dollar loss, wiping out most of the company's stockholders' equity.

OTHER COMPREHENSIVE INCOME

Almost all income and loss items are recorded in net income, on the income statement, and then flow into retained earnings, part of stockholders' equity. We'll call these "front door" items, because they are openly announced to shareholders as part of net income, before they hit stockholders' equity. However, there are "back door" exceptions that are not included in net income, but instead go straight to stockholders' equity. This murky category of items combines to form other comprehensive income. **Other Comprehensive Income (Loss)** consists primarily of three gain/loss items that are not recorded on the income statement,[1] instead they are recorded as part of **Accumulated Other Comprehensive Income (Loss)** in Stockholders' Equity.

There was significant debate over whether these items should be included in net income. It was thought that many of these items are caused by risky investments that fluctuate widely in value, even though they are not directly related to a company's operations. If included in net income, some felt that these items would mislead investors. However, there's nothing to stop investors from adding or subtracting these items from income, just to see what would happen.

During 2010, FCX recorded $50 million in Other Comprehensive Losses during the year, increasing the Accumulated Other Comprehensive Loss to $323 million on December 31, 2010.

---

[1] The specifics of these items are outside the scope of this book. However, the three items are:
1. Unrealized gains/losses on certain securities,
2. Foreign currency translation adjustments, and
3. Certain gains/losses on pension plans.

STOCK SPLITS AND STOCK DIVIDENDS

Stock Splits are proportional increases in the number of shares outstanding. For example, a two-for-one stock split would multiply each share of stock into two new shares of stock in the same company. An investor holding 100 shares would, after a stock split, hold 200 shares.

Consider Harry, Sam, and Tex. Each owns a single share in the gold mine. Let's be generous and give them a **ten**-for-one stock split. Now each owns **ten** shares in the gold mine. Are they better off? Previously, each prospector held 1/3 of the company. Now each prospector holds 10/30 of the company, the same proportional share. Interestingly, research shows that when companies announce planned stock splits, stock prices usually increase.

Stock Dividends are **smaller** proportional increases in the number of shares outstanding. For example, a 10% stock dividend would award the holder of 100 shares of stock 10 new shares of stock. Like stock splits, stock dividends do not increase investors' proportionate share in the company, and therefore, it could be argued, do not provide any value to investors.

FCX declared a stock dividend in December 2010. On February 1, 2011, each stockholder received one new share for every share that they held.

RETURN ON EQUITY

Return on Equity (ROE) measures how effectively stockholders' equity is used to produce net income.[2] To compute this ratio, divide net income by stockholders' equity:

$$\text{Return on Equity} = \frac{\text{Net Income}}{\text{Stockholders' Equity}}$$

Compare the three "Return" ratios: Return on Sales (ROS), Return on Assets (ROA), and Return on Equity (ROE). ROS is computed solely from the income statement, reporting how well the company controlled costs to deliver net income from Sales Revenue. ROA includes the return on liabilities plus stockholders' equity (Assets = Liabilities + Stockholders' Equity), considering profitability from the entire company's perspective, whereas ROE looks at profitability only from the stockholders' perspective.

	Return on Sales	Return on Assets	Return on Equity
Numerator	Net Income	Net Income	Net Income
Denominator	Sales Revenue	Assets	Stockholders' Equity
What do they have in common?	They all have net income in the numerator and measure profitability.		
What's different?	**Income Statement perspective.** *How well did the company control costs?*	**Entire company perspective.** *How much profit was earned with the company's assets, using both creditors' and stockholders' investments?*	**Stockholders' perspective.** *How much profit was earned with stockholders' investments?*

---

[2] Financial Analysts also use the ratio Return on Common Equity to analyze stock performance. It is computed by excluding preferred stock dividends and preferred stock from the ratio:

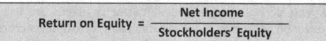

$$\text{Return on Common Equity} = \frac{\text{Net Income - Preferred Dividends}}{\text{Common Stockholders' equity}}$$

Below we compute FCX's return ratios for three years:

FYE December 31,	2010	2009	2008	
Return on Sales	29.2%	23.5%	-58.7%	A/B
Return on Assets	18.9%	13.6%	-44.7%	A/C
Return on Equity	44.3%	38.8%	-181.0%	A/D
Net income (loss)	$ 5,544	$ 3,534	$(10,450)	A
Sales revenue	18,982	15,040	17,796	B
Assets	29,386	25,996	23,353	C
Stockholders' equity	12,504	9,119	5,773	D

Recall that, in 2008, FCX's Stockholders' equity dropped from $18,234 million to $5,773 million because of the tremendous net loss that year. Therefore, we will dismiss 2008 as an aberration. FCX's Return on Equity bounced back to 38.8% in 2009 and 44.3% in 2010.

FINANCIAL LEVERAGE RATIO

In Chapter 2, we explained that a high debt ratio indicates solvency problems and higher financial risk. This is the risk that a company might not be able to pay back its debts. Whether profits are high, low, or losses, the interest payments do not change. These interest payments are fixed and don't vary with profits. Failure to pay interest on debts may result in default and bankruptcy. Accordingly, a company with little or no profit, or even a loss, such as FCX, must still pay interest on its debt, or go into default and possibly bankruptcy.

However, a high debt ratio, and the high financial risk that comes with it, can also boost profits. When profits are high, interest payments do not increase. The company can pay the same fixed interest payments, and then the lion's share of profits will go to the stockholders. Accordingly, high debts increase the variability of net income; when net income is high, only a small portion of the profits go to pay interest, pushing net income higher, and when net income is low or a net loss, high debts will push them further into net loss territory. This can be demonstrated with FCX's results for three years. Consider how a ratio called "Financial Leverage" explains the difference between Return on Assets and Return on Equity. Financial Leverage is computed as:

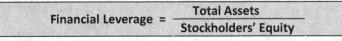

$$\text{Financial Leverage} = \frac{\text{Total Assets}}{\text{Stockholders' Equity}}$$

Financial Leverage is similar to the debt ratio, in the sense that the more debt a company has, the higher the Financial Leverage. It measures how debt "boosts" return on assets to increase return on equity. To demonstrate:

FYE December 31,	2010	2009	2008
Return on Assets	18.9%	13.6%	-44.7%
x Financial Leverage	2.34	2.85	4.05
= Return on Equity	44.3%	38.8%	-181.0%

Return on Equity can be derived by multiplying Return on Assets by Financial Leverage (with a slight rounding difference):

18.9% x 2.34= 44.3%

In 2010, FCX's debts had the effect of multiplying Return on Assets by 2.34 to equal Return on Equity. Back in 2008, the multiplier factor increased to 4.05. Unfortunately for FCX, that was when the company incurred a giant loss. Financial Leverage increased FCX's 44.7% negative Return on Assets to a whopping 181.0% negative Return on Equity.

Simple multiplication can explain this effect, as Total Assets cancel out in each term of the equation:

Return on Equity	=	Return on Assets	X	Financial Leverage
$\dfrac{\text{Net Income}}{\text{Stockholders' equity}}$	=	$\dfrac{\text{Net Income}}{\text{Total Assets}}$	X	$\dfrac{\text{Total Assets}}{\text{Stockholders' Equity}}$
		$\dfrac{\text{Net Income}}{\text{Total Assets}}$	X	$\dfrac{\text{Total Assets}}{\text{Stockholders' Equity}}$

TIMES INTEREST EARNED RATIO

Another risk to a company with high debt is its ability to make timely interest payments. The Times Interest Earned Ratio indicates a company's ability to earn (cover) its periodic interest payments. It compares the amount of income available to make interest payments to interest payment requirements.

$$\text{Times Interest Earned Ratio} = \frac{\text{Operating Income}}{\text{Interest Expense}}$$

($ in millions) FYE December 31,	2010	2009	2008	
Operating income	9,068	6,503	(12,710)	A
Interest expense	462	586	584	B
Times interest earned ratio	19.63	11.10	(21.76)	A/B

In general, a times interest earned ratio of 4 is considered adequate. In 2009, the times interest earned ratio of 11.10 indicates FCX could cover its interest payments with operating income more than 11 times, and in 2010 more than 19 times, which is more than adequate coverage. In 2008, the negative Operating Income indicates interest obligations may be difficult to meet.

($ in millions) December 31,	2010	2009	2008
Total assets	29,386	25,996	23,353
Long-term debt	**4,660**	**6,330**	**7,284**
Total liabilities	14,826	15,239	16,252
Stockholders' equity	14,560	10,757	7,101

An interesting aside is to note the relationship between the amount of interest-bearing long-term debt and interest expense; as the amount of long-term debt increases, interest expense also increases. Can you calculate the average long-term interest rate of 10% during 2010? Can you determine that the average cost of borrowing has increased from 8% in 2008, to 9% in 2009, to 10% in 2010?

Freeport McMoRan Copper & Gold, Inc. CONSOLIDATED STATEMENTS OF OPERATIONS (Excerpts) (In millions, except per share data)			
Year Ended December 31,	**2010**	**2009**	**2008**
Net (loss) income per share of common stock:			
Basic	$4.67	$3.05	$(14.86)
Diluted	$4.57	$2.93	$(14.86)
Average common shares outstanding:			
Basic	915	829	763
Diluted	949	938	763
Dividends declared per share of common stock	$1.125	$0.075	$0.6875

Earnings per share (EPS) is the amount of net income (loss) earned by each individual share of stock held by investors. For example, for each share of stock, FCX lost $4.67 in 2010. An investor holding 100 shares would have earned paper profits of $467. Accountants use the following formula to compute EPS:

$$\text{Earnings per Share} = \frac{\text{Net Income - Preferred Dividends}}{\text{Average Number of Common Shares Outstanding}}$$

FCX, like many companies, reports two earnings per share figures, **basic** and **diluted.** To compute **basic earnings per share,** companies divide net income by the *actual* average number of common shares outstanding. However, as we discussed before, some companies issue **stock options,** which are contracts that give their holders the right to buy or sell shares of stock at a certain market price. Exercise of these stock options increase the number of common shares outstanding and may lower earnings per share. This decrease is similar to the case of Harry, Sam, and Tex, where Tex's new ownership dilutes Harry and Sam's shares. When dilution could occur, companies are required to report both basic and diluted EPS. To compute diluted EPS, companies divide net income by the *potential* average number of common shares outstanding, so Basic EPS will always exceed Diluted EPS. When evaluating performance, investors who want to be on the safe side should use Diluted EPS rather than Basic EPS. In this text, EPS refers to Basic EPS, unless noted otherwise.

Companies with nonrecurring items, such as discontinued operations or extraordinary items (as we discussed in Chapter 3), would report earnings per share from these items separately. FCX is not reporting any nonrecurring items.

Average Number of Common Shares Outstanding indicates how many shares of common stock, on average, were held by investors during the accounting period. This amount is reported at the bottom of the income statement (see above) or in the Notes to the Financial Statements. Do not confuse the *Average* Number of Common Shares Outstanding with the Number of Common Shares Outstanding at *Year End,* (listed in the Balance Sheet and the Statement of Stockholders' Equity).

The **Dividend Rate** is the amount of dividends paid annually for each share of stock held by investors. It can be computed by dividing the annual common stock dividend by the average number of common shares outstanding for the year.

	Annual common stock dividends paid	
Dividend Rate =	Average number of common Shares outstanding	

Companies usually report the dividend rate in the notes to the financial statement or directly on the income statement. Here, FCX reported on the income statement that they issued a dividend of $1.375 even though they incurred a $29.72 loss per share.

Investors often look for a steady stream of dividends, over a long period of time, as a sign that a company has a steady performance record. This is why FCX, even when incurring tremendous losses in 2008, would still make an effort to continue paying steady dividends.

December 31,	2010	2009	2008	
Market price per share	$60.04	$40.14	$ 12.22	A
Earnings per share	$ 4.57	$ 2.93	$ (14.86)	B
Dividend rate per share (as reported on the income statement)	$1.125	$0.075	$ 0.6875	
Price earnings ratio	13.1	13.7	NA	A/B

PRICE EARNINGS RATIO

Investors use the **Price Earnings (PE) Ratio** to measure how "expensive" a company's stock is compared to EPS. It is computed as:

$$\text{Price Earnings Ratio} = \frac{\text{Market Price per Share}}{\text{EPS}}$$

For most stocks, the PE ratio ranges between 10 and 20. A PE ratio below 10 is a "bargain" stock, for which an investor can purchase a share for less than $10 for each $1 of EPS. Here, an investor could buy stock in a company for a low price compared to market value. Alternatively, a PE ratio above 20 would be considered an "expensive" stock because an investor must pay more than $20 for each $1 of EPS.

FCX's market value on December 31, 2010, was $60.04, resulting in a PE ratio of 13.1 ($60.04 / $4.57). This means that FCX's stock was considered to be moderately priced—not too expensive, not too cheap. For each dollar of earnings an investor paid $4.57 in market value.

Contrast this with FCX's performance on December 31, 2008, when the stock was trading at $12.22. Because the company incurred a net loss, the PE ratio on this date would mean nothing. Analysts compute a second PE ratio, based on predicted earnings per share. This is called "Forward PE." In March 2009, analysts estimated a forward PE of 14.27 for FCX (according to Google Finance, March 7, 2009). This is remarkably consistent with actual 2009 performance.

Regrettably, the PE ratio doesn't explain why a stock is expensive or cheap. The PE ratio for a company could be high, because it offers great potential for future earnings. Alternatively, it might be too high, preventing investors from earning a reasonable return on their investments. A low PE ratio might occur because the company is unlikely to grow in the future. Alternatively, this low price could indicate a good opportunity for investors to buy a stock that will rebound and increase in value.

Freeport McMoRan Copper & Gold, Inc. (FCX)									
RATIO	ROS	ROA x	Financial Leverage	= ROE	Times Interest Earned	Market Price	EPS (Basic)	Dividend Rate	PE Ratio
Type	Profit	Profit	Solvency	Profit	Solvency	Invest	Profit	Invest	Invest
Formula	NI / Sales Revenue	NI / Total Assets	Total Assets/ SE	NI / SE	Operating Income / Interest Expense	NA	NI – Preferred Div / Avg CS OS	Annual Div Paid / Avg CS OS	Market Price / EPS
2010	29.2%	18.9%	2.34	44.3%	19.63	$60.04	$4.67	$1.125	13.1
2009	23.5%	13.6%	2.85	38.8%	11.10	40.14	3.05	0.075	13.7
2008	-58.7%	-44.7%	4.04	-181.0%	(21.76)	12.22	(14.86)	0.688	NA
*** Industry	41.7%	21.1%	2.00	38.1%	22.5	NA	NA	NA	11.6
** S&P 500	10.0%	10.0%	2.50	25.0%	30.00	NA	NA	$2.00	14.0

* Industry: *Copper—Industry and S&P 500 ratio averages from moneycentral.msn.com*

** There are no official rules governing how these ratios are calculated. Therefore, the ratio formulas used may differ from the formulas in the text.

SUMMARY

The Statement of Stockholders' Equity provides information about changes in a company's stockholders' equity, including contributed capital and retained earnings. It helps investors understand the structure of a company's ownership.

Contributed Capital reports amounts paid (contributed) for shares of stock by investors. These amounts are classified as either Par Value or Additional Paid-in Capital, amounts paid in addition to the par value. There are two types of stock—preferred and common. Preferred shareholders receive preferential treatment, as they receive dividends before common shareholders. For each type of stock, shares authorized, issued, and outstanding must be disclosed. Shares outstanding are those shares in the hands of shareholders, which equal shares issued less shares repurchased as treasury stock. Stock splits and stock dividends change the number of shares outstanding, but do not change investors' proportionate share of the company.

Retained Earnings is net income earned by the company since incorporation and not yet distributed as dividends. Accordingly, net income increases retained earnings and dividends decrease retained earnings.

Other Comprehensive Income primarily includes gain/loss items not directly related to the company's operations and not reported on the income statement.

U.S. GAAP reports preferred stock as equity, whereas IFRS reports it as debt and the associated dividends as interest expense on the income statement.

There are several ratios introduced in this chapter that help investors further evaluate solvency, profitability, and investment potential. First, the financial leverage ratio (total assets divided by stockholders' equity) measures how debt "boosts" return on assets to increase return on equity. Return on equity (net income divided by stockholders' equity) measures how effectively stockholders' equity is used to produce net income. The Times Interest Earned ratio (operating income divided by interest expense) indicates a company's ability to earn (cover) its periodic interest payments. Earnings per share (net income less preferred dividends divided by the average number of common shares outstanding) is the amount of net income (loss) earned by each share of common stock, whereas the dividend rate is the amount of dividends paid annually for each share of stock. Investors use the price earnings ratio (market price per share divided by EPS) to measure how "expensive" a company's stock is compared to EPS. Regrettably, it does not explain why a stock is expensive or cheap.

American Eagle Outfitters, Inc. (AEO) **STATEMENT OF STOCKHOLDERS' EQUITY** *For the year ended January 28, 2012* (In thousands)							
	Shares Out-standing (1)	**Common Stock (Par)**	**Contributed Capital (APIC)**	**Retained Earnings**	**Treasury Stock (2)**	**Accumulated Other Comprehen-sive Income**	**Total Stockholders' Equity**
Balance at January 29, 2011	194,366	$2,496	$546,597	$1,711,929	$(938,023)	$28,072	$1,351,071
Stock awards	-	-	10,532				10,532
Repurchase of common stock	(1,510)				(17,349)		(17,349)
Reissuance of treasury stock	992				6,549		6,549
Net income				151,705			151,705
Other comprehensive income, net of tax						587	587
Cash dividends				(87,909)			(87,909)
Other (3)			(4,332)	(4,261)	10,258		1,665
Balance at January 28, 2012	**193,848**	**$2,496**	**$552,797**	**$1,771,464**	**$(938,565)**	**$28,659**	**$1,416,851**

(1) $0.01 par value *common stock* at January 28, 2012: 600,000 authorized, 249,566 issued and 193,848 outstanding.

$0.01 par value *common stock* at January 29, 2011: 600,000 authorized, 249,566 issued and 194,366 outstanding.

$0.01 par value *preferred stock* at January 28, 2012 and January 29, 2011: 5,000 authorized, with none issued or outstanding,

(2) *Treasury stock*: 55,718 shares and 55,200 shares [in treasury] at January 28, 2012and January 29, 2011, respectively. During Fiscal 2011, 922 shares were reissued from treasury stock for the issuance of share-based payments.

(3) Reclassified amounts for easier understanding in this text.

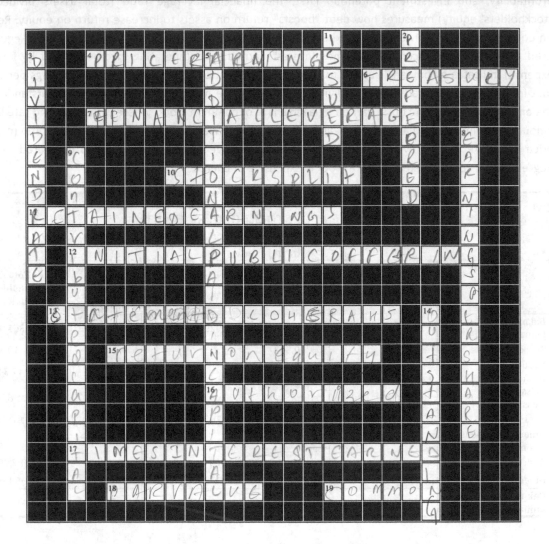

Across

4. Ratio measuring how expensive a company's stock price is compared to EPS (2 words)
6. Shares bought back from investors
7. Solvency ratio that measures how debt boosts ROA to increase ROE (2 words)
10. If three-for-one, an investor holding 100 shares before holds 300 shares after (2 words)
11. Net income not yet distributed as dividends (2 words)
12. First time sale of stock to the public (3 words)
13. Statement reporting changes in shares outstanding, earnings, and the distribution of earnings (2 words)
15. Ratio measuring profitability from the shareholders' perspective (3 words)
16. Maximum number of shares permitted to be issued
17. Ratio measuring the ability to pay periodic interest payments (3 words)
18. Legal value assigned to each share of stock; usually less than the market price of the stock (2 words)
19. Type of stock that all corporations must issue

Down

1. Shares sold to investors
2. Shares receiving dividends before common shares; usually carrying a dividend rate
3. Per share amount of dividends paid annually (2 words)
5. Amounts received in excess of par (4 words)
8. Amount of net income earned by each share of stock (3 words)
9. Total amount paid-in for shares of stock by investors (2 words)
14. Shares held by investors; Issued shares less treasury shares

Purpose:
- Identify three types of stock.
- Identify the number of shares authorized, issued, and outstanding.
- Compute the total cost of contributed capital and the average cost per share.

The **Statement of Stockholders' Equity** provides information about changes in a company's stockholders' equity, including contributed capital and retained earnings. It helps investors understand the structure of a company's ownership.

- **Contributed capital** (CC) includes amounts paid-in (contributed) by stockholders to purchase the stock of a corporation. There are two types of stock: **common stock** and **preferred stock.** Each corporation must issue common stock, whereas preferred stock is optional.

- When originally issued, amounts received from investors are recorded in two separate accounts— the *Par Value* account and an *Additional Paid-in-Capital* account. **Par Value** is a legal value assigned to each share of stock upon incorporation, which must be recorded separately in the financial statements. **Additional Paid-in-Capital** (APIC) is the amount received in excess of par.

> Par Value + Additional Paid-in-Capital = Total Issue Price of Stock

Refer to the Statement of Stockholders' Equity for American Eagle Outfitters, Inc. and accompanying notes on page 107 to answer the following questions.

Q1 For AEO the Par Value account is titled (**Common Stock** / **Contributed Capital**) and is $0.__01__ per share, while the Additional Paid-in-Capital account is titled (**Common Stock** / **Contributed Capital**).

Q2 On January 29, 2011 $__2496__ thousand was reported as Common Stock (Par) and $__546597__ thousand reported as Contributed Capital (APIC) for total contributions of $__549093__ thousand for issued shares.

Q3 During FYE January 28, 2012, AEO repurchased common stock, which (**increased / decreased**) total stockholders' equity by $__17,439__ thousand and reissued treasury stock which (**increased / decreased**) total stockholders' equity by $__6549__ thousand.

Upon incorporation, a company is **authorized** (by the state of incorporation) to **issue** a designated number of shares to investors. Sometimes corporations buy back shares of stock that have been issued; these are referred to as **Treasury Stock. Shares outstanding** are the total number of shares actually held by investors at a given time, equaling shares issued less shares of treasury stock.

> Shares issued - Treasury shares = Shares outstanding

Q4 On January 29, 2011 for *preferred* stock there are (**0** / **5,000** / **600,000**) thousand shares authorized, (**0** / **5,000** / **600,000**) thousand shares issued, and (**0** / **5,000** / **600,000**) thousand shares outstanding. Whereas for *common* stock on January 29, 2011 there are (**600,000** / **249,566** / **194,366**) thousand shares authorized, (**600,000** / **249,566** / **194,366**) thousand shares issued, and (**600,000** / **249,566** / **194,366**) thousand shares outstanding. [*Refer to Note (1)*]

Q5 On January 29, 2011 for *common* stock: __249566__ thousand shares issued - __55200__ thousand shares in treasury [*Refer to Note (2)*] = __194366__ thousand shares outstanding.

Q6 On January 29, 2011 there are __194366__ thousand shares of *common stock* issued for a total contribution of (**$2,496** / **$546,597** / **$549,093** / **$938,023**) thousand, averaging (**$3** / **$17**) per share. Also, there are __55200__ thousand shares of *treasury stock* with a total cost of (**$2,496** / **$546,597** / **$549,093** / **$938,023**) thousand, averaging (**$3** / **$17**) per share.

Why does the average cost of issued common shares differ from the average cost of treasury shares?

Purpose:
- Interpret an increase and decrease in Stockholders' Equity.
- Understand preferred and common stock dividends.
- Compute shares outstanding after a stock split.

Retained earnings (RE) are net income earned by the company since its incorporation and not yet distributed as dividends. It is increased by net income, the earnings of this accounting period, and decreased by dividends, a distribution of earnings.

> Beginning Retained Earnings + Net Income - Dividends = Ending Retained Earnings

Refer to the Statement of Stockholders' Equity for American Eagle Outfitters (AEO), Inc. and accompanying notes presented on page 107 to answer the following questions.

Q1   For fiscal year ended on January 28, 2012 for AEO:
Beginning Retained Earnings, (**January 29**/ **January 28**), 2011 $ _1,711,929_ thousand
+ Net income   _151,705_ thousand
- Dividends   _87,909_ thousand
- Other   (4,261) thousand
= Ending Retained Earnings, January 28, 2012 $ _1,771,464_ thousand

Q2   On January 28, 2012 stockholders' equity totaled $ _1,416,851_ thousand, which is the amount of business assets owned by shareholders.

Q3   Assume that AEO issued 1 million shares of preferred stock with a dividend rate of $5 per share.
a.   Preferred shareholders would expect to receive $ _5_ million in dividends each year.
b.   (**Preferred**/ **Common**) shareholders always receive their dividends first; this is part of the "preferred" treatment. Therefore, if the Board of Directors declared an $80 million dividend, *preferred* shareholders would receive $ _5,954_ million in dividends and *common* shareholders would receive $ _75_ million in dividends.
c.   (**Preferred / Common**) stock usually has a stated dividend rate.

Q4   a.   A company has _170_ million common shares outstanding. Assume there was a two-for-one stock split, after the stock split there would be (**113 / 170 / 255 /(340)/ 510**) million common shares outstanding.
Assume there was a three-for-two stock split, after the stock split there would be (**113 / 170 /(255)/ 340 / 510**) million common shares outstanding.
b.   Because shareholders maintain the same proportionate share of a company's wealth before and after a stock split, the stock split (**increases / decreases /(has no effect)**) on shareholder wealth.
c.   Under International Financial Reporting Standards (IFRS), preferred stock would be classified as (**(a liability)/ stockholders' equity**) and the preferred dividend reported as ((**interest** /
dividends) on the income statement.

Q5   For each of the following events, identify the effect on stockholders' equity.
a.   Net income ((**increases**)/ **decreases / has no effect on**) stockholders' equity.
b.   Cash dividends (**increase / decrease /(have no effect on)**) stockholders' equity.
c.   Repurchase of treasury stock (**increases /(decreases)/ has no effect on**) stockholders' equity.
d.   Reissue of treasury stock ((**increases**)/ **decreases / has no effect on**) stockholders' equity.

Q6   ((**Common**)/ **Preferred**/ **Treasury**) stock is publicly traded, meaning the shares are bought and sold on public stock exchanges such as the New York Stock Exchange and NASDAQ.

Purpose:
- Understand that EPS cannot be used to compare profitability among companies.
- Compute how treasury stock affects EPS.
- Identify EPS trends and compare EPS to Market Price to enhance meaning.

> **Earnings per Share (EPS)** indicates the amount of net income earned by each individual share of stock held by investors.
>
> $$EPS = \frac{\text{Net income - Preferred dividends}}{\text{Average number of common shares outstanding}}$$

Use the EPS information below for Athar and Wagdy Companies to answer the following questions.

Athar Company EPS = $0.50		Wagdy Company EPS = $2.00	
Net income	= $1,000,000	Net income	= $1,000,000
Avg. # of CShares OS	2,000,000	Avg. # of CShares OS	500,000

Q1 Refer to the EPS information immediately above. Even though Wagdy Company reports (**greater** / lower) EPS, both companies have (**the same** / different) net income. A company with greater EPS (does / **does not**) indicate greater profitability.

Q2 If Athar Company *buys back* 1 million shares of common stock, then treasury stock would (**increase** / decrease), common shares outstanding would (increase / **decrease**), and EPS would (**increase** / decrease) to ($0.33 / **$1** / $2) per share. The increase in EPS looks (**good** / bad) to shareholders because their proportionate ownership interest is (**increased** / decreased).

Alternatively, if Athar Company *issues* an additional 1 million shares of common stock then common shares outstanding would (**increase** / decrease) and EPS would (increase / **decrease**) to (**$0.33** / $1 / $2) per share. The decrease in EPS looks (good / **bad**) to shareholders because their proportionate ownership interest is (increased / **decreased**).

Athar Company EPS = $0.50			Wagdy Company EPS = $2.00		
Year 1	Year 2	Year 3	Year 1	Year 2	Year 3
EPS $0.10	$0.20	$0.50	EPS $8	$4	$2

Q3 Refer to the EPS information immediately above. EPS for Athar Company has a/an (**increasing** / decreasing) trend, whereas Wagdy Company has a/an (increasing / **decreasing**) trend. EPS (**can** / cannot) be more meaningful when compared over time.

Athar Company EPS = $0.50		Wagdy Company EPS = $2.00	
Market Price = $6/share = PE Ratio		Market Price $60/share = PE Ratio	
EPS $0.50 of 12		EPS $2.00 of 30	

Q4 Refer to the EPS and the Market Price information immediately above. The PE Ratio measures how expensive a stock is; how much investors are willing to pay for each $1 of EPS. A PE below 10 is considered a "bargain" stock, whereas a PE of more than 20 is considered "expensive." Measured by the PE ratio, Athar Company stock is (a bargain / **moderately-priced** / expensive), while Wagdy Company stock is (a bargain / moderately-priced / **expensive**) EPS (**can** / cannot) be more meaningful when compared to market price per share.

Purpose:
- Understand how debt affects financial leverage and ROE.
- Compute ROS, Asset Turnover, ROA, Financial Leverage, ROE, and the Debt Ratio.

Q1   Review Corporations A through E on page 113. All corporations have the same amount of (**Sales revenue** / **Net income** / **Assets** / **Liabilities** / **Stockholders' equity**), but different amounts of (**Sales revenue** / **Net income** / **Assets** / **Liabilities** / **Stockholders' equity**). Corp A has the (**least** / **greatest**) amount of liabilities, whereas Corp E has the (**least** / **greatest**) amount of liabilities.

Q2   Compute the ratios for Corp C, Corp D, and Corp E and record in the DuPont Analysis of ROE chart on page 113. As liabilities increase (**ROS** / **Asset turnover** / **ROA** / **Financial leverage** / **ROE** / **Debt**) ratios *remain the same*, but the (**ROS** / **Asset turnover** / **ROA** / **Financial leverage** / **ROE** / **Debt**) ratios *increase*.

> **Financial Leverage Ratio = Assets / SE**
>
> **Debt Ratio = Liabilities / Assets**

Because A = L + SE you can convert:

Financial Leverage Ratio = 1 / (1 - Debt Ratio)

Q3   Corp D has a debt ratio of 75%, which results in Financial Leverage of (**2** / **4** / **25**), therefore, ROE is (**2** / **4** / **25**) times greater than ROA.

Corp A has no debt, therefore, ROA (**<** / **=** / **>**) ROE.

Q4   Higher debt results in a (**higher** / **lower**) debt ratio, which leads to (**higher** / **lower**) Financial Leverage, which results in higher (**ROA** / **ROE**) because shareholders are assuming (**higher** / **lower**) risk.

Q5   In the Primary Driver chart on the previous page:

a.   Circle the Primary Driver of ROA as either ROS or Asset Turnover.

b.   Circle the Primary Driver of ROE as either ROA, Financial Leverage, or of equal (=) contribution.

Q6   a.   The primary driver of ROA remains the same because (**sales revenue** / **expenses** / **assets** / **liabilities**) remain the same.

b.   The primary driver of ROE changes because (**sales revenue** / **expenses** / **assets** / **liabilities**) change.

Q7   What is the primary driver of ROE when the debt ratio is:

a.   Less than 50%?   (**ROA** / **=** / **LEV**)

b.   Equal to 50%?   (**ROA** / **=** / **LEV**)

c.   Greater than 50%?   (**ROA** / **=** / **LEV**)

DUPONT ANALYSIS of ROE

	Formula	CORP A	CORP B	CORP C	CORP D	CORP E
Sales revenue		$ 100	$ 100	$ 100	$ 100	$ 100
Net income		10	10	10	10	10
Assets		100	100	100	100	100
Liabilities		0	25	50	75	96
Stockholders' equity		$ 100	$ 75	$ 50	$ 25	$ 4
ROS	NI / Sales revenue	10.00%	10.00%	10%	10%	10%
x Asset turnover	Sales revenue / Assets	1.00	1.00	$1	$1	$1
= ROA	NI / Assets	10.00%	10.00%	.10	.10	.10
x Financial leverage	Assets / SE	1.00	1.33	2800	4.50	25.10
= ROE	NI / SE	10.00%	13.33%	29	40%	250
Debt ratio	Liabilities / Assets	0.00%	25.00%	100		

PRIMARY DRIVER CHART

Primary Driver	CORP A	CORP B	CORP C	CORP D	CORP E
Of ROA?	(ROS / A TO)	(ROS / A TO)	(ROS / A TO)	(ROS / A TO)	(ROS / A TO)
Of ROE?	(ROA/ = /Lev)	(ROA/ = /Lev)	(ROA/ = /Lev)	(ROA/ = /Lev)	(ROA/ = /Lev)

Purpose:
- Understand how debt affects financial leverage and ROE.
- Compute Financial Leverage and ROE.

$ in Millions	Formula	YHOO 12/31/2011	COST 8/29/2011	CAT 12/31/2011
Sales revenue		4,984	88,915	60,138
Net income		1,049	1,462	4,928
Assets		14,783	26,761	81,446
Liabilities		2,242	14,759	68,563
Stockholders' equity		12,541	12,002	12,883
ROS	NI / Sales Revenue	21.05%	1.64%	8.19%
x Asset turnover	Sales Revenue / Assets	0.3371	3.3226	0.7384
= ROA	NI / Assets	7.096%	5.46%	6.05%
x Financial leverage	Assets / SE	1.1788	~~2.23~~	6.32
= ROE	NI / SE	8.36%	12.18	28.25
Debt ratio	Liabilities / Assets	15.17%	55.15%	84.18%

Primary Driver	YHOO	COST	CAT
Of ROA?	(ROS / A TO)	(ROS / A TO)	(ROS / A TO)
Of ROE?	(ROA / = / Lev)	(ROA / = / Lev)	(ROA / = / Lev)

Refer to the financial information above for Yahoo! Inc. (YHOO), Costco Wholesale Corporation (COST), and Caterpillar Inc. (CAT) to answer the following questions.

Q1   Which company offers products to members in a range of merchandise categories that have been purchased directly from manufacturers? (**YHOO / COST / CAT**) The business strategy of this company is to purchase merchandise at (**low / high**) prices and then sell the merchandise to members at (**low / high**) prices to generate (**low / high**) volume. The (**low / high**) pricing strategy is reflected in (**ROS / Asset Turnover / Financial Leverage**) of 1.64%, whereas the (**low / high**) volume strategy is reflected in (**ROS / Asset Turnover / Financial Leverage**) of 3.32

Q2   (**ROS / ROA / ROE**) is the most comprehensive profitability ratio, and of the three companies, (**YHOO / COST / CAT**) has the greatest profitability as measured by this ratio.

Q3   Compute Financial Leverage and ROE for Costco and Caterpillar and record in the chart above. (**YHOO / COST / CAT**) reports the greatest ROE and (**YHOO / COST / CAT**) is assuming the greatest amount of financial risk.

Q4   *Costco* has a debt ratio of approximately (**15% / 55% / 84%**), resulting in a Financial Leverage ratio of around (**1 / 2 / 6**); therefore, ROE is (**1 / 2 / 6**) times greater than ROA.
      Caterpillar has a debt ratio of approximately (**15% / 55% / 84%**), resulting in a Financial Leverage ratio of around (**1 / 2 / 6**); therefore, ROE is (**1 / 2 / 6**) times greater than ROA.

Q5   In the Primary Driver chart above:
      a.   Circle the Primary Driver of ROA as either **ROS** or Asset Turnover.
      b.   Circle the Primary Driver of ROE as either **ROA**, Financial Leverage, or of approximately equal (=) contribution.

Q6   Using only the financial information above, which company would you prefer to invest in? (**YHOO / COST / CAT**) Why?

Purpose:
- Review a number of ratios to better evaluate a company.
- Understand that the expected range of ratios varies by industry.
- Understand that comparing a ratio to industry norms enhances meaning.

Ratios reveal relationships.

Below are ratios with explanations introduced in this chapter. *See Appendix B for additional ratios.*

Financial Leverage is similar to the debt ratio, in the sense that the more debt a company has, the higher the Financial Leverage. It measures how debt "boosts" return on assets to increase return on equity.

Financial Leverage	=	$\dfrac{\text{Total assets}}{\text{Stockholders' equity}}$

The **Return on Equity (ROE)** ratio measures how effectively stockholders' equity is used to produce net income. ROA x Financial Leverage = ROE

ROE	=	$\dfrac{\text{Net income}}{\text{Stockholders' equity}}$

Times Interest Earned indicates a company's ability to earn (cover) its periodic interest payments.

Times Interest Earned	=	$\dfrac{\text{Operating income}}{\text{Interest expense}}$

Earnings per Share (EPS) is the amount of net income (loss) earned by each individual share of stock held by investors.

EPS	=	$\dfrac{\text{Net income - Preferred dividends}}{\text{Average number of common shares outstanding}}$

The **Dividend Rate** is the amount of dividends paid annually for each share of stock held by investors.

Dividend Rate	=	$\dfrac{\text{Annual common stock dividends paid}}{\text{Average number of common shares outstanding}}$

Investors use the **Price Earnings (PE)** ratio to measure how "expensive" a company's stock is compared to EPS. Regrettably, it does not explain why a stock is expensive or cheap.

PE Ratio	=	$\dfrac{\text{Market price per share}}{\text{EPS}}$

Below are ratios and selected financial information for three companies within the Retail Apparel industry: American Eagle Outfitters, Inc. (AEO), GAP Inc. (GPS), and Urban Outfitters Inc.(URBN).

RATIOS for the fiscal year ended January 29, 2011									
RATIO	ROS	ROA x	Financial Leverage	= ROE	Times Interest Earned	Market Price	EPS	Dividend Rate	PE Ratio
Type	Profit	Profit	Solvency	Profit	Solvency	Invest	Profit	Invest	Invest
Formula	NI / Sales Revenue	NI / Total Assets	Total Assets/ SE	NI / SE	Operating Income / Interest Expense	NA	NI – Preferred Div / Avg # of CShares OS	Annual Div paid / Avg # of CShares OS	Market Price / EPS
AEO	4.75%	7.50%	1.39	10.4%	NA	$ 14	$ 0.91	$ 0.44	15
GPS	8.21%	17.04%	1.73	29.5%	NA	$ 19	$ 1.89	$ 0.50	10
URBN	12.01%	15.22%	1.27	19.3%	NA	$ 34	$ 1.64	--	21
Industry * **	6.3%	8.20%	2.01	16.5%	46	NA	NA	NA	15
S&P 500 **	10.0%	10.0%	2.50	25.0%	30	NA	NA	$ 2.00	14

* Industry Averages for *Apparel Stores—Industry and S&P 500 ratio averages from moneycentral.msn.com*
** There are no official rules governing how these ratios are calculated. Therefore, the ratio formulas used may differ from the formulas in the text.

For the fiscal year ended January 29, 2011 (In Millions)	American Eagle Outfitters (AEO)	Gap (GPS)	Urban Outfitters (URBN)
Sales revenue	$ 2,968	$ 14,664	$ 2,274
Operating income	3170	1,968	414
Net income	141	1,204	273
Total assets	1,880	7,065	1,794
Total liabilities	529	2,985	382
Stockholders' equity	1,351	4,080	1,412
Long-term debt	0	0	0
Interest expense	0	0	0
Annual dividends paid	$ 185	$ 252	$ 0
Average number of common shares outstanding	209	588	170

Refer to the ratios and selected financial information for three companies within the Retail Apparel Industry: American Eagle Outfitters, Inc. (AEO), GAP Inc. (GPS), and Urban Outfitters Inc. on the previous page to answer the following questions.

Q1   The strongest ROS ratio is reported by (**AEO / GPS / URBN**). ROS expresses net income as a percentage of (**revenue / expenses / assets**) and measures the firm's ability to control (**revenue / expenses / net income**) to keep (**revenue / expenses / net income**) high.

Q2   Meaning is added to a ratio by comparing it to industry norms because success may vary by industry. An ROA ratio greater than the industry norm is reported by (**AEO / GPS / URBN**), indicating these companies have (**greater / less**) overall profitability than average within the Apparel Store Industry.

Q3   The greatest financial leverage ratio of _____ is reported by (**AEO / GPS / URBN**), which will boost ROA almost (**1 / 2 / 4**) times to increase (**ROS / ROE / EPS / PE**). The average Financial Leverage for the S&P 500 is (**higher / lower**) than the average for the Apparel Store Industry, indicating that the S&P 500 stocks carry (**more / less**) debt on average than the Apparel Store Industry.

Q4   The *strongest* ROE is reported by (**AEO / GPS / URBN**), with ROA contributing 17% to ROE and Financial Leverage contributing _____% to ROE. Therefore, (**ROA / Financial Leverage**) is the primary driver of ROE.

Q5   A Times Interest Earned ratio greater than 4 generally indicates the ability to make interest payments. Companies within the Apparel Store Industry, on average, (**have / don't have**) the ability to make interest payments.

Q6   The higher EPS is reported by (**AEO / URBN**), indicating (**AEO / URBN / can't tell**) is more profitable. EPS (**does / does not**) compare profitability among companies, but (**does / does not**) reflect shareholders' proportionate share of earnings.

Q7   The companies paying dividends are (**AEO / GPS / URBN**). AEO is paying out approximately (**25% / 50% / 75%**) of this year's EPS. The dividend rate of AEO is (**more / less**) than the average for the S&P 500.

> Bargain PE < PE Ratio of 10 to 20 < Expensive PE

Q8   Urban Outfitter's PE Ratio of ___21___ indicates there is $___21___ of market price for each $1 of EPS. As measured by the PE ratio, (**AEO / GPS / URBN**) stock is the most expensive. Using the PE ratio scale immediately above, AEO has (**bargain-priced / moderately-priced / expensive**) stock when compared to EPS. A higher PE ratio indicates (**superior / inferior / can't tell**) stock.

Q9   Overall, which company has the greatest profitability? (**AEO / GPS / URBN**) *How can you tell?*

Which company is assuming the greatest financial risk? (**AEO / GPS / URBN**) *How can you tell?*

Which company would you invest in? (**AEO / GPS / URBN**) *Why?*

Purpose:
- Identify reasons for change in cash, total liabilities, and stockholders' equity.
- Explain how changes in the balance sheet and income statement affect ROA and ROE.
- Explain the effect of a huge cash dividend payment.

Refer to the financial statement and ratio information for Microsoft on page 119 to answer the following questions.

Q1   Study the Statement of Stockholders' Equity for the five years presented.

a.   During fiscal year ended (FYE) 6/30/2003 stockholders' equity increased primarily as a result of (**net income** / **issuing common stock** / **repurchasing common stock** / **paying dividends**).

b.   During FYE 6/30/2004 stockholders' equity (**increased** / **decreased**) primarily as a result of (**net income** / **issuing common stock** / **repurchasing common stock** / **paying dividends**).

c.   During FYE 6/30/2005 stockholders' equity (**increased** / **decreased**) primarily as a result of (**net income** / **issuing common stock** / **repurchasing common stock** / **paying dividends**).

d.   During FYE 6/30/2006 stockholders' equity (**increased** / **decreased**) primarily as a result of (**net income** / **issuing common stock** / **repurchasing common stock** / **paying dividends**).

e.   During FYE 6/30/2007 stockholders' equity (**increased** / **decreased**) primarily as a result of (**net income** / **issuing common stock** / **repurchasing common stock** / **paying dividends**).

Q2   Study the Balance Sheet for the five years presented.

a.   During FYE 6/30/2005 *cash equivalents* (**increased** / **decreased**) significantly as a result of (**a net loss** / **repurchasing common stock** / **paying dividends**).

b.   During FYE 6/30/2006 *cash equivalents* (**increased** / **decreased**) primarily as a result of (**a net loss** / **repurchasing common stock** / **paying dividends**).

c.   From 6/30/2004 to 6/30/2007 *total liabilities* (**increased** / **decreased**) whereas *stockholders' equity* (**increased** / **decreased**), resulting in a(n) (**increasing** / **decreasing**) debt ratio and (**increasing** / **decreasing**) financial leverage.

Q3   Study the Income Statement for the five years presented. From 6/30/2003 to 6/30/2007 revenues (**increased** / **decreased**), net income (**increased** / **decreased**), and EPS (**increased** / **decreased**).

Q4   a.   During FYE (**6-30-2004** / **6-30-2005** / **6-30-2006**) Microsoft paid a huge special one-time $3 per share dividend totaling $ _36968_ billion. To pay this dividend, did Microsoft have enough cash? (**Yes** / **No**) Enough retained earnings? (**Yes** / **No**)

b.   At this time Bill Gates owned 1.12 billion shares of Microsoft stock so his dividend was (**1.12** / **2.24** / **3.36**) billion dollars. What did Bill Gates do with his dividend? (**Buy a super-duper sports car** / **Donate it to charity** / **Give it to his children**)

1.12 × $3 per share

MICROSOFT	STATEMENT OF STOCKHOLDERS' EQUITY				
	Adapted from the Form 10-K, $ in millions				
	6/30/2007	6/30/2006	6/30/2005	6/30/2004	6/30/2003
Beginning CS	$ 59,005	$ 60,413	$ 56,396	$ 49,234	$ 41,845
Issue CS	1,552	(1,408)	4,017	7,162	7,389
Ending CS	60,557	59,005	60,413	56,396	49,234
Beginning RE	11,047	2,239	26,646	20,928	12,997
+ Net income	14,065	12,599	12,254	8,168	7,531
- Dividends	(3,837)	(3,594)	(36,968)	(1,729)	(857)
Other	425	(197)	307	(721)	1,257
Ending RE	21,700	11,047	2,239	26,646	20,928
Beginning TS	(29,948)	(14,537)	(8,217)	(5,250)	--
Repurchase CS	(21,212)	(15,411)	(6,320)	(2,967)	(5,250)
Ending TS	(51,160)	(29,948)	(14,537)	(8,217)	(5,250)
ENDING SE	$ 31,097	$ 40,104	$ 48,115	$ 74,825	$ 64,912

MICROSOFT	BALANCE SHEET				
	Selected Amounts in Millions				
	6/30/2007	6/30/2006	6/30/2005	6/30/2004	6/30/2003
Cash/Assets	37.06%	49.08%	53.31%	64.21%	61.64%
Cash equivalents	$ 23,411	$ 34,161	$ 37,751	$ 60,592	$ 49,048
Assets	$ 63,171	$ 69,597	$ 70,815	$ 94,368	$ 79,571
Liabilities	$ 32,074	$ 29,493	$ 22,700	$ 19,543	$ 14,659
Stockholders' equity	$ 31,097	$ 40,104	$ 48,115	$ 74,825	$ 64,912

MICROSOFT	INCOME STATEMENT				
	Selected Amounts in Millions, Except per Share Data				
Fiscal year ended	6/30/2007	6/30/2006	6/30/2005	6/30/2004	6/30/2003
Revenue	$ 51,122	$ 44,282	$ 39,788	$ 36,835	$ 32,187
Net income	$ 14,065	$ 12,599	$ 12,254	$ 8,168	$ 7,531
EPS	$ 1.44	$ 1.21	$ 1.13	$ 0.76	$ 0.70
Div rate per share	$ 0.40	$ 0.35	$ 3.40	$ 0.16	$ 0.08
Avg C/S O/S	9,742	10,438	10,839	10,803	10,723

MICROSOFT	DUPONT ANALYSIS of ROE				
	6/30/2007	6/30/2006	6/30/2005	6/30/2004	6/30/2003
ROS	27.51%	28.45%	30.80%	22.17%	23.40%
x Asset Turnover	0.8093	0.6363	0.5619	0.3903	0.4045
= ROA	22.26%	18.10%	17.30%	8.66%	9.46%
x Financial Leverage	2.03	1.74	1.47	1.26	1.23
= ROE	45.23%	31.42%	25.47%	10.92%	11.60%
Debt Ratio	50.77%	42.38%	32.06%	20.71%	18.42%

Q5   Review the DuPont Analysis of ROE for the five years presented.

a.   *Asset turnover = Sales revenue / Total assets*. During FYE 6/30/2005 revenue (**increased** /**decreased**). The payment of this special dividend (**increased** /**decreased**) cash, which (**increased** /**decreased**) total assets, resulting in (**increased** /**decreased**) asset turnover.

b.   *ROA = ROS x Asset turnover*. During FYE 6/30/2005 *ROS* (**increased** / **decreased**) and asset turnover (**increased** / **decreased**), resulting in *ROA* (**decreasing** / **doubling** / **more than doubling**).

c.   *Financial Leverage = SE / Total Assets*. During FYE 6/30/2005 liabilities (**increased** /**decreased**), while SE (**increased** /**decreased**), which (**increased** /**decreased**) the debt ratio and (**increased** /**decreased**) financial leverage.

d.   *ROE = ROA x Financial Leverage*. During FYE 6/30/2005 *ROA* (**increased** / **decreased**) and financial leverage (**increased** / **decreased**), resulting in *ROE* (**decreasing** / **doubling** / **more than doubling**).

Q6   What might have prompted this special one-time dividend?

making use of excess money.

Q7   Review the financial information presented for Microsoft. *Explain* how the special one-time $3 dividend affected each of the following items.

a.   Cash, Asset Turnover, and ROA

b.   Debt Ratio, Financial Leverage, and ROE

↓ SE ↑ liabilities

Q8   Cash is a (**high** / **low**) earning asset. *Explain*.

Q9   Review the financial information presented for Microsoft. *Explain* how the purchase of common stock (treasury stock) affected each of the following items.

a.   Cash, Asset Turnover, and ROA

b.   Debt Ratio, Financial Leverage, and ROE

↓ SE ↑ L.

CHAPTER 5

STATEMENT OF CASH FLOWS

LEARNING OBJECTIVES

1. Understand how the Statement of Cash Flows is organized.
2. Identify operating, investing, and financing activities.
3. Understand direct and indirect methods for computing operating cash flows.
4. Compute and interpret cash flow ratios.
5. Prepare and interpret trend and common-size statements of cash flows.

INTRODUCTION

Many investment analysts will tell you that "cash is king." Banks and creditors only take cash—they don't take profits. What's the difference between cash and net income? As we have already learned, many assumptions go into the computation of net income. Revenue is recorded based on the revenue recognition principle; you recognize revenue when it is earned and receivable. Therefore, revenues can often be different from the cash flows that a company receives from customers. Expenses are "matched" to revenues, so that they are recorded when a company gets the benefits from them, not necessarily when they are paid for. Accordingly, expenses generally don't equal cash outflows. Collectively, this means that a company's net income and its cash flows could actually move in opposite directions, so that a profitable company can have net cash *outflows* from its operations; such a company would be earning income but losing money! Similarly, a company can report a net loss but enjoy positive cash inflows from its operations.

The **Statement of Cash Flows** provides information about a company's cash inflows and cash outflows during an accounting period. It helps investors understand how much a company pays its employees, suppliers, creditors, and investors. In this chapter, we evaluate the cash flows of Cedar Fair, L.P., an amusement park operator. Cedar Fair operates 11 amusement parks and other attractions, including Cedar Point in Ohio and Dorney Park in Pennsylvania. We will review the different components of Cedar Fair's Statement of Cash Flows and analyze the company's liquidity and solvency. Here's how Cedar Fair describes itself in its Annual Report:

Cedar Fair, L.P. (together with its affiliated companies, the "Partnership") is a publicly traded Delaware limited partnership formed in 1987 and managed by Cedar Fair Management, Inc., an Ohio corporation (the "General Partner") whose shares are held by an Ohio trust. The Partnership is one of the largest regional amusement park operators in the world and owns eleven amusement parks, six outdoor water parks, one indoor water park and five hotels.

Cedar Fair owns and operates Cedar Point, Kings Island, Canada's Wonderland, Dorney Park & Wildwater Kingdom, Valleyfair, Michigan's Adventure, Kings Dominion, Carowinds, Worlds of Fun, Knott's Berry Farm, California's Great America, and Castaway Bay Indoor Waterpark Resort.

Cedar Fair is a **Limited Partnership**, not a corporation. This means that Cedar Park issues limited partnership units rather than stock. Although limited partners have the same limited liability as common stockholders in a corporation, Cedar Fair also has a general partner, who has personal liability for the company's obligations. Instead of reporting a Stockholders' Equity section on its Balance Sheet, Cedar Fair reports Partners' Equity, as shown:

Cedar Fair, L.P. CONSOLIDATED BALANCE SHEETS ($ in thousands)		
(excerpts)	**12/31/10**	**12/31/09**
Partners' Equity:		
Special L. P. interests	$ 5,290	$ 5,290
General partner	(1)	(1)
Limited partners, 55,334 and 55,234 units outstanding at December 31, 2010 and December 31, 2009, respectively	165,555	209,854
Accumulated other comprehensive loss	(33,708)	(87,281)
	$ 137,136	$ 127,862

Unlike corporations, limited partnerships do not report retained earnings. Instead, profits are credited to general and limited partners' interests listed in the balance sheets. Withdrawals of profits, which are like dividends, are subtracted from these interests.

Cedar Fair, L.P. (FUN) CONSOLIDATED STATEMENTS OF CASH FLOWS ($ in thousands)			
For the years ended December 31,	2010	2009	2008
CASH FLOWS FROM (FOR) OPERATING ACTIVITIES			
Net income (loss)	$ (31,567)	$ 35,429	$ 5,706
Adjustments to reconcile net income (loss) to net cash from operating activities:			
Depreciation and amortization	126,796	132,745	125,838
Noncash equity-based compensation expense	(89)	(26)	716
Loss on early extinguishment of debt	35,289	-	-
Loss on impairment of goodwill and oth. intangibles	2,293	4,500	86,988
Impairment loss on fixed assets / retirement	62,752	244	8,425
Gain on sale of other assets	-	(23,098)	
Net effect of swaps	18,194	9,170	-
Amortization of debt issuance costs	5,671	7,773	7,944
Unrealized foreign currency gain on notes	(17,464)	-	-
Other noncash (income) expense	(1,893)	(257)	(445)
Deferred income taxes	(14,140)	(5,684)	(17,827)
Excess tax benefit from unit-based comp. expense	-	-	(1,729)
Change in assets and liabilities, net of acquisition			
(Increase) decrease in current assets	(11,855)	551	1,674
(Increase) decrease in other assets	6	918	555
Increase (decrease) in accounts payable	652	(2,635)	(5,101)
Increase (decrease) in accrued taxes	(2,242)	1,349	3,725
Increase (decrease) in self-insurance reserves	(383)	857	(559)
Increase (decrease) in deferred revenue and other current liabilities	7,653	20,428	(2,808)
Increase in other liabilities	2,442	2,933	2,486
Net cash from operating activities	182,115	185,197	215,588
CASH FLOWS (FOR) INVESTING ACTIVITIES			
Acquisition of Paramount Parks, net of cash acquired		-	6,431
Sale of Canadian real estate	-	53,831	-
Capital expenditures	(71,706)	(69,136)	(83,481)
Net cash (for) investing activities	(71,706)	(15,305)	(77,050)
CASH FLOWS FROM (FOR) FINANCING ACTIVITIES			
Net (payments) borrowings on revolving credit loans— previous credit agreement	(86,300)	63,600	(11,386)
Net borrowings on revolving credit loans—existing credit agreement	23,200	-	-
Term debt borrowings	1,175,000	-	-
Note borrowings	399,383	-	-
Term debt payments, including early termination penalties	(1,566,890)	(161,329)	(17,450)
Distributions paid to partners	(13,834	(67,864)	(105,078)
Payment of debt issuance costs	(43,264)	(7,694)	-
Exercise of limited partnership unit options	7	4	4,541
Excess tax benefit from unit-based compensation expense	-	-	1,729
Net cash from (for) financing activities	(112,698)	(173,283)	(127,644)
Effect of exchange rate changes	126	1,446	(2,522)
Net increase (decrease) for the year	(2,163)	(1,945)	8,372
Balance, beginning of year	11,928	13,873	5,501
Balance, end of year	$ 9,765	$ 11,928	$ 13,873
SUPPLEMENTAL INFORMATION			
Cash payments for interest expense	$ 129,815	$ 117,008	$ 120,340
Interest capitalized	1,343	1,617	1,623
Cash payments for income taxes	19,074	18,966	14,619

(Handwritten annotation in right margin: "bond pay | 1,000,000 / loss 35289 / Cash 1035")

THREE CATEGORIES OF CASH FLOWS

Accountants classify cash flows into three categories: Financing, Investing, and Operating. As a business prepares to begin operations, it would have to first raise money through **Financing Activities**; issuing capital stock or issuing long-term debt. Financing activities are typically transactions that involve stockholders and creditors, such as receiving common stock investments, paying off loans, and paying dividends.

Then, the business will engage in **Investing Activities,** spending funds on revenue-generating assets, such as property, plant, and equipment. Investing activities are transactions involving noncurrent assets, such as the purchase of property, plant, and equipment or the purchase and sale of stock in other companies.

When the business begins operations, it generates cash flows for **Operating Activities,** using property, plant, and equipment, and other revenue-generating assets to manufacture and sell goods or offer services to customers. Operating activities typically involve cash inflows and outflows from a company's central business, such as receipts from customers and payments to suppliers and employees.

The company might reinvest the funds received from operating activities in more revenue-generating assets (Investing Activities). It could also use the funds to pay off debts or to pay dividends to stockholders (Financing Activities). As the business grows, it could borrow more money (Financing Activities) to purchase more revenue-generating assets (Investing Activities).

Here is a summary of typical **Transactions Reported on the Statement of Cash Flows** for each category:

OPERATING ACTIVITIES (DIRECT METHOD)	
Cash Inflows	**Cash Outflows**
Cash from customers	Cash paid to suppliers
Cash from interest and dividends	Interest paid
Other operating cash receipts	Other operating cash payments
INVESTING ACTIVITIES	
Cash Inflows	**Cash Outflows**
Sell property, plant, and equipment	Purchase property, plant, and equipment
Sell investment securities	Purchase securities
Receive loan repayments	Make loans
FINANCING ACTIVITIES	
Cash Inflows	**Cash Outflows**
Borrow cash from creditors	Repay amounts borrowed (debt principal)
Issue debt securities (bonds)	Repurchase equity shares (treasury stock)
Issue equity securities (capital stock)	Pay cash dividends

(handwritten margin note: "in financest → non operating")

In this chapter, we begin from the bottom and work our way up, starting with financing activities, then discussing investing activities, and then finally discussing operating activities.

Financing activities are transactions that involve owners and creditors, such as borrowing cash from creditors, repaying amounts to creditors, issuing capital stock in exchange for investments by stockholders, repurchasing equity shares (treasury stock), and paying cash dividends. (Note that *paying* dividends is a financing activity, whereas *receiving* cash dividends from investments is an operating activity.)

In a limited partnership such as Cedar Fair, financing activities also include transactions between the partnership and its partners, such as issuing partnership units and paying distributions to partners.

As we discussed in Chapter 2, companies have options when financing their operations, primarily debt or equity. This section of the statement of cash flows summarizes the financing transactions that occur during a year. For example, here is the financing activities section of Cedar Fair's statement of cash flows:

Cedar Fair, L.P. CONSOLIDATED STATEMENTS OF CASH FLOWS ($ in thousands)			
(excerpts) For the years ended December 31,	2010	2009	2008
CASH FLOWS FROM (FOR) FINANCING ACTIVITIES			
Net (payments) borrowings on revolving	$ (86,300)	$ 63,600	$ (11,386)
Net borrowings on revolving credit loans—existing credit agreement	23,200	-	-
Term debt borrowings	1,175,000	-	-
Note borrowings	399,383	-	-
Term debt payments, including early termination penalties	(1,566,890)	(161,329)	(17,450)
Distributions paid to partners	(13,834)	(67,864)	(105,078)
Payment of debt issuance costs	(43,264)	(7,694)	-
Exercise of limited partnership unit options	7	4	4,541
Excess tax benefit from unit-based compensation expense	-	-	1,729
Net cash from (for) financing activities	$ (112,698)	$ (173,283)	$ (127,644)

To understand financial statements, pay careful attention to the largest numbers. Following this strategy, the first item that we notice is the $1,175,000 thousand (that's $1.175 billion) borrowed to repay in full all amounts outstanding under previous credit agreements. In 2010, Cedar Fair used some of this money to make payments on revolving credit loans ($86,300 thousand) and to make term debt payments, ($1,566,890 thousand). In short, Cedar Fair took out one loan and paid back others. Cedar Fair also paid distributions to partners ($13,834 thousand). By the end of the year, Cedar Fair had a net outflow for financing activities of $112,698 thousand.

Investing activities are transactions involving noncurrent assets, such as the purchase or sale of property, plant, and equipment, the purchase or sale of investments, making loans, or receiving loan payments. (Note that the *receipt of loan principal* is classified as an investing activity, whereas the *receipt of interest revenue* on the loan is classified as an operating activity.)

Cedar Fair, L.P. CONSOLIDATED STATEMENTS OF CASH FLOWS (excerpts)			
($ in thousands) For the years ended December 31,	**2010**	**2009**	**2008**
CASH FLOWS (FOR) INVESTING ACTIVITIES			
Acquisition of Paramount Parks, net of cash acquired	$ -	$ -	$ 6,431
Sale of Canadian real estate	-	53,831	-
Capital expenditures	(71,706)	(69,136)	(83,481)
Net cash (for) investing activities	$ (71,706)	$ (15,305)	$ (77,050)

In 2008, Cedar Fair sold Paramount Parks, receiving $6,431 thousand. This section of the statement of cash flows also indicates that Cedar Fair spent $71,706 thousand in 2010 on capital expenditures, which include new land, land improvements, buildings, and, of course, rides and equipment.

When you look at a statement of cash flows, consider whether the company is making adequate investments in new revenue-generating assets. To attract guests, amusement parks advertise exciting new rides and must maintain and upgrade older ones. Let's look more carefully at Cedar Fair's Property and Equipment:

Cedar Fair, L.P. CONSOLIDATED BALANCE SHEETS (excerpts)			
($ in thousands)	**12/31/2010**	**12/31/2009**	**12/31/2008**
Property and Equipment:			
Land	$ 309,980	$ 305,401	$ 320,200
Land improvements	324,734	326,424	315,519
Buildings	575,725	589,219	573,842
Rides and equipment	1,398,403	1,351,595	1,295,076
Construction in progress	16,746	34,468	28,110
	2,625,588	2,607,107	2,532,747
Less accumulated deprec	(948,947)	(826,038)	(707,656)
	$ 1,676,641	$ 1,781,069	$ 1,825,091

Consider that Cedar Fair's "Rides and Equipment" account had a total cost of $1,351,595 thousand at the beginning of 2010 and a total cost of $1,398,403 thousand at the end of 2010. This amounts to a percentage increase of 3.5%, not many new rides at Cedar Park's attractions in 2010.[1] Another useful comparison to determine whether Cedar Fair spends enough on capital expenditures is to compare capital expenditures to depreciation. On its Income Statement, Cedar Fair reports $126,796 thousand in depreciation expense for 2010. However, the company spent only $71,706 thousand in new capital expenditures, so that capital expenditures aren't keeping up with the rate of depreciation on older equipment.

---

[1] (1,398,403 - 1,351,595) / 1,351,595 = 3.5%

OPERATING ACTIVITIES

Operating activities involve cash inflows and outflows from a company's central business, such as receipts from customers and payments to suppliers and employees. There are two methods for preparing the operating activities section of the statement of cash flows, the "direct method" and the "indirect method." We will first discuss the direct method.

OPERATING ACTIVITIES—THE DIRECT METHOD

Using the direct method, the operating activities section of the statement of cash flows is actually similar to an income statement, without the revenue recognition and matching principles. In other words, when preparing the direct method, simply record sales when the company receives cash from customers, rather than when they are earned and received or receivable, as you would for the income statement. Similarly, record expenses when they are paid, rather than when they would be matched to revenues under the revenue recognition principle. To avoid confusion, we avoid the terms "revenues," "sales," "cost of goods sold," and "expenses" on the cash flows statement because these are associated with accrual accounting. Instead use simple cash-related terms, such as "cash received from customers" and "cash paid for such-and-such." Here you can see Cedar Fair's Operating Cash Flows, prepared by the authors using the direct method:

Cedar Fair, L.P. CONSOLIDATED STATEMENTS OF CASH FLOWS (excerpts) ($ in thousands)			
For the years ended December 31,	2010	2009	2008
CASH FLOWS FROM OPERATING ACTIVITIES			
Cash received from customers	$ 974,939	$ 923,644	$ 1,002,976
Cash paid for food and merchandise	(90,749)	(88,201)	(96,272)
Cash paid for operating expenses	(412,190)	(401,542)	(418,255)
Cash paid for selling, general, and admin expenses	(134,001)	(128,473)	(131,882)
Cash paid for interest	(129,815)	(117,008)	(120,340)
Cash paid for taxes	(19,074)	(18,966)	(14,619)
Other operating cash flows	(6,995)	15,743	(6,020)
Net cash from operating activities	$ 182,115	$ 185,197	$ 215,588

In short, this section of the statement of cash flows is similar to the income statement, but the timing is based on the timing of cash flows, rather than the accrual method.

Looking at the direct method operating activities section of the statement of cash flows, we see that Cedar Fair's Cash received from customers decreased over the last three years, from $1,002,976 thousand in 2008 to $974,939 thousand in 2010. In addition, we see that the largest cash outflow of $412,190 is for operating expenses, which is also the greatest expense reported on the income statement. Further similarities include: net revenues (similar to cash received from customers); cost of food, merchandise, and games revenue (similar to cash paid for food and merchandise); operating expenses (similar to cash paid for operating expenses), and so on.

Cedar Fair, L.P. CONSOLIDATED STATEMENTS OF OPERATIONS ($ in thousands)			
For the years ended December 31,	2010	2009	2008
Net revenues:			
Admissions	$ 568,762	$ 532,814	$ 566,266
Food, merchandise, and games	337,356	316,386	355,917
Accommodations and other	71,474	66,875	74,049
	977,592	916,075	996,232
Costs and expenses:			
Cost of food, merchandise, and games revenues	86,619	84,940	90,626
Operating expenses	411,402	402,728	418,550
Selling, general, and administrative	134,001	128,473	131,882
Depreciation and amortization	126,796	132,745	125,838
Loss on impairment of goodwill and other intangibles	2,293	4,500	86,988
Loss on impairment/retirement of fixed assets	62,752	244	8,425
(Gain) on sale of other assets	-	(23,098)	-
	823,863	730,532	862,309
Operating income	153,729	185,543	133,923
Interest expense	150,285	124,706	129,561
Net effect of swaps	18,194	9,170	-
Loss on early debt extinguishment	35,289	-	-
Unrealized/realized foreign currency (gain) loss	(20,563)	445	561
Other income	(1,154)	815	(970)
Income before taxes	(28,322)	50,407	4,771
Provision (benefit) for taxes	3,245	14,978	(935)
Net income (loss)	$ (31,567)	$ 35,429	$ 5,706
Net income (loss) allocated to general partner	-	-	-
Net income (loss) allocated to limited partners	$ (31,567)	$ 35,429	$ 5,706

Revenues decreased by 1.9% over these years[2]. Return on sales increased to 3.2%[3] in 2009 and then decreased to -3.2%[4] in 2010.

Many people think that amusement parks make most of their profits from refreshments, souvenir stands, and arcade games. Let's see if they're right. Compare gross profit from "food, merchandise, and games" with other components of Cedar Fair's income in 2010:

---

[2] (977,592 – 996,232) / 996,232 = -1.9%

[3] 35,429 / 916,075 = 3.9%

[4] (31,567 / 977,592) = 3.2%

2010	Food, Merchandise, and Games		Admissions, Accommodations, and Other[5]	
Net revenue	$337,356	100%	$ 640,236[6]	100%
Costs	86,619	26%	411,402[7]	64%
Gross Profit	$250,737	74%	$ 228,834	36%

Wow! Cedar Fair earned more gross profit on food, merchandise, and games ($250,737 thousand) than on admissions and hotel accommodations ($228,834). Furthermore, take a look at the difference in gross profit margins. The gross profit margin on food, merchandise, and games was a whopping 74%. When it comes to Cedar Fair's profits, those $5 souvenir soft drink cups, $20 T-shirts, and cheap stuffed-animal prizes really do add up!

In Generally Accepted Accounting Principles, the direct method is optional, and most companies do not provide it. Instead, GAAP requires companies to present something called the indirect method, either on the face of the statement of cash flows or as supplemental information which may be in the notes.

OPERATING ACTIVITIES—THE INDIRECT METHOD

When companies prepare the indirect method for computing cash flows for operating activities, they start with net income (or loss), and then list items that reconcile net income (or loss) to cash flows for operating activities, explaining why net income is different from operating cash flows. To the uninitiated, this can be confusing. It does not simply list cash flows, like the direct method, or the format of investing and financing activities. However, this is why the indirect method is so useful. It emphasizes the differences between net income (or net loss) and cash flows from operations, helping you to better understand the sources and uses of a company's cash flows.

In 2010, the statement of cash flows indicates that Cedar Fair received $182,155 thousand in net cash from operating activities, but experienced a loss of net income of $31,567 thousand. How did Cedar Fair receive so much cash flow while earning so little net income? Understanding the difference between cash flow and net income reveals the nature of Cedar Fair's profitability, and the stability of the company's cash flows in what could be called a bad year. The indirect method answers our question, er, directly. Here is the indirect method for Cedar Fair:

---

[5] This category combines "Admissions" with "Accommodations and other." "Accommodations and other" primarily comes from several hotels located on Cedar Fair properties.

[6] $568,762 + 71,474 = $640,236

[7] Here we assume that all operating expenses match to admissions, accommodations, and other.

Cedar Fair, L.P. CONSOLIDATED STATEMENTS OF CASH FLOWS (excerpts) ($ in thousands)			
For the years ended December 31,	2010	2009	2008
CASH FLOWS FROM (FOR) OPERATING ACTIVITIES			
Net income (loss)	$ (31,567)	$ 35,429	$ 5,706
Adjustments to reconcile net income (loss) to net cash from operating activities:			
Depreciation and amortization	126,796	132,745	125,838
Noncash equity-based compensation expense	(89)	(26)	716
Loss on early extinguishment of debt	35,289	-	-
Loss on impairment of goodwill and other intangibles	2,293	4,500	86,988
Impairment loss on fixed assets/retirement fixed assets	62,752	244	9,425
Gain on sale of other assets	-	(23,098)	-
Net effect of swaps	18,194	9,170	-
Amortization of debt issuance costs	5,671	7,773	7,944
Unrealized foreign currency gain on notes	(17,464)	-	-
Other noncash (income) expense	(1,893)	(257)	(445)
Deferred income taxes	(14,140)	(5,684)	(17,827)
Excess tax benefit from unit-based compensation expense	-	-	(1,729)
Change in assets and liabilities, net of effects from acquis:			
(Increase) decrease in current assets	(11,855)	551	1,674
(Increase) decrease in other assets	6	918	555
Increase (decrease) in accounts payable	652	(2,635)	(5,101)
Increase (decrease) in accrued taxes	(2,242)	1,349	3,725
Increase (decrease) in self-insurance reserves	(383)	857	(559)
Increase (decrease) in deferred revenue and other current liabilities	7,653	20,428	(2,808)
Increase in other liabilities	2,442	2,933	2,486
Net cash from operating activities	$ 182,115	$ 185,197	$ 215,588

How did Cedar Fair incur a $31,567,000 net loss while still taking in $185,115,000 in net cash from operations? For 2010, the indirect method starts with Cedar Fair's net loss of $31,567 thousand, and lists all of the reconciling items in arriving at net cash from operating activities of $182,115 thousand.

In the indirect method, there are usually two kinds of reconciling items that explain the difference between net income and cash flows from operations.

- The first kind is noncash expenses. These are expenses reported on the income statement, subtracted in arriving at net income, which have no effect on operating cash flows. The most common noncash expense is depreciation and amortization expense, which is the allocation of the cost of certain noncurrent assets. Although companies subtract depreciation and amortization in arriving at net income, depreciation and amortization expense does not affect operating cash flows because companies **don't pay** for depreciation, but **do pay** for the asset, reported as an investing cash outflow.

- The second category of reconciling items is changes in current assets and liabilities. These typically affect cash flow but don't affect net income. For example, consider inventory, a current asset. An increase in inventory will cost a company money—the company has to pay for that inventory. Therefore, an increase in inventory will reduce operating cash flows. However, it has no effect on income. Therefore, the *increase* in inventory will be *subtracted* in arriving at cash flows from operations. On the other hand, a *decrease* in inventory will be *added* in arriving at cash flows from operations. Now consider a decrease in accounts payable. The only way to decrease accounts payable is to pay off bills. This costs money. Therefore, a *decrease* in accounts payable will be *subtracted* in arriving at cash flows from operations. On the other hand, an *increase* in accounts payable will be *added* in arriving at cash flows from operations.

Accordingly, the indirect method can be explained with the following formula:

Net income	+	Noncash expenses	-	Increases in current assets	+	Decreases in current assets	+	Increases in current liabilities	-	Decreases in current liabilities	=	Cash flows from operations

Looking at Cedar Fair, it's now clear why the company received so much cash flow in 2010, even though it earned a net loss. Cedar Fair recorded $126,796 thousand in depreciation and amortization. This reduced net income but not operating cash flow. The Company also reported a $35,289 thousand loss on early extinguishment of debt. This would be related to the pay-off of debt described in the financing cash flows section. Because payments of debt are a financing activity, and not an operating activity, they would not affect operating cash flows. The Company reported a $62,752 thousand impairment loss on fixed assets/retirement fixed assets. This loss reduced the book value of various assets, by taking their value off of the balance sheet and moving it directly to the income statement. Such an entry would have no effect on cash flow. Accordingly, because of just these three noncash items, cash flows from operations were $224,837 thousand higher than net income.[8]

Cedar Fair also lists changes in seven different current assets and current liabilities. For example, consider the $11,855 thousand increase in current assets reported in 2010. By investing in current assets (such as inventory and accounts receivable), Cedar Fair paid cash flow of $11,855 thousand. Accounts payable increased by $652 thousand. As Cedar Fair allowed its accounts receivable to accumulate, its cash flow increased by $652 thousand.

These reconciling items help explain how a business should manage its current assets and cash flows. As we already noted, buildups in current assets, such as accounts receivable or inventory, are subtractions in arriving at cash flows from operations. This is because such increases absorb a company's cash flow. If a company doesn't collect accounts receivable quickly, as accounts receivable increases, the company will experience cash flow problems. Similarly, a company will also have cash flow problems if it doesn't sell inventory quickly. Buildups of current liabilities, such as accounts payable, will have the opposite effect. As the company chooses to let bills pile up, accounts payable will increase, but the company will have more money in the bank.

INTERNATIONAL FINANCIAL REPORTING STANDARDS (IFRS)

U.S. GAAP and IFRS require similar information but different disclosures for certain items. Reporting cash inflows from interest and dividends received and cash outflows of interest and dividend payments differ between U.S. GAAP and IFRS. Also, a schedule of noncash investing and financing activities is required by both, but the location of disclosure differs. These differences are summarized in the chart below.

---

[8] $126,796 + 35,289 + 62,752 = $224,827.

	U.S. GAAP	IFRS
Interest received	Operating activities	Operating or Investing activities
Dividends received	Operating activities	Operating or Investing activities
Interest paid	Operating activities	Operating or Financing activities
Dividends paid	Financing activities	Operating or Financing activities
Noncash investing and financing activities schedule	Face of the statement of cash flows or the notes	Notes only

As discussed earlier, U.S. GAAP requires the indirect method for operating activities, either displayed on the face of the statement of cash flows or as supplemental information that may be in the notes, whereas IFRS currently encourages the direct method.

In regard to formatting, the FASB and IASB are working on a joint project to establish a common standard for presenting information in the financial statements. The current proposal suggests organizing all financial information into three classifications—operating, investing, and financing. This would mean that the income statement and the balance sheet would be organized in a similar manner to the current statement of cash flows.

ANALYZING THE STATEMENT OF CASH FLOWS

The statement of cash flows provides important insights into how a company raises and spends cash and how its operations generate cash. Analysts commonly use several ratios to better understand a company's ability to generate cash.

FREE CASH FLOW

Free Cash Flow reflects the amount of cash available for business activities after allowances for investing and financing activity requirements to maintain productive capacity at current levels. The formula is based on Net Cash from Operating Activities (NCOA), subtracting both capital expenditures and dividends paid. Adequate free cash flow allows for growth and financial flexibility.

Companies usually disclose total capital expenditures in their statements of cash flow, but rarely disclose capital expenditures required to maintain productive capacity. Accordingly, as a practical matter, analysts often use total capital expenditures in this formula.

Free Cash Flow	=	NCOA	-	(	Capital expenditures	+	Dividends paid)

Let's consider Cedar Fair's free cash flow:

($ in thousands)	2010	2009	2008	
NCOA	$ 182,115	$ 185197	$215,588	A
Capital expenditures	71,706	69,136	83,481	B
Distributions paid to partners	13,834	67,864	105,078	C
Free cash flow	**$ 96,575**	**$ 48,197**	**$ 27,029**	**A-(B+C)**

Note that because Cedar Fair is a partnership, it does not pay dividends. Accordingly, we substitute distributions paid to partners for dividends paid.

Cedar Fair's free cash flow is improving nicely, from $27,029 thousand in 2008 to $48,197 thousand in 2009, to $96,575 thousand in 2010.

CASH FLOW ADEQUACY

The **Cash Flow Adequacy** ratio evaluates whether cash flow from operating activities is sufficient to cover annual payment requirements. Is there enough NCOA to maintain productive capacity at current levels? This ratio presents free cash flow information in a ratio format and is used by credit-rating agencies to identify if there is adequate cash coverage of capital expenditures, dividends, debt, and other annual payments.

$$\text{Cash Flow Adequacy} = \frac{\text{Net cash from operating activities (NCOA)}}{\text{Capital expenditures} + \text{Dividends paid}}$$

A Cash Flow Adequacy Ratio of 1.0 or above indicates cash flows are high enough to pay for capital expenditures and dividends. Below 1.0 would indicate that they are inadequate. As we noted before, as a practical matter, analysts often use total capital expenditures in this formula. (Because Cedar Fair is a partnership, we substitute distributions paid to partners for dividends paid.)

($ in thousands)	2010	2009	2008	
NCOA	$182,115	$185,197	$215,588	A
Capital expenditures	71,706	69,136	83,481	B
Distributions paid to partners	13,834	67,864	105,078	C
Cash flow adequacy	2.129	1.352	1.143	A/(B+C)

In 2010, cash flow adequacy has vastly improved over the previous two years. This can be attributed to the decrease in distribution to partners.

CASH FLOW LIQUIDITY

The **Cash Flow Liquidity** ratio compares cash resources to current liabilities. This ratio uses cash and marketable securities (truly liquid current assets) and NCOA to evaluate whether adequate cash is generated from selling inventory and offering services. Even a profitable business will fail without sufficient cash. This is a cash-basis measure of short-term liquidity that is similar to the current ratio, except that it includes NCOA in its numerator, the likely source of funds that will ultimately be used to pay current liabilities.

$$\text{Cash Flow Liquidity} = \frac{\text{Cash} + \text{Marketable securities} + \text{NCOA}}{\text{Current liabilities}}$$

Like the current ratio, a cash flow liquidity ratio of 1.0 or above indicates cash and operating cash flows are adequate to cover current liabilities. A ratio below 1.0 warns of inadequacy. Let's consider Cedar Fair's Cash Flow Liquidity:

($ in thousands)	2010	2009	2008	
Cash	$ 9,765	$ 11,928	$ 13,873	A
Marketable securities	-	-	-	B
NCOA	182,115	185,197	215,588	C
Current liabilities	168,852	131,520	115,239	D
Cash flow liquidity	1.14	1.50	1.99	(A+B+C)/D

Here we also see Cedar Fair's liquidity worsening, dropping from 1.99 in 2008 to 1.50 in 2009 to 1.14 in 2010.

QUALITY OF INCOME

The **Quality of Income** ratio compares cash flows from operating activities to net income. Ideally, net income should be accompanied by strong cash flows from operations. Profits that don't come with cash flows might have been generated from accounting tricks or from customers who are unable to pay the company later on. A ratio higher than 1.0 indicates high quality income because each dollar of net income is supported by one dollar or more of operating cash flows. It is cash (not accrual-based net income) that is needed to pay suppliers, employees, and so on, to invest in income-producing assets, and to ensure long-term success.

$$\text{Quality of Income} = \frac{\text{Net cash from operating activities (NCOA)}}{\text{Net income}}$$

Computing quality of income for Cedar Fair in 2010 is risky business because the company incurred a loss. Accordingly, we have to focus on 2008 and 2009:

($ in thousands)	2010	2009	2008	
NCOA	$182,115	$185,197	$215,588	A
Net income (Loss)	(31,567)	35,429	5,706	B
Quality of income	NA	5.23	37.78	A/B

Cedar Fair's quality of income fell dramatically in 2010, decreasing from 37.78 in 2008 to just 5.23 in 2009. There's no point in computing quality of income for 2010 because of the net loss reporting that year.

In summary, we learned that, in spite of Cedar Fair's 2010 net loss, this company's operations continue to generate operating cash flow. The investor who looks only at net income, "the bottom line," could miss out on a quality investment.

The Statement of Cash Flows provides information about a company's cash inflows and outflows. It helps investors understand how much a company pays its employees, suppliers, creditors, and investors. The Statement of Cash Flows includes three categories, listed in the following order: (1) operating activities, cash inflows and outflows from a company's central business, such as receipts from customers and payments to suppliers and employees; (2) investing activities, transactions involving long-lived assets, such as the purchase of property, plant, and equipment or the purchase and sale of stock in other companies; and (3) financing activities, transactions that involve owners and creditors, such as issuing common stock, paying off loans, and paying dividends.

Companies are required to report the "indirect method" of computing net cash flows from operating activities. Under the indirect method, companies start with net income, adding and subtracting reconciling items, such as noncash expenses, to arrive at net cash flows from operating activities. These reconciling items can reveal interesting facets of a company's cash flows and net income. Another method, the "direct method," is optional, and rarely provided. Under this method, companies list cash flows such as cash received from customers and cash paid to suppliers.

U.S. GAAP and IFRS require similar information, but different disclosures for certain items. For net cash from operating activities, U.S. GAAP requires the indirect method whereas IFRS encourages the direct method. Under IFRS, interest and dividends received may be reported either as an operating or an investing activity and interest and dividends paid as operating or financing activities. Both require a noncash investing and financing section, but IFRS requires that it be in the notes.

Free Cash Flow is a commonly used measure of liquidity, reflecting the amount of cash available for business activities after allowances for investing and financing activities required to maintain productive capacity. Cash Flow Adequacy is similar to Free Cash Flow, but measured as a ratio that can be compared to other companies, rather than a whole number. Cash Flow Liquidity compares cash resources, including net cash from operating activities, with current liabilities. Quality of Income, a profitability measure, compares net cash from operating activities with net income. High quality of income indicates a company's net income is accompanied by cash flow.

	Cedar Fair, L.P. (FUN)			
RATIO	Free Cash Flow	Cash Flow Adequacy	Cash Flow Liquidity	Quality of Income
Type	Solvency	Solvency	Liquidity	Profitability
Formula	NCOA – (Capital expenditures + Dividends paid)	NCOA / (Capital expenditures + Dividends paid)	(Cash +Marketable securities +NCOA) / Current liabilities	NCOA / Net income
2010	$ 96,575	2.129	1.14	NA
2009	48,197	1.352	1.50	5.23
2008	27,029	1.143	1.99	37.78

ACTIVITY 42 CROSSWORD PUZZLE FOR CHAPTER 5

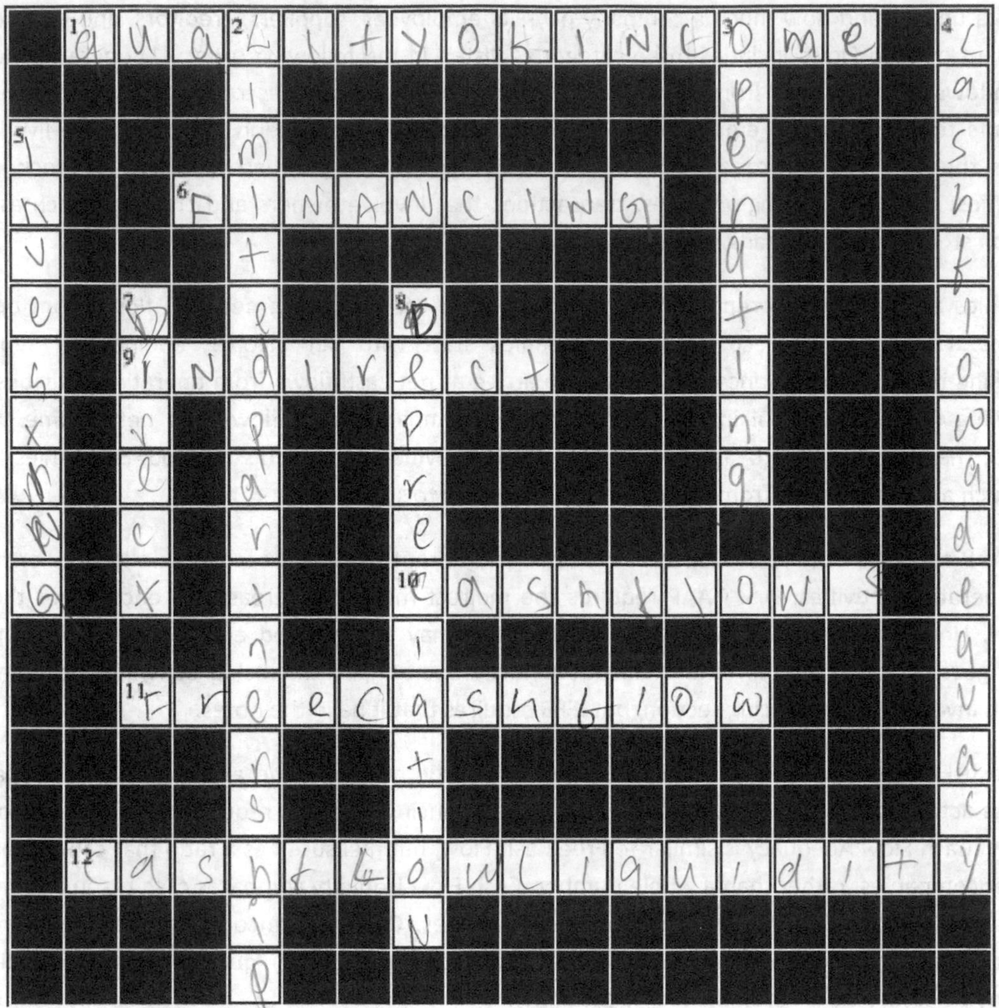

Across

1. Ratio of 1.0 indicating each dollar of profit is supported by a dollar of operating cash flow (3 words)
6. Activities including cash received from issuing common stock
9. Operating activity method reconciling accrual-based net income with cash-based flows from operating activities
10. Statement organized into operating, investing, and financing activities (2 words)
11. Discretionary cash available for pursuing growth opportunities (3 words)
12. Similar to the current ratio; compares cash resources to current liabilities (3 words)

Down

2. Organization that has a general partner and many limited partners; not a corporation (2 words)
3. Activities including cash received from customers
4. Free cash flow in a ratio format; evaluates whether operating cash flow is sufficient to cover annual payment requirements (3 words)
5. Activities including cash paid to purchase property, plant, and equipment
7. Operating activity method reporting a cash-based income statement
8. Noncash expenses, such as _____ expense, have no effect on operating cash flows

Indirect because Net income.

Southwest Airlines (LUV) CONSOLIDATED STATEMENT OF CASH FLOWS ($ in millions)			
For the years ended December 31,	2011	2010	2009
CASH FLOWS FROM (FOR) OPERATING ACTIVITIES			
Net income (loss)	$ 178	$ 459	$ 99
Depreciation expense	715	628	616
(Increase) decrease in accounts receivable	(26)	(26)	40
(Increase) decrease in other current assets	65	49	85
Increase (decrease)in payables	253	193	59
Other operating changes, net	200	258	86
Net cash from operating activities (NCOA)	1,385	1,561	985
CASH FLOWS (FOR) INVESTING ACTIVITIES			
Purchase of property, plant, and equipment, net	(968)	(493)	(585)
Purchase of investments	(5,362)	(5,624)	(6,106)
Proceeds from the sale of investments	5,314	4,852	5,120
Other investing changes, net	(35)	-	2
Net cash (for) investing activities	(1,051)	(1,265)	(1,569)
CASH FLOWS FROM (FOR) FINANCING ACTIVITIES			
Issuance of long-term debt	0	0	455
Issuance of capital stock	39	55	20
Repayment of long-term debt	(577)	(155)	(86)
Repurchase of capital stock	(225)	0	0
Payment of dividends	(14)	(13)	(13)
Other financing changes, net	11	(36)	(46)
Net cash from financing activities (NCFA)	(766)	(149)	330
Effect of exchange rate changes	-	-	-
Net change in cash	(432)	147	(254)
+ Beginning cash and cash equivalents	1,261	1,114	1,368
= Ending cash and cash equivalents	$ 829	$ 1,261	$ 1,114
SUPPLEMENTAL INFORMATION			
Cash interest paid	$ 485	$ 135	$ 152
Cash taxes paid	13	274	5
Free cash flow	403	1,055	387

1385
- 968
= 14

Purpose:
- Understand positive amounts indicate cash inflows and negative amounts indicate cash outflows.
- Identify operating, investing, and financing activities.

The ongoing operation of any business depends on its ability to generate cash from operations. It is *cash* that an organization needs to pay employees, suppliers, creditors, and investors ... *not profits*. Therefore, the real issue is cash. The statement of cash flows organizes cash inflows and cash outflows as operating activities, investing activities, and financing activities because ...

MANAGEMENT uses accounting information to make decisions regarding
Financing —> Investing —> Operating —>

FINANCING ACTIVITIES: Creditors lend and owners contribute $$$ to finance a company.

INVESTING ACTIVITIES: The $$$ obtained through financing is used to purchase revenue-generating assets such as property, plant, and equipment (PPE) and investment securities.

OPERATING ACTIVITIES: PPE and other revenue-producing assets are used to manufacture goods, offer services, and generate dividends and interest, that in turn result in $$$ profits.

FINANCING ACTIVITIES: $$$ profits are reinvested to internally finance the company.

INVESTING ACTIVITIES: $$$ obtained through financing are used to purchase revenue-producing assets ... and the cycle continues.

TRANSACTIONS REPORTED ON THE STATEMENT OF CASH FLOWS	
OPERATING ACTIVITIES (Direct Method)	
CASH INFLOWS	CASH OUTFLOWS
Cash from customers	Cash paid to suppliers
Cash from interest and dividends	Cash paid to employees
Other operating cash receipts	Interest paid
	Other operating cash payments
INVESTING ACTIVITIES	
CASH INFLOWS	CASH OUTFLOWS
Sell property, plant, equipment	Purchase property, plant, equipment
Sell investment securities	Purchase securities
Receive loan repayments	Make loans
FINANCING ACTIVITIES	
CASH INFLOWS	CASH OUTFLOWS
Borrow cash from creditors	Repay amounts borrowed (debt principal)
Issue debt securities (bonds)	Repurchase equity shares (treasury stock)
Issue equity securities (capital stock)	Pay cash dividends

Q1   On the statement of cash flows, a *positive* amount indicates a cash (**inflow** / **outflow**), whereas a *negative* amount indicates a cash (**inflow** / **outflow**).

Q2   Identify the following transactions as Operating, Investing, or Financing activities.

(**O** / I / F)   a.   Receive cash from customers
(O / **I** / F)   b.   Purchase property, plant, and equipment
(**O** / I / F)   c.   Pay employee wages
(O / I / **F**)   d.   Issue common stock
(**O** / I / F)   e.   Pay suppliers
(O / I / **F**)   f.   Pay back long-term debt

Q3   *Refer to the cash flow information displayed below to answer the following questions.*

Southwest Airlines STATEMENT OF CASH FLOWS	($ in millions)		
	2011	**2010**	**2009**
Net cash from *operating* activities	$ 1,385	$ 1,561	$ 985
Net cash from *investing* activities	(1,051)	(1,265)	(1,569)
Net cash from *financing* activities	(766)	(149)	330

a.   For Southwest Airlines, the primary source of cash is (**operating** / **investing** / **financing**) activities, which is considered (**favorable** / **unfavorable** / **depends**).

For an established company, the expected primary source of cash is (**operating** / **investing** / **financing**) activities. Southwest Airlines is a(n) (**young** / **established**) company.

b.   The purchase and sale of long-term assets are reported as (**operating** / **investing** / **financing**) activities, which for this company is a cash (**inflow** / **outflow**). This company is (**purchasing** / **selling**) long-term assets, which is considered (**favorable** / **unfavorable** / **depends**).

c.   Borrowing funds, issuing stock, and paying dividends are reported as (**operating** / **investing** / **financing**) activities.

During 2009, borrowing and repaying debt are the primary financing activities. During 2009, financing activities report a net cash (**inflow** / **outflow**), indicating this company (**borrowed** / **paid off**) more long-term debt.

During 2011, issuing and repurchasing common stock are the primary financing activities. During 2011, financing activities report a net cash (**inflow** / **outflow**), indicating this company (**issued** / **repurchased**) more common stock.

d.   For operating activities, a net cash (**inflow** / **outflow** / **depends**) is preferred. *Why?*

For investing activities, a net cash (**inflow** / **outflow** / **depends**) is preferred. *Why?*

For financing activities, a net cash (**inflow** / **outflow** / **depends**) is preferred. *Why?*

Purpose: • Understand operating activities on the statement of cash flows.

OPERATING ACTIVITIES (Direct Method)	
CASH INFLOWS	**CASH OUTFLOWS**
Cash from customers	Cash paid to suppliers
Cash from interest and dividends	Cash paid to employees
Other operating cash receipts	Interest paid
	Other operating cash payments

Q1   Operating activities include cash transactions that primarily affect (**current asset** / long-term asset/ **current liability** / long-term liability / stockholders' equity) accounts. (Circle *all* that apply)

Q2   Identify transactions recorded in the operating section of the statement of cash flows.

   (**Operating** / Not)   a.   Receive cash from customers paying on account.

   (**Operating** / Not)   b.   Pay rent for the next accounting period.

   (Operating / **Not**)   c.   Receive the utility bill for this accounting period that will be paid next accounting period. *diff. period*

   (Operating / **Not**)   d.   Extend $100,000 of credit to Supplier Barry for a purchase. *Non-cash*

   (**Operating** / Not)   e.   Receive interest payment of $8,000 from Supplier Barry.

   (Operating / **Not**)   f.   Supplier Barry pays off the $100,000.   *Financing*

The operating activity section on the face of the statement of cash flows can be reported using the direct or the indirect method. The **direct method** reports sources and uses of cash during the accounting period. The **indirect method** reconciles accrual-based "Net Income" to cash-based "Net Cash from Operating Activities."

Southwest Airlines (LUV) STATEMENT OF CASH FLOWS—*Operating* Activities						
($ in millions)		**2011**		**2010**		**2009**
Net income (loss)	$	178	$	459	$	99
Depreciation expense		715		628		616
(Increase) decrease in accounts receivable		(26)		(26)		40
(Increase) decrease in other current assets		65		49		85
Increase (decrease)in payables		253		193		59
Other operating changes, net		200		258		86
Net cash from operating activities (NCOA)	$	1,385	$	1,561	$	985

Refer to the information immediately above to answer the following questions.

Q3   Cash flows from operating activities is reported using the (direct / **indirect**) method.

Q4   The *strongest* year for LUV was (**2011**/ 2010 / 2009). *Why?*

Q5   The *weakest* year for LUV was (2011/ 2010 / **2009**). *Why?*

Q6   LUV operates all (**Boeing** / Airbus / Raytheon) aircraft. *Why?*
      (*Hint: Refer to company descriptions in Appendix A—Featured Corporations*)

Purpose: • Understand the direct and indirect method of reporting operating activities

STATEMENT OF CASH FLOWS—*Operating* activities		
STATEMENT A Adapted from COCA-COLA		($ in millions)
Cash received from customers		$ 20,457
Cash paid to suppliers		(6,160)
Cash paid for operating expenses		(8,050)
Other expenses paid		(1,788)
Net cash from operating activities		$ 4,459
STATEMENT B Adapted from COCA-COLA		($ in millions)
Net income (loss)		$ 3,751
Depreciation expense		863
(Increase) decrease in accounts receivable		(37)
(Increase) decrease in inventory		(21)
Increase (decrease) in accounts payable		80
Increase (decrease) in accrued expenses		(177)
Net cash from operating activities		$ 4,459

Refer to the information immediately above to answer the following questions.

Q1   The indirect format of the operating section starts with (**sales revenue** / **net income**). Statement A above reports net cash from operating activities using the (**direct** / **indirect**) method, whereas Statement B uses the (**direct** / **indirect**) method.

Q2   The direct and indirect methods report the (**same** / **different**) amount for net cash from operating activities. However, the (**direct** / **indirect**) method conveys amounts already reported on the income statement and changes in balance sheet accounts, whereas the (**direct** / **indirect**) method reveals new information not found on other financial statements. So no additional information is shared with (**shareholders** / **suppliers** / **competitors**), most companies choose the (**direct** / **indirect**) method.   (*Circle all that apply*)

Q3   Refer to Statement B above. Net cash from operating activities is (**greater** / **less**) than net income. This difference is primarily due to the adjustment for (**depreciation expense** / **change in accounts receivable**). Because most companies report depreciation expense, most companies also report net cash from operating activities as (**greater** / **less**) than net income.

Q4   Is it possible to report a net loss on the income statement and still report a net cash inflow from operating activities? (**Yes** / **No**) *Why?*

Q5 a. *Net income* reported on the income statement is primarily based on (**accrual** / **cash**) accounting, whereas *net cash from operating activities* reported on the statement of cash flows is primarily based on (**accrual** / **cash**) accounting.

b. *Net income* includes (**sales revenue earned** / **cash received from customers**), whereas *net cash from operating activities* includes (**sales revenue earned** / **cash received from customers**).

c. *Net income* includes (**cost of goods sold** / **cash paid to suppliers**), whereas *cash from operating activities* includes (**cost of goods sold** / **cash paid to suppliers**).

Q6 Decision makers compare "net income" to "net cash from operating activities." To make these two amounts more comparable, it is preferable to report the same accounts on both the income statement and the operating activity section of the statement of cash flows.

Which of the following accounts are used to compute net income?
(**Interest revenue** / **Interest expense** / **Dividend revenue** / **Dividends paid**) *(Circle all that apply)*

- *Interest revenue* (**is** / **is not**) reported on the income statement, therefore, on the statement of cash flows *interest received* is reported as a(n) (**operating** / **investing** / **financing**) activity.

- *Interest expense* (**is** / **is not**) reported on the income statement, therefore, on the statement of cash flows *interest payments* are reported as a(n) (**operating** / **investing** / **financing**) activity.

- *Dividend revenue* (**is** / **is not**) reported on the income statement, therefore, on the statement of cash flows *dividends received* are reported as a(n) (**operating** / **investing** / **financing**) activity.

- *Dividends paid* (**are** / **are not**) reported on the income statement, therefore, on the statement of cash flows *dividends paid* are reported as a(n) (**operating** / **investing** / **financing**) activity.

Q7 IFRS allows more flexibility in reporting interest revenue, interest expense, dividend revenue, and dividends paid.

Under IFRS:

- *Interest received* may be reported the same as U.S. GAAP, as a(n) (**operating** / **investing** / **financing**) activity, or because interest is earned by (**current** / **long-term**) assets as a(n) (**operating** / **investing** / **financing**) activity.

- *Interest paid* may be reported the same as U.S. GAAP, as a(n) (**operating** / **investing** / **financing**) activity, or because interest is typically owed as a result of (**short-term** / **long-term**) debt (liabilities) as a(n) (**operating** / **investing** / **financing**) activity.

- *Dividends received* may be reported the same as U.S. GAAP, as a(n) (**operating** / **investing** / **financing**) activity, or because dividends are typically earned by (**current** / **long-term**) assets as a(n) (**operating** / **investing** / **financing**) activity.

- *Dividends paid* may be reported the same as U.S. GAAP, as a(n) (**operating** / **investing** / **financing**) activity, or as a(n) (**operating** / **investing** / **financing**) activity.

Purpose: · Understand investing activities on the statement of cash flows.

INVESTING ACTIVITIES	
CASH INFLOWS	CASH OUTFLOWS
Sell property, plant, equipment	Purchase property, plant, equipment
Sell investment securities	Purchase securities
Receive loan repayments	Make loans

Q1　Investing activities include cash transactions that primarily affect the purchasing and selling of (**current assets** / **long-term assets** / **current liabilities** / **long-term liabilities** / **stockholders' equity**).　(Circle *all* that apply)

Just This　→ Financin

Q2　Identify the transactions that are recorded in the investing section of the statement of cash flows.

(**Investing** / **Not**)　　a.　Sell equipment.
(**Investing** / **Not**)　　b.　Pay rent for the next accounting period.　*Operating*
(**Investing** / **Not**)　　c.　Purchase office building.
(**Investing** / **Not**)　　d.　Issue additional shares of your company's common stock.　*Financing*
(**Investing** / **Not**)　　e.　Purchase 1,000 shares of common stock in Best Buy Company, Inc.
(**Investing** / **Not**)　　f.　Receive $560 in dividends from Best Buy Company, Inc.　*Operating*
(**Investing** / **Not**)　　g.　Sell the 1,000 shares of Best Buy Company, Inc. at a loss.

held in retirece the operating

Q3　A net *cash inflow* results from (**purchasing** / **selling**) more property, plant, and equipment. If a company is selling income-producing assets, resulting future revenues will most likely be (**higher** / **lower**), which is considered (**favorable** / **unfavorable**). However, if the asset being sold is an unprofitable division, then it would be considered (**favorable** / **unfavorable**).

Q4　A net *cash inflow* results from (**purchasing** / **selling**) investment securities. If the reason for selling the investments is to take profits, this is considered (**favorable** / **unfavorable**). If the reason for selling the investments is to finance operations, this is considered (**favorable** / **unfavorable**). If a gain is realized on the sale of assets (**more** / **less** / **the same amount of**) cash will be received if a loss is reported.

Southwest Airlines (LUV) STATEMENT OF CASH FLOWS—*Investing* Activities			
($ in millions)	2011	2010	2009
Purchase of PPE, net	$ (968)	$ (493)	$ (585)
Purchase of investments	(5,362)	(5,624)	(6,106)
Proceeds from the sale of investments	5,314	4,852	5,120
Other investing changes, net	(35)	-	2
Net cash from investing activities (NCIA)	$ (1,051)	$ (1,265)	$ (1,569)

Q5　*Refer to the accounting information immediately above to answer the following questions.*
　　a.　From the sale/purchase of PPE, LUV has a net cash (**inflow** / **outflow**), which indicates the company is (**purchasing** / **selling**) more PPE. This most likely indicates the business is (**expanding** / **down-sizing**). What PPE items is LUV most likely purchasing/selling?

airplanes

　　b.　For investing activities, LUV reports a (**strong** / **weak**) cash position. Why?

ACTIVITY 47   FINANCING ACTIVITIES

Purpose: •   Understand financing activities on the statement of cash flows.

FINANCING ACTIVITIES	
CASH INFLOWS	CASH OUTFLOWS
Borrow cash from creditors	Repay amounts borrowed (debt principal)
Issue debt securities (bonds)	Repurchase equity shares (treasury stock)
Issue equity securities (capital stock)	Pay cash dividends

Q1   Financing activities include cash transactions that primarily affect (**current asset / long-term asset / current liability / long-term liability / stockholders' equity**) accounts. (Circle *all* that apply)

Q2   Identify the transactions that are recorded in the financing section of the statement of cash flows.

(**Financing** / Not)   a.   Issue common stock to Shareholder Adam.
(**Financing** / Not)   b.   Pay dividends to Shareholder Adam.
(**Financing** / Not)   c.   Purchase treasury stock.
(Financing / **Not**)   d.   Record a 2-for-1 stock split.   *Non-cash*
(**Financing** / Not)   e.   Issue note payable #1234.
(Financing / **Not**)   f.   Pay interest on note payable #1234.   *Operating*
(**Financing** / Not)   g.   Repay note payable #1234.   *paying off long-term debt*
(**Financing** / Not)   h.   Issue preferred stock.
(**Financing** / Not)   i.   Call a bond payable currently outstanding.

Southwest Airlines (LUV)			
STATEMENT OF CASH FLOWS—*Financing* Activities			
($ in millions)	2011	2010	2009
Issuance of long-term debt	$ 0	$ 0	$ 455
Issuance of capital stock	39	55	20
Repayment of long-term debt	(540)	(155)	(86)
Repurchase of capital stock	(225)	0	0
Payment of dividends	(14)	(13)	(13)
Other financing changes, net	(26)	(36)	(46)
Net cash from financing activities (NCFA)	$ (766)	$ (149)	$ 330

Refer to the accounting information immediately above to answer the following questions.

Q3   *Debt transactions:* In 2009 LUV had a net cash (**inflow** / outflow), indicating that more debt was (**issued** / repaid), and therefore, is assuming (**more** / less) financial risk. If debt is issued to finance growth and expansion, it is considered (**favorable** / unfavorable). However, if debt is issued because cash from operating activities is insufficient, it is considered (favorable / **unfavorable**). Issuing additional debt (**does** / **does not**) dilute earnings per share.

Q4   *Capital stock transactions:* In 2010 LUV had a net cash (**inflow** / outflow), indicating that more stock was (**issued** / purchased). The ability to attract equity investors is (**favorable** / unfavorable). A company's own stock that is bought back with the intent to reissue to shareholders in the future is referred to as (common / preferred / **treasury**) stock, which (increases / **decreases**) shares outstanding and results in (**higher** / lower) earnings per share for current shareholders. Therefore, buying back a company's own stock is regarded (**favorably** / unfavorably) by current shareholders.

Q5   LUV is paying (**steady** / random) dividends.

Q6   Which year is LUV's cash position most appealing to shareholders? (**2011** / 2010 / 2009) *Why?*

paying off long-term debt

Purpose:
- Identify operating, investing, and financing activities.
- Identify cash inflows and outflows.
- Understand the difference between cash-based and accrual-based accounting.

Kristin Incorporated is preparing her financial statements.
- For each transaction, record the effect on the financial statements, including the amount of change and the title of the account. Record increases as a positive amount and decreases as a negative.
- For the Statement of Cash Flows, also identify whether the amount would be reported as an Operating, Investing, or Financing activity by circling **O, I,** or **F.** A portion of Q1 is completed for you.

Kristin Incorporated			
Financial Statement	Amount		Account Title
Q1 Sell $2,000 of inventory to customers for $5,000 cash.			
Statement of cash flows	$ **5,000**	(**O** / I / F)	**Cash from customers**
Income statement	$ 5000		**Sales revenue**
Income statement	$ 2000		**Cost of goods sold**
Income statement	$ 3000		**Gross profit**
Q2 Sell equipment with a book value (carrying value) of $65,000 for $50,000 cash.			
Statement of cash flows	$ 50,000	(O /(I)/ F)	Cash from sale
Income statement	$ (15,000)		~~accelerated~~ Loss
Q3 Borrow $100,000 from a bank at an annual interest rate of 7%. The note is due in three years.			
Statement of cash flows	$ 100,000	(O / I /(F))	Cash
Income statement	$ 0		Interest
Balance sheet	100,000		~~payable~~ Long-term note
Q4 Issue 1,000 shares of $100 par, 6%, preferred stock for $180 per share.			
Statement of cash flows	$ 180,000	(O / I /(F))	Cash
Income statement	$ 0		N/A
Balance sheet	$ 100,000		~~paid in capital~~ preferred stock, par
Balance sheet	$ 80,000		preferred stock, APIC
Q5 Receive a bill for $60,000 from a supplier. Pay $6,000.			
Statement of cash flows	$ 6,000	((O)/ I / F)	Cash paid
Income statement	$ 60,000		Supply exp.
Balance sheet	$ 54,000		a/c payable
Q6 Sell 500 shares of Microsoft common stock for $12,000 cash, originally acquired for $5,000.			
Statement of cash flows	$ --	(O /(I)/ F)	Cash from Sale
Income statement	$ 7000		Gain on sale
Q7 Purchase equipment for $50,000 cash down and a $150,000 long-term note payable.			
Statement of cash flows	$ 50,000	(O /(I)/ F)	Cash paid
Income statement	$ 0		no interest yet
Balance sheet	$ 200,000		**Equipment**
Balance sheet	$ 150,000		**Note Payable**

ACTIVITY 49   ANALYSIS: RATIOS

Purpose: •   Understand the information provided by cash flow ratios.

Cash Flow Ratios measure a company's ability to generate cash.

Free Cash Flow reflects the amount of cash available for business activities after allowances for investing and financing activity requirements to maintain productive capacity at current levels. Adequate free cash flow allows for growth and financial flexibility
Free Cash Flow   =   NCOA - (Capital expenditures + Dividends paid)

The **Cash-Flow-Adequacy** ratio evaluates whether cash flow from operating activities is sufficient to cover annual payment requirements. The above ratio is defined to evaluate whether net cash from operating activities is adequate to maintain productive capacity at current levels. *It presents free cash flow information in a ratio format.* This ratio (with modifications in the denominator) is used by credit-rating agencies to identify if there is adequate cash coverage of capital expenditures, dividends, debt, and other annual payments.
Cash Flow Adequacy = $\dfrac{\textbf{Net cash from operating activities (NCOA)}}{\textbf{(Capital expenditures + Dividends paid)}}$

The **Cash-Flow-Liquidity** ratio compares cash resources to current liabilities. This ratio uses cash and marketable securities (truly liquid current assets) and net cash from operating activities to evaluate whether adequate cash is generated from selling inventory and offering services to pay current liabilities when they come due. Even a profitable business will fail without sufficient cash. It is a cash-basis measure of short-term liquidity.
Cash Flow Liquidity   = $\dfrac{\textbf{(Cash + Marketable securities + NCOA)}}{\textbf{Current liabilities}}$

The **Quality-of-Income** ratio compares cash flows from operating activities to net income. A ratio higher than 1.0 indicates high-quality income because each dollar of net income is supported by one dollar or more of cash. It is cash (not accrual-based net income) that is needed to pay suppliers, employees, and so on, to invest in income-producing assets, and to ensure long-term success.
Quality of Income   = $\dfrac{\textbf{Net cash from operating activities (NCOA)}}{\textbf{Net income}}$

Southwest Airlines (LUV)—RATIOS				
($ in millions)	2011	2010	2009	2008
FREE CASH FLOW				
Net cash from operating activities (NCOA)	$ 1,385	$ 1,561	$ 985	$ (1,521)
Capital expenditures	(968)	(493)	(585)	(923)
Dividends paid	(14)	(13)	(13)	(13)
NCOA - Capital exp - Dividends paid	**$ 403**	**$ 1,055**	**$ 387**	**$ (2,457)**
CASH FLOW ADEQUACY				
Net cash from operating activities (NCOA)	$ 1,385	$ 1,561	$ 985	$ (1,521)
Capital expenditures + Dividends paid	$ 982	$ 506	$ 598	$ 936
NCOA / (Capital exp + Dividends paid)	**1.41**	**3.09**	**1.65**	**(1.63)**
CASH FLOW LIQUIDITY RATIO				
Cash and cash equivalents	$ 829	$ 1,261	$ 1,114	$ 1,368
Marketable securities (MS)	$ 2,315	$ 2,277	$ 1,479	$ 435
Net cash from operating activities (NCOA)	$ 1,385	$ 1,561	$ 985	$ (1,521)
Current liabilities	$ 4,533	$ 3,305	$ 2,676	$ 2,806
(Cash + MS + NCOA) / Current liabilities	**1.00**	**1.54**	**1.33**	**0.10**
QUALITY OF INCOME				
Net cash from operating activities (NCOA)	$ 1,385	$ 1,561	$ 985	$ (1,521)
Net income	$ 178	$ 459	$ 99	$ 178
NCOA / Net income	**7.78**	**3.40**	**9.95**	**(8.55)**

Refer to the information above to answer the following questions.

Q1 FREE CASH FLOW: Southwest Airlines would have been able to take advantage of a $1 billion opportunity during (2011 / **2010** / 2009 / 2008).

Q2 CASH FLOW ADEQUACY: Southwest Airlines *had* adequate cash for capital expenditures and dividends during (**2011** / **2010** / **2009** / 2008), as indicated by a cash flow adequacy ratio of (**greater** / less) than 1.0.

Q3 CASH FLOW LIQUIDITY RATIO: Southwest Airlines *lacked* cash resources to cover current liability obligations during (2011 / 2010 / 2009 / **2008**), as indicated by a cash flow liquidity ratio of (greater / **less**) than 1.0.

Q4 QUALITY OF INCOME: Southwest Airlines had adequate cash to support each $1 of net income during (**2011** / 2010 / **2009** / 2008), as indicated by a quality of income ratio greater than (0.0 / **1.0** / 2.0).

Q5 The strongest cash position for Southwest Airlines was during (2011 / **2010** / 2009 / 2008).
Why? Support your response with at least two relevant observations.

- had the lowest liabilities / best ratio

- better net income

Purpose:
- Prepare a trend analysis for the statement of cash flows and understand the information provided.

A **trend analysis** compares amounts of a more recent year to a base year. The base year is the earliest year being studied. The analysis measures the percentage of change from the base year.

Refer to the Statement of Cash Flows and the trend analysis below to answer the following questions.

Q1   Complete the trend analysis for 2011. Divide each amount by the amount for the base year. Record the resulting *trend index* in the shaded area. Use 2009 as the base year.

Southwest Airlines (LUV) STATEMENT OF CASH FLOWS Trend Analysis						
	2011		**2010**		**2009**	
($ in millions)	$	Trend Index	$	Trend Index	$	Trend Index
Net cash from operating activities	1,385	141	1,561	158	985	100
(Purchase) proceeds of PPE	(968)	____	(493)	84	(585)	100
(Purchase) proceeds of investments	(48)	____	(772)	78	(986)	100
Other investing changes, net	(35)	____	-	-	2	100
Net cash for investing activities	(1,051)	____	(1,265)	81	(1,569)	100
Issue (payment) of debt	(577)	NA	(155)	NA	369	100
Issue (repurchase) of stock	(186)	NA	55	275	20	100
Payment of dividends	(14)	____	(13)	100	(13)	100
Other financing changes, net	11	NA	(36)	78	(46)	100
Net cash from financing activities	(766)	NA	(149)	NA	330	100
Net change in cash	(432)	____	147	NA	(254)	100

Q2   *Net cash from operating activities* (NCOA): The annual rate of growth in NCOA can be compared among companies.

   Assume less than 5% is low, 5 to 15% is moderate, and more than 15% is high.

   The two-year average rate of growth of NCOA from 2009 to 2011 is (**low / moderate / high**).

Q3   *Net cash from investing activities* (NCIA): In 2011 the trend index for NCOA is _____, indicating NCOA (**increased / decreased**) by _____% since the base year. Whereas the 2011 trend index for NCIA is _____, indicating NCIA (**increased / decreased**) by _____% since the base year.

Q4   *Net cash from financing activities* (NCFA): Since the base year, dividends grew by _____%.

Q5   Trend analysis (**enhances / lacks**) meaning. However, since amounts with opposite signs cannot be accurately compared and division by zero is not applicable, sometimes a trend analysis of the statement of cash flows is less meaningful than for the other financial statements.

Q6   Refer to the information above. The strongest cash position for LUV was in (**2011 / 2010 / 2009**). *Why?* Support your response with at least two valid observations.

Purpose: • Prepare common-size statements using the statement of cash flow and understand the information provided.

The **Common-Size Statement of Cash Flows Statement** compares all amounts to Cash from Operating Activities (NCOA) of that same year. The analysis measures each item as a percentage of NCOA.

Refer to the common-size statement of cash flows below to answer the following questions.

Q1   Complete the common-size statements for 2010 by dividing each amount on the Statement of Cash Flows by the amount of NCOA of the same year.

Southwest Airlines (LUV) STATEMENT OF CASH FLOWS Common-Size			
	2011	**2010**	**2009**
Net income	13%	____%	10%
Depreciation expense	52%	____%	63%
Changes in working capital	21%	____%	20%
Other operating changes, net	14%	____%	7%
Cash from operating activities (NCOA)	**100%**	**100%**	**100%**
(Purchase) proceeds of PPE	-70%	____%	-59%
(Purchase) proceeds of investments	-3%	____%	-100%
Other investing changes, net	-3%	0%	0%
Cash from investing activities (NCIA)	**-76%**	**-81%**	**-159%**
Issue (payment) of debt	-45%	-13%	-5%
Issue (repurchase) of stock	-15%	4%	2%
Payment of dividends	-1%	-1%	-1%
Other financing changes, net	6%	0%	38%
Cash from financing activities (NCFA)	**-55%**	**-10%**	**34%**
Net Change in cash	-31%	9%	-25%

Q2   LUV made payments on long-term debt during (**2011 / 2010 / 2009**).

Q3   LUV issued additional shares of common stock during (**2011 / 2010 / 2009**).

Q4   During 2011 the greatest source of cash was (**NCOA / selling PPE / issuing debt**) and the greatest use of cash was (**purchasing PPE / paying back debt / paying cash dividends**).

Q5   Total cash increased during (**2011 / 2010 / 2009**) and decreased during (**2011 / 2010 / 2009**).

Purpose: • Understand and interpret amounts reported on the statement of cash flows.

DineEquity (DIN) STATEMENT OF CASH FLOWS			
($ in thousands) For the years ended December 31,	Year 9	Year 8	Year 7
Cash flows from operating activities:			
Net (loss) income	$ 31,409	$ (154,459)	$ (480)
Adjustments to reconcile net (loss) income to cash flows provided by operating activities:			
Depreciation and amortization	65,379	112,017	31,829
(Gain) loss on extinguishment of debt	(45,678)	(15,242)	2,223
Loss on derivative financial instrument	-	-	62,131
Impairment and closure charges	105,094	240,630	4,381
Deferred income taxes	(19,875)	(65,226)	(31,324)
Stock-based compensation expense	10,710	12,089	6,958
Tax benefit from stock-based compensation	531	1,864	3,476
Excess tax benefit from stock options exercised	(48)	(315)	(2,693)
Loss (gain) on disposition of assets	(7,355)	259	(98)
Changes in operating assets and liabilities:			
Receivables	11,607	(2,441)	(22,479)
Inventories	(1,474)	182	512
Prepaid expenses	(15,947)	(7,418)	(17,147)
Accounts payable	(14,867)	(23,749)	37,266
Accrued employee compensation and benefits	(8,119)	(11,609)	(21,868)
Deferred revenues	7,180	18,480	43,685
Other accrued expenses	5,287	(2,152)	13,553
Other	34,014	7,929	(3,602)
Cash flows provided by operating activities	157,848	110,839	106,323
Cash flows from investing activities:			
Additions to property and equipment	(15,372)	(31,765)	(11,871)
(Additions) reductions to long-term receivables	-	(4,743)	1,538
Acquisition of business, net of cash acquired	-	(10,261)	(1,943,567)
Collateral released by captive insurance subsidiary	1,549	4,559	345
Proceeds from sale of property and equipment	15,777	61,137	870
Principal receipts from notes and equipment contracts receivable	17,553	15,797	16,617
Reductions (additions) to assets held for sale	-	476	(688)
Other	882	(5)	(636)
Cash flows provided by (used in) investing activities	18,835	35,195	(1,937,392)
Cash flows from financing activities:			
Proceeds from issuance of long-term debt	10,000	405,502	2,296,216
Repayment of long-term debt	(173,777)	(425,300)	(268,199)
Principal payments on capital lease obligations	(16,160)	(5,879)	(5,364)
Dividends paid	(24,091)	(33,362)	(17,293)
(Payment of costs) issuance of preferred stock	-	(1,500)	222,800
Reissuance (purchase) of treasury stock, net	-	1,135	(76,050)
Repurchase of restricted stock	(605)	(540)	-
Proceeds from stock options exercised	324	989	8,928
Excess tax benefit from stock options exercised	48	315	2,694
Payment of debt issuance costs	(52,749)	(48,902)	(138,012)
Payment of early debt extinguishment costs	-	(103)	(1,291)
Restricted cash related to securitization	15,878	49,216	(186,038)
Cash flows (used in) provided by financing activities	(208,812)	(58,429)	1,838,391
Net change in cash and cash equivalents	(32,129)	87,605	7,322
Cash and cash equivalents at beginning of year	114,443	26,838	19,516
Cash and cash equivalents at end of year	$ 82,314	$ 114,443	$ 26,838

Q1   In Year 8 the primary source of cash is (**operating** / investing / financing) activities, which typically indicates a (**strong** / weak) cash position.

Q2   In Year 8, DineEquity purchased property and equipment for $ _31765_ thousand in cash and sold property and equipment for $ _61137_ thousand in cash. Therefore, the company (purchased / **sold**) more property and equipment, which could indicate this business is (expanding / **down-sizing**).

Q3   DineEquity acquired Applebee's in Year (9 / 8 / **7**).

      How much did the company pay to acquire Applebee's? $ _1,983,567_ thousand.

      This acquisition was primarily financed by (operating cash flow / **the issuance of debt** / the issuance of stock).

Q4   DineEquity borrowed more long-term debt than it repaid during Year (9 / 8 / **7**), indicating the assumption of (**more** / less) financial risk.

Q5   DineEquity issued preferred stock during Year (9 / 8 / **7**). _222800_

Q6   DineEquity purchased treasury stock during Year (9 / 8 / **7**). _16050_

      This is generally considered (**favorable** / unfavorable) to stockholders. *Why?*

Q7   DineEquity reissued treasury stock during Year (9 / **8** / 7).

Q8   DineEquity (does / **does not**) pay dividends.

Q9   In Year 8, DineEquity reported (Net income / **a Net loss**) of $ _154459_ thousand. However, the company reported cash (**inflows** / outflows) from operations. This disparity was primarily caused by (**Depreciation and amortization**) / Payment of dividends / **Impairment and closure charges**.
                          (Circle all that apply)

Q10   At December 31, Year 9, DineEquity had $ _82 34_ thousand in cash and cash equivalents.

Q11   DineEquity reports a (**strengthening** / **weakening**) cash position.

      How can you tell? Support your response with at least five observations.

Purpose: • Understand and interpret amounts reported on the statement of cash flows.

Dell (DELL) STATEMENT OF CASH FLOWS			
($ in millions) Fiscal Year Ended	January 28, 2011	January 29, 2010	January 30, 2009
Cash flows from operating activities:			
Net income	$ 2,635	$ 1,433	$ 2,478
Adjustments to reconcile net income to net cash provided by operating activities:			
Depreciation and amortization	970	852	769
Stock-based compensation	332	312	418
Provision for doubtful accounts	382	429	310
Effects of exchange rate changes on monetary assets and liabilities denominated in foreign currencies	(4)	59	(115)
Deferred income taxes	(45)	(52)	86
Other	26	102	34
Changes in operating assets and liabilities, net of effects from acquisitions:			
Accounts receivable	(707)	(660)	480
Financing receivables	(709)	(1,085)	(302)
Inventories	(248)	(183)	309
Other assets	516	(225)	(106)
Accounts payable	(151)	2,833	(3,117)
Deferred service revenue	551	135	663
Accrued and other liabilities	421	(44)	(13)
Change in cash from operating activities	3,969	3,906	1,894
Cash flows from investing activities:			
Investments:			
Purchases	(1,360)	(1,383)	(1,584)
Maturities and sales	1,358	1,538	2,333
Capital expenditures	(444)	(367)	(440)
Proceeds from sale of facility and land	18	16	44
Acquisition of business, net of cash received	(376)	(3,613)	(176)
Purchase of financing receivables	(361)	-	-
Change in cash from investing activities	(1,165)	(3,809)	177
Cash flows from financing activities:			
Repurchase of common stock	(800)	-	(2,867)
Issuance of common stock under employee plans	12	2	79
Issuance (payment) of commercial paper, net	(176)	76	100
Proceeds from issuance of debt	3,069	2,058	1,519
Repayments of debt	(1,630)	(122)	(237)
Other	2	(2)	-
Change in cash from financing activities	477	2,012	(1,406)
Effect of exchange rate changes on cash and cash equivalents	(3)	174	(77)
Change in cash and cash equivalents	3,278	2,283	588
Cash and cash equivalents at beginning of the year	10,635	8,352	7,764
Cash and cash equivalents at end of the year	$ 13,913	$ 10,635	$ 8,352
Income tax paid	$ 435	$ 434	$ 800
Interest paid	$ 188	$ 151	$ 74

Q1   Review <u>operating activities</u> and *comment* on your observations.

Q2   Review <u>investing activities</u> and *comment* on your observations.

Q3   Review <u>financing activities</u> and *comment* on your observations.

Q4   Dell reports a (**strengthening / weakening**) cash position.
           How can you tell? Support your response with at least five observations.

Purpose: • Understand and interpret amounts reported on the statement of cash flows.

Q1   The primary source of cash for an established company with a strong cash position should be (**operating** / **investing** / **financing**) activities.

Q2   a.   OPERATING ACTIVITIES report cash transactions that typically affect (**CA** / **LTA** / **CL** / **LTL** / **SE**) accounts. (*Circle all that apply*)

       b.   INVESTING ACTIVITIES report cash transactions that typically affect (**CA** / **LTA** / **CL** / **LTL** / **SE**) accounts. (*Circle all that apply*)

       c.   FINANCING ACTIVITIES report cash transactions that typically affect (**CA** / **LTA** / **CL** / **LTL** / **SE**) accounts. (*Circle all that apply*)

       Key: CA *current asset*; LTA *long-term asset*; CL *current liability*; LTL *long-term liability*; SE *stockholders' equity*.

Q3   a.   Of the following accounts, circle those that are used to compute net income:
       (**interest revenue** / **interest expense** / **dividend revenue** / **dividends paid**).

       b.   Decision makers compare "net income" to "net cash from operating activities." To make these two amounts more comparable, it is preferable to report the same account information on both the income statement and the operating activity section of the statement of cash flows.

             1.   Because interest revenue, interest expense, and dividend revenue are reported on the income statement, the cash received/paid for these items is reported in the (**operating** / **investing** / **financing**) activity section on the statement of cash flows.

             2.   Because dividends paid are NOT reported on the income statement, they are also NOT reported on the statement of cash flows in the (**operating** / **investing** / **financing**) activity section, but instead, are reported in the (**operating** / **investing** / **financing**) activity section of the statement of cash flows.

Q4   a.   For a note receivable, receiving repayment of principal is a(n) (**operating** / **investing** / **financing**) activity, whereas receiving an interest payment is a(n) (**operating** / **investing** / **financing**) activity.

       b.   For a loan payment, paying the principal is a(n) (**operating** / **investing** / **financing**) activity, whereas paying the interest is a(n) (**operating** / **investing** / **financing**) activity.

       c.   Issuing common stock to shareholders is a(n) (**operating** / **investing** / **financing**) activity and paying cash dividends to those shareholders is a(n) (**operating** / **investing** / **financing**) activity.

Q5   *Answer the questions that follow by referring to the statement of cash flow information below.*

COMPANY ($ in millions)	Ford (F)	Royal Caribbean Cruises (RCL)	United Airlines (UAL)
Net cash from Operating	$ 22,764	$ 634	$ (160)
Net cash from Investing	$ (17,169)	$ (1,784)	$ (1,969)
Net cash from Financing	$ (2,976)	$ 1,700	$ 2,138

a.   The company that appears to be borrowing money to finance operating activities is (Ford / Royal Caribbean / ~~United Airlines~~).

b.   The company that appears to be borrowing money to expand and grow is (Ford / ~~Royal Caribbean~~ / United Airlines).

c.   The company that appears to be using amounts from operating activities to purchase property, plant, and equipment, repay debt, and pay dividends is (~~Ford~~ / Royal Caribbean / United Airlines).

d.   The company that appears to have the *weakest* cash position is (Ford / Royal Caribbean / ~~United Airlines~~). *Why?*

They have the lowest net cash from operating

Q6   a.   List three transactions that result in a *cash inflow* for investing activities.

~~Sale of ppe~~
~~sale of equity & debt inv.~~
~~receipt of loan receipay.~~
Sale of ppe
Selling investments in securities
collecting principal on loans

b.   List three transactions that result in a *cash outflow* from financing activities.

~~repay and long~~
~~purchase treasury~~
~~pay dividend~~
Payment of dividends
purchasing treasury stock
repaying cash loans

Q7   What does the statement of cash flows reveal about a company that the income statement does not? ~~uses & sources of cash~~.

The cash flow statement reflects a firms liquidity whereas the income statement shows profitability.

Q8   Who can use the information on the statement of cash flows? For what purpose?

Anyone but mostly the investment community, and to see how the company is able to generate cash and what those cash funds are used for.

CHAPTER 6

SPECIFIC ACCOUNTS

LEARNING OBJECTIVES

1. Understand the nature of cash and cash equivalents.

2. Learn how companies report short-term and long-term investments.

3. Understand accounts receivable and the accounting for bad debts.

4. Learn to account for inventory, including the FIFO and LIFO methods.

5. Understand accounting for property, plant, and equipment, including the straight-line and double-declining-balance methods.

6. Learn how companies account for current and noncurrent liabilities.

INTRODUCTION

In order to understand a company's liquidity or solvency, you must measure the value of a company's assets and liabilities. But how? How do you measure the value of investments in stocks and bonds? Should they be measured at their cost or most recent stock price? How do you measure the value of inventory as prices change? How do you measure the value of property, plant, and equipment? Should it be measured at cost or an appraised value? How would you appraise the value of equipment? In this chapter, we explore how accountants measure the value of different items on the balance sheet. We learn that, to be practical, accountants often measure assets and liabilities at historical costs, or other values, which don't necessarily reflect their true value.

To demonstrate the concepts in this chapter, we will use the financial statements of Research in Motion Limited ("RIM" or ticker "RIMM"). Headquartered in Waterloo, Ontario, Canada, RIM produces and sells the BlackBerry® device:

> *Research In Motion Limited introduced the BlackBerry® solution in 1999 and quickly became the global leader in wireless innovation. RIM's portfolio of award-winning products, services, and embedded technologies are used by thousands of organizations and millions of consumers around the world and include the BlackBerry» wireless solution, the RIM Wireless Handheld™ product line, software development tools, and other software and hardware. Recently, RIM announced approval of the BlackBerry 7 smartphone for U.S. Department of Defense Networks.*

As shown here, RIMM's Consolidated Balance Sheet was prepared using United States GAAP.

Research In Motion Limited (RIMM) Incorporated under the Laws of Ontario (United States dollars, in millions) CONSOLIDATED BALANCE SHEETS		
As at	February 26, 2011	February 27, 2010
Assets		
Current		
Cash and cash equivalents	$ 1,791	$ 1,551
Short-term investments	330	361
Accounts receivables	3,955	2,594
Other receivables	324	206
Inventories	618	660
Other current assets	241	247
Deferred income tax asset	229	194
	7,488	5,813
Long-term investments	577	958
Property, plant, and equipment, net	2,504	1,957
Intangible assets	1,798	1,326
Goodwill	508	151
	$ 12,875	$ 10,205
Liabilities		
Current		
Accounts payable	$ 832	$ 615
Accrued liabilities	2,511	1,638
Income taxes payable	179	96
Deferred revenue	108	68
Deferred income tax liability	-	15
	3,630	2,432
Long-term debt	276	141
Income taxes payable	31	29
	3,937	2,602
Commitments and contingencies		
Shareholders' Equity		
Capital stock and additional paid-in capital:		
Preferred shares, authorized unlimited number of non-voting, cumulative, redeemable and retractable	-	-
Common shares, authorized unlimited number of non-voting, redeemable, retractable, Class A common shares and unlimited number of voting common shares. Issued—523,868,644 voting common shares (February 27, 2010—557,328,394)	2,359	2,372
Treasury stock February 26, 2011—2,752,890 (February 27, 2010—1,458,950)	(160)	(94)
Retained earnings	6,749	5,274
Accumulated other comprehensive income (loss)	(10)	51
	8,938	7,603
	$ 12,875	$ 10,205

See notes to the consolidated financial statements.

CASH AND CASH EQUIVALENTS

Cash usually refers to physical currency (such as dollar bills, coins, etc.) or bank deposits. Companies need cash to pay for expenses and liabilities. Because many commercial checking accounts today pay no interest, cash produces little or no investment return for companies. Accordingly, cash makes a bad investment for companies.

One way to compensate for this problem is to make overnight investments in money market accounts or other highly liquid investments. Typically, a company will move its entire cash balance to short-term investments at the end of the day and sell those investments for cash the next morning. This way, cash will be available to pay checks outstanding.

Cash not needed for a company's immediate cash needs is often invested in other highly liquid investments, such as time deposits in banks, commercial paper, U.S. government discount notes, mutual funds, or other securities that are relatively safe and can be sold quickly.

On their balance sheets, companies list cash and all of these investments together as "cash and **cash equivalents.**" Cash equivalents are highly liquid investments with maturities of 90 days or less. Companies usually define exactly how they measure cash and cash equivalents in the notes to the financial statements. For example, here is how RIMM describes its cash and cash equivalents:

> *Cash and cash equivalents consist of balances with banks and liquid investments with maturities of three months or less at the date of acquisition.*

International Financial Reporting Standards for cash and cash equivalents are essentially equivalent to U.S. GAAP.

INVESTMENTS

Companies often make **investments** by purchasing other companies' stock and bonds. They may make these investments to store excess cash until they need it or to provide a long-term return. They may also make these investments to strategically buy other companies, such as competitors, suppliers, or customers. Interestingly, the "investments in stock" listed as an asset on one company's balance sheet is "common stock" listed in stockholders' equity on the other company's balance sheet. An investor's acquisition of stock represents an ownership share in an investee, part of the investee's stockholders' equity.

Companies must classify their investments as short term or long term, based on when they intend to sell the securities. If a company purchases an investment intending to sell it within one year, the investment must be classified on the balance sheet as a **short-term investment,** a current asset. Short-term investments are often called **marketable securities.** However, if a company intends to sell the investment after one year, the investment must be classified as a **long-term Investment,** a noncurrent asset.

Companies also must decide whether investments are "trading securities" or "available-for-sale." **Trading securities** are bought and held principally for the purpose of selling them in the near term (thus held for only a short period of time). Trading securities are generally bought and sold with the objective of generating profits on short-term differences in price. They are almost always classified as current assets.

Investments in stocks not classified as trading securities are classified as **available-for-sale.** Available-for-sale securities may be classified as current or noncurrent assets.

Whether they are trading securities or available-for-sale, current or long term, investments are usually recorded at market value, a technique known as **"mark-to-market."** This means reporting the investments on the balance sheet at their most recent stock market price, the closing price on the balance sheet date.

For trading securities, the gains and losses on changes in the market price are listed on the income statement and included in net income. For example, if a stock costing $15 was worth $19 on the balance sheet date, the stock would be listed on the balance sheet as a $19 asset, and a $4 unrealized gain would be placed on the income statement and included in net income.

However, for available-for-sale securities, gains and losses are not included on the income statement until the securities are actually sold. Until the sales date, unrealized gains and losses reflecting changes in market price are placed in accumulated other comprehensive income ("AOCI"), part of stockholders' equity. For example, suppose that an available-for-sale stock costing $15 was worth $19 on the balance sheet date. The $4 appreciation would be placed in AOCI as an unrealized gain, part of stockholders' equity. Then, the next year, the company sold the stock for $25. The $4 unrealized gain would be removed from AOCI and a $10 realized gain would be recorded on the income statement. This is the difference between the $25 proceeds and the $15 cost of the available-for-sale security.

Realized gains and losses result when the security is actually sold and the proceeds have been realized. **Unrealized gains and losses** are the change in market price during an accounting period.

Mark-to-market has been criticized because market prices can fluctuate widely. Large increases or decreases may be temporary, misleading investors into thinking that assets are more valuable or less valuable than they really are. Furthermore, if these large increases or decreases are on trading securities, the gains and losses recorded in the income statement may overstate or understate income. However, many accounting standard-setters consider mark-to-market accounting to be the ideal measure of value, because they reflect the actual value for which assets can be sold on the balance sheet date.

ACCOUNTS RECEIVABLE

Accounts Receivable is monies to be received by the company from previous sales to customers. The most challenging issue in accounts receivable is collection. Inevitably, the company will not be able to collect some portion of accounts receivable from customers. Therefore, if companies presented their **gross,** or total, accounts receivable on the balance sheet, they would mislead investors into thinking that the entire accounts receivable will be collected.

Companies must estimate how much accounts receivable they will not be able to collect and deduct that estimate from Accounts Receivable. This is called the **Allowance for bad debts,** the **Allowance for uncollectibles,** or the **Allowance for doubtful accounts**. It is based on the company's history and especially the "age" of the accounts receivable. "Older" accounts receivable—items sold a long time ago but not yet collected—are less likely to be collected than "newer" accounts receivable. When developing its estimate, a company can also use economic data and information about specific companies, such as their credit ratings.

In the course of business, a company will identify individual accounts receivables that are uncollectible. For example, a customer might declare bankruptcy and have no assets to pay off creditors. When the company identifies this customer account as uncollectible, it will **write off** the account—taking it off the company's books—by subtracting the amount owed from accounts receivable and from the allowance. For example, consider that a company has $1,000,000 in accounts receivable and a $50,000 allowance for bad debts. When it fails to collect a $10,000 receivable, the company decides to write it off. It will reduce accounts receivable to $990,000 and the allowance for bad debts to $40,000.

It should be noted that writing off a bad debt does not mean that the company loses its right to collect the receivable from the customer. This is just a bookkeeping entry to avoid misleading investors.

NOTES to the Financial Statements.

A typical note regarding accounting policy for accounts receivable and bad debts reads:

> _Accounts receivable_
>
> _Accounts receivable are stated at their net realizable value. The allowance against gross accounts receivables reflect the best estimate of probable losses inherent in the receivables portfolio determined on the basis of historical experience, specific allowances for known troubled accounts, and other currently available information. The allowance for bad debts at December 31, 2011 is $2 million (December 31, 2010—$2 million)._

International Financial Reporting Standards for accounts receivable are essentially the same as U.S. GAAP, including the allowance for future bad debts.

ACCOUNTS RECEIVABLE TURNOVER

A chief concern about accounts receivable is how quickly a company collects its accounts receivable. The efficiency associated with speedy collection of accounts receivable indicates that bad debts are not excessive and that accounts receivable assets are being used productively. **Accounts Receivable Turnover** measures how quickly a company collects accounts receivable, specifically, how many times a year, on average, a company makes a sale on a receivable and collects it.

$$\text{Accounts Receivable Turnover} = \frac{\text{Sales revenue}}{\text{Accounts receivable}}$$

In general, the accounts receivable turnover ranges from 6.0 to 12. A ratio of 12.0 indicates that, on average, the company makes 12 collections of accounts receivable every year. Here are accounts receivable turnover ratios for RIMM and Motorola Mobility Holdings (MMI)[1]:

	RIMM			MMI		
	2010	**2009**	**2008**	**2010**	**2009**	**2008**
AR Turnover	5.0 times	5.8 times	5.2 times	7.3 times	7.3 times	8.2 times
AR Days	73	63	70	50	50	45

For example, on average, RIMM collected its accounts receivable 5.2 times per year in 2008, 5.8 times per year in 2009, and 5.0 times per year in 2010. On the other hand, MMI's collections were 8.2 in 2008, 7.3 in 2009, and 7.3 in 2010. MMI collects its accounts receivable, on average, more often, and more quickly, than RIMM.

ACCOUNTS RECEIVABLE DAYS

Because the concept of turnover can be difficult to visualize, analysts sometimes convert it into "days." By dividing the number of days in the year by Accounts Receivable Turnover, you can compute the average number of days it takes for a company to collect accounts receivable.

$$\text{Accounts Receivable Days} = \frac{\text{365 days in the year}}{\text{Accounts receivable turnover}}$$

This measure is much more intuitive than Accounts Receivable Turnover. Below are Accounts Receivable Days for RIMM and MMI. Here we can see more clearly how quickly MMI collects its accounts receivable. By 2010, MMI was collecting its accounts receivable, on average, in 50 days. It took RIMM much longer to collect receivables, 73 days on average.

---

[1] Accounts Receivable Turnover and Accounts Receivable Days are computed as follows:

Fiscal year ending in...	RIMM			MMI			
	2010	**2009**	**2008**	**2010**	**2009**	**2008**	
Sales revenue	$19,907	$14,953	$11,065	$13,064	$11,460	$11,050	A
AR	3,955	2,594	2,112	1,780	1,570	1,341	B
AR Turnover	**5.0**	**5.8**	**5.2**	**7.3**	**7.3**	**8.2**	A/B
AR Days	73	63	70	50	50	45	365/AR Turnover

Inventory, a current asset, is merchandise held for sale to customers. It is classified as inventory based on the company's intention to sell the item. Computers in boxes on the shelf, ready for sale to customers, are inventory. The same model computer, sitting on the sales manager's desk, would be classified as property, plant, and equipment.

Consider how inventory flows through a company. A company usually starts with beginning inventory and then adds to it inventory purchased during the period. Beginning inventory, added to purchases, equals goods available for sale, the total pool of inventory available during the period. Subtract from this the units sold to customers, and you get ending inventory. This can be visualized as follows:

When accounting for inventory, companies must select a **cost flow assumption.** To illustrate, suppose that RIMM assembles three lots of BlackBerry® units. One lot cost $100 each to make, the second cost $110, and the third cost $115. After a customer purchases a single lot, how much did it cost? What was the cost of goods sold? $100? $110? $115? And what is the cost of the lots that remained in RIMM's stock? This requires the company to make an inventory cost flow assumption. The cost of inventory units inevitably changes—what are the costs of units sold, and what are the costs of units kept in inventory?

SPECIFIC IDENTIFICATION

To avoid this assumption, some companies keep track of when each and every inventory item was purchased and sold, the **Specific Identification inventory method.** In our example above, the accountants know exactly which lot of BlackBerry® units the customer purchased and its cost. This method is usually used when dealing with unique and expensive inventory items such as fine jewelry, custom-built homes, or automobiles.

FIRST-IN, FIRST-OUT

When managing inventory, almost all companies use a system of inventory rotation called **First-In, First-Out** or **FIFO.** When restocking shelves, employees move the old inventory up to the front of the shelf, and place the new inventory in the back. This prevents spoilage of the old inventory at the back of the shelf. Think about the milk case in your supermarket. The grocer stocks the new milk at the back of the shelf, and you are encouraged to take the older milk from the front of the shelf. If the grocer stocked the new milk from the front (so that you can take the freshest milk), the older milk at the back of the shelf would eventually spoil.

When *accounting* for inventory, many companies follow FIFO, assuming that the oldest units are sold first, and the newest units are sold last. To illustrate, consider an example where RIMM buys and sells leather cases. As shown below, suppose that RIMM started the year with inventory of 10 units that cost $10 each.

On February 1, RIMM purchased 20 units that cost $20 each. On March 1, RIMM purchased 30 more units that cost $30 each. To summarize:

Date	Event	No. of units	Cost per unit	Total cost
January 1	Beginning inventory	10 units	@$10 each =	$ 100
February 1	Purchase #1	20 units	@$20 each =	400
March 1	Purchase #2	30 units	@$30 each =	900
Goods available for sale		**60 units**		**$ 1,400**

Assume that RIMM sold 45 of these inventory units during the year. The cost of goods sold would be calculated by computing the cost of the first 45 units purchased, because presumably these were the items sold:

Date	Event	No. of units	Cost per unit	Total cost
January 1	Beginning inventory	10 units	@$10 each =	$ 100
February 1	Purchase #1	20 units	@$20 each =	400
March 1	Purchase #2	15 units	@$30 each =	450
Cost of goods sold		**45 units**		**$ 950**

How much did the remaining ending inventory of 15 units cost? This can be calculated by computing the cost of the last 15 units purchased, because presumably these were the items still on hand:

Date	Event	No. of units	Cost per unit	Total cost
January 1	Beginning inventory	0 units	@$10 each =	$ -0-
February 1	Purchase #1	0 units	@$20 each =	-0-
March 1	Purchase #2	15 units	@$30 each =	450
Ending inventory		**15 units**		**$ 450**

Because we are allocating the cost of goods available for sale among the units sold (cost of goods sold) and the units remaining in ending inventory, ending inventory equals cost of goods available for sale minus cost of goods sold: $1400 - $950 = $450.

LAST-IN, FIRST-OUT

When accounting for inventory, many U.S. companies use the opposite of FIFO, called **Last-In, First-Out,** or **LIFO.** This means that they assume that the most recently purchased items are the first to be sold, while the oldest items remain on the shelf. These same companies would use standard inventory management practices, placing the new milk at the back of the dairy case, and so on. However, they account for the inventory in the opposite direction (assuming that savvy customers reach to the back of the case to get their milk). Let's use the same case to illustrate. Here is a list of the beginning inventory and purchases during the year:

Date	Event	No. of units	Cost per unit	Total cost
January 1	Beginning inventory	10 units	@$10 each =	$ 100
February 1	Purchase #1	20 units	@$20 each =	400
March 1	Purchase #2	30 units	@$30 each =	900
Goods available for sale		**60 units**		**$1,400**

Again assume that RIMM sold 45 of these inventory units during the year. The cost of goods sold would be calculated by computing the cost of the *last* 45 units purchased, (which assumes that customers grab the freshest milk):

Date	Event	No. of units	Cost per unit	Total cost
January 1	Beginning inventory	0 units	@$10 each =	$ -0-
February 1	Purchase #1	15 units	@$20 each =	300
March 1	Purchase #2	30 units	@$30 each =	900
Cost of goods sold		**45 units**		**$1,200**

To calculate the cost of the remaining ending inventory of 15 units cost, take the cost of the *oldest* 15 units (the spoiled milk still sitting on the shelf):

Date	Event	No. of units	Cost per unit	Total cost
January 1	Beginning inventory	10 units	@$10 each =	$ 100
February 1	Purchase #1	5 units	@$20 each =	100
March 1	Purchase #2	0 units	@$30 each =	-0-
Ending inventory		**15 units**		**$ 200**

To summarize the flow of inventory for LIFO:

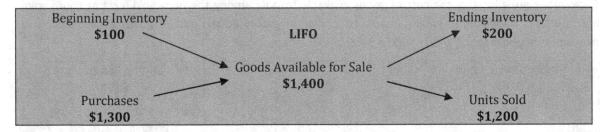

Note that, in this example, prices are increasing from $10 in January, to $20 in February, and to $30 in March. As prices increase, FIFO provides a higher inventory value than LIFO, because under FIFO, the most recent inventory costs (the newest units purchased) are allocated to inventory. Under LIFO, the oldest inventory costs (units purchased a long time ago) are allocated to inventory, resulting in a lower inventory value. FIFO also results in a lower cost of goods sold amount than LIFO. (In a decreasing-prices scenario, these effects will reverse, FIFO providing a lower inventory value than LIFO and higher cost of goods sold.)

The difference between FIFO and LIFO can significantly affect net income. Suppose that RIMM sold the 45 units for $100 each, and incurred $3,000 in operating expenses. Compare RIMM's income statements under the FIFO and LIFO assumptions:

	FIFO	LIFO
Sales	$4,500	$4,500
Cost of goods sold	950	1,200
Gross profit	3,550	3,300
Operating expense	3,000	3,000
Net income	$ 550	$ 300

As prices increase, FIFO results in higher net income than LIFO. This raises a simple question: why use LIFO? LIFO depresses the balance sheet value of inventory because it allocates the cost of the oldest inventory value to ending inventory. Furthermore, it inflates the value of cost of goods sold, thereby depressing net income—LIFO lowers net income. Making matters worse, LIFO doesn't reflect reality. Companies actually manage their inventory using FIFO, first-in, first-out. They always stock their shelves from the back. Why use LIFO accounting?

Companies use LIFO in order to reduce their income tax provision. By reporting lower net income under LIFO, companies pay lower income taxes. The U.S. Internal Revenue Service permits companies to base income tax payments on LIFO accounting as long as they use LIFO for external reporting, their financial statements.

As can be seen in the notes to the financial statements, RIMM uses the FIFO method to account for its inventory. It also provides a breakdown of inventory in the manufacturing process. **Raw materials** are materials to be used in the manufacturing process, such as plastic and individual electronic components. **Work in process** are partially completed units, that have entered the assembly line, but have not yet been completed. **Finished goods** are completed and ready for sale.

Inventories
Raw materials are stated at the lower of cost and replacement cost. Work in process and finished goods inventories are stated at the lower of cost and net realizable value. Cost includes the cost of materials plus direct labour applied to the product and the applicable share of manufacturing overhead. Cost is determined on a first-in-first-out basis.

5. INVENTORIES—Inventories were comprised as follows:

(US$ in thousands)	February 26, 2011	February 27, 2011
Raw materials	$ 552	$ 490
Work in process	222	232
Finished goods	94	55
Provision for excess and obsolete inventories	(250)	(117)
	$ 618	$ 660

The **Provision for excess and obsolete inventories** is a subtraction from inventories, similar to the allowance for bad debts that is subtracted from accounts receivable. Recall that the allowance for bad debts was subtracted from accounts receivable because it represented management's estimate of how much accounts receivable would not be collected. Similarly, the provision for excess and obsolete inventories is management's estimate of the cost of inventories that will not be sold. These could be damaged items or old models that customers are no longer interested in.

INTERNATIONAL FINANCIAL REPORTING STANDARDS

Although U.S. GAAP permits the use of LIFO, IFRS does not. Therefore, international companies that use LIFO in the United States typically use FIFO in other countries.

As we noted before, the Internal Revenue Service (IRS) permits companies to base income tax payments on LIFO accounting as long as they use LIFO for external reporting, their financial statements. However, IFRS prohibits LIFO. Therefore, companies adopting IFRS would not be able to comply with this IRS requirement. They would have to give up LIFO and the tax benefit that it offers. To resolve this issue, either (1) companies need to give up LIFO tax benefits, (2) IFRS needs to permit LIFO usage, or (3) U.S. lawmakers need to eliminate the requirement that companies using LIFO for their tax returns also use LIFO for their financial statements.

GROSS PROFIT MARGIN

The **Gross Profit Margin,** gross profit divided by sales revenue, expresses gross profit as a percentage of sales revenue.

$$\text{Gross Profit Margin} = \frac{\text{Gross profit}}{\text{Sales revenue}}$$

After paying for the cost of purchasing or manufacturing the products sold, how much profit did the company earn? This ratio is the first measure of profitability reported on the income statement. Here we compare RIMM's gross profit percentage with Motorola Mobility Holdings (MMI). MMI offers RAZR smartphones and Motorola Xoom, among many other mobile technology products.

	RIMM			MMI		
	2010	**2009**	**2008**	**2010**	**2009**	**2008**
Sales revenue	$19,907	$14,953	$11,065	$13,064	$11,460	$11,050

RIMM's revenues from 2008 to 2010 increased dramatically, from $11,065 million in 2008, to $14,953 million in 2009, and to $19,907 million in 2010. This is an average increase of 40% per year.[2] During the same period, MMI's sales increased from $11,050 million in 2008 to $13,064 million in 2010.

---

[2] Total increase from 2008 to 2010 is 74.4% [= (19,907 - 11,065) / 11,065]. 79.9% / 2 = 40.0% per year.

Here are the gross profit margins for RIMM and MMI[3]:

	RIMM			MMI		
	2010	**2009**	**2008**	**2010**	**2009**	**2008**
Gross profit margin	44.3%	44.0%	46.1%	25.4%	25.9%	19.5%

Not only is RIMM growing a lot faster than MMI, but it is much more profitable. RIMM's gross profit margin was 44.3% in 2010, 44.0% in 2009, and 46.1% in 2008. For every $100 of sales, RIMM earns $44.30 of gross profit, and incurs $55.70 of cost of goods sold ($100.00 - $44.30). RIMM's products appear to be very profitable. Although the gross profit margin decreased, it is still much higher than MMI's.

INVENTORY TURNOVER

Inventory management requires that companies keep just enough merchandise in stock to satisfy customers' needs. If they keep too much inventory in stock, items may become obsolete or spoiled. Excessive inventory also soaks up financing costs because companies often borrow money to pay for inventory. However, companies that keep too little merchandise inventory in stock might not be able to satisfy customer demand, losing sales as customers shop elsewhere to find the goods they need. The trend has been for companies to use technology and careful coordination with suppliers to keep inventory levels as low as possible.

Inventory turnover indicates the number of times a company sells its average inventory level during the year. It measures how efficiently a company uses its investment in inventory. It is computed by dividing cost of goods sold by inventory:

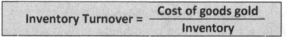

$$\text{Inventory Turnover} = \frac{\text{Cost of goods gold}}{\text{Inventory}}$$

For example, the department store industry reports an average inventory turnover of 6.3, meaning that department stores typically sell their average inventory level about six times per year. Department stores generally restock their shelves four times a year, for four seasons: Spring, Summer, Back-to-School, and Holiday. At the beginning of the season, new clothes are brought out to the front of each department, and clothes from the prior season, are put on sale, with increasing discounts until they are sold. The industry's inventory turnover, however, is higher than 4.0 because certain items (such as cosmetics and accessories) sell more quickly.

---

[3] Computed as follows.

Fiscal year ending in...	RIMM			MMI			
	2010	**2009**	**2008**	**2010**	**2009**	**2008**	
Sales revenue	$16,416	$12,536	$9,411	$13,064	$11,460	$11,050	A
Gross profit	8,825	6,584	5,097	3,317	2,965	2,153	B
Gross profit margin	**53.7%**	**52.5%**	**54.2%**	**25.4%**	**25.9%**	**19.5%**	**B/A**

Here is the Inventory Turnover for RIMM and MMI[4]:

	RIMM			MMI		
	2010	**2009**	**2008**	**2010**	**2009**	**2008**
Inventory turnover	6.9 times	5.4 times	7.3 times	18.2 times	25.1 times	13.6 times

When it comes to efficiency in handling inventory, MMI performs much better than RIMM. At 18.2 in 2010, MMI's inventory turnover is much higher than RIMM's 6.9. Meanwhile, RIMM's inventory turnover dropped from 7.3 in 2008 to just 6.9 in 2010.

INVENTORY DAYS

As with accounts receivable turnover, analysts can convert inventory turnover into "days." By dividing the number of days in the year by the Inventory Turnover, you can compute the average number of days it takes for a company to sell inventory.

$$\text{Inventory Days} = \frac{365 \text{ days in the year}}{\text{Inventory turnover}}$$

This measure is easier to understand than Inventory Turnover. Here are Inventory Days for RIMM and MMI:

	RIMM			MMI		
	2010	**2009**	**2008**	**2010**	**2009**	**2008**
Inventory days	20 days	29 days	41 days	26 days	36 days	28 days

Here we can see more clearly how quickly the companies sell their inventory. In 2010, RIMM needed just 20 days, on average, to sell inventory. MMI, on the other hand, was selling each unit of inventory within 26 days. RIMM now manages its inventory more efficiently than MMI.

---

[4] Inventory Turnover and inventory Days are computed as follows.

	RIMM			MMI			
	2010	**2009**	**2008**	**2010**	**2009**	**2008**	
COGS	$11,082	$8,369	$5,968	$9,747	$8,495	$8,897	A
Inventory	618	660	682	701	843	688	B
Inventory turnover	**17.9**	**12.7**	**8.8**	**13.9**	**10.1**	**12.9**	A/B
Inventory days	**20**	**29**	**41**	**26**	**36**	**28**	365/Inv TO

PROPERTY, PLANT, AND EQUIPMENT

Property, plant, and equipment are long-term assets expected to benefit future years. This asset category is also called **PPE, fixed assets,** or **capital assets.** Land, buildings, machines, computers, and vehicles, when used in a company's business, are all classified as property, plant, and equipment. As with inventory, a company's intent and use are very important. For example, dairy cattle—cows that produce milk—are PPE. Beef cattle—cows raised for consumption—would be classified as inventory.

PPE is recorded at **acquisition cost,** also called **original cost** or **historical cost.** This includes all costs necessary to prepare the asset for use, including the purchase price, delivery, and set-up costs.

Depreciation expense is the systematic allocation of the cost of an asset over the expected useful life of the asset. To illustrate, suppose a company buys a truck costing $20,000 with a five-year life. Recording the whole cost of the truck as an expense of $20,000 in one year would make little sense because the truck will run for four more years. Therefore, the company could record $4,000 depreciation expense in each of five years. This simplifies matters, and a few other considerations need to be made.

Land is not depreciated because it is considered to have an indefinite life.

Before an asset can be depreciated, a company must estimate the **residual value,** also known as the **salvage value** or **scrap value.** This is the estimated value of the asset at the end of its estimated useful life. The **depreciable base,** computed as acquisition cost less residual value, is the total amount of depreciation that will be recorded over an asset's life. On the balance sheet, the account accumulated depreciation appears as a subtraction from the asset's cost. **Accumulated depreciation** is the total amount of depreciation expensed since acquisition. **Book value** is the acquisition cost less accumulated depreciation, the value at which the asset is recorded on the balance sheet. It is also called **carrying value; PPE, net;** or the **cost not yet depreciated.**

The two most widely used depreciation methods are called **Straight-Line (SL)** and **Double-Declining-Balance (DDB).** Straight-line spreads depreciation out equally over all periods. Double-declining-balance is an accelerated method, meaning that it records more depreciation early in the life of an asset, when it is new, and less depreciation when the asset is old.

STRAIGHT-LINE DEPRECIATION

Straight-line depreciation divides the depreciable base by the life of the asset, recording equal amounts of depreciation expense each year:

$$\frac{\text{Depreciation}}{\text{Expense}} = \frac{\text{Depreciable base}}{\text{Expected useful life}} = \frac{\text{Acquisition cost - Residual value}}{\text{Expected useful life}}$$

To illustrate, suppose that RIMM purchased equipment costing $500,000, with an estimated useful life of five years and residual value of $50,000. Annual depreciation expense would be computed as:

$$\frac{\text{Depreciation}}{\text{Expense}} = \frac{\$500,000 - \$50,000}{5 \text{ years}} = \$90,000 \text{ / year}$$

Over the life of the asset, depreciation expense would be recorded at $90,000 per year, increasing accumulated depreciation, and decreasing book value down to the residual value:

SL	Depreciation Expense	Accumulated Depreciation	Book Value (Acq Cost - Acc Dep) = Book Value	
Year 1	$ 90,000	$ 90,000	($500,000 - 90,000 =)	$410,000
Year 2	90,000	180,000	($500,000 - 180,000 =)	320,000
Year 3	90,000	270,000	($500,000 - 270,000 =)	230,000
Year 4	90,000	360,000	($500,000 - 360,000 =)	140,000
Year 5	90,000	450,000	($500,000 - 450,000 =)	50,000
Total	$450,000			

After Year 5, when the asset has been fully depreciated, there is no more need to record depreciation expense; there is no depreciable base left to depreciate. The asset will be reported on the balance sheet at its acquisition cost, less accumulated depreciation, with a book value of $50,000.

On the income statement, annual depreciation expense is reported. On the balance sheet, the company will report the acquisition cost, accumulated depreciation, and book value.

Our Company BALANCE SHEET (excerpt) December 31, Year 3	
Property, plant, and equipment	$500,000
Less: Accumulated Depreciation	(270,000)
Property, plant, and equipment, net	$230,000

DOUBLE-DECLINING-BALANCE DEPRECIATION

Double-declining-balance is an accelerated depreciation method that records more depreciation expense when an asset is new, and less when the asset is older. It is computed by multiplying the asset's book value by two times (double) the straight-line depreciation rate:

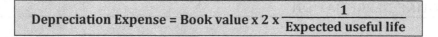

$$\text{Depreciation Expense} = \text{Book value} \times 2 \times \frac{1}{\text{Expected useful life}}$$

As the book value decreases each year, depreciation expense will also decrease.

To illustrate, again suppose that RIMM purchased equipment costing $500,000, with an estimated useful life of five years and residual value of $50,000. The first year's depreciation expense would be computed as:

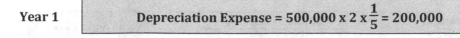

Year 1 $$\text{Depreciation Expense} = 500,000 \times 2 \times \frac{1}{5} = 200,000$$

This would reduce the book value to $300,000 (= $500,000 - $200,000), so that the second year's depreciation expense would be computed as:

Year 2	Depreciation Expense = $300,000 \times 2 \times \dfrac{1}{5}$ = 120,000

After recording this depreciation expense, book value would decline to $180,000 (= $300,000 - 120,000). The third year's depreciation expense would be:

Year 3	Depreciation Expense = $180,000 \times 2 \times \dfrac{1}{5}$ = 72,000

For the Year 4 computation, book value equals $108,000 (= $180,000 - $72,000). Fourth-year depreciation expense would be:

Year 4	Depreciation Expense = $108,000 \times 2 \times \dfrac{1}{5}$ = 43,200

However, this creates a problem. Year 5 depreciation would be $25,920 (64,800 x 2 x 1/5) and the new book value would equal $38,800 ($64,800 - 25,920). This is below the $50,000 residual value. Therefore, we would stop using DDB depreciation in Year 5, and decrease the book value until it hit the $50,000 residual value. Depreciation in Year 5 would equal $14,800 ($64,800, the Year 4 book value, less the $50,000 residual value).

Year 5	Year 4 Book Value – Residual Value = $64,800 - $50,000 = $14,800

The following amounts will be reported in each year's income statement and balance sheet:

DDB	Depreciation Expense	Accumulated Depreciation	Book Value Acq. Cost – Acc. Dep. = Book Value
Year 1	$200,000	$200,000	($500,000 - 200,000 =) $300,000
Year 2	120,000	320,000	($500,000 - 320,000 =) 180,000
Year 3	72,000	392,000	($500,000 - 392,000 =) 108,000
Year 4	43,200	435,200	($500,000 - 435,200 =) 64,800
Year 5	14,800	450,000	($500,000 - 450,000 =) 50,000
Total	$450,000		

Our Company BALANCE SHEET (excerpt) December 31, Year 3	
Property, plant, and equipment	$500,000
Less: Accumulated Depreciation	(392,000)
Property, plant, and equipment, net	$108,000

By Year 5, the asset has been fully depreciated. No depreciation expense will be recorded in subsequent years.

COMPARING STRAIGHT-LINE WITH DOUBLE-DECLINING-BALANCE

Comparing Straight-line (SL) to Double-declining-balance (DDB) depreciation illustrates the differences between these two depreciation methods. DDB reports much higher depreciation expense when the asset is new: In Year 1, the company records $200,000 in DDB depreciation, and $90,000 in SL depreciation. This means that in Year 1, a company using DDB would report *lower* net income than under SL. Furthermore, under DDB, book value is lower when the asset is new. In Year 1, the company reports $300,000 in DDB book value, versus $410,000 in SL book value. This means that under DDB, total assets will be lower than under SL.

As the asset ages, however, the trend reverses. To illustrate, in Year 4, DDB reports lower depreciation expense than SL, $25,000 versus $90,000. This would mean *higher* income under DDB, and *lower* income under SL. In Year 4, DDB also reports lower book value than SL, $50,000 versus $140,000, and therefore lower total assets.

	Straight-Line		Double-Declining-Balance	
	Depreciation Expense	Book Value	Depreciation Expense	Book Value
Year 1	$ 90,000	$410,000	$200,000	$300,000
Year 2	90,000	320,000	120,000	180,000
Year 3	90,000	230,000	72,000	108,000
Year 4	90,000	140,000	43,200	64,800
Year 5	90,000	50,000	14,800	50,000
Total	$450,000		$450,000	

In short, the accounting method used for depreciation has tremendous effect on both net income and total assets. However, regardless of which depreciation method is used, total depreciation *over the life of the asset* will be the same; it will equal the depreciable base. Furthermore, after the asset is fully depreciated, its book value will be the same under either method; it will equal the residual value.

Companies can choose among Straight-Line, Double-declining-balance, or other depreciation methods. GAAP requires them to select the method that appropriately allocates costs to the periods benefited. For example, assets that rapidly become obsolete, or that are more productive when new, and less productive when old, would be better depreciated under Double-declining-balance. On the other hand, assets that provide fairly stable levels of productivity over their useful lives would be better depreciated under Straight-line. Most companies use one method or the other for all of their assets. Therefore, this decision is made very carefully.

GAINS AND LOSSES ON SALE OF PPE

The **gain** or **loss** on the sale of PPE is computed as the selling price less the book value. If the difference is positive, it is a gain. If it's negative, it's a loss. For example, suppose a company acquires an asset for $500,000, and then depreciates it down to its residual value, $50,000, as shown above. Then, suppose that the company sells the asset for $60,000. It would record a gain of $10,000 (= $60,000 - $50,000). Now, suppose that the company sold this asset for $30,000. It would record a loss of $20,000. A gain or loss on disposal would be reported on the income statement as part of nonoperating revenues and expenses.

Consider the nature of this gain or loss. In the first example, the company sold the asset for $60,000, recording a $10,000 gain. However, recall that the company paid $500,000 for the asset. This means that *the company really lost $440,000 on the asset* (= the $60,000 proceeds less the $500,000 original cost of the asset). After considering depreciation of $450,000, however, accountants would actually report a $10,000 gain, *the difference between the proceeds ($60,000) and the book value ($50,000)*. Accordingly, the gain or loss on the sale of PPE is not a true gain or loss, as would be recorded when a company buys a stock one day for $50 a share and sells it for $75, and would report a $25 gain. Rather, the gain or loss on the sale of PPE indicates whether the company recorded too much or too little depreciation on the asset. If it recorded too much depreciation, book value would be below the fair value of the asset, and the company would report a gain on disposal. If the company recorded too little depreciation on the asset, book value would exceed the fair value of the asset, and the company would report a loss on disposal.

NOTES to the Financial Statements.

A typical note regarding accounting policy for PPE reads:

Property, plant, and equipment

We state property, plant, and equipment at cost less accumulated amortization. We do not amortize construction in progress until the assets are ready for use. Depreciation and amortization are recorded using the following rates and methods:

Buildings, leaseholds and other	Straight-line between 5 and 40 years
Cloud operations and other	
information technology	Straight-line between 3 and 5 years
Manufacturing equipment, research and	
development equipment	Straight-line between 2 and 8 years
Furniture and fixtures	Declining balance at 20% per annum

This company uses straight-line depreciation for all categories of PPE except for furniture and fixtures, where it uses declining balance. By "Declining balance at 20% per annum," the company means that book value is multiplied by 20% each year to determine depreciation expense.

NOTES to the Financial Statements continue for PPE:

Property, plant, and equipment, net
Property, plant, and equipment comprised the following:

Cost	December 31, 2011	December 31, 2010
Land	$ 100	$ 100
Buildings, leaseholds, and other	1,200	900
Cloud operations and other information technology	1,800	1,200
Manufacturing equipment, research and development equipment	400	300
Furniture and fixtures	500	300
	4,000	2,800
Accumulated depreciation and amortization	1,400	900
Net book value	$ 2,600	$ 1,900

At December 31, 2011, the carrying amount of assets under construction was $300 million (December 31, 2010—$250 million). Of this amount, $150 million (December 31, 2010—$100 million) was included in buildings, leaseholds and other; $130 million (December 31, 2010—$100 million) was included in Cloud operations and other information technology; and $20 million (December 31, 2010—$50 million) was included in manufacturing equipment, research and development equipment.

INTERNATIONAL FINANCIAL REPORTING STANDARDS

Under U.S. GAAP, companies record assets at historical cost. If the assets decline in value, they may be deemed "impaired," and written down to a lower book value. However, under International Financial Reporting Standards, companies have the option to revalue PPE to market value on their financial statements. Companies choosing to revalue their assets must revalue all assets within a class of PPE on a regular basis.

CURRENT AND NONCURRENT LIABILITIES

Liabilities are amounts owed to creditors. They arise from transactions that occurred in the past. For example, if RIMM purchased and received a shipment of raw materials, it would have a liability to pay for the shipment. If RIMM received a loan from the bank, it would now have a liability to the bank.

Current liabilities are those due within a year. All other liabilities are classified as noncurrent. A single debt can be split up between these categories. For example, if a company has a long-term debt requiring monthly payments for the next 30 years, the next 12 months' payments would be classified as current, and the remaining payments would be classified as noncurrent.

Most companies record some kind of **accounts payable,** a current liability. These are amounts due to suppliers in the future for the purchase of inventory.

Many liabilities require careful estimates. For example, suppose that RIMM provides a free 90-day warranty for parts and services on all of its products. This, of course, creates a liability, **warranty payable.** But how can it be estimated? RIMM will need to look at sales and past payments made because of the warranty program, and the cost of parts and labor needed to repair or replace defective units. As such, companies need to update the warranty payable balance every year, based on their best estimates of the amounts likely to be paid. Any new amounts added to the warranty payable would be recorded as warranty expense.

Employee pensions, called **post-retirement benefits,** require many estimates. These occur when companies promise employees payments or other benefits after they retire. For example, a company might offer employees 50% of their last year's salary, for the rest of their lives after they retire. This **post-retirement benefit liability** requires careful estimation. How long are employees expected to live? How much will employees' last years' salaries be? If the company invests money now to cover this liability, how much return will it earn on these investments?

The most difficult estimates involve **contingent liabilities.** These are for potential liabilities from lawsuits and especially for environmental cleanups. For example, if a company is a defendant in a lawsuit, it has to consider whether it will have to pay damages, and whether or not to record a liability on its balance sheet. For such lawsuits, it can be extremely difficult to predict a jury's outcome. However, accountants may need to predict that outcome—and estimate the payments as a liability—before the lawsuit even goes to trial. Similarly, for an environmental clean-up site, a company needs to estimate the liability, even before it can fully determine the damage or cost of cleanup.

When accounting for contingent liabilities, accountants record a liability when the payment is probable and estimable. Here, "probable" means that the company will most likely have to make a payment. "Estimable" means that it is possible to estimate how much the company will have to pay. Inevitably, these estimates may turn out to be incorrect. If so, a company can continue to adjust the liability as the situation develops. For loss contingences, IFRS uses the lower standard of "more likely than not," meaning that there is a greater than 50% chance that a company will have to make a payment.

NOTES to the Financial Statements.
 A typical note regarding litigation reads:

> <u>Litigation</u>
> There are a number of patent disputes with third parties who claim the Company's products infringed on patents. In April 2010, ABC Company filed a lawsuit. In June 2011, a jury found the Company had willfully infringed the patent and awarded approximately $2 billion in past compensation damages. The Company has appealed the jury's verdict. The Company is confident in the merits of its case and believes that it will prevail on appeal. As a result, no reserves have been recorded in this case.
> In addition, the Company is subject to legal proceedings, claims, and litigation arising in the ordinary course of business, including intellectual property litigation. While the outcome of these matters is currently not determinable, the Company does not expect that the ultimate costs to resolve these matters will have a material adverse effect on its financial position, results of operations, or cash flows.

Needless to say, companies usually owe some form of income taxes. As they say, only two things in life are certain: death and taxes. In most countries, companies periodically pay estimated taxes during each year, say, every three months. Then, after the end of the year, the company prepares a tax return to compute the exact amount of taxes owed. If the company paid more than that amount during the year, it will receive a refund. If it paid less, then it will have to pay the remainder. For example, if a company paid $1 million in estimated taxes during the year, and then computed total income taxes of $1,150,000 for the year, it would owe an additional $150,000 payment with the tax return, an **income tax payable.**

Most companies use legal "tax planning" strategies to put off paying taxes until future periods or to avoid paying them completely. For example, accelerated depreciation methods (such as an IRS-sanctioned version of double-declining-balance) can help a company to put off taxes until a future period. Recall that, when an asset is new, DDB delivers higher depreciation and lower net income than straight-line. This means lower taxes when the asset is new. However, this effect reverses when the asset is older. When the asset is older, DDB delivers lower depreciation expense, and higher net income, resulting in higher taxes. This is one strategy companies may use to push tax payments off to future years.

We know the company will have to pay the taxes—it has just managed to legally defer them to future periods. These strategies create a liability, called a **deferred tax liability.**

Long-term debt usually refers to bank loans that are due over more than one year. They may require annual or monthly payments. If so, as we stated before, the coming year's payments would be classified as "current portion of long-term debt," a current liability. Any payments due after that would be classified with noncurrent liabilities.

One specific type of long-term debt is called **bonds payable.** A company issues bonds to raise large amounts of capital (money). These are loans with certificates that can be traded among investors. Then, investors holding the bonds can sell them on bond markets. Companies must make two types of payments for bonds payable. First, when a bond **matures,** or comes due, debtors must pay the **principal,** or the amount due when the loan matures. Second, companies must pay interest, usually a rate printed on the face of the bond certificate. Interest payments may be due monthly, semi-annually, or upon maturity.

One issue is that investors often expect a higher or lower interest rate than that printed on the face of the bond certificate.

> For example, suppose that RIMM issued $1 billion bonds payable with a rate of 8% printed on the bond. When it prepared to sell the bond to creditors, creditors were expecting a rate of 10%, called the market interest rate; the face rate of 8% was too low. Accordingly, creditors would require RIMM to sell the bonds at a discount, and RIMM would collect less than the $1 billion principal of the bonds.
>
> On the other hand, suppose that creditors were expecting a rate of 7%, less than the 8% rate printed on the face of the bond. The creditors would be willing to pay a premium on the bond. RIMM would collect more than the $1 billion principal of the bonds.

When issuing bonds, companies usually receive a premium (because the face rate was higher than the market was expecting) or accept a discount (because the face rate was lower than the market expected). On the balance sheet, bonds payable are reported as liabilities, with premiums added to the principal. Discounts would be subtracted from the principal. However, when the bond becomes due, the company is required only to pay the principal amount, not the discount or premium, back to the creditor. Therefore, the premium or discount is amortized as an adjustment to interest expense, in a fashion similar to how long-lived assets are depreciated. Over the life of the bond, a premium or discount is reduced to zero.

	Research in Motion Limited (RIMM)				
RATIO	**Accounts Receivable Turnover**	**Accounts Receivable Days**	**Gross Profit Margin**	**Inventory Turnover**	**Inventory Days**
Type	*Efficiency*	*Efficiency*	*Profitability*	*Efficiency*	*Efficiency*
Formula	Sales Revenue / AR	365 / AR Turnover	Gross Profit / Sales Revenue	Cost of Goods Sold / Inventory	365 / Inventory Turnover
2010	5.0 times	73 days	44%	6.9 times	20 days
2009	5.8 times	63 days	44%	5.4 times	29 days
2008	5.2 times	70 days	46%	7.3 times	41 days
Industry (1) (2)	10.4 times	35 days	60%	31.0 times	12 days
S&P 500 (2)	14.2 times	26 days	39%	10.0 times	37 days

(1) Industry: *Diversified Communications Services. Industry and S&P 500 ratio averages from moneycentral.msn.com*

(2) There are no official rules governing how these ratios are calculated. Therefore, the ratio formulas used may differ from the formulas in the text.

SUMMARY

This chapter reviews the accounting for cash; investments; accounts receivable; inventory; property, plant, and equipment (PPE); and liabilities.

Cash and cash equivalents includes physical currency, bank deposits, and highly-liquid investments with short maturities. This is usually a company's most liquid asset.

Companies' investments are typically in the stocks and bonds of other companies. Companies must classify investments in two ways: as short term or long term, and as trading securities or available-for-sale securities. Investments intended to be held for only a short time, usually within a year, are classified as short term. Investments intended to be held for longer periods of time are classified as long term. Trading securities are bought and held principally for the purpose of selling them in the near term. They are recorded on the balance sheet at their market value. Any gains or losses on trading securities, whether realized on sale or unrealized (as the investments increase or decrease in market value), are recorded as part of net income on the income statement. Investments in stock not classified as trading securities are classified as available-for-sale securities. These are also recorded at market value on the balance sheet. For available-for-sale securities, realized gains and losses are recorded on the income statement, but unrealized gains and losses are recorded as part of stockholders' equity.

Accounts receivable are moneys to be received by the company from customers. The allowance for bad debts records an estimate of the total receivables that are unlikely to be collected. This will be subtracted in arriving at net accounts receivable on the balance sheet. Accounts Receivable Turnover and Accounts Receivable Days measure the speed with which a company collects accounts receivable.

Inventory is merchandise held for sale to customers. Companies can use different cost-flow assumptions to measure the value of inventory. These assumptions include Specific Identification, First-In, First-Out (FIFO), and Last-In, Last-Out (LIFO). IFRS does not permit use of LIFO. The Gross Profit Margin measures the profitability on sales of inventory items. Inventory Turnover and Inventory Days measure how quickly a company sells inventory, on average.

PPE are noncurrent assets expected to benefit future years, such as land, factories, and vehicles. Companies can choose between the straight-line and double-declining-balance methods of depreciation, among others. Gains and losses on PPE are recorded as the difference between the selling price and the book value.

Liabilities are amounts owed to creditors. Companies list many types of liabilities on their balance sheets. Accounts payable are due to suppliers. Warranty payable is an estimate of warranty repairs owed to customers for items that they purchased. Post-retirement benefits are owed to workers when they retire. Contingent liabilities are estimated liabilities for lawsuits and environmental clean-ups. Income taxes payable are owed for tax payments on income earned during the year. Long-term debt refers to bank loans due over more than one year.

Across

3. Cost-flow assumption reporting recently purchased inventory on the balance sheet (4 words) *FiFo*
5. Beginning inventory + Purchases = Goods _____ for Sale *Available*
6. Marketable Securities are _____ investments (2 words) *Short term*
7. Asset cost not yet depreciated (2 words) *Book Value*
8. Valuing investments at the closing stock price (3 words) *market to market*
10. Securities bought and sold for profit in the near term
11. Subtotal that is the first indication of profitability (2 words) *Gross profit*
14. 360 divided by AR Turnover = AR _____ *a/c days residual*
17. Salvage value or scrap value or _____ value *residual*
20. Huge amount of debt that can be traded in smaller denominations (2 words) *Bonds Payable*
22. AR _____ measures how quickly a company collects amounts from customers *Turnover*
23. Gains and losses recorded when a security is sold and cash received *Realized*
25. Keeping track of each inventory item purchased and sold (2 words) *Specific Identification*
27. Investments intended to be held for more than one year (2 words) *long-term*
28. How long it takes to sell merchandise (2 words) *Inventory for sale*
30. Not trading securities (3 words) *available for sale*
31. When sold is reported as COGS on the income statement *inventory*

Down

1. Tangible long-term assets whose cost includes the purchase price, delivery, and set-up costs (4 words) *PPE*
2. Estimate of accounts receivable that may go bad in the future is the _____ for Uncollectibles *Allowance*
4. Gains and losses reflecting changes in market price *unrealized*
9. Take uncollectible accounts receivable off the company books (2 words) *write off*
12. Physical currency (such as dollar bills, coins, etc.) and bank deposits *Cash*
13. Double-declining balance is an _____ method of depreciation *accelerated depn method*
15. Depreciation method spreading cost equally over all periods (2 words) *straight-line method*
16. Measures the number of times a company sells its average inventory level during the year (2 words) *inventory turn*
18. Bank loans due in more than one year (3 words) *long term debt*
19. Highly-liquid investments with maturities of 90 days or less (2 words) *Cash & cash equ*
21. Historical cost is also referred to as _____ cost *acquisitn*
24. Inventory cost-flow assumption used to reduce tax liabilities in a period of inflation (abbreviation) *LIFO last in first out*
26. Another companies' stock or bond used to store excess cash or provide a long-term return *Investment*
29. Report when sales proceeds exceed book value *Gain*

ACTIVITY 56   CASH AND CASH EQUIVALENTS

Purpose: • Reinforce understanding of cash and cash equivalents.

ORACLE CORPORATION (ORCL)			
($ in millions)	05/31/11	05/31/10	05/31/09
Cash and cash equivalents	$ 16,163	$ 9,914	$ 8,995
Short-term investments	12,685	8,555	3,629
Receivables	6,628	5,585	4,430
Other current assets	3,698	2,950	1,527
Property, plant, equipment, net	2,857	2,763	1,922
Other noncurrent assets	31,504	31,811	26,913
TOTAL Assets	$73,535	$61,578	$47,416

NOTES to the Financial Statements.

A typical note regarding accounting policy for Cash, Cash Equivalents, and Short-term Investments reads:

> *Cash, Cash Equivalents, and Short-term Investments.*
> Cash and cash equivalents primarily consist of highly-liquid investments in time deposits and certificates of deposit with original maturities of 3 months or less. Short-term investments, which include marketable equity securities, time deposits, and government and corporate bonds with original maturities of greater than 3 months but less than one year when purchased, are classified as available-for-sale and are recorded at fair value using the specific identification method.

Refer to the information presented above to answer the following questions:

Q1   Highly-liquid investments with maturities of 3 months or less are classified as (**cash and cash equivalents** / short-term investments / long-term investments) and investments with maturities of greater than 3 months but less than one year are classified as (cash and cash equivalents / **short-term investments** / long-term investments).

The definition of cash equivalents is reported (on the balance sheet / on the income statement / **in the notes to the financial statements**).

Q2   For Oracle, cash and cash equivalents plus short-term investments total $ _28,848_ million on 5/31/11 that is __39.22__ % of total assets, which seems like a (**high** / low) percentage.

Q3   One measure of cash flow adequacy is (**free cash flow** / the debt ratio / return on sales), which is the amount of cash available from operations after paying for planned investments in property, plant, and equipment and dividends.

Q4   Can a company ever have too much cash? (**Yes** / No) *Why?*
Could have to much to keep track of and could become a target for robbery

Too little cash? (**Yes** / No) *Why?*
They wouldn't be able to make certain payments and would have a low liquidity.

Purpose: • Reinforce understanding of amounts reported for short-term investments.

BALANCE SHEET ACCOUNTS—December 31, Year 1	
Cash	$ 30,000
Short-term investments—Trading securities	200,000
Interest receivable	1,000
Total current assets	$ 231,000
INCOME STATEMENT ACCOUNTS—Year 1	
Interest revenue	$ 4,000
Dividend revenue	5,000
Unrealized loss on trading securities	12,000

Refer to the information presented above to answer the following questions. Assume this is the *first year* of operation.

Q1   Investments classified as short term are intended to be sold or liquidated in (**one year or less /** **more than one year**).

Q2   Trading securities are reported on the balance sheet at their (**acquisition cost /** **market value**). The fair market value of the trading securities reported above is $ 200 000 . During this accounting period the market value of these trading securities has (**increased /** **decreased** **/ can't tell**) by $ 12 000 . Because this is the first year of operation, these securities must have been originally purchased for $ 212 000 .

Q3   If these securities were sold next year, a(n) (**realized /** **unrealized**) loss would be reported if the selling price was less than the (**acquisition cost /** **market value at the end of last year /** **current market value**).

Q4   The amount of interest *earned* during this accounting period was $ 4000 . Of this amount, $ 3000 was collected in cash during this accounting period and $ 1000 is the amount of cash to be received in the future.

Q5   The income statement accounts listed above would be reported on a multi-step income statement as (**operating /** **nonoperating**) revenues and expenses, indicating these are revenues and expenses from (**operating /** **investing /** **financing**). (Circle *all* that apply.)

Q6   As a result of the financial statement information listed above, Year 1 net income will (**increase /** **decrease**) by $ 3000 .

                3,000

Purpose: • Reinforce understanding of amounts reported on the financial statements for accounts receivable.

BALANCE SHEET ACCOUNTS—December 31, Year 5	
Accounts receivable	$ 90,000
Allowance for bad debts	(4,000)
Accounts receivable, net	86,000
INCOME STATEMENT ACCOUNTS—Year 5	
Sales revenue	$ 800,000
Bad debt expense	15,000

Refer to the information presented above to answer the following questions:

Q1   The *allowance* for bad debts is the portion of (**accounts receivable** / **sales revenue**) that is estimated as uncollectible and is reported on the balance sheet as a (**current asset** / **noncurrent asset** / **current liability** / **noncurrent liability** / **stockholders' equity**).

Q2   The total amount customers owe the company on account on December 31, Year 5 is $ 90 000 . Of this amount, $ 4 000 is estimated to be uncollectible and $ 86 000 is estimated to be collectible. As a result of the financial statement information listed above, total assets will increase by $ 86 000 .

Q3   Bad debt *expense* is the portion of (**accounts receivable** / **sales revenue**) that is estimated as uncollectible and reported as a(n) (**operating** / **nonoperating**) expenses on a multi-step income statement. Above, sales revenue earned during Year 5 totals $ 800 000 , and of that amount, $ 15 000 is estimated to be uncollectible.

Q4   Bad debt expense is a(n) (**estimated** / **known**) amount calculated (**at the end of** / **during**) each accounting period and recorded as an adjustment. This is an application of the (**cost** / **matching** / **historical cost**) principle. The adjustment to record bad debt expense changes (**total assets** / **net income** / **both** / **neither**). *Why?*

Q5   Above, the (**allowance** / **direct write-off**) method is used to report uncollectible accounts. Using the above amounts, assume that $2,000 owed by Customer Ryan was written off as uncollectible. After the write-off, the accounts would report: Accounts receivable (**$88,000** / **$90,000** / **$92,000**), Allowance for bad debts (**$2,000** / **$4,000** / **$6,000**), and Accounts receivable, net (**$84,000** / **$86,000** / **$88,000**). The write-off of an uncollectible account changes (**total assets** / **net income** / **both** / **neither**). *Why?*

Note: *Accounts receivable, net* is also referred to as *net realizable value*.
Bad debt expense is also referred to as *doubtful-account expense* or *uncollectible account expense*.
Nonoperating revenues and expenses are also referred to as *other gains and losses*.

Purpose: • Analyze trends in Accounts Receivable and the Allowance for Bad Debt accounts.

Assume you work in the corporate loan office of Lanford Bank. Chris Ives, owner of CI Manufacturing, Inc. has come to you seeking a loan of $350,000 for new manufacturing equipment to expand his operations. He proposes to use his accounts receivable as collateral for the loan and has provided you with the following financial statements.

($ in thousands)	Year 7	Year 6	Year 5
Income Statement			
Sales revenue	$1,475	$1,589	$1,502
Cost of goods sold	876	947	905
Gross profit	599	642	597
Operating expenses	518	487	453
Operating income	$ 81	$ 155	$ 144
Balance Sheet			
Accounts receivable	$ 458	$ 387	$ 374
Allowance for bad debts	23	31	29
Ratio Analysis			
Accounts receivable turnover ratio	3.22	4.10	4.01
Allowance as a percentage of sales revenue	1.56	1.95	1.93

[handwritten notes in margin: SR / AR, 1589 / 387, larger estimat, low]

Q1   Examine the trend in each of the following accounts.

   a.   *Sales revenue:*
             In Year 6 it (**increased / decreased**), and then in Year 7 it (**increased / decreased**).
   b.   *Cost of goods sold:*
             In Year 6 it (**increased / decreased**), and then in Year 7 it (**increased / decreased**).
   c.   *Operating income:*
             In Year 6 it (**increased / decreased**), and then in Year 7 it (**increased / decreased**).
   d.   *Accounts receivable:*
             In Year 6 it (**increased / decreased**), and then in Year 7 it (**increased / decreased**).
   e.   *Allowance for bad debts:*
             In Year 6 it (**increased / decreased**), and then in Year 7 it (**increased / decreased**).

   f.   *Comment* on any unexpected or suspicious observations.

Q2   Compute the Accounts Receivable Turnover ratio and the Allowance as a Percentage of Sales ratio for each of the three years. Record in the chart above. *What* information do these ratios reveal?

Q3   The amount reported for the *allowance for bad debts* is a(n) (**known / estimated**) amount so this amount (**can / cannot**) be manipulated.

Q4   Would you feel comfortable granting a loan based on the information above? (**Yes / No**).
        If not, what additional information would you request before granting a loan? *Explain.*

Purpose: • Understand the effect ethical decisions have on amounts reported for accounts receivable.

A manager of a small electronics store would like to expand and also sell computers. The expansion would require seeking a loan from a local bank. The manager knows net income for this year is lower than what is needed to qualify for additional financing at his current bank. The manager also realizes some of the estimates used to calculate net income could be adjusted to make *net income* come within the qualifying range for an additional loan.

Q1   On the income statement, overestimating bad debt expense will result in (**understating / having no affect on / overstating**) operating expenses and (**understating / having no affect on / overstating**) net income.

Q2   On the balance sheet, overestimating bad debt expense will result in (**understating / having no affect on / overstating**) the allowance for bad debts and (**understating / having no affect on / overstating**) accounts receivable, net.

Q3   To qualify for the bank loan, the manager should (**over / under**) estimate bad debt expense. *Why?*

Q4   Is intentionally misstating an estimate ethical? (**Yes / No / Maybe**) *Why?*

Q5   Is intentionally misstating an estimate legal? (**Yes / No / Maybe**) *Why?*

Q6   List some possible consequences if bank officials detect the misstatement of the estimate.

Q7   Discuss some ways the misstatement of bad debt expense could be detected by bank officials.

Q8   In general, unethical decisions make the (**short term / long term**) appear better, but may result in huge (**short-term / long-term**) costs.

Purpose:
- Reinforce understanding of amounts reported for inventory from using different cost-flow assumption; LIFO or FIFO.

GENERAL ELECTRIC COMPANY (GE)

> **Note 1**: *Summary of Significant Accounting Policies Inventories.*
> All inventories are stated at the lower of cost or realizable values. Cost for substantially all of GE's U.S. inventories is determined on a last-in, first-out (LIFO) basis. Cost of other GE inventories is primarily determined on a first-in, first-out (FIFO) basis.

Note 11: GE Inventories (Adapted)		
($ in millions) December 31,	**Year 6**	**Year 5**
Raw material and work in process	$4,894	$4,708
Finished goods	4,379	3,951
Unbilled shipments	372	312
	9,645	8,971
Less revaluation to LIFO	(606)	(676)
	$9,039	$8,295

Refer to Note 1 above to answer Q1 and Q2.

Q1 General Electric uses the (**FIFO** / **Weighted Average** / **LIFO**) inventory cost-flow assumption(s).
(*Circle all that apply.*)

Q2 Does the answer for Q1 comply with the Consistency Principle? (**Yes** / **No**) *Explain.*

Refer to Note 11 above to answer Q3 through Q7.

Q3 On December 31, Year 6, the balance sheet would have reported inventories of (**$9,645** / **$9,039**) million if the first-in, first-out (FIFO) method had been used to value all inventories and (**$9,645** / **$9,039**) million if the last-in, first-out (LIFO) method were used to value the domestic portion of inventories.

Q4 Circle the effect the LIFO cost-flow assumption has had on reported financial statement amounts since GE began operations. As a result of using LIFO, GE has reported:

    a. $606 million (**more** / **less**) in ending inventory.

    b. $606 million (**more** / **less**) in cost of goods sold (COGS).

    c. $606 million (**more** / **less**) in income before income tax.

    d.   assuming a 40% tax rate, $242 million ($606 million x 40%) (**more** / **less**) in tax expense.

Q5 The revaluation to LIFO (**decreased** / **increased**) from Year 5 to Year 6, which indicates there probably (**was** / **was not**) a LIFO liquidation. ⟶ *if company sell more than they buy*

Q6 In a period of inflation, the cost-flow assumption resulting in the lowest taxable income is (**FIFO** / **Weighted Average** / **LIFO**). This tax benefit is achieved by allocating the higher, more current inventory costs to (**COGS** / **Ending Inventory**).

Q7 General Electric would appear more profitable if it used (**FIFO** / **LIFO**) to determine the value of all inventories. Would it really be more profitable? (**Yes** / **No**) *Explain.*

total inv. cost remains constant

If prices are falling

Purpose: • Compute COGS and Ending Inventory when using the LIFO and FIFO cost-flow assumptions.

At the end of the accounting period inventory costs must be assigned to either cost of goods sold or ending inventory so the financial statements can be prepared.

The **specific identification inventory method** tracks when each inventory item is purchased and sold. This method is used when dealing with unique and expensive inventory items such as jewelry, custom-built homes, or automobiles.

Many times tracking individual units is not cost effective, and GAAP allows companies to select an **inventory cost-flow assumption** to allocate costs between cost of goods sold and ending inventory. In a craft store, imagine trying to track when each wooden bead or Styrofoam cone is purchased and then sold.

Two commonly used cost-flow assumptions are **first-in, first-out (FIFO)** and **last-in, first-out (LIFO)**. FIFO assumes the *first* units purchased are the *first* units sold during the accounting period, whereas LIFO assumes the *last* units purchased are the *first* units sold during the accounting period.

Use the information in the chart immediately below to answer the following questions.

Jan 1 Beg inventory	20 units @ $20 per unit =	$ 400
Feb 1 Purchase #1	30 units @ $30 per unit =	900
Mar 1 Purchase #2	40 units @ $40 per unit =	1,600
Goods available for sale	90 units	$2,900

Q1   Assume 60 units were sold. Using FIFO and LIFO, calculate the cost allocated to cost of goods sold (COGS) and ending inventory in the space provided below.

	FIFO	LIFO
COGS	$ 20 units 1,700	$ 2,200
ENDING INVENTORY	$ 1,200	$ 700

Q2   Examine the results above. In a period of inflation:

a.   (**FIFO / (LIFO)**) reports the greatest amount for COGS (Cost of goods sold).

b.   (**(FIFO) / LIFO**) allocates the higher, more recent costs to the balance sheet.

c.   Which 60 units were really sold?

Q3 Assume the 60 units in Q1 sold for $100 each and operating expenses total $3,500. Using FIFO and LIFO, complete the income statement in the space provided below.

INCOME STATEMENT—Sell 60 units for $100 each		
	FIFO	LIFO
Sales revenue	$ 6000	$ 6000
COGS	17000	2200
Gross profit	1400	3800
Operating expenses	3,500	3,500
Operating income	$ 800	$ 300

Q4 Examine the income statement above. In a period of inflation:

a. FIFO allocates the (**recent / older**) inventory costs to COGS, which results in (**lower / higher**) COGS and, therefore, (**lower / higher**) operating income.

b. LIFO allocates the (**recent / older**) inventory costs to COGS, which results in (**lower / higher**) COGS and, therefore, (**lower / higher**) operating income.

c. (**FIFO / LIFO**) results in less income tax expense.

Q5 International Financial Reporting Standards allow (**FIFO / LIFO**), but do not allow (**FIFO / LIFO**)

Purpose:
- Understand if recent or older costs are allocated to the income statement or the balance sheet when using LIFO and FIFO.

Q1   Use the LIFO cost-flow assumption to answer the following questions.

YEAR 1:   Purchase #1   1,000 units @ $1 = $1,000

Purchase #2   1,000 units @ $1 = $1,000

   a.   *How much is goods available for sale?* $ 2000

   Sell 1,000 units.

   b.   *What costs remain in ending inventory?* $ 1,000

YEAR 2:   Beginning inventory ___1000___ units @ $ _1000_ per unit = $ 1,000

Purchase 2,000 units @ $2 = $4,000

   a.   *How much is goods available for sale?* $ 5,000

   Sell 2,000 units.

   b.   *What costs remain in ending inventory?* $ 1000

YEAR 3:   Beginning inventory _1 000_ units @ $ _1_ per unit = $ 1000

Purchase 3,000 units @ $3 = $9,000

   a.   *How much is goods available for sale?* $ 10000

   Sell 3,000 units.

   b.   *What costs remain in ending inventory?* $ 1000

Q2   The Coca-Cola Company is more than 100 years old. Coca-Cola uses the LIFO cost-flow assumption.

   a.   So how old are those inventory costs on the balance sheet?

   b.   *When* will Coca-Cola get those "ancient" LIFO inventory costs off of the balance sheet?

   c.   Because Coca-Cola uses LIFO, does it have cans of Coca-Cola that have been sitting in the warehouse since the company started business? **(Yes / No)**

Q3   Summarize the effects of using the FIFO and LIFO cost-flow assumptions on COGS and Ending Inventory by circling the type of costs allocated to each below.

	FIFO	LIFO
COGS	(Recent / Older / Ancient)	(Recent / Older / Ancient)
Ending inventory	(Recent / Older / Ancient)	(Recent / Older / Ancient)

Q4   May a company use LIFO for tax purposes and FIFO for external reporting to shareholders?

(Yes / No) *Why* would a company want to do this?

Purpose:
- Understanding that gross profit margin, ROS, and inventory turnover ratios vary by industry.

The **gross profit margin (GP%)** compares gross profit to sales revenue. It expresses gross profit as a percentage of sales. This ratio is the first measure of profitability reported on the income statement.

$$\text{GROSS PROFIT MARGIN} = \frac{\text{Gross profit}}{\text{Sales revenue}}$$

Q1   Guess the GP% and ROS for each of the following companies:

		GP%	ROS
a.	Bristol-Myers Squibb (BMY) (*pharmaceuticals*)	(70% / 40% / 20%)	(25% /20% / 2%)
b.	Apple (AAPL) (*computers*)	(70% / 40% / 20%)	(25% / 20% / 2%)
c.	Kroger (KR) (*grocery*)	(70% / 40% / 20%)	(25% /20% / 2%)

d.   *What* do the above ratios reveal about each of the companies?

e.   The information for both the numerator and denominator of the ratios above come from the (**balance sheet / income statement / statement of cash flows**).

f.   Gross profit margin is the (**first** / **second** / **last**) indication of profitability on the income statement.

INVENTORY TURNOVER RATIO

The **inventory turnover ratio** indicates the number of times a company sells its average inventory level during the year. It measures how efficiently a company uses its investment in inventory. It is a measure of efficiency.

$$\text{INVENTORY TURNOVER RATIO} = \frac{\text{Cost of goods sold}}{\text{Inventory}}$$

Q2   Guess the inventory turnover ratio for each of the following companies:

a.	Wal-Mart—(*discount retailer*)	(4 / 8 / 12 / 35)
b.	Kroger—(*grocery*)	(4 / 8 / 12 / 35)
c.	Dell Computer—(*computer*)	(4 / 8 / 12 / 35)
d.	JC Penney—(*department store*)	(4 / 8 / 12 / 35)

Q3   *What* does the inventory turnover ratio reveal about each of the companies?

Q4   *What* are some of the costs of holding inventory?

Purpose: • Understand the effect ethical decisions have on amounts reported for inventory.

A manager of a men's clothing store receives a bonus based on the amount of *gross profit* earned by the department. This year the manager is only two thousand dollars short from qualifying for a sizable year-end bonus. The manager is in a position to have a portion of the inventory counted twice in the year-end physical inventory count. Cost of goods sold is adjusted for any changes to year-end inventory.

Q1   On the balance sheet, double counting a portion of ending inventory will result in
       (**understating / having no affect on / overstating**) ending inventory and
       (**understating / having no affect on / overstating**) total assets.

Q2   On the income statement, double counting a portion of ending inventory will result in
       (**understating / having no affect on / overstating**) cost of goods sold (COGS) and
       (**understating / having no affect on / overstating**) gross profit.

Q3   To qualify for the year-end bonus, the manager (**should / should not**) double count over two
       thousand dollars of ending inventory.
       Why?

Q4   Is intentionally double counting ending inventory ethical? (**Yes / No / Maybe**)
       Why?

Q5   Is intentionally double counting ending inventory legal? (**Yes / No / Maybe**)
       Why?

Q6   List some possible consequences if upper management detects double counting of ending
       inventory.

Q7   Discuss some ways the double counting of inventory could be detected by management.

Purpose:
- Reinforce understanding of property, plant, and equipment amounts reported on the financial statements.

BALANCE SHEET ACCOUNTS—12/31/Year 5	
Equipment	$ 400,000
Accumulated depreciation	(150,000)
Book value	$ 250,000
INCOME STATEMENT ACCOUNTS—Year 5	
Depreciation expense	$ (50,000)
Gain on sale of equipment	7,000
Loss on sale of land	(3,000)

Refer to the financial statement information presented above to answer the following questions.

Q1   The amount originally paid (acquisition cost) to purchase the equipment was $ 400,000 , which was capitalized and recorded as a(n) (**noncurrent asset** / **expense**).

Q2   The portion of the equipment's original cost expensed since it was purchased is $ 150,000 . The cost allocated to Year 5 for use of the equipment is $ 50,000 . Assuming straight-line depreciation is used, it appears the equipment was purchased 3 years ago.

Q3   Depreciation expense is a(n) (**estimated** / **known**) amount recorded (**at the end of** / **during**) each accounting period as an adjustment, which is an application of the (**cost** / **matching** / **consistency**) principle. On a multi-step income statement, depreciation expense is reported as an (**operating expense** / **nonoperating revenues and expenses**).

Q4   The (**straight-line** / **double-declining-balance** / **neither**) method(s) of depreciation will result in greater depreciation the *first* year of an asset's useful life and the (**straight-line** / **double-declining-balance** / **neither**) method(s) will result in greater *total* depreciation over the asset's useful life.

Q5   Book value (**is** / **is not**) the same as current value. The primary purpose of depreciation is (**cost allocation** / **current valuation**). *Explain* what this means.

Q6   During the year, equipment was sold for $ 7,000 more than (**acquisition cost** / **book value** / **market value**) whereas land was sold for $ 3,600 less than (**acquisition cost** / **market value**). The company got a better deal on the sale of the (**equipment** / **land** / **can't tell**) *Explain.*

acquisition cost
(what amt they paid for

Q7   As a result of the financial statement information above, $ 250,000 will be added into total assets and Year 5 net income will (**increase** / **decrease**) by $ 46,000

Q8   By purchasing additional property, plant, and equipment, the company is investing in (**short-term** / **long-term**) income-producing assets that are expected to (**increase** / **decrease**) future revenues.

Purpose:
- Compute depreciation using the straight-line method.
- Understand what amounts are reported for depreciation on the financial statements.

Property, Plant, and Equipment = PPE = fixed assets = capital assets

Acquisition Cost = Original cost = Historical cost = The amount reported as the acquisition cost of PPE includes all costs to make the asset operational including purchase, delivery, and set-up costs.

Residual Value = salvage value = scrap value
The estimated value of the asset at the end of the estimated useful life.

Depreciable Base = *Acquisition Cost - Residual Value*

Depreciation is the allocation of the *Depreciable Base* over the *expected useful life* of the asset. Two widely used depreciation methods include straight-line (SL) and double-declining balance (DDB). **Straight-Line (SL)** depreciation allocates an equal amount of expense to each year of the asset's expected useful life. **Double-Declining-Balance (DDB)** depreciation is an accelerated method, which allocates more expense to the early years of the asset's useful life.

Accumulated Depreciation is the total amount of depreciation expensed since acquisition.

Book value	= *Acquisition Cost* minus *Accumulated Depreciation*
	= Carrying value = PPE, net = Cost not yet depreciated
	= Amount reported on the balance sheet and added to arrive at total assets

STRAIGHT-LINE DEPRECIATION

Q1 Equipment costing $400,000 has an estimated useful life of five years and a residual value of $50,000. Record depreciation expense, accumulated depreciation, and book value in the chart below for each year of the five-year useful life using the straight-line method of depreciation.

SL	Depreciation Expense	Accumulated Depreciation	Book Value = Acquisition Cost – Accumulated Dep	
Year 1	70,000	970,000	330 – 70,000	
Year 2	70,000	140,000	260	260,000
Year 3	70,000	210	190	
Year 4	70,000	280	120	
Year 5	70,000	350	50 0	
Total	350,000	double		

Q2 Record amounts reported on the income statement and the balance sheet over a six-year period in the chart below.

	Year 1	Year 2	Year 3	Year 4	Year 5	Year 6
Income Statement						
Depreciation Expense	$70	$70	$70	$70	$70	$0
Balance Sheet						
Acquisition Cost	$400,000	$400,000	$400,000	$400,000	$400,000	$400,000
Accumulated Dep	70,000	140,000	21	280	350	350
Book Value	$330,000	$260,000	$190,000	$120,000	$50,000	$50,000

Purpose:
- Compute depreciation using the double-declining-balance method.
- Understand what amounts are reported for depreciation on the financial statements.

Q1   Compute the Double-Declining-Balance (DDB) Rate for each useful life below.

Straight-Line Rate = (1 / Useful Life)

DDB Rate = Straight-Line Rate x 2 = Double the Straight-line Rate

		SL Rate	Double It =	DDB Rate
a.	5 year life	1/5 = 20%	x 2	40%
b.	10 year life	$\frac{1}{10} \times 100 = 10\%$	x 2	70%
c.	3 year life	33.3%	x 2	67%

Q2   Equipment costing $400,000 has an estimated useful life of five years and a residual value of $50,000. Complete the table below for Years 2–5 using the DDB method of depreciation.

> **Beginning Book Value x DDB Rate = DDB Depreciation Expense**

DDB	Depreciation Expense	Accumulated Depreciation	Book Value = Acquisition Cost – Accumulated Dep
Acquisition	400,000 * 40% =		400,000 - 0 = 400,000
Year 1	160,000	160,000	400,000 - 160,000 = 240,000
Year 2	96000 2 96,000	256,000	144 000
Year 3	144000 x 57,600	313,600	86,400
Year 4	35486 34,560	348160	51,840
Year 5	14,840	350,000	50,000
Total	350,000		

Q3   Record the amounts reported on the income statement and the balance sheet over a six-year period.

	Year 1	Year 2	Year 3	Year 4	Year 5	Year 6
Income Statement						
Depreciation Expense	$ 160	$ 96	$ 576	$ 3459	$840	$ 0
Balance Sheet						
Acquisition Cost	$ 40600	$400,000	$ r r	$ r r	$ r r	$ r r
Accumulated Dep	160,000	256,000	313	348160	350	350
Book Value	$ 240	$144,000	$86.4	$51480	$ 50 rw	$ 50 rw

Purpose: • Understand how SL and DDB depreciation methods affect the financial statements.

Q1   In the *first* year of an asset's useful life, the DDB depreciation method reports:

a.   *depreciation expense* that is (**higher** / **lower**) than the SL depreciation method.

b.   *net income* that is (**higher** / **lower**) than the SL depreciation method.

c.   *accumulated depreciation* that is (**higher** / **lower**) than the SL depreciation method.

d.   *total assets* that are (**higher** / **lower**) than the SL depreciation method.

Q2   In the *final* year of an asset's useful life, the DDB depreciation method reports:

a.   *depreciation expense* that is (**higher** / **equal** / **lower**) than the SL depreciation method.

b.   *net income* that is (**higher** / **equal** / **lower**) than the SL depreciation method.

c.   *accumulated depreciation* that is (**higher** / **equal** / **lower**) than the SL depreciation method.

d.   *total assets* that are (**higher** / **equal** / **lower**) than the SL depreciation method.

Q3   Book value (**does** / **does not**) depend on the depreciation method used.

Q4   Book value (**is** / **is not**) the same as the current selling price of the asset.

Q5   If an asset has an acquisition cost of $20,000, accumulated depreciation of $10,000, and no residual value, then on average, the assets are (**recently purchased** / **about half way through their useful lives** / **old and ready to be disposed of** / **can't tell**).

Q6   An accelerated depreciation method is (**SL** / **DDB**), which means that a greater amount of depreciation expense is reported at the (**beginning** / **end**) of the asset's useful life.

Q7   If a building is being depreciated, the (**SL** / **DDB** / **either**) method can be used.

        If an auto is being depreciated, the (**SL** / **DDB** / **either**) method can be used.

Q8   Land (**is** / **is not**) depreciated because it has an indefinite life.

Q9   The company generally appears better to shareholders when using (**SL** / **DDB**). *Why?* It shows a more equal distribution of depreciation for expenses

Q10   For tax purposes, (**SL** / **DDB**) is usually preferred. *Why?* It allocates depreciation to the earlier years of the business.

Q11   May a company choose one depreciation method for reporting to shareholders and a different depreciation method for tax purposes? (**Yes** / **No**)

ACTIVITY 70   PPE: GAINS AND LOSSES

Purpose:
- Compute gains and losses on the sale of PPE.
- Understand that the effect on net income equals the cost of using the asset over the useful life of the asset.

Gain (Loss) = Selling Price - Book Value

Revenues are earned when engaging in the *primary* business activity and reported at their *gross* amount. *Gains (Losses)* are reported when a *peripheral* asset is sold and the selling price is reported *net* of book value as of the date of sale.

Q1   Compute the gain (loss) for Fancy Florist on the sale of a van with a:
- a.   book value of $8,000 and a selling price of $10,000.   (**Gain** / Loss) of $ ___2000___
- b.   book value of $10,000 and a selling price of $10,000.   (Gain / Loss) of $ ___0___
- c.   book value of $11,000 and a selling price of $10,000.   (Gain / **Loss**) of $ ___1000___

Q2   Equipment purchased for $30,000 with a 10-year estimated useful life and no estimated residual value is sold at the end of Year 2 for $22,000.
- a.   Compute the book value at the time of sale (at the end of Year 2).

    SL $ ___6000___ → 24,000   DDB $ ___19,200___   22,000
- b.   1.   At the end of Year 2, the market value of the equipment is $ ___22,000___.
  2.   The market value and the book value are (the same / **different**) for SL.
  3.   The market value and the book value are (the same / **different**) for DDB.
  4.   *Why?*

Q3   Compute the gain (loss) on the sale for the SL and DDB depreciation methods.

	Straight-line	Double-declining-balance
Selling Price	$ 22,000	$ 22,000
- Book Value	$ 24,000	$ 19,200
= Gain (Loss) on the Sale	$ (2000)	$ 2800

Q4   a.   Compute the effect on net income for SL and DDB from purchase to sale of the asset. Record in the chart below.

	Straight-line	Double-declining-balance
Year 1 Depreciation Expense	$ (3,000)	$ (6,000)
Year 2 Depreciation Expense	$ (3,000)	$ (4,800)
Gain (Loss) on the Sale	$ (2,000)	$ 2,800
= Increase (Decrease) in Net Income	$ (8,000)	$ (8,000)

- b.   Over the life of this asset, the effect on net income is the (**same** / different) for SL and DDB. *Why?*

Purpose: • Understand the effect ethical decisions have on amounts reported for property, plant, and equipment.

Financial analysts have predicted that net income will increase by 5% for a major corporation. Corporate management has suggested that the controller do what is necessary to meet these predictions. The controller decides to examine depreciation expense because the amount is based on estimates of useful life and residual value and GAAP allows choices with regard to depreciation methods.

Q1   GAAP allows choices with regard to depreciation methods. In the first year of an asset's useful life, if the *straight-line* rather than the double-declining-balance depreciation method is used then:

     a.   reported depreciation expense will be (**lower** / **higher**), which leads to (**lower** / **higher**) net income.

     b.   reported accumulated depreciation will be (**lower** / **higher**), which leads to (**lower** / **higher**) book value and (**lower** / **higher**) total assets.

Q2   To make net income appear as favorable as possible, the controller would choose the (**straight-line** / **double-declining-balance**) depreciation method for assets placed in service during the current year.

Q3   Is intentionally choosing a depreciation method that reports higher net income ethical? (**Yes** / **No** / **Maybe**)   Legal? (**Yes** / **No** / **Maybe**) *Explain.*

Q4   Depreciation expense is based on estimates of useful life and residual value. To make net income appear as *favorable* as possible, the controller would (**shorten** / **lengthen**) the useful life and (**raise** / **lower**) the residual value of the asset.

Q5   Is intentionally choosing an estimated useful life and residual value that report higher net income ethical? (**Yes** / **No** / **Maybe**)   Legal? (**Yes** / **No** / **Maybe**) *Explain.*

Q6   a.   For financial statement purposes, a company generally prefers to report (**lower** / **higher**) net income and therefore would choose the (**straight-line** / **double-declining-balance**) depreciation method.

     b.   For income tax purposes, a company generally prefers to report (**lower** / **higher**) taxable income and therefore would choose the (**straight-line** / **double-declining-balance**) depreciation method.

     c.   Is intentionally choosing one depreciation method for financial statement purposes and a different method for income tax purposes ethical? (**Yes** / **No** / **Maybe**)   Legal? (**Yes** / **No** / **Maybe**)

Q7   Identify at least three items that the controller could use to make *net income appear more favorable* with regard to the depreciation of assets placed in service during the current year that are both ethical and legal.

Purpose: • Reinforce understanding of investments classified as available-for-sale securities

Q1   Assume Winfield Corporation purchased 100 shares of Coca-Cola stock and 100 shares of IBM stock on January 2, Year 1. These equity securities are classified as available-for-sale because the intent is to hold them for several years. *Refer to the related financial information below to answer the following questions.*

	Fair Market Value			Cost
	Dec 31, Year 3	Dec 31, Year 2	Dec 31, Year 1	Jan 2, Year 1
COCA-COLA (100 shares)	$ 7,400	$ 5,300	$ 4,500	$ 4,600
IBM (100 shares)	11,400	7,600	6,000	10,000
Total	$ 18,800	$ 12,900	$ 10,500	$ 14,600

Q2   Complete the chart below to reflect how the above information would be reported on the financial statements.

BALANCE SHEET	Dec 31, Year 3	Dec 31, Year 2	Dec 31, Year 1
ASSETS: Long-term investments	$ 18 800	$ 12 900	$ 10 500
SE: Accumulated other comprehensive income—*Unrealized gain/(loss) on investments*	$ 4,200	$ (1,700)	$ (4,100)
INCOME STATEMENT	Year 3	Year 2	Year 1
Other comprehensive income—*Unrealized gain/(loss) on investments*	$ 5,900	$ 2,400	$ (4,100)
STATEMENT OF CASH FLOWS	Year 3	Year 2	Year 1
INVESTING ACTIVITIES: *Cash inflows (outflows)*	$ 0	$ 0	$ (14,600)

Q3   When available-for-sale securities increase in value, this event will:

debt securities
no eff in ↑ change market
↑ change/market

a.   (**increase** / decrease / **have no effect on**) total assets,

b.   (increase / decrease / **have no effect on**) net income,

c.   (**increase** / decrease / have no effect on) comprehensive income, and

d.   (**increase** / decrease / have no effect on) stockholders' equity.

Q4   Assume the 100 shares of Coca-Cola stock were sold for $76 per share during Year 4. As a result, the Year 4 income statement would report a (**realized** / unrealized) gain of $ _____ as an **3,000** (operating / **nonoperating**) revenue and the Year 4 statement of cash flows would report a cash (**inflow** / outflow) of $ _____ 7,600 in the (operating / **investing** / financing) activity section.

Q5   When available-for-sale securities are sold at a gain, this event will:

if equity

a.   (increase / decrease / **depends**) total assets,

b.   (**increase** / decrease / depends) net income,

c.   (increase / decrease / **depends**) comprehensive income, and

d.   (increase / decrease / **depends**) stockholders' equity.

Purpose: •   Reinforce understanding of amounts reported on the financial statements for current and noncurrent liabilities.

BALANCE SHEET ACCOUNTS—Dec 31, Year 5	($ in millions)
Accounts payable	$ 6,245
Warranty liability	510
Income taxes payable	389
Current portion of long-term debt	271
Total current liabilities	7,415
Deferred income taxes	51
Post-retirement benefit liabilities	2,390
Bonds payable, 8%, mature in 2030	2,500
Bond discount	(156)
	2,344
Long-term debt	631
INCOME STATEMENT ACCOUNTS—Year 5	
Sales revenue	$ 50,000
Post-retirement benefit expense	698
Warranty expense	275
Interest expense (related to the bond payable)	220

Refer to the information presented above to answer the following questions.

Q1   (**Current** / **Noncurrent**) liabilities are obligations due within one year or within the company's normal operating cycle if longer. Obligations due beyond that time are classified as (**current** / **noncurrent**) liabilities.

Q2   The purchase of inventory will usually increase the (**accounts** / **notes** / **mortgage**) payable account.

Q3   Warranty costs related to Year 5 sales total (**$275** / **$510** / **$785**) million and warranty costs expected to be incurred in the future total (**$275** / **$510** / **$785**) million. These amounts are (**known** / **estimated**).

Q4   There is (**$271** / **$631** / **$902**) million of total debt outstanding (not including bonds). Of this amount, the company plans to pay (**$271** / **$631** / **$902**) million during the following year and pay (**$271** / **$631** / **$902**) million in later years.

Q5   When bonds payable are issued, they are recorded at their (**face** / **present**) value. After issuance, they are reported at their (**present** / **fair market** / **amortized**) value. The above bond has a current carrying value of $___2344___ million that will continue to (**increase** / **decrease**) until maturity. At maturity, the issuing corporation will pay $___2500___ million to the holder of the bond.

Q6   The bond payable was issued at a discount because the market interest rates were (**higher than** / **equal to** / **lower than**) 8%, and therefore, the actual cost of borrowing is (**greater than** / **equal to** / **less than**) 8%. This year's interest payment totaled (**$156** / **$200** / **$220** / **$250**) million while this year's cost of borrowing totaled (**$156** / **$200** / **$220** / **$250**) million.   8%. $\times$ 2500

Q7   Post-retirement benefits are expensed and recorded as a liability in the year of (**employment** / **retirement**). This is an application of the (**matching** / **cost** / **reliability**) principle.

Purpose: • Benchmark current market rates and understand why they differ among various financial instruments.

Q1   Research the following current interest rates. These rates are available on the Internet and at a local bank or credit union.

> The current rates banks/credit unions are offering/asking are:
>
> a. _____%   for a traditional savings account.
>
> b. _____%   for a one-year certificate of deposit (CD).
>
> c. _____%   for a 30-year fixed-rate mortgage with no points.
>
> d. _____%   for a standard credit card.
>
> Please note the source of your information: (financial institution, newspaper, Website, etc.)
>
> _____

Q2

> The current prime-lending rate is _____%, which is the interest rate charged by banks to their most creditworthy customers (usually the most prominent and stable business customers).
>
> Please note the source of your information: (financial institution, newspaper, Website, etc.)
>
> _____

Q3   Explain why the reported interest rates differ between (a) and (b) above.

Q4   Explain why the reported interest rates differ between (b) and (c) above.

Q5   Explain why the reported interest rates differ between (c) and (d) above.

Q6   Explain the prime lending rate and its importance with regard to other lending rates.

Purpose:
- Reinforce understanding of bonds payable amounts reported on the financial statements.
- Compute interest payments on a bond payable.
- Understand why a bond sells at a premium, par, or a discount.

Q1 **Bond Prices**

For example, if a $100,000 bond is issued at 102 the bond will sell for 102% of the face value or for $102,000.

a. A $100,000 bond issued at 99 will sell for ___99___ % of the face value, which is $ _99,000_ .

b. A $50,000 bond issued at 103 will sell for _103_ % of the face value, which is $ _51,500_ .

A **Bond Issuance** raises large amounts of capital ($$$) by issuing many bonds of small denominations (e.g. $1,000).

Principal = Maturity Value = Face Value = the amount the issuing corporation pays to the holder of the bond at maturity

Stated Rate = Coupon Rate = the rate of the required annual interest payment

> **Principal x Stated Rate = Annual Interest Payment**

Use the information on the bond payable below to answer the following question.

> **Bond Payable**
> Principal $10,000
>
> Stated rate 10%
>
> Matures in 10 years

Q2 The issuing corporation makes
interest payments of (**$1,000** / $10,000 / $20,000) annually to the holder of this bond.

Over the life of the bond, the corporation will pay out ($1,000 / **$10,000** / $20,000) in interest payments and repay ($1,000 / **$10,000** / $20,000) of principal at maturity, for a total cash outflow of ($1,000 / $10,000 / **$20,000**) over the life of the bond.

Q3   Assume the bond was originally issued for $10,000 and held to maturity.

    a.   The corporation *paid out* $____10,000____ in total interest payments + *paid out* $____10,000____ of principal at maturity = total amounts paid of $__20,000__

    b.   At issuance the corporation *received* from the investor   (__10,000__)

    c.   The difference is the cost of borrowing over the ten years = $__10,000__

    d.   T

          his bond was issued at (**a premium /(par)/ a discount**) because the market rate of interest was (**less than 10% /(10%)/ more than 10%**).

Q4   Assume the bond was originally issued for $8,000 and held to maturity.

    a.   The corporation *paid out* $__10,000__ in total interest payments + *paid out* $__10,000__ of principal at maturity = total amounts paid of $__20,000__

    b.   At issuance the corporation *received* from the investor   (__8,000__)

    c.   The difference is the cost of borrowing over the ten years = $__12,000__

    d.   This bond was issued at (**a premium / par /(a discount)**) because the market rate of interest was (**less than 10% / 10% / more than 10%**).

Q5   Assume the bond was originally issued for $12,000 and held to maturity.

    a.   The corporation *paid out* $__10,000__ in total interest payments + *paid out* $__10,000__ of principal at maturity = total amounts paid of $__20,000__

    b.   At issuance the corporation *received* from the investor   (__12,000__)

    c.   The difference is the cost of borrowing over the ten years = $__8,000__

    d.   This bond was issued at ((**a premium**)/ par / a discount) because the market rate of interest was (**less than 10%**/ 10% / more than 10%).

Q6   The issuing corporation would prefer to borrow money in a (**(4%)** / 8% / 12%) market, whereas an investor would prefer a (4% / 8% /(**12%**)) market.

Q7   When will a bond be issued at a premium? Par? A discount?

Q8   A corporation would prefer to issue bonds at a ((**premium**)/ par / discount). *Why?*

Purpose: • Understand why bond yields differ.

YIELD COMPARISONS					
CORPORATE BONDS			**NEW TAX-EXEMPT BONDS**		
Maturity	**Rating**	**Yield**	**Maturity**	**Rating**	**Yield**
1–10 years	High quality (AAA-AA)	2.95%	7–12 years	G.O. (AA)	3.30%
1–10 years	Medium quality (A-BBB/Baa)	3.92%	2–22 years	G.O. (AA)	4.19%
10+ years	High quality (AAA-AA)	5.34%	22+years	G.O. (AA)	4.70%
10+ years	Medium quality (A-BBB/Baa)	5.95%			
All years	High yield (BB/Ba-C)	9.23%			

Refer to the information in the table above to answer the following questions.

Q1   *Yield* is the cost to the issuing entity for borrowing and the return to the investor/creditor for lending the money. Yield is also referred to as the market rate and the effective rate of borrowing. Record the yield of a *high-quality* corporate bond that matures in *1–10 years*.   _2.95_ %

Q2   *Ratings* are a measure of risk. Standard & Poor's and Moody's are two companies that assess the amount of risk. A rating of AAA indicates very low risk and a rating of C indicates very high risk.
   a.   Record the yield of a *high-quality* corporate bond that matures in 1–10 years. _2.95_ %
   b.   Record the yield of a *high-yield* corporate bond.   _9.23_ %
   c.   *Explain* why one yield is higher than the other for these two types of corporate bonds.

Q3   Bonds have different lengths of *time to maturity*.
   a.   Record the yield of a high-quality corporate bond that *matures in 1–10 years*. _7.95_ %
   b.   Record the yield of a high-quality corporate bond that *matures in more than 10 years*.   _5.34_ %
   c.   *Explain* why one yield is higher than the other for these two types of corporate bonds.

Q4   Bonds issued by corporations are usually not *tax-exempt,* whereas bonds issued by municipalities usually are tax-exempt.
   a.   Record the yield of a high-quality *corporate bond* that matures in 10+ years. _5.34_ %
   b.   Record the yield of a high-quality *tax-exempt bond* that matures in 7–12 years. _3.30_ %
   c.   *Explain* the advantage of tax-exempt bonds to the investor/creditor.

   d.   *Explain* why one yield is higher than the other for these two types of bonds.

Purpose: • Understand why bonds sell at a premium, at par, or at a discount.

HIGH-YIELD BONDS					
Name	**Rating**	**Coupon Rate**	**Maturity**	**Bid Price**	**Yield***
Allied Waste	B+	10.00%	8/2014	104.50	8.71%
Trump AC	CCC+	11.25%	5/2011	79.00	21.13%
* Yield is the lower of yield to maturity and yield to call.					

Refer to the information in the table above to answer the following questions.

Q1   The Allied Waste bond has a _____% coupon rate (also referred to as the stated rate or the face rate) that determines the (**cash interest payment / effective interest rate**). An investor/creditor holding a $100,000 Allied Waste bond will receive $_____ in interest payments each year.

Q2   The Allied Waste bond is currently rated a B+ and returning a _____% yield, whereas the Trump AC bond is rated _____ and returning a _____% yield. The CCC+ rating indicates (**more / less**) financial risk than a B+ rating. Therefore, to attract investors/creditors the Trump AC bond must offer a (**higher / lower**) rate of return (yield).

Q3   An investor/creditor purchasing the Allied Waste bond is expecting a(n) _____ % annual return. Assuming investments with the same amount of risk, an investor/creditor would prefer a (**high / low**) yield whereas the issuing corporation would prefer a (**high / low**) yield.

Q4   The amount paid by the issuing corporation at maturity is referred to as the face value, the par value, and the maturity value. Bond bid (selling) price is quoted as a percentage of par.

For example, the Bid Price of the Allied Waste bond is 104.50. This indicates an investor/creditor could purchase or sell a $100,000 Allied Waste bond for $104,500. ($100,000 x 104.50%). This bond is selling at a (**premium / par / discount**).

A $100,000 Trump AC bond would sell for $_____. This bond is selling at a (**premium / par / discount**).

Q5   The Allied Waste bond is selling at a premium because the coupon rate (stated rate, face rate) is (**greater than / less than**) the yield (market rate, effective rate) for this investment. To achieve the (**higher / lower**) yield, the investor/creditor pays the issuing corporation an additional amount (premium) at the beginning of the investment.

The Trump AC bond is selling at a discount because the coupon rate (stated rate, face rate) is (**greater than / less than**) the yield (market rate, effective rate) for this investment. To achieve the (**higher / lower**) yield, the initial investment of the investor/creditor is less than face value (discount) and at maturity the higher face value is received.

Q6   Would you prefer to invest in the Allied Waste or the Trump AC bond? *Why?*

Purpose:
- Reinforce understanding of amounts reported on the financial statements for stockholders' equity.

The COCA-COLA COMPANY	
Shareowners' Equity December 31, 2011 $ in millions	
Common stock, $.25 par value	
Authorized: 5,600 shares	
Issued: 3,520 shares	$ 880
Capital surplus*	11,212
Reinvested earnings	53,550
Accumulated other comprehensive income (loss)	(2,703)
Treasury shares, at cost (1,257 shares)	(31,302)
Assume capital surplus is all from issuing common stock above par value.	

Refer to the financial information above to answer the following questions.

Q1 The total amount of financing received from shareholders since incorporation is $ _12092_ million and is generally referred to as _Contributed Capital_. Common stock of the Coca-Cola Company was originally issued (**above** / **at** / **below** / **can't tell**) par at an average price of $ _3.44_ per share.

Q2 When additional shares of common stock are issued, this event will:
- a. (**increase** / decrease / have no effect on) total assets,
- b. (increase / decrease / **have no effect on**) net income,
- c. (**increase** / decrease / have no effect on) stockholders' equity, and
- d. (increase / **decrease** / have no effect on) earnings per share.

Q3 The amount of net income retained in the business and not yet distributed as dividends to the shareholders is $ _53550_ million, which is generally referred to as _retained earnings_.

Q4 Retained earnings (**is** / **is not**) a reservoir of cash available for dividends.

Q5 Treasury stock is considered (**issued** / outstanding / retired) but no longer (issued / **outstanding** / retired). The average price paid for treasury stock is approximately $ _24.90_ per share.

Q6 When a company buys back its own stock, this event will:
- a. (increase / **decrease** / have no effect on) total assets,
- b. (increase / decrease / **have no effect on**) net income,
- c. (increase / **decrease** / have no effect on) stockholders' equity, and
- d. (**increase** / decrease / have no effect on) earnings per share.

Q7 The number of common shares currently *outstanding* is # _2263_ million shares, which represents 100% ownership of the company.

Q8 Total stockholders' equity is $ _31,637_ million, which is the amount of business assets owned by shareholders.

Q9 *List* several factors that would attract you to purchase shares of stock in a particular corporation.

↑ market price
dividends
future potential
reputation

Using the Internet

Purpose:
- Understand how the DJIA is computed.
- Understand the information provided by the DJIA average.

Q1 **Companies comprising the Dow Jones Industrial Average (DJIA).** The DJIA is the most quoted stock market index. On October 1, 1928 the first DJIA was computed using (**10 / 20 / 30**) industrial stocks traded on the New York Stock Exchange. Since then the corporations comprising the index have changed many times to reflect the changing economy. What stocks currently comprise the DJIA? Use the Internet to find out and list 6 of the 30 companies that currently comprise the DJIA.

_____ _____ _____ _____ _____ _____

Q2 **Computing the DJIA.** The index started as a true average of the market values of the stocks comprising the index. In 1928, the sum of the market values of the each of the 30 stocks totaled $6,000 / 30 stocks = 200 DJIA points. However, the average computation needed to be adjusted for stock splits and stock dividends. On May 31, 2012 the market values added together totaled $1,637.54 divided by a divisor of 0.132129493 = DJIA of 12,393 points.

On May 31, 2012 if each of the 30 DJIA stocks increased in value by one dollar per share then the DJIA would increase by approximately 227 points (30/0. 132129493 = 227). On May 31, 2012 assume the DJIA increased by approximately 450 points. This means that on average, each DJIA company would have increased in value by $_____ per share. When the DJIA increases in value, then the majority of stocks traded on the New York Stock Exchange would also be expected to (**increase / decrease**) in value.

Q3 **Historical Summary of the DJIA.** The following chart summarizes the DJIA at various points in history. Using the information presented in the chart, complete the graph outlined below.

Date	DJIA
1928	200
1981	1,000
1986	2,000
1991	3,000
1995	4,000
1996	6,000
1997	8,000
1999	11,000
2002	7,000
2004	10,000
2007 Oct 9	14,164
2008	8,000
2009 March 9	6,547
2011	12,000

```
14,000 |              DJIA

12,000 |

10,000 |

 8,000 |

 6,000 |

 4,000 |

 2,000 |_____
         1928 '38 '48 '58 '68  '81 '91 2001 2006 2011
```

Q4 Use the Internet to find the current DJIA. DJIA closed at _____ points on _____ (date).

Q5 In the chart above, draw a line graph of the DJIA using the historical data above and the current DJIA information you just found.

Q6 Over the years the DJIA has had its ups and downs, but since 1928 the general direction of the DJIA has been (**increasing / decreasing**).
- a.   What is the significance of the trend to investors?
- b.   To the corporations issuing the stock?

Using the Internet

Purpose:
- Follow the stock market quotes for three companies and the Dow Jones Industrial Average (DJIA) for four weeks.
- Understand market value per share.

Q1   Select three publicly traded corporations. For each of the next four weeks record in the chart below the (a) date of the stock information, (b) the closing stock price of the three companies you selected, and (c) the DJIA as of the close (end) of that business day.

Free stock quote information can be found on the Internet at money.msn.com; finance.yahoo.com; and other sites.

Corporation Name	Company #1	Company #2	Company #3	DJIA
WEEK ONE: Closing Market Price on _____ (a)				
WEEK TWO: Closing Market Price on _____				
WEEK THREE: Closing Market Price on _____				
WEEK FOUR: Closing Market Price on _____ (b)				
Four week change in market price (b) - (a)				
Four week % change in market price (b - a) / (a)	%	%	%	%

Q2   At the end of the four weeks complete the following:

a.   Compute the information requested in the bottom two rows of the above chart.

b.   Over the four weeks you observed the DJIA (**increased / stayed the same / decreased**).

c.   Did the stocks you selected move in the same direction as the Dow Jones Industrial Average? (**Yes / No**)

d.   Would you expect your stocks to move in the same direction as the DJIA? (**Yes / No**)

    Why?

e.   Comment on at least two interesting results you noted while following the stock market.

Purpose: •   Analyze profitability, efficiency, and solvency ratios of various companies.

Where's the Cash?

2011	CC*	BBY	WMT	DELL	AAPL
Accounts receivable (A/R) days	10.3	17.0	4.4	38.0	18.1
Inventory days	61.7	57.2	42.0	10.6	4.4

Efficiency Ratios

2011	CC*	BBY	WMT	DELL	AAPL
A/R turnover	35.5	21.4	82.9	9.6	20.2
Inventory turnover	5.9	6.4	8.7	34.4	83.0
Asset turnover	3.1	2.8	2.3	1.4	0.9

DuPont Analysis of ROE

2011	CC*	BBY	WMT	DELL	AAPL
ROS	-2.72%	2.54%	3.89%	5.63%	23.95%
Asset turnover	3.1	2.8	2.3	1.4	0.9
ROA	-8.54%	7.15%	9.07%	7.84%	22.28%
Financial leverage	2.5	2.7	2.6	5.0	1.5
ROE	-21.29%	19.34%	23.91%	39.16%	33.83%
Debt Ratio	59.88%	63.01%	62.06%	79.98%	34.16%

Selected Accounts	CC*	BBY	WMT	DELL	AAPL
($ in Millions)	2/28/2008	2/1/11	1/31/11	1/1/12	9/29/11
Accounts receivable	$ 331	$ 2,348	$ 5,089	$ 6,476	$ 5,369
Inventory	1,574	5,897	36,318	1,404	776
Total assets	3,746	17,849	180,663	44,533	116,371
Total liabilities	2,243	11,247	112,121	35,616	39,756
Stockholders' equity	1,503	6,602	68,542	8,917	76,615
Revenue	11,744	50,272	421,849	62,071	108,249
Cost of goods sold	9,319	37,635	315,287	48,260	64,431
Net income	$ (320)	$ 1,277	$ 16,389	$ 3,492	$25,922

Circuit City (CC)	SIC #5731	Retail—Radio TV and Consumer Electronics Stores
Best Buy (BBY)	SIC #5731	Retail—Radio TV and Consumer Electronics Stores
Wal-Mart (WMT)	SIC #5331	Retail—Variety Stores
Dell (DELL)	SIC #3571	Electronic Computers
Apple (AAPL)	SIC #3571	Electronic Computers

* CC amounts from 2007, the year before the company filed for bankruptcy.

Use the information on the previous page regarding Circuit City (CC), Best Buy (BBY), Wal-Mart (WMT), Dell (DELL), and Apple (AAPL) to answer the following questions.

Q1 Wal-Mart generates profits from a (**high mark up** / **high volume of sales**). What other companies have a low-cost high-volume strategy? (**CC** / **BBY** / **DELL** / **AAPL**) Contributing to CC and BBY's high asset turnover is their high (**accounts receivable** / **inventory**) turnover.

Q2 Inventory turnover is *faster* for (**BBY** / **DELL**) because it assembles the product after the order is received from the customer, thereby needing very little inventory on hand. Whereas inventory turnover is slower for (**BBY** / **DELL**) because inventory sits on the shelf an average of 57.2 days, almost 2 months before it is sold.

Q3 The company with the *strongest* ROA is (**CC** / **BBY** / **WMT** / **DELL** / **AAPL**). The primary driver of ROA for BBY is (**ROS** / **asset turnover**) whereas for AAPL it is (**ROS** / **asset turnover**). Branding of AAPL allows it to charge (**more** / **less**) for its products, resulting in a higher (**ROS** / **asset turnover**).

Q4 The company with the *greatest* financial leverage is (**CC** / **BBY** / **WMT** / **DELL** / **AAPL**), indicating it relies primarily on (**debt** / **equity**) to finance assets. Creditors, those who finance debt, (**do** / **do not**) have ownership rights. Therefore, there are (**more** / **less**) profits for the shareholders, who (**do** / **do not**) have ownership rights.

Q5 The company with the *highest* ROE is (**CC** / **BBY** / **WMT** / **DELL** / **AAPL**). The driver of ROE for Dell is (**ROA** / **financial leverage**), as ROA contributes 7.84 % to ROE, whereas financial leverage contributes 31.32 % to ROE.

Q6 The company with the *weakest* ROE is (**CC** / **BBY** / **WMT** / **DELL** / **AAPL**). Circuit City filed for bankruptcy on November 10, 2008. Impending signs of bankruptcy include weak (**efficiency** / **profitability** / **both**). *How* can you tell?

Q7 Best Buy has its cash tied up in (**accounts receivable** / **inventory**) whereas Dell has its cash tied up in (**accounts receivable** / **inventory**). Which company is managing its cash most efficiently? (**CC** / **BBY** / **WMT** / **DELL** / **AAPL**) *How* can you tell?

Q8 Overall the company with the greatest profitability is (**CC** / **BBY** / **WMT** / **DELL** / **AAPL**). *How* can you tell?

Has the highest net income and the best ratio percentages.

Q9 Of the 5 companies, which one would you choose to invest in? (**CC** / **BBY** / **WMT** / **DELL** / **AAPL**) *Why*? Support your choice by discussing at least 3 good reasons.

-AAPL
1. Has highest net income
2. Better ratios
3. Lowest debt.

Purpose:
- Compare effects of the inventory cost-flow assumptions FIFO and LIFO on the financial statements.
- Compare effects of the depreciation method (SL or DDB) on the financial statements.
- Prepare the income statement, balance sheet, and the statement of cash flows using different accounting methods.
- Understand how the choice of different accounting methods affects cash and accrual accounting.

Frasco and Lasco are virtually identical; both companies began operations at the beginning of the current year and during the year purchased inventory as follows:

Jan 4	10,000	units at $4 =	$ 40,000
Apr 6	10,000	units at $5 =	50,000
Aug 9	10,000	units at $6 =	60,000
Nov 3	10,000	units at $7 =	70,000
	40,000		$220,000

During the first year, both companies **sold 25,000 units** of inventory. **Frasco** uses the first-in, first-out **(FIFO)** method, and **Lasco** uses last-in, first-out **(LIFO)** method for inventory.

In early January both companies **purchased equipment costing $200,000** with a 10-year estimated useful life and no residual value. **Frasco** uses **straight-line** depreciation, and **Lasco** uses **double-declining-balance** depreciation for equipment.

$= \dfrac{Cost - resi}{useful\ lif}$ $\hookrightarrow BooV. x2x \dfrac{1}{usf}$

> Both companies' trial balances at December 31st include the following:
> Sales revenue.. $300,000
> Purchases (see above).. $220,000
> COGS ....compute
> Operating expenses:
>   Depreciation expense..compute
>   Other than depreciation 80,000

200

Use the above information to answer the following questions.

Q1   Prepare a multi-step Income Statement for both companies in the space provided below.

INCOME STATEMENT	FRASCO	LASCO
Sales revenue	300 000	300 000
COGS	120 000	155 000
Operating expenses:	GP 180 000	145 000
Depreciation expense	20 000	40 000
Other	80 000	80 000
Net income	$80,000	25 000

Q2 Assuming all transactions are cash transactions, prepare a Statement of Cash Flows. Also prepare the Supplement Schedule—Indirect Method that reconciles net income and net cash from operating activities.

STATEMENT OF CASH FLOWS	FRASCO	LASCO
Net cash from *operating* activities		
Cash from customers	$ 300,000	$ 800,000
Cash paid to suppliers	220,000	220,000
Cash paid for operating expenses	80,000	80,000
Total net cash from operating activities	0	50,000
Net cash from investing activities		
Cash paid for equipment	(200,000)	(200,000)
Net cash from financing activities		
Issued long-term debt	350,000	350,000
Net change in cash		150,000
+ Beginning cash	0	0
= Ending cash	$ 150,000	$ 150,000

Supplemental Schedule—Indirect Method	FRASCO	LASCO
Net Income	$ 60,000	$ 25,000
+ Depreciation expense		40,000
(Increase) decrease in inventory	20,000 — 10,000	(65,000)
Net cash from operating activities	$ 0	$ 0

Q3 Prepare a Balance Sheet for both companies in the space provided below.

BALANCE SHEET	FRASCO	LASCO
Cash	$ 150,000	$ 150,000
Inventory	100,000	45,000
Equipment	180,000	160,000
Total assets	430,000	375,000
Long-term debt	350,000	350,000
Retained earnings	80,000	25,000
Total liabilities and stockholders' equity	$ 430,000	$ 375,000

Q4 a. Which company appears to be more profitable? (**Frasco / Lasco / the same**)

b. Which company generated more cash during the year? (**Frasco / Lasco / the same**)

c. Which company presents a stronger balance sheet? (**Frasco / Lasco / the same**)

Why?

Q5 On the Income Statement, *why* is net income different for Frasco and Lasco?

Q6 On the balance sheet, which accounts report different amounts?

(**Cash / Inventory / Equipment / Notes payable / Retained earnings**)
Why?

Q7 On the Statement of Cash Flows, which totals differ between Frasco and Lasco?

Net cash from (**operating / investing / financing / none**)

What conclusions can you draw from this Activity?

Q8 Different accounting methods, such as FIFO or LIFO and SL or DDB, affect (**cash- / accrual-**) basis accounting.

CHAPTER 7

THE ACCOUNTING CYCLE

LEARNING OBJECTIVES

1. Describe the 10 steps of the accounting cycle.
2. Analyze transactions using the accounting equation.
3. Prepare journal entries using debits and credits.
4. Post journal entries to the general ledger.
5. Prepare a trial balance.
6. Prepare adjusting journal entries and understand why they are made.
7. Prepare closing journal entries and understand the closing process.
8. Understand how specific events and transactions affect the financial statements.

INTRODUCTION

For literally thousands of years, accountants have been recording, classifying, and reporting transactions. The Biblical book of Exodus accounts for items donated to and used for the building of the tabernacle in the desert. Egyptian hieroglyphics recount the collection and distribution of grain. By 1494, in Renaissance Venice, the Franciscan friar Luca Pacioli authored *Summa de Arithmetica, Geometria, Proportioni et Proportionalita*, a mathematical treatise that explains how to keep financial records and prepare an income statement and balance sheet.

In this chapter, we will give a brief introduction to the accounting cycle, explaining how to record, classify, and report transactions. This chapter was written with you in mind—it was designed not only for the future accountant, but also for all business people who will one day work with accountants.

THE 10-STEP ACCOUNTING CYCLE

How does the accounting system gather data and convert this data into useful information? Through the use of accounts, journals, and ledgers.

Accounts are used to classify and record economic events and transactions. Accounts appear in financial statements as line items, such as "cash," "accounts receivable," "accounts payable," "sales revenue," and "income tax expense." Accountants typically number accounts. A financial statement line item can be broken down into several accounts, in order to keep more detailed records.

A **Chart of Accounts** is a list of all accounts used by a company.

A **Journal** is a book listing the accounts affected by each transaction recorded by a company. In a computer program, it is a database of transactions. To record a journal entry, simply list the accounts affected, and whether each account is increased or decreased.

A **Ledger** is a book with one page for each account, keeping track of the balance or amount in each account. A computer program would typically set up a general ledger as a database.

The goal of the accounting system is to transform a list of transactions into financial statements.

THE GOAL (Transactions) ⟹ (Financial Statements)

This is accomplished through the 10-Step Accounting Cycle.

THE ACCOUNTING CYCLE

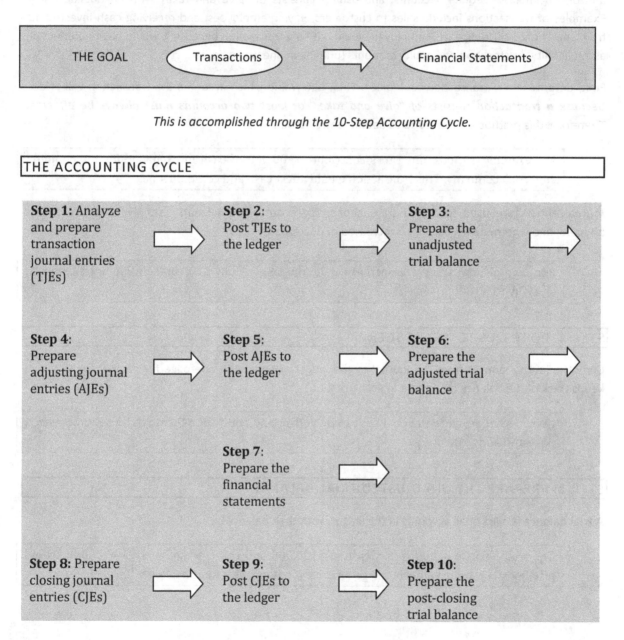

Step 1: Analyze and prepare transaction journal entries (TJEs) ⟹ **Step 2:** Post TJEs to the ledger ⟹ **Step 3:** Prepare the unadjusted trial balance ⟹

Step 4: Prepare adjusting journal entries (AJEs) ⟹ **Step 5:** Post AJEs to the ledger ⟹ **Step 6:** Prepare the adjusted trial balance ⟹

Step 7: Prepare the financial statements ⟹

Step 8: Prepare closing journal entries (CJEs) ⟹ **Step 9:** Post CJEs to the ledger ⟹ **Step 10:** Prepare the post-closing trial balance

STEP 1: ANALYZE AND PREPARE TRANSACTION JOURNAL ENTRIES (TJES)

A **transaction** is an event that affects the financial position of an enterprise; it changes asset, liability, and/or stockholders' equity accounts, and usually consists of "give and take" with an outside party. Examples of transactions include sales to customers, paying employees, and receiving cash investments from shareholders. Hiring a new employee would *not* be a transaction because it would have no effect on asset, liability, or stockholders' equity accounts (until he or she was paid).

First, determine if a transaction took place. Then determine which accounts the transaction will affect. ***Because a transaction consists of "give and take," at least two accounts must always be affected.*** Therefore, this method is referred to as double-entry accounting.

> For example, suppose investors contribute $100,000 of cash in exchange for the common stock of a company. This transaction would affect cash and common stock.

Journal entries are used to record transactions. To record a journal entry, simply list the accounts affected, and whether each account is increased or decreased.

> For example, the above transaction would increase cash by $100,000 and increase common stock by $100,000.

STEP 2: POST TJES TO THE LEDGER

Copy the journal entries from the journal to the ledger, a book with one page for each account, which keeps track of the balance or amount in each account.

> In our example, go to the cash page in the ledger and add $100,000. Go to the common stock page and add $100,000.

STEP 3: PREPARE THE UNADJUSTED TRIAL BALANCE

A **trial balance** is a list of all accounts in the ledger, with their balances.

> The trial balance would report cash of $100,000 and common stock of $100,000. It would also list all other accounts in the general ledger along with their balances.

STEP 4: PREPARE ADJUSTING JOURNAL ENTRIES (AJES)

STEP 5: POST AJES TO THE LEDGER

At the end of the accounting period, accountants adjust accounts to reflect accrued amounts and unrecorded transactions. This entails recording more journal entries, like in Step 2, and posting them to the ledger, as in Step 3.

> For example, suppose that a company owed salaries of $40,000 to employees at the end of the month, but because pay day is Friday, in two days, employees have not yet received their paychecks. Therefore, the company's bookkeeper did not record the transaction. The accountant would record a journal entry that increases wage expense and increases wages payable by $40,000.

STEP 6: PREPARE THE ADJUSTED TRIAL BALANCE

Just as in Step 3, list all accounts in the ledger, with their balances. The difference is that the *adjusted* trial balance includes the adjustments in Step 4.

> The adjusted trial balance includes an additional $40,000 in wage expense and wages payable recorded in Step 5.

STEP 7: PREPARE THE FINANCIAL STATEMENTS

Using the adjusted trial balance from Step 6, the accountant transcribes the accounts listed into an:

- Income Statement,

- Statement of Stockholders' Equity, and

- Balance Sheet.

The accountant also uses information from the financial statements and general ledger to prepare a **Statement of Cash Flows.**

STEP 8: PREPARE CLOSING JOURNAL ENTRIES (CJES)

Record closing journal entries to zero out temporary accounts. **Temporary accounts** are dividends and all accounts appearing on the income statement. These need to be "closed," or zeroed out so that, at the beginning of the year, new amounts for that year can accumulate.

STEP 9: POST CJES TO THE LEDGER

As in Steps 2 and 5, closing entries need to be posted to the ledger.

STEP 10: PREPARE THE POST-CLOSING TRIAL BALANCE

The final trial balance indicates that all temporary accounts (accounts appearing on the income statement and dividends) have been brought down to zero, and **permanent accounts** (balance sheet accounts), are reported at their correct ending balances. This trial balance will take us to the beginning of next year, returning the company to Step 1.

ANALYZE TRANSACTIONS USING THE ACCOUNTING EQUATION

This section uses the transactions of Lincoln's Tax Accounting Corporation (LTAC) to explain how accounting data goes through the accounting cycle. LTAC uses accrual accounting. Initially, these transactions will be organized using the accounting equation, and later recorded using debits and credits in an accounting journal. Revenue, expense, and dividend account data appear in the retained earnings column as Net Income (Revenues - Expenses) increases retained earnings and dividends decrease retained earnings.

A **chart of accounts** is a list of all accounts used by a company. For example:

Lincoln's Tax Accounting Corporation
Chart of Accounts

100	Cash
110	Accounts receivable
200	Notes payable
210	Interest payable
300	Common stock
310	Retained earnings
320	Dividends
400	Revenue
500	Rent expense
510	Salary expense
520	Interest expense
600	Income Summary

TRANSACTION #1: Lincoln's Tax Accounting Corporation started on January 1, 2010, when investors contributed $20,000 in cash in exchange for the common stock of LTAC.

The issuance of stock for cash affects the company's assets (cash) and its stockholders' equity (common stock). This transaction would increase cash by $20,000 and increase common stock by $20,000.

Assets		=	Liabilities		+	Stockholders' Equity	
Cash	Other Assets	Notes Payable	Other Liabilities		Common Stock	Retained Earnings
+20,000					+20,000	

TRANSACTION #2: LTAC borrowed $10,000 from the bank. The signed promissory note states that the amount borrowed is due January 1, 2011, one year from now.

The signing of a note for cash affects the company's assets (cash) and its liabilities (notes payable). This transaction would increase cash by $10,000 and increase notes payable by $10,000.

Assets		=	Liabilities		+	Stockholders' Equity	
Cash	Other Assets	Notes Payable	Other Liabilities		Common Stock	Retained Earnings
+10,000		+10,000				

TRANSACTION #3: During January, LTAC received $80,000 in cash payments from clients for preparing tax returns.

The preparation of tax returns is the primary business activity of Lincoln's Tax Accounting Corporation; therefore, the company has earned $80,000 in revenue. The earning of revenue for cash affects assets (cash) and retained earnings (revenue). This transaction would increase cash by $80,000 and increase revenue by $80,000, thus increasing net income by $80,000, which in turn, increases retained earnings and stockholders' equity.

Assets		=	Liabilities		+	Stockholders' Equity	
Cash	Other Assets	Notes Payable	Other Liabilities		Common Stock	Retained Earnings
+80,000						+80,000

<u>TRANSACTION #4</u>: **During January, LTAC billed clients for $25,000 for the preparation of tax returns but has not received payment.**

Again, the preparation of tax returns is the primary business activity of Lincoln's Tax Accounting Corporation; therefore, the company has earned $25,000 in revenue. The earning of revenue on account affects assets (accounts receivable) and retained earnings (revenue), as retained earnings is increased by revenues and decreased by expenses and dividends. This transaction would increase accounts receivable by $25,000 and increase revenue by $25,000.

Assets		=	Liabilities		+	Stockholders' Equity	
Cash	Other Assets	Notes Payable	Other Liabilities		Common Stock	Retained Earnings
	Accounts Receivable +25,000					Revenue +25,000

<u>TRANSACTION #5</u>: **During the month, LTAC paid January rent of $2,000 and paid employees $60,000 in salaries.**

The costs incurred to earn revenues are referred to as expenses. Here, LTAC has paid expenses totaling $62,000. The payment of expenses affects assets (cash) and retained earnings (expenses). This transaction would decrease cash by $62,000 and decrease retained earnings by $62,000, because expenses decrease net income, which in turn decreases retained earnings and stockholders' equity. (Note that the parentheses indicate negative amounts.)

Assets		=	Liabilities		+	Stockholders' Equity	
Cash	Other Assets	Notes Payable	Other Liabilities		Common Stock	Retained Earnings
(62,000)						Rent expense (2,000) Salary expense (60,000)

<u>TRANSACTION #6</u>: **LTAC paid a $3,000 cash dividend to stockholders.**

The payment of a cash dividend affects the company's assets (cash) and retained earnings (dividends). This transaction would decrease cash by $3,000 and decrease retained earnings by $3,000.

Assets		=	Liabilities		+	Stockholders' Equity	
Cash	Other Assets	Notes Payable	Other Liabilities		Common Stock	Retained Earnings
(3,000)						Dividends (3,000)

<u>TRANSACTION SUMMARY</u>: **The business transactions of Lincoln's Tax Accounting Corporation (LTAC) for January are summarized below. Revenue, expense, and dividend account data appear in the retained earnings column.**

Assets		=	Liabilities		+	Stockholders' Equity	
Cash	Other Assets		Notes Payable	Other Liabilities		Common Stock	Retained Earnings
#1 Investors contributed $20,000 in cash in exchange for the common stock of LTAC.							
+20,000						+20,000	
#2 LTAC borrowed $10,000 from the bank and signed a promissory note.							
+10,000			+10,000				
#3 LTAC received cash payments totaling $80,000 from clients for preparing tax returns.							
+80,000							Revenue +80,000
#4 LTAC billed clients for $25,000 for the preparation of tax returns, but have not received payment.							
	Accounts Receivable +25,000						Revenue +25,000
#5 LTAC paid January rent of $2,000 and paid employees $60,000 in salaries.							
(62,000)							Rent Expense (2,000) Salary Expense (60,000)
#6 LTAC paid a $3,000 cash dividend to stockholders.							
(3,000)							Dividends (3,000)
BALANCE in each account at the end of January.							
$45,000	$25,000		$10,000			$20,000	$40,000

Cash $45,000 + A/R $25,000 = N/P $10,000 + Common stock $20,000 + Retained Earnings $40,000

Assets $70,000 = Liabilities $10,000 + Stockholders' Equity $60,000

Note that within each transaction the accounting equation is in balance, and therefore, at the end of January the accounting equation is also in balance. In his treatise on accounting, Luca Pacioli said that a person should never go to sleep until their accounts balance.

To record a large volume of accounts, we use the debit/credit system, which builds off of the accounting equation.

ASSETS = LIABILITIES + STOCKHOLDERS' EQUITY

DEBITS = CREDITS

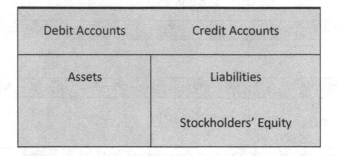

Debit Accounts	Credit Accounts
Assets	Liabilities
	Stockholders' Equity

DEBIT ACCOUNTS		CREDIT ACCOUNTS	
Debit	Credit	Debit	Credit
Increase	Decrease	Decrease	Increase
To increase a debit account, debit it. To decrease a debit account, credit it.		To increase a credit account, credit it. To decrease a credit account, debit it.	

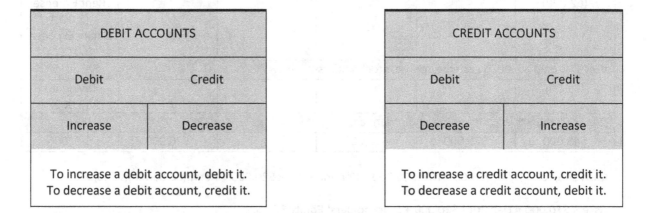

DEBIT ACCOUNTS	CREDIT ACCOUNTS
Assets	Liabilities
Expenses	Stockholders' Equity
Dividends	Revenues

Therefore, to record an increase in cash (an asset), debit it. To record a decrease in cash (an asset), credit it. As an example of a credit account, to record an increase in notes payable (a liability account), credit it. To record a decrease, debit it. In theory, expenses could be subtracted from the credit side. However, to avoid subtraction, we add them to the left side.

Retained Earnings is increased by revenues and decreased by expenses and dividends. Because retained earnings is a stockholders' equity account (a credit account), revenue is also a credit account. Revenue is increased by a credit. Expenses, which reduce net income and stockholders' equity, are increased by debits. Similarly, dividends, which reduce stockholders' equity, are increased by debits.

Forget any notions that "credits are good, debits are bad." Credits represent increases in revenues, but they also represent increases in liabilities. Debits represent increases in expenses, but also represent increases in assets. A more useful intuition is that credits tend to be **sources** of funds, whereas debits usually represent **uses** of funds.

STEP 1: ANALYZE AND PREPARE TRANSACTION JOURNAL ENTRIES (TJES)

We will again use the transactions of Lincoln's Tax Accounting Corporation to explain the accounting cycle. In the last section, to record transactions, we used the accounting equation. In this section, we will instead use debits and credits. The account that is debited should always be listed first. The account that is credited should be indented and listed second. Continue to use the same Chart of Accounts for Lincoln's Tax Accounting Corporation.

TRANSACTION #1: **Lincoln's Tax Accounting Corporation started on January 1, 2010, when investors contributed $20,000 in cash in exchange for the common stock of LTAC.**

Cash is increased by $20,000 ... cash is an asset ... assets are debit accounts ... increased with a debit. Common stock is increased by $20,000 ... common stock is a stockholders' equity (SE) account ... SE are a credit accounts ... increased with a credit.

Date	Accounts	Debit	Credit
Jan 1	Cash	20,000	
	Common stock		20,000

TRANSACTION #2: **LTAC borrowed $10,000 from the bank. The signed promissory note states that the amount borrowed is due January 1, 2011, one year from now.**

Cash is increased by $10,000 ... cash is an asset ... assets are debit accounts ... increased by a debit. Notes payable is increased by $10,000 ... notes payable is a liability ... liabilities are credit accounts ... increased with a credit.

Date	Accounts	Debit	Credit
Jan 1	Cash	10,000	
	Notes Payable		10,000

TRANSACTION #3: **During January, LTAC received $80,000 in cash payments from clients for the preparing tax returns.**

Cash is increased by $80,000 … cash is an asset … assets are debit accounts … increased with a debit. Revenue is increased by $80,000 … revenues increase retained earnings … retained earnings is an SE account … increased with a credit.

Date	Accounts	Debit	Credit
January	Cash	80,000	
	Revenue		80,000

TRANSACTION #4: **During January, LTAC billed clients for $25,000 for the preparation of tax returns, but has not received payment.**

Accounts receivable is increased by $25,000 … accounts receivable is an asset account … assets are debit accounts … increased with a debit. Revenue is increased by $25,000 … revenues increase retained earnings … retained earnings is an SE account … increased with a credit.

Date	Accounts	Debit	Credit
January	Accounts Receivable	25,000	
	Revenue		25,000

TRANSACTION #5: **During the month, LTAC paid January rent of $2,000 and paid employees $60,000 in salaries.**

Cash is decreased by $62,000 … cash is an asset account … assets are debit accounts … decreased with a credit. Rent Expense and Salary Expense decrease retained earnings by $62,000 … retained earnings is an SE account … decreased with a debit.

Date	Accounts	Debit	Credit
January	Rent Expense Salary Expense	2,000 60,000	
	Cash		62,000

TRANSACTION #6: **LTAC paid a $3,000 cash dividend to stockholders.**

Cash is decreased by $3,000 ... cash is an asset ... assets are debit accounts ... decreased with a credit. Dividends decrease retained earnings by $3,000 ... retained earnings is an SE account ... SE accounts are credit accounts ... decreased with a debit.

Date	Accounts	Debit	Credit
Jan 31	Dividends	3,000	
	Cash		3,000

STEP 2: POST TJES TO THE LEDGER

Recall that a **ledger** is a book with one page for each account, to keep track of the balance or amount in each account. **Posting** is copying each of the journal entries to the appropriate ledger account, noting whether the account is debited or credited. A T-account is used to represent each account in the general ledger; each account from the Chart of Accounts for Lincoln's Tax Accounting Corporation. Transactions #1 through #6 have been posted from the journal to the ledger.

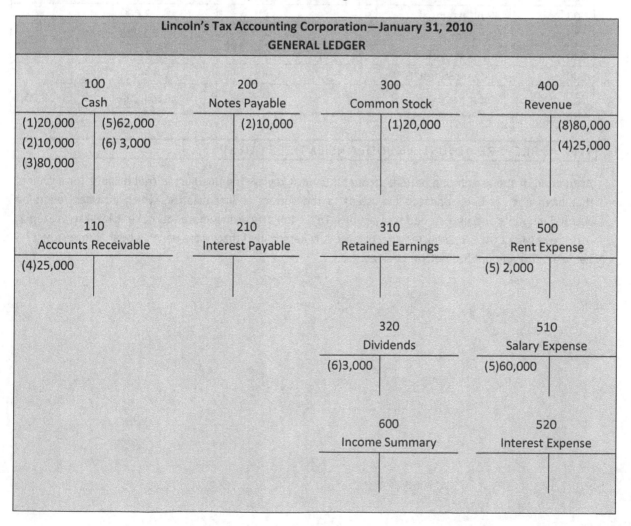

Lincoln's Tax Accounting Corporation—January 31, 2010
GENERAL LEDGER

100 Cash		200 Notes Payable	300 Common Stock	400 Revenue	
(1)20,000	(5)62,000	(2)10,000	(1)20,000		(8)80,000
(2)10,000	(6) 3,000				(4)25,000
(3)80,000					

110 Accounts Receivable	210 Interest Payable	310 Retained Earnings	500 Rent Expense	
(4)25,000			(5) 2,000	

		320 Dividends	510 Salary Expense	
		(6)3,000	(5)60,000	

| | | 600 Income Summary | 520 Interest Expense | |

STEP 3: PREPARE THE UNADJUSTED TRIAL BALANCE

Recall that a **trial balance** is a list of all accounts in the general ledger, with their balances. Below is the unadjusted trial balance for Lincoln's Tax Accounting Corporation. To check the accuracy of the postings, make certain that total debits equal total credits.

No.	Account	Debit	Credit
\multicolumn{4}{c}{**Lincoln's Tax Accounting Corporation—January 31, 2010**}
100	Cash	$ 45,000	
110	Accounts receivable	25,000	
200	Notes payable		$ 10,000
210	Interest payable		
300	Common stock		20,000
310	Retained earnings		
320	Dividends	3,000	
400	Revenue		105,000
500	Rent expense	2,000	
510	Salary expense	60,000	
520	Interest expense		
600	Income summary		
	Total	$135,000	$135,000

STEP 4: PREPARE ADJUSTING JOURNAL ENTRIES (AJES)

At the end of the accounting period, accountants must review the unadjusted trial balance for accounts that have not yet been updated (adjusted) to the correct ending balance, which includes recording accrued amounts and unrecorded transactions. This entails recording more journal entries, like in Step 2. After reviewing LTAC's unadjusted trial balance it is determined that notes payable bears interest of 12% per year. This amount has not yet been accrued.

<u>AJE #1</u>: **LTAC borrowed $10,000 from the bank on January 1, 2010, signed a promissory note due January 1, 2011, bearing 12% interest annually. One month of accrued interest needs to be recorded.**

At the end of January, one month of accrued interest totals $100. (If 12 months of interest totals 12%, then one month of interest is 1%. $10,000 x 1% = $100 of accrued interest. **Principal x Rate x Time = Interest**) Interest expense is increased by $100 ... interest expense decreases retained earnings ... retained earnings is an SE account ... SE accounts are credit accounts ... decreased with a debit. Interest payable (not due until January 1, 2011) is increased ... liabilities are credit accounts ... increased with a credit.

Date	Accounts	Debit	Credit
Jan 31	Interest expense	100	
	Interest payable		100

STEP 5: POST AJES TO THE LEDGER

As in Step 2, post amounts from the journal to the ledger.

Lincoln's Tax Accounting Corporation—January 31, 2010
GENERAL LEDGER

100 Cash	200 Notes Payable	300 Common Stock	400 Revenue
(1)20,000 (5)62,000	(2)10,000	(1)20,000	(8)80,000
(2)10,000 (6) 3,000			(4)25,000
(3)80,000			

110 Accounts Receivable	210 Interest Payable	310 Retained Earnings	500 Rent Expense
(4)25,000	(A1)100		(5) 2,000

	320 Dividends	510 Salary Expense
	(6)3,000	(5)60,000

	600 Income Summary	520 Interest Expense
		(A1)100

STEP 6: PREPARE THE ADJUSTED TRIAL BALANCE

As in Step 3, list all accounts in the general ledger, with their balances. The difference here is that the *adjusted* trial balance includes the adjustments in Step 4, an additional $100 in interest expense and interest payable.

No.	Account	Debit	Credit
	Lincoln's Tax Accounting Corporation—January 31, 2010 **ADJUSTED TRIAL BALANCE**		
100	Cash	$ 45,000	
110	Accounts receivable	25,000	
200	Notes payable		$ 10,000
210	Interest payable		100
300	Common stock		20,000
310	Retained earnings		
320	Dividends	3,000	
400	Revenue		105,000
500	Rent expense	2,000	
510	Salary expense	60,000	
520	Interest expense	100	
600	Income summary		
	Total	$ 135,100	$ 135,100

STEP 7: PREPARE THE FINANCIAL STATEMENTS

Using the adjusted trial balance from Step 6, with all amounts correctly updated, the accountant transcribes the accounts listed into the following financial statements.

(1) Income Statement

(2) Statement of Stockholders' Equity

(3) Balance Sheet

The accountant also uses information from the financial statements and general ledger to prepare a **Statement of Cash Flows.**

Lincoln's Tax Accounting Corporation—January 2010 INCOME STATEMENT		
Revenue		$ 105,000
Operating expenses:		
Rent expense	2,000	
Salary expense	60,000	
Total operating expense		62,000
Operating income		43,000
Nonoperating revenues and expenses:		
Interest expense		(100)
Net income		$ 42,900

Lincoln's Tax Accounting Corporation—January 2010 STATEMENT OF STOCKHOLDERS' EQUITY			
	Common Stock	Retained Earnings	Total SEquity
Balance, January 1, 2010	$ 0	$ 0	$ 0
Stock issued	20,000		20,000
Net income		42,900	42,900
Dividends		(3,000)	(3,000)
Balance, January 31, 2010	$ 20,000	$39,900	$59,900

Lincoln's Tax Accounting Corporation—January 31, 2010 BALANCE SHEET		
ASSETS		
Cash	$ 45,000	
Accounts receivable	25,000	
Total assets		$ 70,000
LIABILITIES		
Notes payable	10,000	
Interest payable	100	
Total liabilities		10,100
STOCKHOLDERS' EQUITY		
Common stock	20,000	
Retained earnings	39,900	
Total stockholders' equity		59,900
Total liabilities & stockholders' equity		$ 70,000

Lincoln's Tax Accounting Corporation—January 2010 STATEMENT OF CASH FLOWS		
CASH FROM OPERATING ACTIVITIES		
Cash from customers	$ 80,000	
Rent paid	(2,000)	
Salaries paid	(60,000)	
Net cash from operating activities		$ 18,000
CASH FROM FINANCING ACTIVITIES		
Cash from issuing a note payable	10,000	
Cash from issuing common stock	20,000	
Dividends paid	(3,000)	
Net cash from financing activities		27,000
Net change in cash		45,000
Beginning cash balance		-0-
Ending cash balance		$ 45,000

STEP 8: PREPARE CLOSING JOURNAL ENTRIES (CJES)

After the financial statements are prepared, the accounts must be made ready for the next accounting period. This means that all temporary accounts (income statement accounts and dividends) must be closed, brought to zero balances, so they are ready to start accumulating amounts during the next accounting period. Permanent (balance sheet) accounts have already been updated to their correct ending balances, which become the beginning balances of the next accounting period.

CJE #1: **Close all revenue and gain accounts to income summary.**

Revenue has a credit balance; therefore, to close it (zero it out), this account must be debited. All revenue and gain accounts are closed to income summary.

Date	Accounts	Debit	Credit
Jan. 31	Revenue	105,000	
	Income Summary		105,000

CJE #2: **Close all expense and loss accounts to income summary.**

Expenses have a debit balance; therefore, to close them (zero them out), these accounts must be credited. All expense and loss accounts are closed to income summary.

Date	Accounts	Debit	Credit
Jan. 31	Income summary	62,100	
	Rent expense		2,000
	Salary expense		60,000
	Interest expense		100

<u>CJE #3</u>: **Close the income summary account to retained earnings.**

After closing all revenue and gain accounts and expenses and loss accounts, Income Summary has a credit balance equal to net income. Therefore, to close Income Summary (zero it out), this account must be debited. Income Summary is closed and Retained Earnings increased by net income.

Date	Accounts	Debit	Credit
Jan. 31	Income Summary	42,900	
	Retained earnings		42,900

<u>CJE #4</u>: **Close the dividends account to retained earnings.**

Dividends are closed and Retained Earnings updated and reduced by the amount of dividends declared during the accounting period. Dividends have a debit balance; therefore, to close dividends (zero it out), this account must be credited.

Date	Accounts	Debit	Credit
Jan. 31	Retained earnings	3,000	
	Dividends		3,000

STEP 9: POST CJES TO THE LEDGER

Lincoln's Tax Accounting Corporation—January 31, 2010
GENERAL LEDGER

100 Cash		200 Notes Payable		300 Common Stock		400 Revenue	
(1)20,000	(5)62,000		(2)10,000		(1)20,000		(8)80,000
(2)10,000	(6) 3,000						(4)25,000
(3)80,000						**(C1)105,000**	
Bal. 45,000							**Bal. 0**

110 Accounts Receivable		210 Interest Payable		310 Retained Earnings		500 Rent Expense	
(4)25,000			(A1)100	**(C4)3,000**	**(C3)42,900**	(5) 2,000	**(C2)2,000**
					Bal. 39,300		**Bal. 0**

320 Dividends		510 Salary Expense	
(6)3,000	**(C4)3,000**	(5)60,000	**(C2)60,000**
Bal. 0			**Bal. 0**

600 Income Summary		520 Interest Expense	
(C2)62,000	**(C1)105,000**	(A1)100	**(C2)100**
	Bal. 42,900		**Bal. 0**
(C3)42,900			
	Bal. 0		

STEP 10: PREPARE THE POST-CLOSING TRIAL BALANCE

The post-closing trial balance shows all temporary accounts with zero balances and permanent accounts with the correct ending balances. The accounts of LTAC are ready to start the next accounting period.

No.	Account	Debit	Credit
\multicolumn{4}{c|}{**Lincoln's Tax Accounting Corporation—January 31, 2010**}			
100	Cash	$ 45,000	
110	Accounts receivable	25,000	
200	Notes payable		$ 10,000
210	Interest payable		100
300	Common stock		20,000
310	Retained earnings		39,900
320	Dividends	-0-	
400	Revenue		-0-
500	Rent expense	-0-	
510	Salary expense	-0-	
520	Interest expense	-0-	
600	Income summary	-0-	
	Total	$ 70,000	$ 70,000

TRANSACTION JOURNAL ENTRIES OF A MERCHANDISE RETAILER

Our example, Lincoln's Tax Accounting Corporation, was a service corporation. What about the transactions of a retailer, which buys and sells inventory? Recording the sale of merchandise involves four different accounts. Two of the accounts, sales revenue and cash (or accounts receivable), record the amount paid by the customer at retail. The other two accounts record the amount paid by the retailer to the supplier, cost of goods sold and merchandise inventory. The difference between sales revenue (amount at retail) and cost of goods sold (amount at wholesale) is gross profit, the amount of profit or markup on the goods sold.

Pirate Company, a costume retailer, sold merchandise that cost $3,000 for cash of $5,000.

Date	Accounts	Debit	Credit
Feb 1	Cash	5,000	
	Sales revenue		5,000
	Cost of goods sold	3,000	
	Merchandise inventory		3,000

Suppose that, prior to this entry, Pirate Company had $12,000 in cash and $17,000 in merchandise inventory.

Cash		Sales Revenue	
Bal. 10,000			
5,000			5,000

Merchandise Inventory		Cost of Goods Sold	
Bal. 17,000	3,000	3,000	

When assets are used to produce revenue, an asset is reduced (merchandise inventory) and an expense (cost of goods sold) is increased. The asset is "moved" to the income statement. The reduction in the asset indicates the asset has been used to help produce revenue. This reduction will equal the amount of the expense.

MORE ADJUSTING JOURNAL ENTRIES

Adjusting journal entries (AJEs) are made at the end of the accounting period to update account balances before preparing the financial statements. The adjusting process consists of four steps:

1. Review the unadjusted trial balance for accounts that need to be updated.
2. Determine the appropriate ending balance for each account that needs to be updated.
3. Determine the required increase or decrease to achieve the appropriate ending balance.
4. Make the adjusting journal entry.

AJE #2: The company did not pay its employees until February 3 for their work on January 29, 30, and 31. Employees earn $200 per day. The ending balance in salaries payable should be $600 (3 days x $200 per day.

Date	Accounts	Debit	Credit
Jan. 31	Salary expense	600	
	Salaries payable		600

Salaries Payable		Salary Expense	
	-0-	5,600	
	600 (A2)	(A2) 600	
	600 Bal.	Bal. 6,200	

AJE #3: **The company's $3,600 insurance policy covers a 12-month time period. January has now passed and only 11 months remain.** The company has consumed one month's worth of insurance, costing $300 ($3,600 / 12 months). This $300 asset is moved to the income statement, as an expense. The ending balance of $3,300 represents the remaining 11 months (11 months x $300 per month) of prepaid insurance premiums.

Date	Accounts	Debit	Credit
Jan. 31	Insurance expense	300	
	Prepaid insurance		300

Prepaid Insurance		Insurance Expense	
3,600			
	300 (A3)	(A3) 300	
Bal. 3,300		Bal. 300	

AJE #4: **Pirate Company's truck, costing $20,000, has a five-year, or 60-month life, and a residual value of $1,400. Depreciate one month using straight-line depreciation.** Accumulated depreciation is called a contra-asset account, because it is a "negative asset."

> **(Cost - Residual value) / Estimated useful life = Depreciation Expense**
> **(20,000 - 1,400) / 60 = $310**

The journal entry to record depreciation expense is always the same:

Date	Accounts	Debit	Credit
Jan. 31	Depreciation expense	310	
	Accumulated depreciation		310

Truck		Accumulated Depreciation		Depreciation Expense	
60,000					
		310 (A4)		(A4) 310	
Bal. 60,000		310 Bal.		Bal. 310	

<u>AJE #5</u>: **The company counted $500 worth of unused office supplies in its supply closet. The company had originally purchased $1,200 in supplies.** The company has used $700 ($1,200 - 500) worth of supplies.

Date	Accounts	Debit	Credit
Jan. 31	Office supplies expense	700	
	Office supplies		700

Office Supplies		Office Supplies Expense	
1,200			
	700 (A5)	(A5) 700	
Bal. 500		Bal. 700	

SUMMARY

The accounting system gathers data and converts it into financial statements through the 10-step accounting cycle.

Step 1: Analyze and Prepare Transaction Journal Entries (TJEs)—First, determine if the event changed an asset, liability, or stockholders' equity account. If it did, it is a **transaction** that is recorded in the **journal,** a book listing transactions in chronological order using debits and credits. Assets, Expenses, and Dividends are debit accounts, increased with a debit and decreased with a credit. Liabilities, Stockholders' Equity, and Revenues are credit accounts, increased with a credit and decreased with a debit.

Recording the sale of merchandise involves four different accounts: Sales Revenue and Cash (or accounts receivable) to record the price paid by the customer and Cost of Goods Sold and Merchandise Inventory to record the amount paid to the supplier. The difference between sales revenue (amount at retail) and cost of goods sold (amount at wholesale) is gross profit.

Step 2: Post TJEs to the Ledger—Copy the journal entries from the journal to the **ledger,** a book with one page for each account, which tracks the balance.

Step 3: Prepare the Unadjusted Trial Balance—The trial balance is a list of all accounts in the general ledger with their balances.

Step 4: Prepare Adjusting Journal Entries (AJEs)—At the end of the accounting period, accountants adjust accounts to reflect accrues amounts and unrecorded transactions.

Step 5: Post AJEs to the Ledger—Like in Step 2, post amounts from the journal to the ledger.

Step 6: Prepare the Adjusted Trial Balance—Like in Step 3, list each account balance in a trial balance.

Step 7: Prepare the Financial Statements using amounts from the Adjusted Trial Balance.

Step 8: Prepare Closing Journal Entries (CJEs)—After the financial statements are prepared, zero out or close the temporary accounts, all income statement accounts and dividends, so that amounts for coming year can accumulate.

Step 9: Post CJEs to the Ledger—Like in Step 2, post amounts from the journal to the ledger.

Step 10: Prepare the Post-Closing Trial Balance—Like in Step 3, list each account balance in a trial balance.

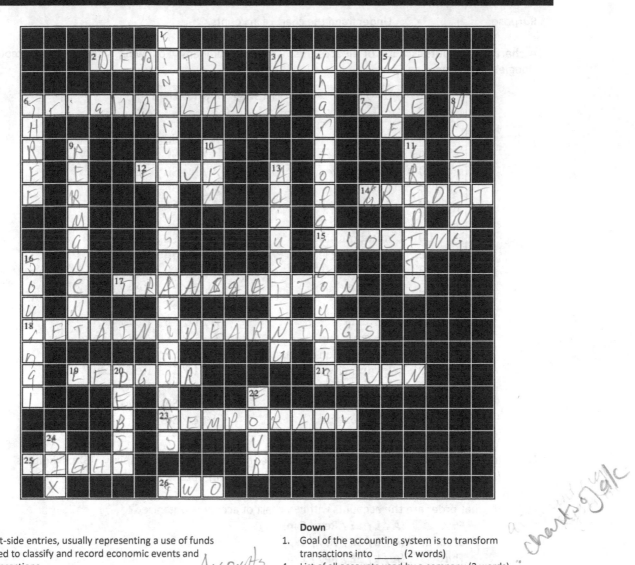

Across

2. Left-side entries, usually representing a use of funds
3. Used to classify and record economic events and transactions
6. List of all ledger accounts and their balances (2 words)
7. Step _____ Analyzing and Preparing Transaction Journal Entries (TJEs)
12. Step _____ Posting AJEs to the Ledger
14. The inventory account is decreased with a _____
15. Journal entries bringing all temporary accounts to a zero balance
17. Event changing an asset, liability, or stockholders' equity account
18. Account increased by revenues and decreased by expenses and dividends (2 words)
19. Database of accounts, keeping track of the balance in each
21. Step _____ Preparing the Financial Statements using amounts from the Adjusted Trial Balance
23. Accounts including all income statement accounts and dividends
25. Step _____ Preparing Closing Journal Entries (CJEs) that zero out all temporary accounts
26. Step _____ Posting TJEs to the Ledger

Down

1. Goal of the accounting system is to transform transactions into _____ (2 words)
4. List of all accounts used by a company (3 words)
5. Step _____ Posting CJEs to the Ledger
6. Step _____ Preparing the Unadjusted Trial Balance
8. Copying journal entries to the ledger, noting debit or credit
9. Accounts where ending balances become beginning balances of the next accounting period
10. Step _____ Preparing the Post-Closing Trial Balance
11. Debits must always equal _____
13. Journal entries generally affecting one income statement account and one balance sheet account; never cash
16. Chronological listing of all transactions
20. The sales revenue account is closed using a _____
22. Step _____ Preparing Adjusting Journal Entries (AJEs) at the end of the accounting period
24. Step _____ Preparing the Adjusted Trial Balance

accrual — cash transaction takes before ~~cash~~ to ~~record~~ recorded.

Purpose: •   Understand the chart of accounts.

A **chart of accounts** is a list of all accounts used by a company. Following is the chart of accounts for Doogie's Dog Grooming Corporation.

Doogie's Dog Grooming Corporation Chart of Accounts		
100	Cash	(**A** / L / SE / Rev / Exp)
110	Accounts receivable	(**A** / L / SE / Rev / Exp)
120	Supply inventory	(**A** / L / SE / Rev / Exp)
130	Equipment	(**A** / L / SE / Rev / Exp)
140	Accumulated depreciation	(**A** / L / SE / Rev / Exp)
150	Prepaid insurance	(**A** / L / SE / Rev / Exp)
200	Accounts payable	(A / **L** / SE / Rev / Exp)
210	Rent payable	(A / **L** / SE / Rev / Exp)
220	Wages payable	(A / **L** / SE / Rev / Exp)
300	Common stock	(A / L / **SE** / Rev / Exp)
350	Retained earnings	(A / L / **SE** / Rev / Exp)
360	Dividends	(A / L / **SE** / Rev / Exp)
400	Revenue	(A / L / SE / **Rev** / Exp)
500	Depreciation expense	(A / L / SE / Rev / **Exp**)
510	Insurance expense	(A / L / SE / Rev / **Exp**)
520	Rent expense	(A / L / SE / Rev / **Exp**)
530	Supply expense	(A / L / SE / Rev / **Exp**)
540	Wage expense	(A / L / SE / Rev / **Exp**)

Q1   Identify each of the above accounts as either a(n) (A)sset, (L)iability, (S)tockholders' (E)quity, (Rev)enue, or (Exp)ense account by circling the appropriate response.

Q2   In what order are the accounts within a chart of accounts organized?
   First   (**A** / L / SE / Rev / Exp)
   Second   (A / **L** / SE / Rev / Exp)
   Third   (A / L / **SE** / Rev / Exp)
   Fourth   (A / L / SE / **Rev** / Exp)
   Last   (A / L / SE / Rev / **Exp**)

Q3   Within Doogie's Chart of Accounts, account numbers for:
   a.   (A)sset accounts.........start with (**100** / 200 / 300 / 400 / 500)
   b.   (L)iability accounts.....start with (100 / **200** / 300 / 400 / 500)
   c.   (SE)quity accounts......start with (100 / 200 / **300** / 400 / 500)
   d.   (Rev)enue accounts ...start with (100 / 200 / 300 / **400** / 500)
   e.   (Exp)ense accounts ....start with (100 / 200 / 300 / 400 / **500**)

Q4   Within Doogie's Chart of Accounts the account numbers increase by (ones / **tens**) so that additional accounts can be easily added. For example, if the company received a utility bill, the most appropriate account number for *utilities payable* would be (**201** / 230) and for *utilities expense* would be (160 / **230** / 370 / 410 / 550).

Purpose: • Analyze transactions and events using the accounting equation.

Q1   A **transaction** is an event that affects the financial position of an enterprise; it changes an asset (A), liability (L), or stockholders' equity (SE) account. A company is not liable for payment of supplies until the supplies (**are ordered** / **arrive**). Therefore, an order (**is** / **is not**) a transaction and (**is** / **is not**) recorded. Because the arrival of supplies increases an asset and creates a liability this event (**is** / **is not**) a transaction and (**is** / **is not**) recorded.

Q2   Because a transaction consists of *"give and take,"* at least (**one** / **two** / **three**) accounts are always affected. Therefore, this method is referred to as (**the give-'n-take method** / **double-entry accounting**).

Q3   "Investors contribute $30,000 of cash in exchange for the common stock of a company" (**is** / **is not**) a transaction that affects (**cash** / **accounts receivable**) and (**retained earnings** / **common stock**). Cash is a(n) (**A** / **L** / **SE**) account that would (**increase** / **decrease**) by $30,000. Common stock is a(n) (**A** / **L** / **SE**) account that would (**increase** / **decrease**) by $30,000.

Q4   Revenue, expense, and dividend account data are recorded in the Retained Earnings column. Retained earnings is increased by (**net income** / **dividends**) and decreased by (**net income** / **dividends**). Therefore, "Doogie's provided dog grooming services for $20,000 cash" is a transaction that affects (**cash** / **accounts receivable**) and (**revenue** / **expense**). Because revenue (**increases** / **decreases**) net income and net income (**increases** / **decreases**) (**retained earnings** / **common stock**), the revenue portion of this transaction is listed under the Retained Earnings column.

Q5   Doogie's Dog Grooming Corporation started business in July. The chart on the following page lists eight events that occurred during July for Doogie's. For each transaction, indicate which accounts increased or decreased and identify the amount and account title under the appropriate heading. If an event is not a transaction, record "No Transaction." In the Retained Earnings column record revenue, expense, and dividend account data. Use the Chart of Accounts on the previous page. Transaction #1 is completed for you.

Q6   For each of the six columns in the chart, compute the ending balance for July and record in the bottom row of the chart.

Q7   For each balance sheet classification listed below, compute the ending balance for July.

   a.   Total assets $ 47,300

   b.   Total liabilities $ 1,200

   c.   Total stockholders' equity $ 46,100

Q8   Is the accounting equation in balance at the end of July? (**Yes** / **No**)

Doogie's Dog Grooming Corporation TRANSACTIONS—July				
ASSETS	**=**	**LIABILITIES +**	**STOCKHOLDERS' EQUITY**	
Cash	Other Assets	Accounts Payable	Common Stock	Retained Earnings
#1 July 1 Doogie's Dog Grooming Corporation began by issuing 1,000 shares of common stock in exchange for $30,000 cash.				
+ 30,000			+ 30,000	
#2 July 1 Doogie purchased a grooming table and other equipment for $18,000 cash.				
-18000	equip. +18000			
#3 July 1 Doogie purchased a one-year insurance policy for $2,400 cash.				
-2400	Prepaid insurance + 2,400			
#4 July 1 Doogie ordered doggie treats and other supplies totaling $1,200.				
		No Trans.		
#5 July 6 The doggie treats and other supplies arrived along with a bill for $1,200.				
	supply Inv. +1200	(+)1200		
#6 July Doogie's provided dog grooming services for $20,000 cash.				
+20000		2 3		Revenue + 20,000
#7 July 31 Doogie paid employee wages of $2,000 and rent of $1,500 for July.				
-3500				wage exp. -2,000 Rent Exp. (1,500)
#8 July 31 Doogie paid a $400 cash dividend to shareholders.				
(400)				Div. Paid (400)
Compute the BALANCE in each account at the end of July.				
25,700	21,600	1,200	30,000	16,100

Q9   Transaction #6 affects (1 / 2 / 3) accounts and is referred to as a ((double) / compound) entry, whereas Transaction #7 affects (1 / 2 / 3) accounts and is referred to as a (double / compound) entry.

more than 2

Right

Purpose:
- Prepare journal entries using debits and credits.
- Post transaction journal entries to the general ledger.
- Prepare an unadjusted trial balance.

To record a large volume of accounts, we use the debit/credit system, which builds off of the accounting equation.

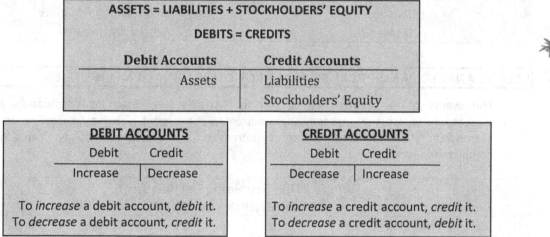

ASSETS = LIABILITIES + STOCKHOLDERS' EQUITY

DEBITS = CREDITS

Debit Accounts	Credit Accounts
Assets	Liabilities
	Stockholders' Equity

DEBIT ACCOUNTS

Debit	Credit
Increase	Decrease

To *increase* a debit account, *debit* it.
To *decrease* a debit account, *credit* it.

CREDIT ACCOUNTS

Debit	Credit
Decrease	Increase

To *increase* a credit account, *credit* it.
To *decrease* a credit account, *debit* it.

Q1 When amounts are correct, the accounting equation, Assets = Liabilities + Stockholders' Equity, (**will** / **will not**) always be in balance. Similarly, Debits (**will** / **will not**) always equal Credits.

Q2 Assets are (**debit** / **credit**) accounts, which are increased with a (**debit** / **credit**) and decreased with a (**debit** / **credit**). Whereas liabilities and stockholders' equity are (**debit** / **credit**) accounts, which are increased with a (**debit** / **credit**) and decreased with a (**debit** / **credit**).

Q3 Cash is a(n) (**A** / **L** / **SE**) account, which is a (**debit** / **credit**) account, which is increased with a (**debit** / **credit**). Therefore, to record an increase of $30,000 in cash, the journal entry should (**debit** / **credit**) cash.

Q4 Common stock is a(n) (**A** / **L** / **SE**) account, which is a (**debit** / **credit**) account, which is increased with a (**debit** / **credit**). Therefore, to record an increase of $30,000 in common stock, the journal entry should (**debit** / **credit**) stockholders' equity.

ASSETS = LIABILITIES + **STOCKHOLDERS' EQUITY**

STOCKHOLDERS' EQUITY = COMMON STOCK + **RETAINED EARNINGS**

Beginning RETAINED EARNINGS + NET INCOME - DIVIDENDS = Ending **RETAINED EARNINGS**

Beginning R/E + (REVENUE - EXPENSES) - DIVIDENDS = Ending **RETAINED EARNINGS**

Debit Accounts	Credit Accounts
Expenses	*Stockholders' Equity*
Dividends	Revenue

Q5 Retained Earnings is increased by net income (revenues - expenses) and decreased by dividends. Hence, revenues (**increase** / **decrease**) retained earnings whereas expenses and dividends (**increase** / **decrease**) retained earnings.

Q6   Retained Earnings is a Stockholders' Equity account. Because revenue increases stockholders' equity, revenue is recorded with a (**debit / credit**). Because expenses and dividends decrease stockholders' equity, they are recorded with a (**debit / credit**). In summary, revenue is increased with a credit and expenses and dividends are increased with a debit.

Debit Accounts	Credit Accounts
Assets	Liabilities
Expenses	Stockholders' Equity
Dividends	Revenues

STEP 1: ANALYZE AND PREPARE TRANSACTION JOURNAL ENTRIES (TJES)

Q7   The events below occurred during July for Doogie's Dog Grooming Corporation. For each transaction, record the appropriate journal entry. If an event is not a transaction, record "No Transaction." Use the Chart of Accounts introduced in the previous Activity. Transaction #1 is completed for you.

<table>
<tr><th colspan="4">Doogie's Dog Grooming Corporation
GENERAL JOURNAL—JULY</th></tr>
<tr><th>Date</th><th>Accounts</th><th>Debit</th><th>Credit</th></tr>
<tr><td>TJE #1 July 1</td><td colspan="3">Doogie's Dog Grooming Corporation began by issuing 1,000 shares of common stock in exchange for $30,000 cash.</td></tr>
<tr><td>July 1</td><td>Cash</td><td>30,000</td><td></td></tr>
<tr><td></td><td>Common stock</td><td></td><td>30,000</td></tr>
<tr><td>TJE #2 July 1</td><td colspan="3">Doogie purchased a grooming table and other equipment for $18,000 cash.</td></tr>
<tr><td></td><td>table + equipment</td><td>18,000</td><td></td></tr>
<tr><td></td><td>Cash</td><td></td><td>18,000</td></tr>
<tr><td>TJE #3 July 1</td><td colspan="3">Doogie purchased a one-year insurance policy for $2,400 cash.</td></tr>
<tr><td></td><td>Insurance</td><td>2400</td><td></td></tr>
<tr><td></td><td>cash</td><td></td><td>2400</td></tr>
<tr><td>TJE #4 July 1</td><td colspan="3">Doogie ordered doggie treats and other supplies totaling $1,200.</td></tr>
<tr><td></td><td>No entry</td><td></td><td></td></tr>
<tr><td>TJE #5 July 6</td><td colspan="3">The doggie treats and other supplies arrived along with a bill for $1,200.</td></tr>
<tr><td></td><td>Supp
a/c pay</td><td>1200</td><td>1200</td></tr>
<tr><td>TJE #6 July</td><td colspan="3">Doogie's provided dog grooming services for $20,000 cash.</td></tr>
<tr><td>July</td><td>Cash
A/R</td><td>20000</td><td>20000</td></tr>
<tr><td>TJE #7 July 31</td><td colspan="3">Doogie paid employee wages of $2,000 and rent of $1,500 for July.</td></tr>
<tr><td></td><td>Wage Exp.</td><td>2,000</td><td></td></tr>
<tr><td></td><td>Rent expense</td><td>1,500</td><td></td></tr>
<tr><td></td><td>Cash</td><td></td><td>3,500</td></tr>
<tr><td>TJE #8 July 31</td><td colspan="3">Doogie paid a $400 cash dividend to shareholders.</td></tr>
<tr><td></td><td>Div. Retained Earning</td><td>400</td><td></td></tr>
<tr><td></td><td>Cash Dividend</td><td></td><td>400</td></tr>
</table>

cash

Recall that a **ledger** is a book with one page for each account, keeping track of the balance or amount in each account. **Posting** is copying each of the journal entries to the appropriate ledger account, noting whether the account is debited or credited. A T-account is used to represent each account in the general ledger; each account from the Chart of Accounts for Doogie's Dog Grooming Corporation.

Q8   Post each transaction recorded in the General Journal on the previous page to the General Ledger below, noting whether the account is debited or credited. Transaction #1 is completed for you.

Q9   Compute the ending balance of the cash account below, noting whether the balance is debited or credited.

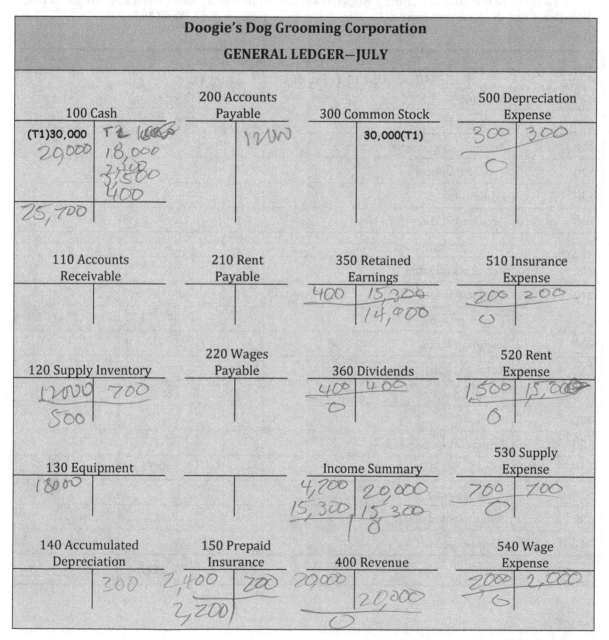

Doogie's Dog Grooming Corporation

GENERAL LEDGER—JULY

A **trial balance** is a list of all accounts in the general ledger, with their debit or credit balances.

Q10 In the unadjusted trial balance below, record the ending balance of each account in the General Ledger of Doogie's Dog Grooming Corporation on the previous page. The ending balance in cash is completed for you.

Q11 Compute total debits and total credits and record in the last row below. Total debits are completed for you.

Q12 As a check to the accuracy of the postings, make certain that total debits equal total credits. If not, please find the error and correct. Do total debits equal total credits? **(Yes / No)**

No.	Account	Debit	Credit
	Doogie's Dog Grooming Corporation **UNADJUSTED TRIAL BALANCE—July 31**		
100	Cash	$25,700	
110	Accounts receivable	-0-	
120	Supply inventory	1,200	
130	Equipment	18,000	
140	Accumulated depreciation		-0-
150	Prepaid insurance	2,400	
200	Accounts payable		1,200
210	Rent payable		-0-
220	Wages payable		-0-
300	Common stock		30,000
350	Retained earnings		-0-
360	Dividends	400	~~20,000~~
400	Revenue		20,000
500	Depreciation expense	-0-	
510	Insurance expense	-0-	
520	Rent expense	1,500	
530	Supply expense	-0-	
540	Wage expense	2,000	
	Total	$51,200	51,200

ACTIVITY 87   DOOGIE'S … STEPS 4, 5, AND 6 USING DEBITS AND CREDITS

Purpose:
- Prepare adjusting journal entries using debits and credits.
- Post adjusting journal entries to the general ledger.
- Prepare an adjusted trial balance.

STEP 4: PREPARE ADJUSTING JOURNAL ENTRIES (AJES)

Q1   At the end of the accounting period, accountants adjust accounts to reflect accrued amounts and unrecorded transactions. This entails recording more journal entries, like in Step 2, and posting them, like in Step 3.

Review the accounts in Doogie's unadjusted trial balance on the previous page. There are three balance sheet accounts that need to be adjusted (updated to the correct ending balance), which are (**cash / supply inventory / accumulated depreciation / prepaid insurance / common stock**). There are (**1 / 2 / 3 / 4**) income statement accounts that need to be adjusted, which are (**revenue / depreciation expense / insurance expense / rent expense / supply expense**).

Q2   Use the information below to prepare general journal entries needed to record the adjustments for Doogie's Dog Grooming Corporation on July 31. The Chart of Accounts for Doogie's is presented in a previous activity.

<table>
<tr><th colspan="4">Doogie's Dog Grooming Corporation
GENERAL JOURNAL—July</th></tr>
<tr><th>Date</th><th>Accounts</th><th>Debit</th><th>Credit</th></tr>
<tr><td colspan="4">AJE #1 Doogie purchased a grooming table and other equipment for $18,000 cash on July 1. This equipment has a five-year life with no residual value. Straight-line depreciation is used. Record depreciation expense for July.</td></tr>
<tr><td>July 31</td><td>Dep^y</td><td>300</td><td></td></tr>
<tr><td></td><td>accumul depⁿ</td><td></td><td>300</td></tr>
<tr><td colspan="4">AJE #2 Doogie purchased a one-year insurance policy for $2,400 cash on July 1. On July 31, one month of insurance coverage has been used. Record insurance expense for July.</td></tr>
<tr><td>July 31</td><td>Insurance exp</td><td>200</td><td></td></tr>
<tr><td></td><td>prepaid exp</td><td></td><td>200</td></tr>
<tr><td colspan="4">AJE #3 Doogie treats and other supplies arrived along with a bill for $1,200 on July 6. On July 31 there were $500 of doggie treats and other supplies remaining. What amount of supplies was used during July? Record supply expense for July.</td></tr>
<tr><td>July 31</td><td>Supply exp</td><td>700</td><td></td></tr>
<tr><td></td><td>Sup. Inv.</td><td></td><td>700</td></tr>
</table>

Balance sheet & Income st

Q3   Post each adjusting journal entry recorded in the General Journal on July 31 for Doogie's Dog Grooming Corporation (on the previous page) to the **General Ledger on Page 241**, noting whether the account is debited or credited.

Q4   After posting adjustments compute the ending balance for Supply Inventory and Prepaid Insurance, recording it as a debit or credit balance in the **General Ledger on Page 241.**

STEP 6: PREPARE THE ADJUSTED TRIAL BALANCE

A **trial balance** is a list of all accounts in the general ledger, with their debit or credit balances.

Just like in Step 3, list all accounts in the general ledger, with their balances. The difference is that the *adjusted* trial balance includes the adjustments in Step 4.

Q5   In the adjusted trial balance below, record the ending balance of each account in the General Ledger of Doogie's Dog Grooming Corporation (Question 4). The ending balance in cash is completed for you.

Q6   Compute total debits and total credits and record below. As a check to the accuracy of the postings, make certain that total debits equal total credits. If not, please find the error and correct. Do total debits equal total credits? **(Yes / No)**

No.	Account	Debit	Credit
	Doogie's Dog Grooming Corporation **ADJUSTED TRIAL BALANCE—July 31**		
100	Cash	$25,700	
110	Accounts receivable	-0-	
120	Supply inventory	500	
130	Equipment		
140	Accumulated depreciation	300	300
150	Prepaid insurance	2400	
200	Accounts payable		
210	Rent payable		-0-
220	Wages payable		-0-
300	Common stock		
350	Retained earnings		-0-
360	Dividends		
400	Revenue		
500	Depreciation expense		
510	Insurance expense		
520	Rent expense		
530	Supply expense		
540	Wage expense		
	Total	$51,500	

Purpose:
- Prepare the financial statements.
- Post transaction journal entries to the general ledger.
- Prepare an unadjusted trial balance.

STEP 7: PREPARE THE FINANCIAL STATEMENTS

Q1   Use the information from Activities 86 and 87 and prepare the:
- a.   Income Statement
- b.   Statement of Stockholders' Equity
- c.   Balance Sheet
- d.   Statement of Cash Flows

Doogie's Dog Grooming Corporation INCOME STATEMENT—July		
Revenue	2000	$
Operating expenses:		
Wage Expense	$ 2,000	
Rent Expense	1500	
Supply Expense	700	
Depreciation Expense	300	
Insurance Expense	200	
Total operating expense		4,700
Net income		$

Doogie's Dog Grooming Corporation STATEMENT OF STOCKHOLDERS' EQUITY—July			
	Common Stock	Retained Earnings	Total SEquity
Balance, July 1	$ -0-	$ -0-	$ -0-
Stock issued	3000		
Net income			
Dividends			
Balance, July 31	$	$	$ 44,900

Doogie's Dog Grooming Corporation BALANCE SHEET—July 31		
ASSETS		
Cash		$
Supply Inventory		
Equipment	$18,000	
Accumulated Depreciation	( )	
Prepaid Insurance		
Total assets		
LIABILITIES		
Accounts Payable		$
STOCKHOLDERS' EQUITY		
Common Stock		
Retained Earnings		
Total liabilities & stockholders' equity		$ 46,100

Doogie's Dog Grooming Corporation STATEMENT OF CASH FLOWS—July		
CASH FROM OPERATING ACTIVITIES		
Cash from customers	$20,000	
Insurance paid	( )	
Rent paid	( )	
Wages paid	( )	
Net cash from operating activities		$ 14,100
CASH FROM INVESTING ACTIVITIES		
Cash used to purchase equipment		( )
CASH FROM FINANCING ACTIVITIES		
Cash from issuing common stock	30,000	
Dividends paid	( )	
Net cash from financing activities		$
Net change in cash		25,700
Beginning cash balance		-0-
Ending cash balance		$

Direct?

Purpose:
- Prepare closing journal entries using debits and credits.
- Post closing journal entries to the general ledger.
- Prepare a post-closing trial balance.

STEP 8: PREPARE CLOSING JOURNAL ENTRIES (CJES)

Q1 Record closing journal entries that zero out temporary accounts. **Temporary accounts** include all income statement accounts and dividends. These need to be zeroed out or closed so that, at the beginning of the year, new amounts for that year can accumulated.

Date	Accounts	Debit	Credit
Doogie's Dog Grooming Corporation **GENERAL JOURNAL—July**			
CJE #1	Close all revenue and gain accounts to income summary.		
July 31	Revenue	20,000	
	Income Summary		20,000
CJE #2	Close all expense and loss accounts to income summary.		
July 31			
	Rent Expense		1,500
CJE #3	Close the income summary account to retained earnings.		
July 31	Income Summary	15,300	
CJE #4	Close the dividends account to retained earnings.		
July 31			

STEP 9: POST CJES TO THE LEDGER

Closing Entries are journal entries, like in Steps 2 and 5, which need to be posted to the general ledger.

Q2 Post each closing journal entry recorded in the General Journal on July 31 for Doogie's Dog Grooming Corporation (on the previous page) to the **General Ledger on Page 241,** noting whether the account is debited or credited.

Q3 After posting closing entries compute the ending balances, recording as a debit or credit balance in the **General Ledger on Page 241.**

One last trial balance, this one shows that all temporary accounts (accounts appearing on the income statement and dividends) have been brought down to zero, and **permanent accounts** (balance sheet accounts), are reported at their correct ending balances. This trial balance will start the next year, returning the company to Step 1.

	Doogie's Dog Grooming Corporation POST-CLOSING TRIAL BALANCE—July 31		
No.	Account	Debit	Credit
100	Cash	$25,700	$
110	Accounts receivable	-0-	
120	Supply inventory		
130	Equipment		
140	Accumulated depreciation		
150	Prepaid insurance		
200	Accounts payable		
210	Rent payable		-0-
220	Wages payable		-0-
300	Common stock		
350	Retained earnings		
360	Dividends		
400	Revenue		
500	Depreciation expense		
510	Insurance expense		
520	Rent expense		
530	Supply expense		
540	Wage expense		
	Total	$	$ 46,400

Purpose:
- Analyze merchandising transactions.
- Prepare journal entries using debits and credits.
- Understand how merchandising transactions affect the income statement and the balance sheet.

Recording the sale of merchandise involves four different accounts. Two of the accounts, **sales revenue** and **cash** (or **accounts receivable**), record the amount paid by the customer at retail. The other two accounts record the amount paid by the retailer to the supplier, **cost of goods sold** and **merchandise inventory.** The difference between sales revenue (amount at retail) and cost of goods sold (amount at wholesale) is gross profit, the amount of profit or markup on the goods sold.

Q1   Prepare general journal entries for the following transactions.

Date	Accounts	Debit	Credit
\multicolumn{4}{c}{**Scott King's Sporting Goods Retailer**}		
\multicolumn{4}{c}{**GENERAL JOURNAL—AUGUST**}		
TJE #1 Aug 1	Sold 2,000 shares of no-par common stock for cash of $12,000.		
Aug 1	**Cash**	**12,000**	
	Common stock		**12,000**
TJE #2 Aug 3	Purchased store equipment for $3,000 cash.		
	E	3	
	C		3
TJE #3 Aug 3	Purchased merchandise inventory on account for $9,000.		
	m	9	
	a/c		9
TJE #4 Aug 10	Sold merchandise that cost $3,000 for $5,000 in cash.		
	cash	5000	
	S-rev.	5000	5000
	cost y goods sold	3000	
	Merchandise Inventory		**3,000**
TJE #5 Aug 30	Sold merchandise that cost $2,000 for $4,000 on account.		
	a/c rec.	4000	
	sales rev.		4000
	cost of goods	2000	
	mch.		2000
TJE #6 Aug 30	Paid August salaries of $1,500.		
	wages	1500	
	cash		1500

Q2   The general ledger reported $10,000 as the August 1 balance for cash. On August 31, the general ledger would report cash of $ _25000_ .

Q3   The August Income Statement would report Sales Revenue of $(**4,000 / 5,000 / 9,000**), Cost of Goods Sold of $(**2,000 / 3,000 / 5,000**), and Operating Expenses totaling $(**1,500 / 3,500 / 6,500**).

Q3   The August income statement would report gross profit of $_____ and net income of $_____.

Purpose:
- Analyze adjusting journal entries.
- Prepare adjusting journal entries using debits and credits.

Q1   Prepare general journal entries to record the adjustments below as of December 31, 2012 for the Perry Corporation.

| \multicolumn{4}{c}{**Perry Corporation**} | | | |

| \multicolumn{4}{c}{**GENERAL JOURNAL—2012**} | | | |

Date	Accounts	Debit	Credit
\multicolumn{4}{l}{AJE #1 The accountant completed the depreciation schedule for 2012, which showed total depreciation expense of \$10,520 for the year. The depreciation expense account already has a balance of \$8,500. Record the remaining depreciation expense for the year.}			
Dec 31	Dep^n exp		
	accum. ~~ext~~ dep.		2,020
\multicolumn{4}{l}{AJE #2 Commissions for December of \$22,000 will be paid to Perry's sales staff on January 5, 2013. The commissions payable account has a zero balance. Record commission expense for December.}			
	com ~~exp~~		
	com payable		
\multicolumn{4}{l}{AJE #3 The company loaned \$20,000 to a customer on July 1, 2012 for one year at 8% interest. The customer will pay the principal and interest on the loan on June 30 of next year. No interest in connection with this loan has been recorded. Record interest revenue for the year.}			
	Interest exp	800	
	Interest		
\multicolumn{4}{l}{AJE #4 On July 1, 2012 Perry paid an entire year's rent of \$14,000 for a warehouse, which the bookkeeper recorded as Prepaid Rent. Record rent expense for 2012.}			

$20000 × 8\% × \frac{6}{12}$

Q2   Review the adjusting journal entries (AJEs) above. Identify each journal entry account as either a balance sheet account or an income statement account. In total there are (**3 / 4 / 5**) balance sheet accounts and (**3 / 4 / 5**) income statement accounts. Each AJE includes (**1 / 2 / 3**) balance sheet accounts and (**1 / 2 / 3**) income statement account and (**always / sometimes / never**) includes the cash account.

Q3   Prepare part of the December 31, 2012 adjusted trial balance for the expense accounts below.

| \multicolumn{4}{c}{**ADJUSTED TRIAL BALANCE—Dec 31, 2012**} | | | |

No.	Account	Debit	Credit
400	Interest revenue	800	
500	Depreciation expense	10,520	
510	Commission expense	22,000	
520	Rent expense	7,000	

Purpose: • Prepare an adjusted trial balance.

The following account information from Lelescu Corporation's adjusted trial balance at December 31 is arranged in alphabetical order by account:

Accounts Receivable	$18,000
Accounts Payable	7,000
Accumulated Depreciation, Equipment	3,000
Additional Paid-in Capital	31,000
Cash	9,000
Common Stock	5,000
Cost of Goods Sold	11,000
Dividends	2,000
Equipment	22,000
Loss on Sale of Equipment	5,800
Interest Expense	100
Inventory	5,000
Notes Payable	4,100
Retained Earnings, beginning	4,000
Sales Revenue	20,000
Supply Expense	1,200

Required: Prepare an adjusted trial balance in proper form using the above information.

Lelescu Corporation		
ADJUSTED TRIAL BALANCE—December 31		
Account	Debit	Credit
Cash	$ 9,000	$
Accounts Payable		7,000
Sales Revenue		20,000
Total	$ 74,100	

Purpose: • Prepare closing entries.

The following account information from Oza Corporation's adjusted trial balance at December 31 is arranged in alphabetical order by account:

Accounts Receivable	$18,000
Accounts Payable	7,000
Accumulated Depreciation, Equipment	3,000
Additional Paid-in Capital	31,000
Cash	9,000
Common Stock	5,000
Cost of Goods Sold	11,000
Dividends	2,000
Equipment	22,000
Interest Expense	100
Inventory	5,000
Loss on Sale of Equipment	5,800
Notes Payable	4,100
Retained Earnings, beginning	4,000
Sales Revenue	20,000
Supply Expense	1,200

Q1   Prepare closing entries for year-end.

Oza Corporation GENERAL JOURNAL			
Date	Accounts	Debit	Credit
CJE #1 Close all revenue and gain accounts to income summary.			
Dec 31	Sales Rev.	20,000	
	Income Summary		**20,000**
CJE #2 Close all expense and loss accounts to income summary.			
	Income Summary	18,100	
	COGS		11,000
	Supp. Exp.		1,200
	Int. Exp		100
	Loss on Sale of Equipment		**5,800**
CJE #3 Close the income summary account to retained earnings.			
	Income Summary	1,900	
	Ret. Earnings		1,900
CJE #4 Close the dividends account to retained earnings.			
	Ret. Earnings	2,000	
	Div.		2,000

Q2   Retained earnings on the December 31 Balance Sheet will report $[(100) / 3,900 / 4,000 / 5,900].

Purpose: •   Comprehensive review the 10-step accounting cycle—Year 1.

Nancy Nanny opened a child-care facility on January 1, Year 1. Use the Chart of Accounts below to complete the requirements on the following pages for Nancy Nanny Child Care.

NANCY NANNY CHILD CARE

CHART OF ACCOUNTS

110	Cash
120	Accounts receivable
130	Note receivable
135	Interest receivable
140	Supply inventory
150	Prepaid rent
170	Property, plant, and equipment
171	Accumulated depreciation—PPE
210	Accounts payable
220	Notes payable
230	Interest payable
240	Unearned revenue
310	Common stock
320	Retained earnings
330	Dividends
410	Revenue
420	Interest revenue
510	Cost of goods sold
520	Depreciation expense
530	Rent expense
540	Supply expense
550	Wage expense
560	Interest expense

Note: *Add other accounts if needed.*

Q1   The following transactions occurred during Year 1, the first year of business, for Nancy Nanny Child Care. Record each transaction in proper journal entry format below using debits and credits.

	Nancy Nanny Child Care GENERAL JOURNAL—Year 1			
Date	Accounts		Debit	Credit
TJE #1 On January 2, Nancy Nanny received $100,000 in cash from investors in exchange for shares of Nancy Nanny common stock.				
Jan 2	Cash		100,000	
	Common stock			100,000
TJE #2 On January 2, Nancy Nanny paid $30,000 for a two-year lease of the building. The prepaid rent account was used to record this entry.				
Jan 2				
TJE #3 On February 1, Nancy Nanny purchased tables, chairs, cots, and other furniture for $18,000. $5,000 was paid in cash with the balance on a note payable due in one year bearing 12% annual interest. This furniture has an estimated useful life of five years and is depreciated monthly using the straight-line method with no expected residual value.				
Feb 1				
TJE #4 On February 1, Nancy Nanny purchased supplies at a cost of $40,000. Paid cash.				
Feb 1				
TJE #5 During Year 1, Nancy Nanny provided child-care services on account totaling $150,000.				
Year 1				
TJE #6 During Year 1, collections from receivable customers totaled $146,000.				
Year 1				
TJE #7 During Year 1, paid employees $70,000.				
Year 1				

NANCY NANNY CHILD CARE—Year 1

Q2   At the end of Year 1, Nancy Nanny made the following adjusting journal entries. Record each adjusting entry in proper journal entry format below using debits and credits.

<table>
<tr><th colspan="4">Nancy Nanny Child Care
GENERAL JOURNAL—Year 1</th></tr>
<tr><th>Date</th><th>Accounts</th><th>Debit</th><th>Credit</th></tr>
<tr><td colspan="4">AJE #1   Record rent expense for the year. (Refer to TJE #2.)</td></tr>
<tr><td>Dec 31</td><td></td><td></td><td></td></tr>
<tr><td></td><td></td><td></td><td></td></tr>
<tr><td colspan="4">AJE #2   Record depreciation expense for the year. (Refer to TJE #3.)</td></tr>
<tr><td></td><td></td><td></td><td></td></tr>
<tr><td></td><td></td><td></td><td></td></tr>
<tr><td colspan="4">AJE #3 Record interest expense for the year. (Refer to TJE #3.)</td></tr>
<tr><td></td><td></td><td></td><td></td></tr>
<tr><td></td><td></td><td></td><td></td></tr>
<tr><td colspan="4">AJE #4 At the end of the first year, Nancy Nanny had $6,000 of supplies still on hand that had not been used. (Refer to TJE #4.)</td></tr>
<tr><td></td><td></td><td></td><td></td></tr>
<tr><td></td><td></td><td></td><td></td></tr>
</table>

Q3   Post the Transaction Journal Entries from Q1 and the Adjusting Journal Entries from Q2 to the General Ledger below.

Q4   Compute the ending balance for each account.

Nancy Nanny Child Care
GENERAL LEDGER—Year 1

110 Cash	220 Notes Payable	310 Common Stock	520 Depreciation Expense

120 Accounts Receivable	230 Interest Payable	320 Retained Earnings	530 Rent Expense

140 Supply Inventory		330 Dividends	540 Supply Expense

150 Prepaid Rent		Income Summary	550 Wage Expense

170 PPE	171 Accumulated Depreciation—PPE	410 Revenue	560 Interest Expense

Q5   Use the ending balances computed in the General Ledgèr to prepare the Adjusted Trial Balance below.

	Nancy Nanny Child Care ADJUSTED TRIAL BALANCE—Year 1		
No.	Account	Debit	Credit
110	Cash	$ 101,000	
120	Accounts receivable	4000	
140	Supply inventory	6000	
150	Prepaid rent	1500	
170	Property, plant, and equipment	78000	
171	Accumulated depreciation—PPE		3300
220	Notes payable		13500
230	Interest payable		1430
310	Common stock		100000
410	Revenue		150000
520	Depreciation expense	3300	
530	Rent expense	1500	
540	Supply expense	3400	
550	Wage expense	7000	
560	Interest expense	1430	
	Total	**$267,730**	

NANCY NANNY CHILD CARE—Year 1

Q6   Use amounts from the Adjusted Trial Balance to prepare the Income Statement and the Statement of Stockholders' Equity. Use the forms provided below.

Nancy Nanny Child Care INCOME STATEMENT—Year 1		
Revenue		$
Operating expenses:		
	$	
Total operating expense		122,300
Operating income		
Nonoperating expenses:		
Net income		$ 26,270

Nancy Nanny Child Care STATEMENT OF STOCKHOLDERS' EQUITY—Year 1			
	Common Stock	Retained Earnings	Total SEquity
Balance, January 1, Year 1	$ -0-	$ -0-	$ -0-
Stock issued			
Net income			
Dividends			
Balance, December 31, Year 1			

Q7   Use amounts from the General Ledger, Adjusted Trial Balance, and the Statement of Stockholders' Equity to prepare the Balance Sheet and the Statement of Cash Flows. Use the forms provided below.

Nancy Nanny Child Care BALANCE SHEET—Year 1		
ASSETS		
Cash		$ 101,000
Property, plant, and equipment	$	
Accumulated depreciation—PPE	( )	14,700
Total assets		140,700
LIABILITIES		
Total liabilities		
STOCKHOLDERS' EQUITY		
Total stockholders' equity		
Total liabilities and stockholders' equity		$

Nancy Nanny Child Care STATEMENT OF CASH FLOWS—Year 1		
CASH FROM OPERATING ACTIVITIES		
Cash from customers	$ 146,000	
Rent paid	( )	
Cash paid for supplies	( )	
Wages paid	( )	
Net cash from operating activities		$
CASH FROM INVESTING ACTIVITIES		
Cash paid for property, plant, and equipment		( )
CASH FROM FINANCING ACTIVITIES		
Cash from issuing common stock		$
Net change in cash		$
Beginning cash balance		-0-
Ending cash balance		$ 101,000

Q8 Use amounts from the Adjusted Trial Balance to prepare Closing Journal Entries and the Post-Closing Trial Balance. Use the forms provided below.

	Nancy Nanny Child Care—GENERAL JOURNAL—Year 1		
Date	Accounts	Debit	Credit
CJE #1 Close all revenue and gain accounts to income summary.			
Dec 31			
	Income summary		**150,000**
CJE #2 Close all expense and loss accounts to income summary.			
	Income summary	**123,730**	
CJE #3 Close the income summary account to retained earnings.			
CJE #4 Close the dividends account to retained earnings.			
	Retained earnings	**-0-**	
	Dividends		**-0-**

	Nancy Nanny Child Care—POST-CLOSING TRIAL BALANCE—Year 1		
No.	Account	Debit	Credit
110	Cash	$ 101,000	
120	Accounts receivable		
140	Supply inventory		
150	Prepaid rent		
170	Property, plant, and equipment		
171	Accumulated depreciation—PPE		
220	Note payable		
230	Interest payable		
310	Common stock		
320	Retained earnings		
	Total	$ 144,000	

Purpose: •   Comprehensive review of the 10-step accounting cycle—Year 2.

NANCY NANNY CHILD CARE—Year 2

Nancy Nanny opened a child-care facility on January 1, Year 1. The previous Activity covered the accounting cycle for Year 1. This activity covers the accounting cycle for Year 2. Continue to use the chart of accounts for Nancy Nanny Child Care provided in the previous Activity.

Q1   The following transactions occurred during Year 2, the second year of business for Nancy Nanny Child Care. Record each transaction in proper journal entry format below using debits and credits.

Nancy Nanny Child Care GENERAL JOURNAL—Year 2			
Date	Accounts	Debit	Credit
TJE #1 On January 2, Nancy Nanny purchased a computer, printer, server, and related accessories for $10,000 cash. Due to fast changing computer technologies, Nancy Nanny decided to use the double-declining method of depreciation over a five-year life with no expected residual value.			
Jan 2	Property, plant, and equipment	10,000	
	Cash		10,000
TJE #2 On February 1, Nancy Nanny repaid the note payable from Year 1 plus interest.			
	Interest expense	130	
TJE #3 On February 1, Nancy Nanny purchased supplies at a cost of $45,000. Paid cash.			
TJE #4 On December 8, Grandpa Meyer prepaid $6,000 toward next year's child care costs for Jason, his grandson, a child who regularly attends Nancy Nanny's.			
TJE #5 On December 14, Nancy Nanny declares and distributes $20,000 of dividends to her investors.			
TJE #6 During Year 2, Nancy Nanny provided child care services on account totaling $180,000.			
Year 2			
TJE #7 During Year 2, collections from customer receivables totaled $182,000.			
Year 2			
TJE #8 During Year 2, paid employees $80,000.			
Year 2			

Q2 At the end of Year 2, Nancy Nanny made the following adjusting journal entries. Record each adjusting entry in proper journal entry format below using debits and credits.

<table>
<tr><td colspan="4" align="center">**Nancy Nanny Child Care
GENERAL JOURNAL—Year 2**</td></tr>
<tr><td>Date</td><td>Accounts</td><td>Debit</td><td>Credit</td></tr>
<tr><td colspan="4">AJE #1 Record rent expense for the year. (*Refer to Year 1 TJE #2.*)</td></tr>
<tr><td>Dec 31</td><td></td><td></td><td></td></tr>
<tr><td></td><td></td><td></td><td></td></tr>
<tr><td colspan="4">AJE #2 Record depreciation expense for the year. (*Refer to Year 1 TJE #3 and Year 2 TJE #1.*)</td></tr>
<tr><td>Dec 31</td><td></td><td></td><td></td></tr>
<tr><td></td><td></td><td></td><td></td></tr>
<tr><td colspan="4">AJE #3 At the end of the second year, Nancy Nanny had $5,000 of supplies on hand that had not been used. (*What amount of supplies did Nancy Nanny use during Year 2?*)</td></tr>
<tr><td>Dec 31</td><td></td><td></td><td></td></tr>
<tr><td></td><td></td><td></td><td></td></tr>
</table>

NANCY NANNY CHILD CARE—Year 2

Q3   Use the Post-Closing Trial Balance amounts of Year 1 (from the previous Activity) as the beginning balances of Year 2. Record below.

Q4   Post the Transaction Journal Entries from Q1 Year 2 and the Adjusting Journal Entries from Q2 Year 2 to the General Ledger below.

Q5   Compute the ending balance for each account.

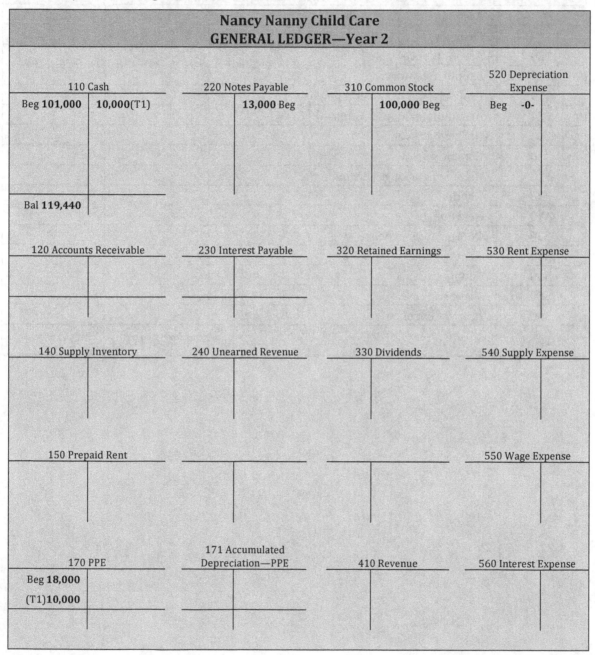

Nancy Nanny Child Care
GENERAL LEDGER—Year 2

110 Cash		
Beg **101,000**	**10,000**(T1)	
Bal **119,440**		

220 Notes Payable	
	13,000 Beg

310 Common Stock	
	100,000 Beg

520 Depreciation Expense	
Beg -0-	

120 Accounts Receivable

230 Interest Payable

320 Retained Earnings

530 Rent Expense

140 Supply Inventory

240 Unearned Revenue

330 Dividends

540 Supply Expense

150 Prepaid Rent

550 Wage Expense

170 PPE	
Beg **18,000**	
(T1)**10,000**	

171 Accumulated Depreciation—PPE

410 Revenue

560 Interest Expense

Q6   Use the ending balances from the General Ledger to prepare the Adjusted Trial Balance below.

	Nancy Nanny Child Care		
	ADJUSTED TRIAL BALANCE—Year 2		
No.	Account	Debit	Credit
110	Cash	$ 119,440	
120	Accounts receivable		
140	Supply inventory		
170	Property, plant, and equipment		
171	Accumulated depreciation—PPE		
240	Unearned revenue		
310	Common stock		
320	Retained earnings (Beginning)		
330	Dividends		
410	Revenue		
520	Depreciation expense		
530	Rent expense		
540	Supply expense		
550	Wage expense		
560	Interest expense		
	Total	$ 323,170	

Q7   Use amounts from the Adjusted Trial Balance to prepare the Income Statement and the Statement of Stockholders' Equity. Use the forms provided below.

Nancy Nanny Child Care INCOME STATEMENT—Year 2		
Revenue		$
Operating expenses:		
	$	
Total operating expense		148,600
Operating income		
Nonoperating expenses:		
Net income		$

Nancy Nanny Child Care STATEMENT OF STOCKHOLDERS' EQUITY—Year 2			
	Common Stock	Retained Earnings	Total SEquity
Balance, January 1, Year 2	$	$	$ 126,270
Stock issued	0		0
Net income			
Dividends		( )	( )
Balance, December 31, Year 2	$	$	$

Q8 Use amounts from the General Ledger, Adjusted Trial Balance, and the Statement of Stockholders' Equity to prepare the Balance Sheet and the Statement of Cash Flows. Use the forms provided below.

Nancy Nanny Child Care BALANCE SHEET—Year 2		
ASSETS		
		$
	$	
	( )	
Total assets		$
LIABILITIES		
STOCKHOLDERS' EQUITY		
Total liabilities & stockholders' equity		$ 143,540

Nancy Nanny Child Care STATEMENT OF CASH FLOWS—Year 2		
CASH FROM OPERATING ACTIVITIES		
Cash from customers	$	
Cash paid for supplies	( )	
Wages paid	( )	
Interest paid	(1,560)	
Net cash from operating activities		$ 61,440
CASH FROM INVESTING ACTIVITIES		
Cash paid for property, plant, and equipment		( )
CASH FROM FINANCING ACTIVITIES		
Paid note payable	( )	
Dividends paid	( )	
Net cash used for financing activities		( )
Net change in cash		18,440
Beginning cash balance		
Ending cash balance		$

Q9   Use amounts from the Adjusted Trial Balance to prepare the Closing Journal Entries and the Post-Closing Trial Balance. Use the forms provided below.

\multicolumn{4}{l}{**Nancy Nanny Child Care—GENERAL JOURNAL—Year 2**}			
Date	Accounts	Debit	Credit
CJE #1	Close all revenue and gain accounts to income summary.		
Dec 31			
Dec 31	**Income Summary**	**148,730**	
CJE #3	Close the income summary account to retained earnings.		
Dec 31	**Income Summary**	**31,270**	
CJE #4	Close the dividends account to retained earnings.		
Dec 31			

\multicolumn{5}{l}{**Nancy Nanny Child Care—POST-CLOSING TRIAL BALANCE—Year 2**}				
No.	Account	Debit	Credit
110	Cash	$	$
120	Accounts receivable		
140	Supply inventory		
170	Property, plant, and equipment		
171	Accumulated depreciation—PPE		
240	Unearned revenue		
310	Common stock		
320	Retained earnings		
	Total	$ 154,440	$

Purpose:
- Post journal entries directly into T-accounts.
- Prepare financial statements.
- Prepare the Statement of Cash Flows using the direct method.
- Prepare the Statement of Cash Flows using the indirect method.

Brian was ready to start business on September 1 after issuing common stock for $30,000 and purchasing a delivery van for $24,000.

Brian Nelson's Delivery Service Corporation
GENERAL LEDGER—September

100 Cash	200 Salaries Payable	300 Common Stock	400 Revenue
Beg. 6,000	Beg. -0-	Beg. 30,000	Beg. -0-

110 Accounts Receivable		350 Retained Earnings	500 Depreciation Expense
Beg. -0-		Beg. -0-	Beg. -0-

130 Delivery Van	140 Accumulated Depreciation		510 Salary Expense
Beg. 24,000	Beg. -0-		Beg. -0-

Q1 Record the following transaction journal entries for September directly into the T-accounts above.

TJE #1 Bill customers for deliveries that total $2,000 during September.

TJE #2 For accounts receivable, the ending balance on September 30 is $100. Prepare the TJE for cash received from customers.

TJE #3 Employees earn $700 in salaries during September. Record as Salaries Payable.

TJE #4 For Salaries Payable, the ending balance on September 30 is $150. Prepare the TJE for cash paid to employees.

Q2 Record the adjusting journal entry for September directly into the T-accounts above:

AJE #1 Record September depreciation expense for the delivery van, which has a four-year (48-month) life, using straight-line depreciation.

Q3 Compute the ending balance for each account, recording it as a debit or credit balance in the General Ledger above. These ending balances would appear on the (**unadjusted / adjusted / post-closing**) trial balance and (**be / not be**) reported on the financial statements.

What amounts would be recorded on the September balance sheet?

REarnings $_____   Total Assets $_____   Total Liabilities $_____   SEquity $_____

Q4   Using amounts from the General Ledger on the previous page, (A) prepare the Income Statement and (B) prepare the Operating Activity section of the Statement of Cash Flows below.

INCOME STATEMENT		ADJUSTMENTS	STATEMENT OF CASH FLOWS	
Revenue	$ 2,000	$ (100)	Cash received from customers	$
Salary expense	( )		Salaries paid	( )
Depreciation expense	( )		Depreciation paid	( )
Net income	$	Total $ 550	Net cash from operating activities	$ 1,350

Q5   What adjustments are needed to get from accrual-based net income to cash-based Net Cash from Operating Activities?

a.   The difference between (**accrual- / cash-**) based "Revenue" reported on the (**Income Statement / Statement of Cash Flows**) and (**accrual- / cash-**) based "Cash received from customers" reported on the (**Income Statement / Statement of Cash Flows**) is $_____. This adjustment is (**added / subtracted**). Record in the Adjustments Column.

b.   During September, Accounts Receivable had a beginning balance of $_____ and an ending balance of $_____, a difference of $_____. This difference will (**always** / **sometimes**) be the same as the amount in the Adjustments Column.

c.   The difference between (**accrual- / cash-**) based "Salary expense" reported on the (**Income Statement / Statement of Cash Flows**) and (**accrual- / cash-**) based "Salaries paid" reported on the (**Income Statement / Statement of Cash Flows**) is $_____. This adjustment is (**added / subtracted**). Record in the Adjustments Column above.

d.   During September, Salaries Payable had a beginning balance of $_____ and an ending balance of $_____, a difference of $_____. This difference will (**always / sometimes**) be the same as the amount in the Adjustments Column.

e.   Complete the Adjustments Column for Depreciation in the chart above.

Q6   The indirect method of preparing the Statement of Cash Flows reconciles accrual-based Net Income with cash-based Net Cash from Operating Activities (NCOA). Use amounts from the Adjustments Column above to prepare the Operating Activities section of the Statement of Cash Flows below.

Statement of Cash Flows (Indirect Method)	Amounts
Net income	$ 800
Add depreciation expense	500
(Increase) decrease in accounts receivable	(100)
Increase (decrease) in salaries payable	150
Net cash from operating activities (NCOA)	$ 1,350

Q7   Amounts from the Adjustments Column are used to reconcile accrual-based Net Income with cash-based Net Cash from Operating Activities, which is the purpose of the (**direct / indirect**) method.

Q8   In the Statement of Cash Flows, *operating activities* may be reported using the (**direct / indirect / either**) method, *investing activities* may be reported using the (**direct / indirect / either**) method, and *financing activities* may be reported using the (**direct / indirect / either**) method.

CHAPTER 8

COMPREHENSIVE REVIEW

INTRODUCTION

This chapter presents a series of activities designed to review and integrate the concepts learned throughout the course. It would be relatively easy to look at one aspect of a company, to the exclusion of others. For example, research has shown that some investors only look at net income. They don't care about revenue, or liquidity, or solvency, or even how net income was calculated. They focus almost exclusively on net income. This chapter emphasizes how important it is to look at the whole picture, to review all of the financial statements, and to jointly assess a company's profitability, efficiency, liquidity, and solvency.

First of all, consider how the financial statements interact with one another. The Statement of Stockholders' Equity describes how net income (reported on the income statement) increases retained earnings (reported on the balance sheet). The operating cash flows section of the Statement of Cash Flows, under the indirect method, describes how net income (reported on the income statement) increases cash and cash equivalents (reported on the balance sheet). The financial statements link with and explain one another.

When considering a company's investment potential, profitability is generally considered the most important factor. Well-run companies earn profits that grow reliably at a steady pace. That said, the DuPont Model demonstrates how efficiency (as measured by asset turnover) and solvency (as measured by financial leverage) can be multiplied by return on sales to increase return on equity; efficiency and solvency can boost returns. Remember that efficiency and solvency can also boost losses.

In addition to profitability and efficiency, it is important to track financial risk. Solvency and liquidity indicate financial risk. A company must eventually pay back its debts. Solvency indicates a company's ability to pay back debts in the long term, whereas liquidity indicates a company's ability to pay back debts in the short term. If a company can't pay back debts, it could close, ending all future opportunities of returns.

These measures change over time. For example, as a company grows, its return on equity could be increasing, but due to increased financial leverage rather than increased profitability. So even though ROE is increasing, the additional financial leverage is increasing financial risk, and may spell trouble later on. This is why it's especially important to consider trends, changes in financial statements, and ratios measured over time.

Chapter 9, the Capstone Project, provides further comprehensive review, using a company of your choice.

Purpose: •   Review the effect of various transactions on total assets.

Circle whether each of the following events/transactions will (I)ncrease, (D)ecrease, or have (No) effect on total assets.

		TOTAL ASSETS *(Circle the answer)*
a.	Record a cash sale to Customer Grant.	(**I** / D / No)
b.	Record a sale on account to Customer Casey.	(**I** / D / No)
c.	Record the receipt of cash from Customer Casey in (b).	(I / D / **No**)
d.	Purchase supplies for cash.	(I / D / **No**)
e.	Purchase equipment on account.	(**I** / D / No)
f.	Record depreciation for the equipment.	(I / **D** / No)
g.	Sell equipment at a gain for cash.	(**I** / D / No)
h.	Purchase short-term trading securities for cash.	(I / D / **No**)
i.	At the end of the accounting period, the short-term trading securities purchased in (h) have increased in market value.	(**I** / D / No)
j.	Land purchased ten years ago has increased in market value.	(I / D / **No**)
k.	The current market value of high-tech inventory is less than acquisition cost.	(I / **D** / No)
l.	Issue a bond payable at a discount for cash.	(**I** / D / No)
m.	Purchase treasury stock for cash.	(I / **D** / No)
n.	Pay cash dividends.	(I / **D** / No)

Handwritten annotations: "↑ cash" (a), "↑ equipment" (e), "if loss ↓" (f), "↓ ppe net" (f), "10,000 - 12,000 = 8,000" (g), "historical cost" (j)

Purpose: • Review the effect of various transactions on total liabilities.

Circle whether each of the following events/transactions will (I)ncrease, (D)ecrease, or have (No) effect on total liabilities.

TOTAL LIABILITIES
(Circle the answer)

a.   Purchase inventory on account.   (I / D / No)

b.   Pay for the inventory purchased in (a).   (I / D / No)

c.   Sell inventory to customers for cash.   (I / D / No)

d.   Issue bond payable at a discount.   (I / D / No)

e.   At the end of the accounting period,
     record accrued interest expense on the bond payable.   (I / D / No)

f.   Bond payable matures and is paid in full.   (I / D / No)

g.   Hire a new employee for an annual salary of $20,000.
     The employee will start next Monday.   (I / D / No)

h.   The end of the accounting period is on Wednesday.
     Record accrued employee wage expense. Employees
     get paid on Friday.   (I / D / No)

i.   Retirement costs for current employees are recorded.
     These costs will not be paid until an employee retires
     in a future accounting period.   (I / D / No)

j.   At the end of the accounting period, estimate the
     amount of income taxes owed for the fiscal year.   (I / D / No)

k.   Company ABC files a lawsuit. Company lawyers
     evaluate the case and estimate the company will
     probably win a substantial amount for damages.
     The case will be tried in a future accounting period.   (I / D / No)

l.   A lawsuit is filed against Company ABC. Company
     lawyers evaluate the case and estimate the company will
     probably lose and owe a substantial amount for damages.
     The case will be tried in a future accounting period.   (I / D / No)

Purpose: • Review the effect of various transactions on stockholders' equity.

Circle whether each of the following events/transactions will (I)ncrease, (D)ecrease, or have (No) effect on stockholders' equity.

STOCKHOLDERS' EQUITY
(*Circle the answer*)

a.   Issue preferred stock at par value.   (**I** / D / No)

b.   Issue common stock at more than par value.   (**I** / D / No)

c.   Purchase treasury stock.   (I / **D** / No)

d.   During the accounting period, the market price of the
       company's common stock increases.   (I / D / **No**)

e.   Declare and issue a *cash* dividend.   (I / **D** / No)

f.   Declare and issue a *stock* dividend.   (I / D / **No**)

g.   Record net income for the accounting period.   (**I** / D / No)

h.   Purchase inventory on account.   (I / D / **No**)

i.   Issue bonds payable at a premium.   (I / D / **No**)

j.   Correct an error that understated
       depreciation expense in the previous accounting period.   (I / **D** / No)

Purpose: •   Review the effect of various transactions on net income.

Circle whether each of the following events/transactions will (I)ncrease, (D)ecrease, or have (No) effect on net income.

NET INCOME
(*Circle the answer*)

a.   Record a sale for Customer Ashley paying cash.   (**I** / D / No)

b1.   Record a sale for Customer Ewa on account.   (**I** / D / No)
b2.   Record cash received from Customer Ewa for the sale recorded in (b1).   (I / D / **No**)

c1.   Purchase equipment.   (I / D / **No**)
c2.   At the end of the accounting period, make the adjusting entry
       to record depreciation for the equipment.   (I / **D** / No)
c3.   Record a loss on the sale of equipment.   (I / **D** / No)

d1.   Borrow $10,000 from the bank and sign a note.   (I / D / **No**)
d2.   At the end of the accounting period, make the adjusting entry
       to record accrued interest expense on the note in (d1).   (I / **D** / No)
d3.   Repay the $10,000 note.   (I / D / **No**)

e.   Pay rent for this accounting period.   (I / **D** / No)

f.   Record an extraordinary gain.   (**I** / D / No)

g.   Declare and issue a cash dividend.   (I / D / **No**)

h.   Issue common stock for more than the par value.   (I / D / **No**)

i.   At the end of the accounting period, record the portion of sales
       estimated as uncollectible.   (I / **D** / No)

j.   At the end of the accounting period, record an unrealized gain
       on the short-term trading securities portfolio.   (**I** / D / No)

Purpose: • Reinforce understanding of the information provided by each financial statement.

Circle the financial statement you would consult to find the following information.

BS	= Balance sheet
IS	= Income statement
SE	= Statement of stockholders' equity
CF	= Statement of cash flows
Not	= Not found on any of the financial statements

FINANCIAL STATEMENTS
(Circle only one correct answer)

a.   Rental costs incurred this year.   (BS / **IS** / SE / CF / Not)

b.   Rental costs paid this year.   (BS / IS / SE / **CF** / Not)

c.   Rental costs still owed.   (**BS** / IS / SE / CF / Not)

d.   Cost of equipment allocated to this accounting period.   (BS / **IS** / SE / CF / Not)

e.   Equipment book value (carrying value).   (**BS** / IS / SE / CF / Not)

f.   Market value of equipment purchased ten years ago.   (BS / IS / SE / CF / **Not**)

g.   Accrual-basis accounting used to compute operating results.   (BS / **IS** / SE / CF / Not)

h.   Cash-basis accounting used to compute operating results.   (BS / IS / SE / **CF** / Not)

i.   Noncash investing and financing activities.   (BS / IS / SE / **CF** / Not)

j.   Market value of investments in the short-term trading portfolio.   (**BS** / IS / SE / CF / Not)

k.   Market value of the common stock issued by the corporation.   (**BS** / IS / SE / CF / **Not**)

l.   Amounts contributed by common shareholders this year.   (**BS** / IS / SE / CF / Not)

m.   Inventory remaining unsold at the end of the accounting period.   (**BS** / IS / SE / CF / Not)

n.   Cost of inventory sold during the accounting period.   (BS / **IS** / SE / CF / Not)

o.   If we use the FIFO inventory cost flow assumption, the
       most recent inventory costs will end up on this statement.   (**BS** / IS / SE / CF / Not)

p.   Evaluate how assets are currently being financed.   (**BS** / IS / SE / CF / Not)

q.   Financial statement reporting amounts as of a certain date.   (**BS** / IS / SE / CF / Not)

Purpose:
- Apply the revenue recognition and the matching principles.
- Differentiate between accrual accounting and cash accounting.
- Prepare a multi-step income statement, the statement of retained earnings, a classified balance sheet, and the statement of cash flows.

Yonghong opened Books Galore, Inc., for business on January 1, Year 1. The following financial items summarize the first year of operations. Use these items to prepare the Year 1 multi-step income statement, the Year 1 statement of stockholders' equity, the December 31, Year 1 classified balance sheet, and the Year 1 statement of cash flows in the space provided.

a.   Yonghong and her friend each invested $50,000 in cash (for a total of $100,000) in exchange for shares of common stock in Books Galore, Inc.

b.   On January 1, Year 1, purchased new equipment costing $70,000 with a 10-year useful life and no residual value. Paid cash. Straight-line depreciation is used.

c.   Rental costs for the year total $48,000. Of that amount, $4,000 remains unpaid at the end of the year, December 31, Year 1.

d.   January 1, Year 1, purchased and paid $2,000 for a two-year property insurance policy.

e.   January 1, Year 1, purchased a piece of land next to the store for $20,000 in cash. Later in the year, the land was sold to another small business owner for $30,000 in cash.

f.   During Year 1, customers purchased $300,000 of books. Of that amount, $250,000 has been collected from customers in cash and the remaining amounts will be collected next year.

g.   Inventory purchases totaled $200,000 for the year. All purchases have been paid for, and $18,000 of those purchases remain in inventory at the end of the year.

h.   On July 1, Year 1, borrowed $25,000 from a local bank and signed a one-year, 10% note payable. Principal and interest are due on June 30, Year 2.

i.   During Year 1, the company paid shareholders cash dividends totaling $8,000.

j.   At the end of the year, adjusting entries were recorded for depreciation expense and interest expense.

Multi-Step Income Statement Year 1	
Sales revenue	300,000
Cost of goods sold	182,000
Gross profit	118,000
Operating expenses:	
Rent	48,000
Insurance	1,000
dep, insurance	9,000
Nonoperating revenues (expenses):	62,000
interest exp + gain on sale	-(1250+10,000)
Net income	70,750

Handwritten margin notes:
USC
Left right Method

300,000
operating 182,000
Rent 48K
Dep. exp 7K
Int. exp 1,250
Ins. exp 1,000
(57,250)

Non op
Gain on Sale + 10K

Net Income: $70,750

62000 - 1250 + 10,000
= 70,750

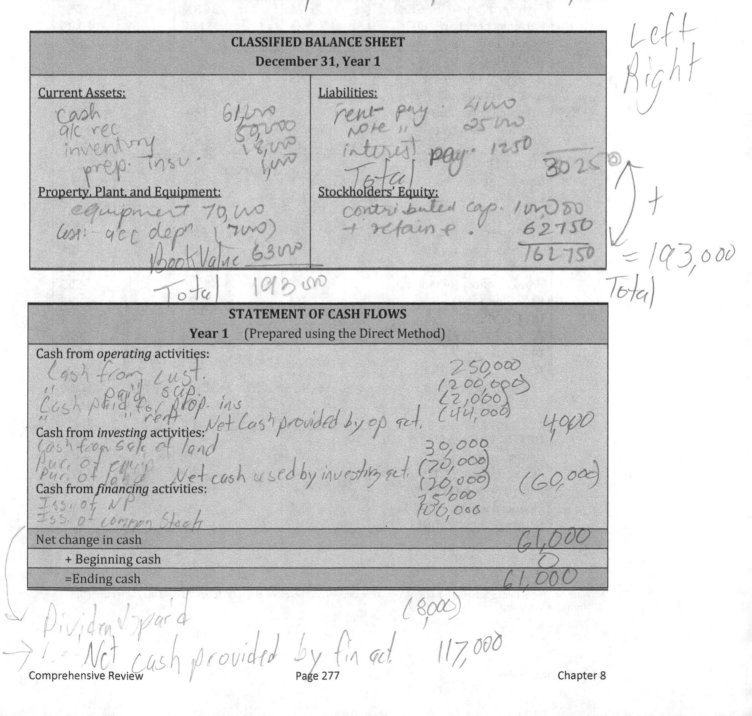

STATEMENT OF STOCKHOLDERS' EQUITY
Year 1

	Contributed Capital	Retained Earnings	Total SE
Beginning balances	$ -0-	$ -0-	$ -0-
Additions: Issue of common stock Net Income	100,000	70,750	100,000 70750
Deductions: Dividends		(8,000)	(8,000)
Ending balances	$ 100,000	$ 62,750	$ 162,750

CLASSIFIED BALANCE SHEET
December 31, Year 1

Current Assets:
Cash 61,000
a/c rec 50,000
inventory 18,000
prep. insu. 4,000

Property, Plant, and Equipment:
equipment 70,000
Less: acc depr (7,000)
Book Value 63,000

Total 193,000

Liabilities:
rent pay. 4,000
note " 25,000
interest pay. 1250
Total 30,250

Stockholders' Equity:
contributed cap. 100,000
+ retain e. 62750
162750

Left
Right

} + } = 193,000
Total

STATEMENT OF CASH FLOWS
Year 1   (Prepared using the Direct Method)

Cash from *operating* activities:
Cash from cust. 250,000
" paid s.cap. (200,000)
Cash paid for prop. ins (2,000)
" " rent (44,000)
Net Cash provided by op act. 4,000

Cash from *investing* activities:
Cash from sale of land 30,000
Pur. of equip (70,000)
Pur. of land Net cash used by investing act. (20,000) (60,000)

Cash from *financing* activities:
Iss. of NP 75,000
Iss. of common stock 100,000

Net change in cash	61,000
+ Beginning cash	0
=Ending cash	61,000

Dividends paid (8,000)
" Net cash provided by fin act. 117,000

Purpose:
- Understand that reviewing many ratios helps give an overall impression of corporate financial strength.
- Understand that meaning is added to a ratio by comparing that ratio to industry norms or to a company within the same industry because norms may vary by industry.
- Analyze profitability, efficiency, liquidity, solvency, and investment ratios.

RATIOS As of January 28, 2012	Industry Average*	The GAP (GPS)	American Eagle Outfitters (AEO)
PROFITABILITY			
Return on sales (ROS)	6.5%	5.7%	4.8%
Return on assets (ROA)	9.9%	11.2%	7.8%
Return on equity (ROE)	20.9%	30.2%	10.9%
Gross profit margin (GP%)	39.9%	36.3%	35.7%
Earnings per share (EPS)	XXXXX	$1.57	$0.85
Quality of income	NA	1.64	1.58
EFFICIENCY			
Asset turnover (A TO)	1.53	1.96	1.62
Accounts receivable turnover	55	--	78
Accounts receivable days	6.6 days	--	4.67 days
Inventory turnover	4.5	5.7	5.4
Inventory days	81.1 days	64 days	67.59 days
LIQUIDITY			
Current ratio	2.1	2.0	3.2
Cash flow liquidity	NA	1.53	2.43
SOLVENCY			
Debt ratio	52%	63%	27%
Financial leverage (LEV)	2.1	2.7	1.4
Times interest earned	117	20.8	NA
Free cash flow (in millions)	XXXXX	$579	$53
Cash flow adequacy	NA	1.74	1.28
INVESTMENT			
Price earnings ratio (PE)	**19.3	14.4	16.9
Dividend rate	NA	$0.40	$0.43
Market value per share:			
Close March, 2012	NA	$25.00	$16.10
52-week high	NA	$25.43	$16.43
52-week low	NA	$15.08	$10.00
DUPONT ANALYSIS OF ROE			
Return on sales (ROS)	6.5%	5.7%	4.8%
Asset turnover (A TO)	1.53	1.96	1.62
Return on assets (ROA)	9.9%	11.2%	7.8%
Financial leverage (LEV)	2.1	2.7	1.4
Return on equity (ROE)	20.9%	30.2%	10.9%

NA = Not available

XXXXX = Not comparable among companies

*   Industry: Apparel Stores—*Industry averages from money.msn.com*

** Industry: Apparel Stores—*Industry ratio averages from morningstar.com*

There are no official rules governing how these ratios are calculated. Therefore, the ratio formulas used may differ from the formulas in the text.

Refer to the ratio information on the previous page to answer the following questions.
For ratio formulas and explanations refer to Appendix B—Ratios.

$365/78 = 4.679$

Q1   For American Eagle Outfitters, compute account receivable days _____ and inventory days

$365/54$ _____. Enter these amounts in the appropriate location in the ratio chart on the previous page. Compared to the industry average, AEO collects accounts receivable **(quicker / slower)** and sells inventory **(quicker / slower)**.

Q2   Compare The GAP and American Eagle Outfitters.

check

a.   For profitability and efficiency ratios … *Circle* the stronger ratio.

b.   For liquidity and solvency ratios … *Circle* the ratio reporting the least amount of risk.

Q3   Compare The GAP and American Eagle Outfitters to industry averages.

check

a.   For profitability and efficiency ratios … *Cross out* any company ratio weaker than the industry average.

b.   For liquidity and solvency ratios … *Cross out* any company ratio reporting higher risk.

Q4   Review the DUPONT ANALYSIS of ROE for American Eagle Outfitters.

check

a.   Regarding overall profitability (ROA), the most significant influence can be attributed to **(ROS / Asset Turnover / both contribute about equally)**.

b.   Regarding ROE, the most significant influence can be attributed to **(ROA / Financial Leverage / both contribute about equally)**.

Q5   Analyze American Eagle Outfitters by reviewing each category of ratio information presented on the previous page to answer the following questions.

a.   PROFITABILITY RATIOS measure the overall performance of a firm. Is American Eagle Outfitters earning sufficient profits? **(Yes / No)** *How can you tell?*

Under performing industry average.

b.   EFFICIENCY RATIOS measure the effectiveness of managing cash, accounts receivable, inventory, PPE, and other assets. Is American Eagle Outfitters efficiently managing its assets?

check

(Yes / No) *How can you tell?* Accounts receivables beats industry average

c.   LIQUIDITY RATIOS measure a firm's ability to meet cash needs as they arise. Does American Eagle Outfitters have the ability to make payments as they come due? **(Yes / No)**
How can you tell? High current assets ratio and high cash flow liquidity

d.   SOLVENCY RATIOS measure the extent of debt relative to equity, if financial leverage is being used effectively, and the ability to cover required payments for interest, capital expenditures, dividends, and other fixed payments.
Is American Eagle Outfitters effectively managing its debt? **(Yes / No)**
Able to adequately cover capital expenditures and pay dividends? **(Yes / No)**
How can you tell?

e.   INVESTMENT RATIOS compare the market value per share to other per share amounts and the level of dividend payment. Is American Eagle Outfitters providing an adequate return to shareholders? **(Yes / No)** *How can you tell?* PE higher than Gap & are able to pay off debt faster

Q6   Based on all of the information presented on the previous page, would you recommend investing in American Eagle Outfitters? **(Yes / No)** *Why?*

Purpose:
- Analyze the income statement, the balance sheet, and the statement of cash flows.
- Prepare a statement of retained earnings.

Google (GOOG) BALANCE SHEET ($ in millions)				
ASSETS	12/31/2011	12/31/2010	12/31/2009	12/31/2008
Cash and cash equivalents	$ 9,983	$ 13,630	$ 10,198	$ 8,657
Short-term investments	34,643	21,345	14,287	7,189
Accounts receivable	5,427	4,252	3,178	2,642
Inventories	0	0	0	0
Other current assets	2705	750	1,504	1,690
TOTAL Current assets	52,758	41,562	29,167	20,178
Property, plant, and equipment, net	9,603	7,759	4,845	5,234
Goodwill	7,346	6,256	4,903	4,840
Intangibles	1,578	1,044	775	997
Other noncurrent assets	1,289	1,223	808	519
TOTAL Assets	$ 72,574	$ 57,851	$ 40,497	$ 31,768
LIABILITIES				
Accounts payable	$ 588	$ 483	$ 216	$ 178
Short-term debt	1,218	3,465	0	0
Accrued expenses	4,356	3,256	2,247	1,824
Other current liabilities	2,751	2,792	285	300
TOTAL Current liabilities	8,913	9,996	2,748	2,302
Long-term debt	2986	0	0	0
Deferred income taxes	287	0	0	13
Other noncurrent liabilities	2,243	1,614	1,745	1,214
TOTAL Noncurrent liabilities	5,516	1,614	1,745	1,227
TOTAL Liabilities	14,429	11,610	4,493	3,529
STOCKHOLDERS' EQUITY				
Preferred stock	0	0	0	0
Common stock	20,264	18,235	15,817	14,450
Retained earnings	37,605	27,868	20,082	13,562
Other stockholders' equity	276	138	105	227
Treasury stock	0	0	0	0
TOTAL Stockholders' equity	58,145	46,241	36,004	28,239
TOTAL L & SE	$ 72,574	$ 57,851	$ 40,497	$ 31,768

Google (GOOG) INCOME STATEMENT ($ in millions)				
For the years ended December 31,	2011	2010	2009	2008
Revenue	$ 37,905	$ 29,321	$ 23,651	$ 21,796
Cost of goods sold (COGS)	13,188	10,417	8,844	8,622
Gross profit	24,717	18,904	14,807	13,174
Sales and marketing	4,589	2,799	1,984	1,946
General and administrative	2,724	1,962	1,668	1,803
Research and development	5,162	3,762	2,843	2,793
Unusual expense	500	0	0	0
Total operating expenses	12,975	8,523	6,495	6,542
Operating income	11,742	10,381	8,312	6,632
Other revenues and expenses, net	+584	+415	+69	(778)
Income before income tax	12,326	10,796	8,381	5,854
Provision for income tax	2,589	2,291	1,861	1,627
Net income	$ 9,737	$ 8,505	$ 6,520	$ 4,227
Outstanding Shares (in millions)	323	319	316	314

Google (GOOG) STATEMENT OF CASH FLOWS ($ in millions)				
For the years ended December 31,	2011	2010	2009	2008
Cash flows from (for) *operating* activities				
Net income (loss)	$ 9,737	$ 8,505	$ 6,520	$ 4,227
Depreciation and amortization	1,851	1,396	1,524	1,500
Deferred income tax	343	9	(268)	(225)
Operating (gains) losses	2,004	1,270	1,054	2,024
Changes in working capital	630	(99)	486	327
Net cash from operating activities (NCOA)	14,565	11,081	9,316	7,853
Cash flows from (for) *investing* activities				
Sale of investments	48,746	37,099	22,103	15,763
Purchase of PPE, net	(3,438)	(4,018)	(810)	(2,358)
Purchase of investments	(62,095)	(45,055)	(29,204)	(15,403)
Other investing cash flow items	(2,254)	1,294	(108)	(3,321)
Net cash (for) investing activities (NCIA)	(19,041)	(10,680)	(8,019)	(5,319)
Cash flows from (for) *financing* activities				
Issuance (repayment) of debt, net	726	3,463	0	0
Issuance (repurchase) of capital stock, net	0	(801)	0	(72)
Cash dividends paid	0	0	0	0
Other financing cash flow items	81	388	233	160
Net cash from financing activities (NCFA)	807	3,050	233	88
Effect of exchange rate changes	22	(19)	11	(46)
Net change in cash	(3,647)	3,432	1,541	2,575
+ Beginning cash and cash equivalents	13,630	10,198	8,657	6,082
= Ending cash and cash equivalents	$ 9,983	$ 13,630	$ 10,198	$ 8,657
Supplemental information				
Cash interest paid	$ 795	$ 959	$ 243	$ 1,336
Cash taxes paid	731	102	217	883
Free cash flow	11,127	7,063	8,506	3,373

Refer to the financial statements presented for Google on the previous two pages to answer the following questions.

BALANCE SHEET

Q1   Review the following accounts, subtotals, and totals; (1) describe your observations; and then (2) identify what your observations indicate. A response is given for Cash and Short-term Investments to help with understanding.

      a.   Cash and short-term investments … ***more than doubled*** *from 12/31/2008 to 12/31/2011, comprising more than 80% of total assets on 12/31/2011,* **indicating** *a company that is rich in cash.*

      b.   Goodwill...

      c.   Total assets...

      d.   Contributed capital...

      e.   Retained earnings...

Q2   Compute the ratios requested in the chart below. *For ratio formulas and explanation refer to Appendix B—Ratios.*

Google	Industry Norm*	12/31/2011	12/31/2008
Current ratio	5.0		
Debt ratio	29%	%	%

   *   Industry: *Internet Information Provider—Industry ratio averages from* <u>money.msn.com</u>

For each ratio, (a) compare the two years of company ratios and *circle* the ratio indicating lower financial risk, (b) *cross out* any company ratio indicating greater financial risk than the industry norm, and (c) *comment* on the results.

Q3   Overall, the balance sheet and related ratios indicate a (**strengthening / steady / weakening**) financial position. *Why?* List observations that support your conclusion and explain why.

INCOME STATEMENT

Q4   Compute the ratios requested in the chart below. *For ratio formulas and explanation refer to Appendix B—Ratios.*

Google DUPONT ANALYSIS of ROE	Industry Norm*	2011	2008
ROS	22.4%	%	%
Asset turnover	0.63		
ROA	14.1%	%	%
Financial leverage	1.24		
ROE	17.5%	%	%

   *   Industry: *Internet Information Provider—Industry ratio averages from* <u>money.msn.com</u>

Q5 Review the DUPONT ANALYSIS of ROE for Google on the previous page.

    a. Regarding overall profitability (ROA), the most significant influence can be attributed to
        (**ROS / Asset Turnover / both contribute about equally**).

    b. Regarding ROE, the most significant influence can be attributed to
        (**ROA / Financial Leverage / both contribute about equally**).

    c. For each ratio, (a) *circle* the stronger ratio, (b) *cross out* any ratio that is weaker than the industry norm, and (c) *comment* on the results.

Q6 Compute the missing information for 2011 in Google's common-size income statements below.

Google Common-Size INCOME STATEMENT	2011	2010	2009	2008
Revenue	_100_ %	100%	100%	100%
Cost of goods sold	_35_ %	36%	37%	40%
Operating expenses	_34_ %	29%	29%	30%
Nonoperating revenues (expense)	_2_ %	+1%	+0%	-4%
Provision for income tax	_7_ %	8%	8%	8%
Net income	25.7%	29%	28%	19%

    a. Operating expenses have been (**increasing** / **decreasing**), indicating that (**sales and marketing** / **general and administrative** / **R&D** / **interest income** / **provision for income tax**) has been increasing as a percentage of revenue.   *(Circle all that apply.)*

    b. Provision for income tax has been (**increasing / decreasing**) as a percentage of revenue.

    c. Since 2009, ROS has been (**increasing / decreasing**), indicating profitability is (**down / up**).

Q7 The income statement and related information indicate (**strengthening / mixed / weakening**) earnings potential. *Why?* List observations that support your conclusion and explain why.

    · ROS Increase   · Non operating rev increase   · Operating - exp increase.

STATEMENT OF CASH FLOWS

Q8 The primary source of cash was (**operating activities** / **issuing debt** / **issuing capital stock**) and the primary use of cash was (**purchasing PPE** / **purchasing investments** / **paying dividends**).

    For investments, there was a net cash outflow during (**2011 / 2010 / 2009** / **2008**), indicating that more investments were (**purchased** / **sold**).

Q9 Compute the ratios requested in the chart below. *For ratio formulas and explanation refer to Appendix B—Ratios.*

Google RATIOS	*Industry Norm*	2011	2008
Free cash flow ($ in millions)	*NA*	$ 11,127	$ 5,445
Cash flow adequacy	*NA*	4.24	3.33
Cash flow liquidity	*NA*	6.64	10.30
Quality of income	*NA*	1.50	1.86

For each ratio, (a) *circle* the company ratio indicating the strongest cash position and (b) *comment* on the results.

Q10   a.   Complete the missing information in the common-sized statement of cash flows for 2011.

Google STATEMENT OF CASH FLOWS	Common-Size		($ in millions)	
	2011	**2010**	**2009**	**2008**
Net cash from operating activities	_100_ %	100%	100%	100%
Sale of investments	_335_ %	335%	237%	201%
Purchase of investments	_-426_ %	-407%	-313%	-196%
Purchase of PPE, net	_-24_ %	36%	-9%	-30%
Issuance (repayment) of debt, net	_5_ %	31%	0%	0%
Cash dividends paid	_0_ %	0%	0%	0%
Net change in cash	-25%	31%	17%	33%

     * Only select amounts are listed above so will not sum to the total.

     b.   In what year did Google issue a significant amount of debt?   2010

     c.   In what year did Google report a net decrease in cash? (**2011** / **2010** / **2009** / **2008**)
        What was the cause of the decrease?   Purchased shrt trm invstmnts

Q11   The statement of cash flows and related information report a (**strengthening** / steady / **weakening**) cash position. *Why?* List observations that support your conclusion and explain why.

     · Increase in NCOA.

     · The ratios remain strong

STATEMENT OF RETAINED EARNINGS

Q12   a.   Complete the statement of retained earnings below.

Google STATEMENT OF RETAINED EARNINGS	($ in millions)			
For the years ended December 31,	**2011**	**2010**	**2009**	**2008**
Retained earnings, beginning	$ 27,868	$ 20,082	$ 13,562	$ 9,335
Net income	9,737	8505	6520	4,227
Dividends paid	0	0	0	0
Other adjustments	0	(719)	0	0
Retained earnings, ending	$ 37,605	$ 27,868	$ 20,082	$ 13,562

     b.   As of 12/31/2011, since incorporation Google has earned profits and losses totaling $ 37,605 million.

     c.   Does Google pay dividends? (**Yes** / **No**) What might be the reason for this?

        The retained the money for expantion

OTHER

Q13   Based on the financial statements presented for Google, would you invest in this company? (**Yes** / **No**) *Why? Support* your response with at least five good observations.

     · NI slowed down   · ROE & ROA are below industry norms

     · Cash from CS has decresd.   · No divdnd.

Purpose:
- Analyze the income statement, the balance sheet, and the statement of cash flows
- Prepare a statement of retained earnings

Chipotle Mexican Grill (CMG) BALANCE SHEET ($ in millions)				
ASSETS	**12/31/2011**	**12/31/2010**	**12/31/2009**	**12/31/2008**
Cash and cash equivalents	$ 401	$ 225	$ 220	$ 88
Short-term investments	55	125	50	100
Accounts receivable	8	6	5	4
Inventories	9	7	6	5
Other current assets	28	43	17	14
TOTAL Current assets	501	406	298	211
Property, plant, and equipment	1,122	982	882	777
Accumulated depreciation	-370	-305	-246	-191
PPE, net	752	677	636	586
Goodwill and other intangibles	22	22	22	22
Long-term investments	0	0	0	0
Other noncurrent assets	150	17	6	6
TOTAL Noncurrent assets	924	716	664	614
TOTAL Assets	$ 1,425	$ 1,122	$ 962	$ 825
LIABILITIES				
Accounts payable	$ 46	$ 34	$ 25	$ 24
Short-term debt	0	0	0	0
Current portion of long-term debt	0	0	0	0
Accrued expenses	77	89	73	53
Other current liabilities	34	0	4	0
TOTAL Current liabilities	157	123	102	77
Long-term debt	0	4	4	4
Deferred income taxes	64	51	39	30
Other noncurrent liabilities	160	133	113	92
TOTAL Noncurrent liabilities	224	188	156	126
TOTAL Liabilities	381	311	258	202
STOCKHOLDERS' EQUITY				
Preferred stock	0	0	0	0
Common stock	677	594	540	502
Retained earnings	671	457	278	151
Other stockholders' equity	(304)	(240)	(114)	(30)
TOTAL Stockholders' equity	1044	811	704	623
TOTAL L & SE	$ 1,425	$ 1,122	$ 962	$ 825

Chipotle Mexican Grill (CMG) INCOME STATEMENT ($ in millions)				
For the years ended December 31,	2011	2010	2009	2008
Revenue	$ 2,270	$ 1,836	$ 1,518	$ 1,332
Cost of goods sold (COGS)	1,680	1,347	1,140	1,045
Gross profit	590	489	379	287
Selling, general, and admin expense (SGA)	158	126	108	101
Depreciation and amortization expense	75	69	61	53
Other operating expenses	6	6	6	9
Total operating expenses	239	201	175	163
Operating income	351	288	204	124
Interest income (expense) and other	(1)	1	0	3
Income before income tax	350	289	204	127
Provision for income tax	135	110	77	49
Income from continuing operations	215	0	0	0
Nonrecurring items / Minority interest	0	0	0	0
Net income	$ 215	$ 179	$ 127	$ 78

Chipotle Mexican Grill (CMG) STATEMENT OF CASH FLOWS ($ in millions)				
For the years ended December 31,	2011	2010	2009	2008
Cash flows from (for) *operating* activities				
Net income (loss)	$ 215	$ 179	$ 127	$ 78
Depreciation and amortization	75	69	61	53
Deferred income tax	11	10	8	13
Operating (gains) losses	12	13	21	21
Changes in working capital	98	18	43	33
Net cash from (for) operating activities	411	289	261	199
Cash flows from (for) *investing* activities				
Sale of property, plant, and equipment	0	0	0	0
Sale of investments	125	50	100	20
Purchase of property, plant, and equipment	(151)	(113)	(117)	(152)
Purchase of investments	(183)	(127)	(50)	(100)
Other investing cash flow items	(1)	0	0	0
Net cash from (for) investing activities	(210)	(190)	(67)	(232)
Cash flows from (for) *financing* activities				
Issuance of debt	0	0	0	0
Issuance of capital stock	0	0	0	0
Repayment of debt	0	0	0	0
Repurchase of capital stock	(64)	(109)	(72)	(30)
Cash dividends paid	0	0	0	0
Other financing cash flow items	40	14	10	0
Net cash (for) financing activities	(24)	(95)	(62)	(30)
Effect of exchange rate changes	0	0	0	0
Net change in cash	176	5	132	(63)
+ Beginning cash and cash equivalents	225	220	88	151
= Ending cash and cash equivalents	$ 401	$ 225	$ 220	$ 88
Supplemental information				
Free cash flow	$ 260	$ 176	$ 144	$ 47

Refer to the financial statements presented for Chipotle on the previous two pages to answer the following questions.

BALANCE SHEET

Q1 Review the following accounts, subtotals, and totals; (1) describe your observations; and then (2) identify what your observations indicate. A response is given for Cash and Cash Equivalents to help with understanding.

a. Cash and Cash Equivalents ... ***more than tripled*** *from $88 million in 2008 to $401 million in 2011. Also, cash and cash equivalents moved from being 10% of total assets in 2008 up to more than 25% of total assets in 2011,* ***indicating*** *this company is cash rich!*

b. Noncurrent assets... ·Non current assets have increased by 150 90% indicates growth and the company is investing in its future.

c. Total assets... Total assets have almost dubled vhich indicates growth.

d. Total liabilities... They have increased with assets vhich indicates the debt ratio stays the same.

e. Retained earnings... They have shy rockited vhich indicates a big increase in profitbility

f. Stockholders' equity... stoch holders has almost dubled. It mostly came from R&E

Q2 Compute the ratios requested in the chart below. *For ratio formulas and explanation refer to Appendix B – Ratios.*

Chipotle	Industry Norm*	12/31/2011	12/31/2008
Current ratio	1.3	3.19	2.79
Debt ratio	66%	27%	

* Industry: *Restaurants —Industry ratio averages from* <u>money.msn.com</u>

For each ratio, (a) compare the two years of ratios and *circle* the ratio indicating lower financial risk, (b) *cross out* any ratio indicating greater financial risk than the industry norm, and (c) *comment* on the results.

Q3 Overall, the balance sheet and related ratios indicate a (strengthening / steady / weakening) financial position. *Why?* List observations that support your conclusion and explain why.

INCOME STATEMENT

Q4 <u>Revenues</u> were $_____ million for the earliest year reported and $_____ million for the most recent year reported. Since the earliest year reported, this account has changed by $_____ million, which is a _____% (**increase / decrease**). During the same time period, *COGS* (**increased / decreased**) by _____%, *total operating expenses (other than COGS)* (**increased / decreased**) by _____%, resulting in *net income* (**increasing / decreasing**) by _____%.

Q5   Compute the ratios requested in the chart below. *For ratio formulas and explanation refer to Appendix B – Ratios.*

Chipotle	Industry Norm*	12/31/2011	12/31/2008
ROS	14.0 %		
ROA	14.0 %		
ROE	37.8 %		
Gross profit margin	33.5 %		
Accounts receivable turnover	71.2		
Inventory turnover	99		
Asset turnover	1.2		

*   Industry: *Restaurants —Industry ratio averages from* money.msn.com

For each ratio, (a) *circle* the stronger company ratio, (b) *cross out* any company ratio that is weaker than the industry norm, and (c) *comment* on the results.

Q6   The income statement and related ratios indicate (**strengthening / steady / weakening**) earnings potential. *Why?* List observations that support your conclusion and explain why.

STATEMENT OF CASH FLOWS

Q7   During 2011, the primary source of cash was (**operating activities / issuing debt / issuing capital stock**) and the primary use of cash was (**purchasing PPE / purchasing investments /paying dividends**).

For investments, there was a net cash outflow during (**2011 / 2010 / 2009 / 2008**), indicating that more investments were (**purchased / sold**).

A *net cash outflow for capital stock* occurred during (**2011 / 2010 / 2009 / 2008**), meaning more capital stock was (**issued / repurchased**). Repurchased common stock is referred to as (**common / preferred / treasury**) stock. Treasury stock (**increases / decreases**) total stockholders' equity on the balance sheet and decreases total shares outstanding, which is (**favorable / unfavorable**) for shareholders because earnings per share (**increases / decreases**).

Q8   Compute the ratios requested in the chart below. *For ratio formulas and explanation refer to Appendix B – Ratios.*

Chipotle RATIOS	Industry Norm	2011	2008
Free cash flow	NA	$	$
Cash flow adequacy	NA		
Cash flow liquidity	NA		
Quality of income	NA		

For each ratio, (a) *circle* the company ratio indicating the strongest cash position and (b) *comment* on the results.

Q9   The statement of cash flows reports a net increase in cash during (**2011 / 2010 / 2009 / 2008**). The statement of cash flows and related information report a (**strengthening / steady / weakening**) cash position.

Why?   List observations that support your conclusion and explain why.

STATEMENT OF RETAINED EARNINGS

Q10   a.   Complete the statement of retained earnings below.

Chipotle STATEMENT OF RETAINED EARNINGS ($ in millions)				
For the years ended December 31,	**2011**	**2010**	**2009**	**2008**
Retained earnings, beginning	$	$	$	$ 73
Net income				78
Dividends paid				0
Other adjustments	(1)	0	0	0
Retained earnings, ending	$	$	$	$ 151

b.   Retained earnings increased during (**2011 / 2010 / 2009**). *Why?*

OTHER

Q11   Based on the financial statements presented for Chipotle, would you invest in this company? (**Yes / No**) *Why?* *Support* your response with at least five good observations.

Purpose:
- Analyze the income statement, the balance sheet, and the statement of cash flows.
- Prepare a statement of retained earnings.

Carnival Corporation (CCL) BALANCE SHEET ($ in millions)				
ASSETS	**11/30/Year 5**	**11/30/Year 4**	**11/30/Year 3**	**11/30/Year 2**
Cash and cash equivalents	$ 1,178	$ 643	$ 610	$ 667
Short-term investments	9	17	461	39
Accounts receivable	408	409	403	108
Inventories	250	240	171	91
Other current assets	370	419	487	227
TOTAL Current assets	2,215	1,728	2,132	1,132
Property, plant, and equipment	25,331	24,184	20,073	12,103
Accumulated depreciation	(4,019)	(3,361)	(2,551)	(1,987)
PPE, net	21,312	20,823	17,522	10,116
Goodwill and other intangibles	4,488	4,627	4,355	681
Long-term investments	0	0	0	0
Other noncurrent assets	417	458	482	406
TOTAL Assets	$ 28,432	$ 27,636	$ 24,491	$ 12,335
LIABILITIES				
Accounts payable	$ 690	$ 631	$ 634	$ 269
Short-term debt	583	981	94	0
Current portion of long-term debt	1,042	681	392	155
Accrued expenses	832	721	568	290
Other current liabilities	2,045	2,020	1,622	906
TOTAL Current liabilities	5,192	5,034	3,310	1,620
Long-term debt	5,727	6,291	6,918	3,014
Deferred income taxes	0	0	0	0
Other noncurrent liabilities	541	551	470	283
TOTAL Noncurrent liabilities	6,268	6,842	7,388	3,297
TOTAL Liabilities	11,460	11,876	10,698	4,917
STOCKHOLDERS' EQUITY				
Preferred stock	0	0	0	0
Common stock, par	359	359	355	6
Additional paid-in capital	7,381	7,311	7,163	1,089
Retained earnings	10,233	8,623	7,191	6,326
Other stockholders' equity	143	525	142	(3)
Treasury stock	(1,144)	(1,058)	(1,058)	0
TOTAL Stockholders' equity	16,972	15,760	13,793	7,418
TOTAL L & SE	$ 28,432	$ 27,636	$ 24,491	$ 12,335

Carnival Corporation (CCL) INCOME STATEMENT ($ in millions)				
For the years ended November 30,	Year 5	Year 4	Year 3	Year 2
Revenue	$ 10,735	$ 9,427	$ 6,459	$ 4,244
Cost of goods sold (COGS)	4,822	4,244	2,880	1,764
Gross profit	5,913	5,183	3,579	2,480
Selling, general, and admin expense (SGA)	2,474	2,288	1,680	1,067
Depreciation and amortization expense	902	812	585	382
Other operating expenses	(102)	(90)	(69)	(11)
Total operating expenses	3,274	3,010	2,196	1,438
Operating income	2,639	2,173	2,173	1,042
Interest income (expense) and other	(330)	(284)	(195)	(111)
Total nonoperating revenue (expense)	21	12	35	28
Income before income tax	2,330	1,901	1,223	959
Provision for income tax	73	47	29	(57)
Income from continuing operations	2,257	1,854	1,194	1,016
Nonrecurring items / Minority interest	0	0	0	0
Net income	$ 2,257	$ 1,854	$ 1,194	$ 1,016
Outstanding shares (in millions)	806	802	718	587

Carnival Corporation(CCL) STATEMENT OF CASH FLOWS ($ in millions)				
For the years ended November 30,	Year 5	Year 4	Year 3	Year 2
Cash flows from (for) *operating* activities				
Net income (loss)	$ 2,257	$ 1,854	$ 1,194	$ 1,016
Depreciation and amortization	902	812	585	382
Operating (gains) losses	45	28	22	54
Changes in working capital	206	522	132	17
Net cash from operating activities	3,410	3,216	1,933	1,469
Cash flows from (for) *investing* activities				
Sale of property, plant, and equipment	0	0	0	0
Sale of investments	0	0	0	0
Purchase of property, plant, and equipment	(1,977)	(3,586)	(2,516)	(1,986)
Purchase of investments	0	0	0	0
Other investing cash flow items	7	497	83	(75)
Net cash (for) investing activities	(1,970)	(3,089)	(2,433)	(2,061)
Cash flows from (for) *financing* activities				
Issuance of debt	910	881	1,751	232
Issuance of capital stock	50	112	42	7
Repayment of debt	(912)	(736)	(898)	(190)
Repurchase of capital stock	(305)	0	0	0
Cash dividends paid	(566)	(400)	(292)	(246)
Other financing cash flow items	(69)	64	(137)	(1)
Net cash from (for) financing activities	(892)	(79)	466	(198)
Effect of exchange rate changes	(13)	(15)	(23)	(5)
Net change in cash	535	33	(57)	(795)
+ Beginning cash and cash equivalents	643	610	667	1,421
= Ending cash and cash equivalents	$ 1,178	$ 643	$ 610	$ 667
Supplemental information				
Cash interest paid	$ 314	$ 250	$ 156	$ 110
Cash taxes paid	15	8	20	0
Free cash flow	867	(770)	(875)	(763)

Refer to the financial statements presented for Carnival Corporation on the previous two pages to answer the following questions.

BALANCE SHEET

Q1   Review the following accounts, subtotals, and totals; (1) describe your observations; and then (2) identify what your observations indicate. A response is given for PPE, net to help with understanding.

   a.   Property, plant, and equipment, net … ***increased*** *from $10,116 million in Year 2 to $21,312 million in Year 5, an increase of 111%,* **indicating** *purchases of additional cruise ships for expansion. The greatest increase was in Year 3, when PPE increased by more than 50%.*

   b.   Goodwill and other intangibles…

   c.   Long-term debt…

   d.   Contributed capital totals $_____ million on Year 5…

   e.   Retained earnings…

Q2   Compute the ratios requested in the chart below. *For ratio formulas and explanation refer to Appendix B—Ratios.*

Carnival Corporation	*Industry Norm**	Year 5	Year 3
Current ratio	*0.50*		
Debt ratio	63%		
Times Interest Earned	*8.00*		

   *   Industry: *Resorts and Casinos—Industry and S&P 500 ratio averages from* *money.msn.com*

For each ratio, (a) compare the two years of ratios and *circle* the ratio indicating lower financial risk, (b) *cross out* any ratio indicating greater financial risk than the industry norm, and (c) *comment* on the results.

Q3   Overall, the balance sheet and related ratios indicate a (**strengthening / steady / weakening**) financial position. *Why?* List observations that support your conclusion and explain why.

INCOME STATEMENT

Q4   *Revenues* were $_____ million for the earliest year reported and $_____ million for the most recent year reported. Since the earliest year reported, this account has changed by $_____ million, which is a(n) _____% (**increase / decrease**). During the same time period, *COGS* (**increased / decreased**) by _____%, *operating expenses (other than COGS)* (**increased / decreased**) by _____%, and *net income* (**increased / decreased**) by _____%.

Q5 Compute the ratios requested in the chart below. *For ratio formulas and explanation refer to Appendix B—Ratios.*

Carnival Corporation	Industry Norm*	Year 5	Year 3
Gross profit margin	50.8%		
ROS	16.8%		
ROA	6.7%		
ROE	12.2%		
Asset turnover	0.40		

* Industry: *Resorts and Casinos—Industry and S&P 500 ratio averages from* <u>money.msn.com</u>

For each ratio, (a) circle the stronger company ratio, (b) *cross out* any company ratio that is weaker than the industry norm, and (c) *comment* on the results.

Q6 The income statement and related ratios indicate (**strengthening / steady / weakening**) earnings potential. *Why?* List observations that support your conclusion and explain why.

STATEMENT OF CASH FLOWS

Q7 The primary source of cash was (**operating / investing / financing**), which is a(n) (**favorable / unfavorable**) sign.

For *property, plant, and equipment* a net cash (**inflow / outflow**) was reported in the (**operating / investing / financing**) activity section so PPE was (**purchased / sold**), which is a(n) (**favorable / unfavorable**) sign *indicating...*

A *net cash inflow for debt* occurred during FYE (**5 / 4 / 3 / 2**), indicating more debt was (**borrowed / repaid**). These amounts appear to have primarily financed (**operations / the purchase of PPE / the repurchase of common stock**).

A *net cash inflow for capital stock* occurred during FYE (**5 / 4 / 3 / 2**), indicating more capital stock was (**issued / repurchased**). This is a(n) (**favorable / unfavorable**) sign *indicating...*

Q8 *Net cash from operating activities* (**increased / decreased**) by $_____ million or _____%. During the same time period, *dividends paid* (**increased / decreased**) by _____%.

Q9 Compute the ratios requested in the chart below. *For ratio formulas and explanation refer to Appendix B—Ratios.*

Carnival Corporation	Industry Norm	Year 5	Year 3
Free cash flow ($ in millions)	NA	$	$
Cash flow adequacy ratio	NA		
Cash flow liquidity ratio	NA		
Quality of income ratio	NA		

For each ratio, (a) *circle* the company ratio indicating the strongest cash position and (b) *comment* on the results.

Q10   Complete the common-size Statement of Cash Flows for Year 5. Only select accounts are reported.

Carnival Corporation STATEMENT OF CASH FLOWS Common-Size ($ in millions)				
For the years ended November 30,	Year 5	Year 5	Year 3	Year 3
Net cash from operating activities	$ _____	100.00%	$ 1,933	100.00%
Purchase of PPE	_____	____%	(2,516)	-130.16%
Issuance of debt	_____	____%	1,751	90.58%
Issuance of capital stock	_____	____%	42	2.17%
Repayment of debt	_____	____%	(898)	-46.46%
Repurchase of capital stock	_____	____%	0	0.00%
Cash dividends paid	_____	____%	(292)	-15.11%
Net change in cash	$ 535	____%	$ (57)	-1.50%

* Only select amounts are listed above and will not necessarily sum to the total.

In Year 3, the primary use of cash was (**purchasing PPE / repaying debt / paying dividends**) using _____% of NCOA, whereas in Year 5, the primary use of cash was (**purchasing PPE / repaying debt / paying dividends**) using _____% of NCOA,

Q11   The statement of cash flows indicates a (**strengthening / steady / weakening**) cash position. *Why? Comment* on your observations.

STATEMENT OF RETAINED EARNINGS

Q12   Complete the statement of retained earnings below.

Carnival Corporation STATEMENT OF RETAINED EARNINGS ($ in millions)				
For the years ended November 30,	Year 5	Year 4	Year 3	Year 2
Retained earnings, beginning	$	$	$	$ 5,556
Net income				1,016
Dividends				(246)
Other adjustments	(81)	(22)	(37)	(0)
Retained earnings, ending	$	$	$	$ 6,326

Net income is initially reported on the (**balance sheet / income statement / statement of cash flows**) and dividends paid are initially reported on the (**balance sheet / income statement / statement of cash flows**).

OTHER

Q13   Based on the financial statements presented for Carnival Corporation, would you invest in this company? (**Yes / No**) *Why? Support* your response by listing at least five significant observations.

Purpose:
- Analyze the income statement, the balance sheet, and the statement of cash flows.
- Prepare a statement of retained earnings.

Circuit City Stores (CCYTQ) BALANCE SHEET ($ in millions)				
ASSETS	**2/28/Year 7**	**2/28/Year 6**	**2/28/Year 5**	**2/28/Year 4**
Cash and cash equivalents	$ 296	$ 141	$ 316	$ 880
Short-term investments	1	600	522	125
Accounts receivable	489	424	221	231
Inventories	1,574	1,637	1,698	1,455
Other current assets	80	82	76	54
TOTAL Current assets	2,440	2,884	2,833	2,745
Property, plant, and equipment	2,485	2,220	2,019	1,820
Accumulated depreciation	(1,448)	(1,300)	(1,179)	(1,093)
PPE, net	1,037	920	840	727
Goodwill and other intangibles	136	141	254	247
Long-term investments	0	0	0	0
Other noncurrent assets	132	62	142	121
TOTAL Noncurrent assets	1,305	1,123	1,236	1,095
TOTAL Assets	$ 3,745	$ 4,007	$ 4,069	$ 3,840
LIABILITIES				
Accounts payable	$ 912	$ 922	$ 850	$ 636
Short-term debt	0	0	22	0
Current portion of long-term debt	12	7	7	1
Accrued expenses	318	380	287	171
Other current liabilities	365	404	456	508
TOTAL Current liabilities	1,607	1,713	1,622	1,316
Long-term debt	57	50	52	20
Deferred income taxes	36	0	0	0
Other noncurrent liabilities	542	453	440	425
TOTAL Noncurrent liabilities	635	503	492	445
TOTAL Liabilities	2,242	2,216	2,114	1,761
STOCKHOLDERS' EQUITY				
Preferred stock	0	0	0	0
Common stock, par	84	86	87	94
Additional paid-in capital	320	344	459	720
Retained earnings	981	1,336	1,365	1,240
Other stockholders' equity	118	25	44	25
TOTAL Stockholders' equity	1,503	1,791	1,955	2,079
TOTAL L & SE	$ 3,745	$ 4,007	$ 4,069	$ 3,840

Circuit City Stores (CCYTQ) INCOME STATEMENT ($ in millions)				
For the years ended February 28,	Year 7	Year 6	Year 5	Year 4
Revenue	$ 11,744	$ 12,430	$ 11,514	$ 10,470
Cost of goods sold (COGS)	9,318	9,501	8,704	7,901
Gross profit	2,426	2,928	2,810	2,569
Selling, general, and admin expense (SGA)	2,587	2,664	2,435	2,322
Depreciation and amortization expense	183	178	161	154
Other operating expenses	26	92	0	(15)
Total operating expenses	2796	2934	2,596	2,461
Operating income	(370)	(6)	214	108
Interest income (expense) and other	17	26	19	(5)
Income before income tax	(353)	20	233	103
Provision for income tax	(32)	31	86	38
Income from continuing operations	(321)	(11)	147	65
Nonrecurring items / Minority interest	1	2	(11)	(3)
Net income	$ (320)	$ (9)	$ 136	$ 62

Circuit City (CCYTQ) STATEMENT OF CASH FLOWS ($ in millions)				
For the years ended February 28,	Year 7	Year 6	Year 5	Year 4
Cash flows from (for) *operating* activities				
Net income (loss)	$ (320)	$ (9)	$ 136	$ 62
Depreciation and amortization	187	182	164	154
Deferred income tax	28	72	(14)	(116)
Operating (gains) losses	71	120	27	10
Changes in working capital	4	(46)	43	274
Net cash from (for) operating activities	(30)	319	356	384
Cash flows from (for) *investing* activities				
Sale of property, plant, and equipment	71	39	55	61
Sale of investments	3,246	1,926	1,015	--
Purchase of property, plant, and equipment	(325)	(286)	(254)	(151)
Purchase of investments	(2,650)	(2,002)	(1,410)	--
Other investing cash flow items	(1)	(12)	--	--
Net cash from (for) investing activities	341	(335)	(594)	(90)
Cash flows from (for) *financing* activities				
Issuance of debt	256	37	19	--
Issuance of capital stock	5	90	38	9
Repayment of debt	(295)	(64)	(58)	(25)
Repurchase of capital stock	(47)	(237)	(339)	--
Cash dividends paid	(27)	(20)	(13)	(14)
Other financing cash flow items	(49)	36	25	(632)
Net cash (for) financing activities	(157)	(158)	(328)	(662)
Effect of exchange rate changes	1	(1)	2	--
Net change in cash	155	(175)	(564)	(368)
+ Beginning cash and cash equivalents	141	316	880	1,248
= Ending cash and cash equivalents	$ 296	$ 141	$ 316	$ 880
Supplemental information				
Free cash flow	$ (382)	$ 13	$ 89	$ 219

Refer to the financial statements presented for Circuit City on the previous two pages to answer the following questions.

BALANCE SHEET

Q1   Review the following accounts, subtotals, and totals; (1) describe your observations; and then (2) identify what your observations indicate. A response is given for Current Assets to help with understanding.

a.   Current assets... ***decreased*** *in Year 7 due to a sharp decline in short-term investments and a dip in inventory. The buildup of accounts receivable accompanied by a decrease in inventory is cause for concern,* **indicating** *credit terms might be too lax.*

b.   Noncurrent assets...

c.   Total assets...

d.   Total liabilities...

e.   Retained earnings...

f.   Stockholders' equity...

Q2   Compute the ratios requested in the chart below. *For ratio formulas and explanation refer to Appendix B—Ratios.*

Circuit City	Industry Norm*	Year 7	Year 4
Current ratio	1.3		
Debt ratio	29%		

    *   Industry: *Electronics Stores—Industry ratio averages from* money.msn.com

For each ratio, (a) compare the two years of company ratios and *circle* the ratio indicating lower financial risk, (b) *cross out* any company ratio indicating greater financial risk than the industry norm, and (c) *comment* on the results.

Q3   Overall, the balance sheet and related ratios indicate a (**strengthening / steady / weakening**) financial position. *Why?* List observations that support your conclusion and explain why.

INCOME STATEMENT

Q4   *Revenues* were $_____ million for the earliest year reported and $_____ million for the most recent year reported. Since the earliest year reported, this account has changed by $_____ million, which is a _____% (**increase / decrease**). During the same time period, *COGS* (**increased / decreased**) by _____%, *total operating expenses (other than COGS)* (**increased / decreased**) by _____%, and *net income* (**increased / decreased**).

Q5 Compute the ratios requested in the chart below.
For ratio formulas and explanation refer to Appendix B—Ratios.

Circuit City	Industry Norm*	Year 7	Year 4
ROS	2.9%		
ROA	7.8%		
ROE	21.3%		
Gross profit margin	27.5%		
Accounts receivable turnover	63		
Inventory turnover	6.3		
Asset turnover	2.8		

*   Industry: *Electronics Stores—Industry ratio averages from* <u>money.msn.com</u>

For each ratio, (a) *circle* the stronger ratio, (b) *cross out* any ratio that is weaker than the industry norm, and (c) *comment* on the results.

Q6 The income statement and related ratios indicate (**strengthening / steady / weakening**) earnings potential. *Why?* List observations that support your conclusion and explain why.

STATEMENT OF CASH FLOWS

Q7 The primary source of cash was operating activities during Year (**7 / 6 / 5 / 4**).
Investing activities provided a source of cash during Year (**7 / 6 / 5 / 4**), *indicating ...*

A *net cash outflow for capital stock* occurred during Year (**7 / 6 / 5 / 4**), meaning more capital stock was (**issued / repurchased**). Repurchased common stock is referred to as (**common / preferred / treasury**) stock. Treasury stock (**increases / decreases**) total stockholders' equity on the balance sheet and decreases total shares outstanding, which is (**favorable / unfavorable**) for shareholders because earnings per share (**increases / decreases**).

Q8 Compute the ratios requested in the chart below. *For ratio formulas and explanation refer to Appendix B—Ratios.*

Circuit City RATIOS	Industry Norm	Year 7	Year 4
Free cash flow ($ in millions)	NA	$	$
Cash flow adequacy	NA		
Cash flow liquidity	NA		
Quality of income	NA		

For each ratio, (a) *circle* the company ratio indicating the strongest cash position and (b) *comment* on the results.

Q9   The statement of cash flows and related information report a (**strengthening / steady / weakening**) cash position. *Why?* List observations that support your conclusion and explain why.

STATEMENT OF RETAINED EARNINGS

Q10   Complete the statement of retained earnings below.

Circuit City STATEMENT OF RETAINED EARNINGS ($ in millions)				
For the years ended February 28,	Year 7	Year 6	Year 5	Year 4
Retained earnings, beginning	$	$	$	$ 1,199
Net income				62
Dividends paid				(14)
Other adjustments	(8)	0	2	(7)
Retained earnings, ending	$	$	$	$ 1,240

  a.   A net loss was reported during Year (**7 / 6 / 5 / 4**) and dividends increased during Year (**7 / 6 / 5 / 4**). What might be one reason that dividends paid increased?

  b.   Retained earnings decreased during Year (**7 / 6 / 5**). *Why?*

OTHER

Q11   Circuit City filed for bankruptcy 6 months into Year 8. What signs of this impending bankruptcy do you find in these financial statements? When did these signs start to appear?

CAPSTONE PROJECT

WOULD YOU ADVISE A FRIEND TO INVEST IN THIS COMPANY?

PURPOSE: This chapter outlines a capstone project that includes researching and analyzing a publicly-traded corporation of your choice.

In this project, you will use your understanding of financial accounting to analyze a company's financial statements. To prepare this analysis, you will use data from the Internet and organize it using 5 worksheets. Then, you will communicate the results of your analysis in a detailed written report and highlight the results in a presentation. Accordingly, this project will help you build your critical thinking, technology, and communication skills.

You will be responsible for the following parts of this project:

PART 1 – WRITTEN REPORT AND COMPANY RESEARCH (Activity 108)

   A.   **Tell Me About Your Company:** Choose a company to research. Write a brief description of your company, its industry, its products, and its markets.

   B.   **Company News:** Search for at least 2 major events that have affected your company or its industry over the past year.

   C.   **Stock Market Activity:** Summarize your company's market activity over the past 10 years.

   D.   **Financial Statement Analysis:** Prepare and analyze condensed, trend, and common-size financial statements for your company.

   E.   **Ratio Analysis:** Compute financial statement ratios for your company to analyze its profitability, efficiency, liquidity, and solvency. Compare to industry norms.

   F.   **Research Summary:** Would You Advise a Friend to Invest in This Company? Prepare a 2-page written summary of your analysis and investment recommendation.

PART 2 – PRESENTATION AND POWERPOINT SLIDES (Activity 109)

Would you advise a friend to invest in this company? Prepare and deliver a short presentation highlighting information that supports your investment recommendation.

Have fun with this project! Be creative!
Include graphs, charts, and other items to enhance the overall project.

Purpose:
- Use a variety of resources to research a corporation.
- Research the current stock quote of your company and analyze past market activity.
- Prepare a financial statement analysis using condensed, trend, and common-size financial statements.
- Compute financial statement ratios and analyze.
- Compare company ratios to industry averages.
- Support your investing advice with three to five significant points based on previous research, analysis, and sound reasoning.
- Prepare a well-written report analyzing your corporation using appropriate business and accounting vocabulary.

A.   Tell me about your company ... its industry, its products, and its market (1-3 pages)

Choose a company to research. The company must be publicly traded but not regulated. Each student will select a different company. The Instructor must approve the company. If you are undecided about which company to select, choose one of the 30 corporations comprising the Dow Jones Industrial Average (DJIA) listed below or one of the companies used in this text, which can be found in Appendix A.

"30 INDUSTRIAL" STOCKS
that currently comprise the
DOW JONES INDUSTRIAL AVERAGE

3M (MMM)	ExxonMobil (XOM)	Merck (MRK)
Alcoa (AA)	General Electric (GE)	Microsoft (MSFT)
American Express (AXP)	Hewlett-Packard (HPQ)	Pfizer (PFE)
AT&T (T)	Home Depot (HD)	Procter & Gamble (PG)
Bank of America (BAC)	Intel (INTC)	The Coca-Cola Company (KO)
Boeing (BA)	IBM (IBM)	Travelers Companies (TRV)
Caterpillar (CAT)	Johnson & Johnson (JNJ)	United Technologies (UTX)
Chevron Corporation (CVX)	JPMorgan Chase (JPM)	Verizon Communications (VZ)
Cisco Systems (CSCO)	Kraft Foods (KFT)	Wal-Mart Stores (WMT)
DuPont (DD)	McDonald's (MCD)	Walt Disney (DIS)

Research your company using a variety of resources.

1.   **Explore the corporate website,** which usually provides updated comprehensive information including links to current news items and financial information. Note that the company provides the information posted on the website and, therefore, may be biased in favor of the company.

2.   **Review the Annual Report,** especially the *Letter to Shareholders* and *Management's Discussion & Analysis,* which summarizes the past year and highlights future opportunities. Links to the Annual Report are usually found on the company website under Investor Relations.

3.   **Consult the Form 10-K filed with the SEC.** This form contains a wealth of information. Read through PART 1 Item 1. *Business* to find information regarding the business, product offerings, marketing strategy, competition, and market share. Form 10-K information is available at *http://www.sec.gov/edgar/searchedgar/companysearch.html.*

Summarize your research in a 1-3 page written report of your company … its industry, its products, and its markets. This should be a well-written paper with introductory and concluding paragraphs.

Appropriately cite all sources and include a print-out of each cited page in Appendix 3.

B.   **Company News (1-2 pages)**

Search for *at least two* significant news items or events that have affected your company or its industry over the past year. Briefly describe each event. Next, discuss how this event will affect the company's operations and the financial ratios. Make certain that the item is truly newsworthy. For example, the announcement of a dividend is not newsworthy unless it is a major surprise.

Appropriately cite all sources and include a print-out of each cited page in Appendix 3.

C.   **Stock Market Activity (1-2 pages)**

Summarize the market activity of your company's stock, including the current stock quote and market activity over the most recent 10 years. In addition, explain trends and events influencing the stock chart.

       Include your company's 10-year stock chart.

       Find stock market activity information and charts at:

           http://money.msn.com

           http://finance.yahoo.com

           http://www.google.com/finance

Appropriately cite all sources and include a print-out of each cited page in Appendix 3.

D.   **Financial Statement Analysis (4 pages)**

Collect three years of financial statement information to prepare the condensed balance sheet, the condensed income statement, and the condensed statement of cash flows. Use the three most recent years available. Organize your information using Worksheets A, B, and C found on pages 306 to 308.

Financial Statement information can be found at:

       http://money.msn.com

       http://finance.yahoo.com

       http://www.google.com/finance

Prepare Trend Analyses and Common-Size Financial Statements

Balance Sheet: Prepare a trend analysis and common-size balance sheet using the amounts from the condensed balance sheet. Enter the results in Worksheet A on page 306.

Income Statement: Prepare the trend analysis and common-size income statement using the amounts from the condensed balance sheet. Enter the results in Worksheet B on page 307.

Statement of Cash Flows: Prepare the trend analysis and common-size income statement using the amounts from the condensed statement of cash flows. Enter the results in Worksheet C on page 308.

Analyze each Financial Statement (1-page each)

Balance Sheet: Review the condensed, trend, and common-size balance sheet. Summarize your analysis in a one-page written report. Comment on trends in the growth of assets, liabilities, and stockholders' equity, and overall financial risk.

Income Statement: Review the condensed, trend, and common-size balance sheet. Summarize your analysis in a one-page written report. Comment on trends in the growth of revenues, expenses, and net income, and overall profitability.

Statement of Cash Flows: Review the condensed, trend, and common-size balance sheet. Summarize your analysis in a one-page written report. Comment on trends in the growth of operating, investing, and financing activities, and the overall cash position.

Summarize your results in a 1-page written report.

Review the information reported on Worksheets A, B, and C.
Write a report summarizing the overall story of the financial statements (1 page).

Appropriately cite all sources.
In Appendix 1, include a copy of Worksheets A, B, and C.
In Appendix 2, include a copy of the company's financial statements.
In Appendix 3, include a print-out of each cited page.

(Optional) Create a Microsoft Excel workbook based on the tables provided on the following pages.

Create a separate worksheet tab for the balance sheet, income statement, and statement of cash flows. Use Excel formulas for all computations within the condensed financial statements. Create the trend and common-size financial statements using Excel formulas that reference the condensed financial statement.

E.   **Ratio Analysis (2-4 pages)**

Collect the additional data needed for ratio computations listed below.   *MSN. Money*
- Accounts receivable
  Inventory
  Interest expense
  Capital expenditures
  Dividends paid

Record this information on Worksheet D – Ratio Analysis (page 309).

Compute two years of ratios for each ratio listed below.

1.	Return on Sales	7.	Asset Turnover
2.	Return on Assets	8.	Current Ratio
3.	Return on Equity	9.	Debt Ratio
4.	Gross Profit Margin	10.	Financial Leverage
5.	Accounts Receivable Turnover	11.	Times Interest Earned
6.	Inventory Turnover	12.	Free Cash Flow

Ratio formulas can be found in Appendix B. Record your results on Worksheet D – Ratio Analysis found on page 309. Note that all ratios may not apply to your company.

Analyze ratio trends.

Compare the two years of ratio information. Indicate whether each ratio is stronger/weaker, quicker/slower, more/less liquid, or more/less risk on Worksheet D – Ratio Analysis.

Obtain industry averages.

Industry average information can be found at _money.msn.com_* and _finance.yahoo.com_.** Note the industry and record at the top of Worksheet D – Ratio Analysis. Record the industry averages in the first column of Worksheet D – Ratio Analysis. (page 309. Note: Because free cash flow is not comparable among companies, no industry average is available.)

*   At _money.msn.com_ to find industry average ratios: (1) Type in the Ticker Symbol or Company Name in the GET QUOTE box, then (2) in the left-hand column menu under Fundamentals click on Key Ratios.

**   At _finance.yahoo.com_ to find industry average ratios: (1) Type in the Ticker Symbol or Company Name in the Get Quotes box, then (2) in the left-hand column menu under COMPANY click on Competitors.

Summarize your results in a 1-3 page written report.

Refer to the information reported on Worksheet D – Ratio Analysis.

Write a 1-3 page report discussing:

What information each ratio reveals about your company.

Your company's profitability, efficiency, liquidity, and solvency, and noting whether they are improving or deteriorating.

Your company's profitability, efficiency, liquidity, and solvency, are noting whether they are better than or worse than its peers.

In Appendix 1, include a copy of Worksheet D – Ratio Analysis.

Appropriately cite all sources and include a print-out of each cited page in Appendix 3.

(Optional)   Add a Ratios tab to your Microsoft Excel workbook formatted similar to Worksheet D – Ratio Analysis.

F. **Research Summary (2 pages)**

Use the format shown in Worksheet E – Research Summary (page 310) to prepare a two-page summary of your analysis. This conclusion should summarize your research in a clear and concise manner. As a part of this analysis:

1. Indicate whether the overall profitability, efficiency, liquidity, and solvency of the company are strong, average, or weak. Briefly explain why you came to this conclusion.

2. Prepare the DuPont Analysis of ROE for your company and its industry. Indicate the primary driver of ROA and ROE for your company.

3. Summarize current events and other items of importance.

4. Indicate whether you would invest in your company, identifying three to five significant points that justify your conclusion.

In Appendix 1, include a copy of Worksheet E – Research Summary.

Place your Written Report, including a title page, in a binder.

Set apart the following sections, in this order:
*   Title Page
*   Research Summary   (Part F)
*   Tell Me About Your Company   (Part A)
*   Company News   (Part B)
*   Stock Market Activity   (Part C)
*   Financial Statement Analysis   (Part D)
*   Ratio Analysis   (Part E)
*   Sources Used
*   Appendix 1 – Copies of Worksheets A, B, C, D, and E
*   Appendix 2 – Copies of your company's financial statements
*   Appendix 3 – Printouts of materials cited in report (such as company information and news events)

Written reports will be graded on comprehensive coverage, accuracy of the analysis, use of a clear and concise writing style that is easy to understand and professional in appearance.

Professional Quality. Prepare your report as a professional-looking document for which you were paid a great deal of money. Be careful with grammar and spelling; business leaders have a "zero tolerance" policy regarding basic spelling and grammar mistakes. Use Microsoft Word, double-space the paper and leave one-inch margins.

Proper Referencing. Copying or rewording another report without proper citation and quotation is considered plagiarism. In the body of the paper, include proper references to all written materials and internet sources, with a complete page of sources used. Include printouts from cited sources in Appendix 3.

Format: Typed, double-spaced with one-inch margins, using a 12-point Times New Roman font.

(Your Company Name) CONDENSED CLASSIFIED BALANCE SHEET (Month) (Day)			
($ in millions) Year-End	2023 (Most recent)	2022	2021
Current assets	$17.85 B	$ 21.57 B	$ 20.76 B
PPE, net	35.49 B	32.24 B	30.49 B
Goodwill and intangibles	14.00 M	25.00 M	668.00 M
Other assets			
TOTAL ASSETS	$	$	$
Current liabilities	$ 19.50 B	$ 21.75 B	$ 20.13 B
Noncurrent liabilities	14.07 B	11.58 B	9.77 B
Contributed capital			
Retained earnings			
Treasury stock and other SE	11.23 B	12.83 B	14.44 B
TOTAL L & SE	$	$	$

(Your Company Name) CONDENSED TREND ANALYSIS BALANCE SHEET (Month) (Day)			
Year-End	(Most recent)		
Current assets			100
PPE, net			100
Goodwill and intangibles			100
Other assets			100
TOTAL ASSETS			100
Current liabilities			100
Noncurrent liabilities			100
Contributed capital			100
Retained earnings			100
Treasury stock and other SE			100
TOTAL L & SE			100

(Your Company Name) CONDENSED COMMON-SIZE BALANCE SHEET (Month) (Day)			
Year-End	(Most recent)		
Current assets	%	%	%
PPE, net	%	%	%
Goodwill and intangibles	%	%	%
Other assets	%	%	%
TOTAL ASSETS	100.0%	100.0%	100.0%
Current liabilities	%	%	%
Noncurrent liabilities	%	%	%
Contributed capital	%	%	%
Retained earnings	%	%	%
Treasury stock and other SE	%	%	%
TOTAL L & SE	100.0%	100.0%	100.0%

(Your Company Name)
CONDENSED MULTISTEP INCOME STATEMENT
Fiscal Year Ended (Month) (Day)

($ in millions) Year-End	2023 (Most recent)	2022	2021
Sales revenue	$ 109.12B	$ 106.01B	$ 93.56 B
Cost of goods sold	82.23B	74.96B	105.95B
Gross profit	26.89 B	31.04 B	27.61 B
Operating expenses	23.04 B	21.76 B	21.58 B
Operating income	3.85B	9.28 B	6.03B
Nonoperating revenues and expenses	48.00 M	47.00 M	-16.00M
Income before income tax	3.42 B	8.9 B	5.55 B
Provision for income tax	638,000	1,961,000	1,178,000
Income from continuing operations	2,780,000	6,946,000	4,368,000
Nonrecurring items			
NET INCOME	$ 2.78 B	$ 6.95 B	$ 4.37B
Earnings per share	$ 6.02	$ 14.23	$ 8.72

(Your Company Name)
CONDENSED TREND ANALYSIS INCOME STATEMENT
Fiscal Year Ended (Month) (Day)

Year-End	(Most recent)		
Sales revenue			100
Cost of goods sold			100
Gross profit			100
Operating expenses			100
Operating income			100
Nonoperating revenues and expenses			100
Income before income tax			100
Provision for income tax			100
Income from continuing operations			100
Nonrecurring items			100
NET INCOME			100
Earnings per share			100

(Your Company Name)
CONDENSED COMMON-SIZE INCOME STATEMENT
Fiscal Year Ended (Month) (Day)

Year-End	(Most recent)		
Sales revenue	100.0%	100.0%	100.0%
Cost of goods sold	%	%	%
Gross profit	%	%	%
Operating expenses	%	%	%
Operating income	%	%	%
Nonoperating revenues and expenses	%	%	%
Income before income tax	%	%	%
Provision for income tax	%	%	%
Income from continuing operations	%	%	%
Nonrecurring items	%	%	%

WORKSHEET C:		STATEMENT OF CASH FLOWS ANALYSIS

(Your Company Name)
CONDENSED STATEMENT OF CASH FLOWS
Fiscal Year Ended (Month) (Day)

($ in millions)	Year-End	2023 (Most recent)	2022	2021
Net cash from *operating* activities		$4.02B	$8.63B	$10.53B
Net cash from *investing* activities		-5.50B	-3.15B	-2.59B
Net cash from *financing* activities		-2.20B	-8.07B	-2.00B
Effect of *exchange rate* on cash				
Net change in cash				
Cash, beginning				
Cash, ending		$2.3B	$5.9B	$8.5B

(Your Company Name)
CONDENSED TREND ANALYSIS STATEMENT OF CASH FLOWS
Fiscal Year Ended (Month) (Day)

	Year-End	(Most recent)		
Net cash from *operating* activities				100
Net cash from *investing* activities				100
Net cash from *financing* activities				100
Effect of *exchange rate* on cash				100
Net change in cash				100

(Your Company Name)
CONDENSED COMMON-SIZE STATEMENT OF CASH FLOWS
Fiscal Year Ended (Month) (Day)

	Year-End	(Most recent)		
Net cash from *operating* activities		100.0%	100.0%	100.0%
Net cash from *investing* activities		%	%	%
Net cash from *financing* activities		%	%	%
Effect of *exchange rate* on cash		%	%	%
Net change in cash		%	%	%

Company Name: **Walmart**
Industry Name: **Retail**

	Industry Ratios Average	Change	Company Ratios	
Title of Ratio -301 87			Current Year	Prior Year
Profitability Ratios				
Return on sales (ROS) 0.08	~~5.2~~ %	Stronger / ~~Weaker~~	38.13 %	42.45 %
Return on assets (ROA) 0.18	~~7~~ %	Stronger / ~~Weaker~~	8.10 %	12.68 %
Return on equity (ROE) 04.4	~~12.8~~ %	Stronger / ~~Weaker~~	-66.45 %	-73.38 %
Gross profit margin -2630	~~48.7~~ %	Stronger / ~~Weaker~~	1.40 %	4.8 %
Efficiency Ratios				
Accounts receivable turnover 669	~~14.13~~	Quicker / Slower	9.10	9.60
Inventory turnover 771	~~84.84~~	Quicker / Slower	185.04	202.88
Asset turnover 241.802	0.~~284~~	Quicker / Slower	0.365	0.449
Liquidity Ratios				
Current ratio 95.14		More / Less Liquid	1.01	0.98
Solvency Ratios				
Debt ratio 126.34	%	More / Less Risk	4.78 %	4.16 %
Financial leverage ~~850.00~~ 6.04		More / Less Risk	17.28	23.25
Times interest earned -387.10		More / Less Risk	1.28	1.31
Free cash flow ($ in millions)	XXXXX	More / Less Risk	$ -1.48	$ 2.10

(margin notes: 114.7)

(right margin notes: millions / 15,080 / 478,614)

Additional data needed for ratio computations:

($ in millions)	Year...	(Most recent)		
Accounts receivable		$	$	$
Inventory				
Interest expense				
Capital expenditures				
Dividends paid				

Company Name: _____

Industry Name: _____

1. **FINANCIAL ANALYSIS** of your company:

Profitability (~~Strong~~ / Average / ~~Weak~~) Explain:	
Efficiency (~~Strong~~ / Average / Weak) Explain:	
Liquidity (~~Strong~~ / Average / Weak) Explain:	
Solvency (Strong / Average / Weak) Explain:	

2. **DuPont Analysis of ROE**

Ratio	ROS	x Asset Turnover	= ROA	x Financial Leverage	= ROE
Type	Profitability	Efficiency		Solvency	
Formula	NI / Rev	Rev / A	NI / A	A / SE	NI / SE
Your Company	-3.71.22 %	0.56	-2.1 %	2.96	− 6.1 %
Your Industry	%		%		%

For your company, the primary driver of ROA is [**ROS** (mark-up) / **Asset Turnover** (volume)]

For your company, the primary driver of ROE is [**ROA** (profit) / **Financial Leverage** (use of debt)]

3. **SIGNIFICANT** current events and other information of importance:

4. **INVESTMENT DECISION**

Your Company: (**Invest / Not invest**)
Why?   1 –   2 –   3 –   4 –   5 –

WRITTEN REPORT — GRADING RUBRIC

Student Name _____

Company Name _____

Industry Name_____

Item	Maximum Score	Improve	Average	Great
CONTENT				
F. Research Summary (2 pages)	10			
1. Financial analysis...Profitability, Efficiency, Liquidity, Solvency				
2. DuPont Analysis of ROE...primary drivers				
3. Significant current events.... other significant information				
4. Your company...Invest? Not invest? Why?				
A. Tell Me About Your Company (1-3 pages)	5			
Description of company ... its industry, products, and markets				
B. Company News (1-2 pages)	5			
Search for 2-3 major items/events occurring over the past year				
Discuss how each affects the company's operations and the financial ratios				
C. Stock Market Activity (1-2 pages)	5			
10-year stock chart with explanation of trends				
Use a variety of sources				
D. Financial Statement Analysis (4 pages)	20			
Prepare the condensed, trend, and common-size statements				
BS ... Analyze the Balance Sheet and RISK (1 page)				
IS ... Analyze the Income Statement and PROFITABILITY (1 page)				
CF ... Analyze the Stmt of CFlows and CASH Position (1 page)				
Summarize your analysis in a written report ... What's the Story?				
E. Ratio Analysis (1-3 pages)	20			
Compute ratios ... 2 years				
Collect industry averages for each ratio				
Aanalyze your company's a. Profitability b. Efficiency c. Liquidity d. Solvency				
Summarize your analysis in a written report				
Appendices	5			
App 1: Copies of Worksheets A, B, C, D, E App 2: Copy of company financial statements App 3: Copies of cited materials App 4: PowerPoint slides				
Professional quality ... comprehensive coverage, accuracy, grammar				
Proper referencing ... sources used page				
TOTAL POINTS	70			

Purpose:
- Prepare and deliver a presentation titled **"Would You Advise a Friend to Invest in This Company?"** that is based on research, analysis, and sound reasoning.
- Prepare PowerPoint slides as a visual aid using at least 2 graphs

Prepare and deliver a presentation titled "Would You Advise a Friend to Invest in This Company?" based upon your research and analysis of this company's financial information. Include:

- Use the Research Summary to help organize your presentation.
- Convince the audience to invest or not invest in your company.
- Present the *highlights* of your research, not a broad summary.
- Focus on the financial information and key ratios.
- The presentation should be well delivered with a strong opening and a closing that is evident.
- Make your presentation interesting.
- Please support your fellow students by being attentive and courteous during their presentations.

Use PowerPoint slides as your visual aid, including at least 2 graphs.

- Remember that PowerPoint slides are visual aids.
- A rule of thumb is one slide per minute.
- Another rule of thumb is no more than 7 items across and 7 items down.
- Slides should contain bullet points, not sentences or paragraphs.

Conduct a Q&A session at the conclusion of your presentation. Each student should listen attentively to the other presentations and jot down questions. During each *class* of presentations, every student is expected to ask at least one question.

In Appendix 4, include a copy of your PowerPoint slides.
Provide hard-copy of your PowerPoint slides to the instructor on the day of presentation.

1. Opening should grab the audience's attention. Opening techniques include asking a question, stating an interesting fact, or telling a story. The story could be about an incident that led you to choose this company to research.

2. Identify three to five main points that you want the audience to remember. Support these points with good explanation and examples.

3. Introduction, Body, and Conclusion: State what you are going to say, say it, and then summarize what you just said.

4. A visual aid is just that—an aid that supports the presentation. If using PowerPoint—no more than one slide per minute (maximum eight). Keep aids uncluttered and readable—no more than seven items across and seven items down.

5. Closing is evident and leaves a definite impression.

6. Practice your opening and closing—as these are critical.

7. Talk to your audience. You may use note cards with key points and key statistics. Do not read your presentation.

8. Speak slowly and clearly. If you look at the last row your voice will project to the last row.

9. Achieve eye contact with your audience. If eye contact is intimidating, look at foreheads. For encouragement, plant a smiling friend at the back of the audience for you to look at during the presentation.

10. Stand with your feet planted squarely on the ground, not leaning against the podium or swaying back and forth.

11. Please be courteous and attentive during other student presentations.

12. Consider: **P**urpose, **A**udience, **I**nformation, **B**enefits, **O**bjections, **C**ontext

13. If your presentation is videotaped, review the video five different times, each time using one of the following techniques. View it ...

    a. As yourself
    b. As a boss
    c. With just sound—Listen (turn your back to the screen so that you cannot see the video)
    d. With no sound—Just the visual
    e. With someone else

PRESENTATION — GRADING RUBRIC

Student Name _____

Company Name _____

Industry Name_____

Item	Maximum Score	Improve	Average	Great
CONTENT	**10**			
Strong OPENING ... vivid and compelling ... should grab the audience's attention				
BODY is well organized				
Information is appealing to the audience and can be easily followed				
Include a description of the company, its industry, its products, its markets				
Include several innovative or interesting facts about the company				
Focus on the financials and key ratios				
INVESTING ADVICE is clearly stated and well supported				
Explain amounts and ratios				
Information is accurate				
CLOSING is evident and leaves a definite impression of investment advice				
Question & Answer ... answers questions thoughtfully				
PRESENTATION	**10**			
Presenter is confident, relaxed, and in control				
Appropriate gestures, tone, volume, and delivery rate are used				
Appropriate eye contact with the audience				
Voice is projected to the back row				
Delivery is energetic				
Conversational voice style is used				
Professional language and few "ums," "okays," and "likes"				
Note cards may be used, but not read				
Professional appearance ... business casual attire				
Adheres to time limits				
POWERPOINT	**10**			
Helps to clarify and emphasize content				
Includes at least two graphs to highlight significant financial results				
Slides are attractive				
Uses key words, not full sentences				
Not more than one PowerPoint slide per minute				
Not cluttered—not more than seven items across and seven items down				
GROUP COORDINATION (if applicable)				
Presentation is well-coordinated among members				
All members speak				
Provide hard-copy of PowerPoint slides to your instructor to follow during the presentation				
TOTAL POINTS	**30**			

APPENDIX A – FEATURED CORPORATIONS

A brief description of the company, its stock symbol, and the corporate website follow for each corporation used in the text.

Adidas AG (ADDYY OTC) is a global producer of sportswear and sports equipment. The Company offers its products through three main brands: Adidas, Reebok, and TaylorMade. Each brand specializes in a certain area. Adidas focuses on running, football, basketball, tennis, and training, for performance athletes. The Reebok brand covers sports and lifestyle products. The TaylorMade Adidas Golf brand covers a range of golf clubs, accessories, footwear, and apparel. www.adidas-group.com

Amazon.com, Inc. (AMZN NASDAQ) is the world's largest online bookstore offering millions of books, CDs, DVDs, videos, and other products at its website. After years of expansion, the company is now focusing on profits. Founder Jeff Bezos and his family own about one-third of the company. www.amazon.com

American Eagle Outfitters, Inc. (AEO NYSE) is a retailer that designs, markets, and sells its own brand of clothing targeting 15- to 25-year-olds in the United States and Canada. American Eagle operates over 800 stores in the United States and Canada and also distributes merchandise via its e-commerce operation. www.ae.com

Anheuser-Busch InBev NV/SA (ABI EBR) is a publicly traded company based in Leuven, Belgium. It is the leading global brewer and one of the world's top five consumer products companies. A true consumer-centric, sales-driven company, Anheuser-Busch InBev manages a portfolio of nearly 300 brands that includes global flagship brands Budweiser®, Stella Artois®, and Beck's®. Anheuser-Busch InBev's dedication to heritage and quality is rooted in brewing traditions that originate from the Den Hoorn brewery in Leuven, Belgium, dating back to 1366, and the pioneering spirit of the Anheuser & Co brewery established in 1860 in St. Louis, Missouri, USA. www.abinbev.com

Apple Computer, Inc. (AAPL NASDAQ) designs, manufactures, and markets mobile communication devices, personal computers, and personal entertainment devices. The company now also offers an online music store (iTunes). Other products include servers (Xserve), wireless networking equipment (Airport), and publishing and multimedia software. www.apple.com

Barnes & Noble (BKS NYSE) is a bookseller. The Company's principal business is the sale of trade books (such as mystery, romance, science fiction, and other fiction), children's books, bargain books, magazines, gifts, cafe products and services, music, and movies. As of October 2011, the Company operated 703 bookstores, 637 college bookstores, and a website. Barnes and Noble are aggressively marketing their eReader, the Nook, in an attempt to capture a larger ebook market share. www.barnesandnoble.com

Best Buy (BBY NYSE) is a specialty retailer of consumer electronics, home office products, entertainment software, appliances, and related services. The Company operates retail stores and websites under the brand name Best Buy. They currently operate domestically and internationally. www.bestbuy.com

Brinker International (EAT NYSE) owns, develops, operates, and franchises the Chili's Grill & Bar (Chili's) and Maggiano's Little Italy (Maggiano's) restaurant brands. During fiscal year 2011, the Company's international franchisees opened 37 Chili's restaurants. As of June 2011, company owned and franchisee restaurants totaled 1,579. Of that, 868 are Company operated. www.brinker.com

Bristol-Myers Squibb (BMY NYSE) is engaged in the discovery, development, licensing, manufacturing, marketing, distribution, and sale of biopharmaceutical products. The Company sold off all non-pharmaceutical brands to focus their efforts on next generation products. To that end, the company is acquiring businesses and acquiring licensing for next generation technologies. www.bms.com

Carnival Corporation (CCL NYSE) (previously Carnival Cruise Lines Inc.) provides cruises to major vacation destinations outside the Far East. It also markets and operates hotels and lodges, motor coaches for sightseeing and charters, domed rail cars, and luxury day boats. The company operates 99 cruise ships with about 196,000 passenger capacity in North America, Europe, the United Kingdom, Germany, Australia, and New Zealand. www.carnivalcorp.com

Caterpillar Inc. (CAT NYSE) operates in three principal lines of business: Machinery, Engines, and Financial Products. The Company is focusing on growth initiatives for mining, rail, and engines. They have announced plans to increase capacity, increase production, and make acquisitions in those growth areas. www.cat.com

Cedar Fair, L.P. (FUN NYSE) is one of the largest regional amusement park operators in the world. It owns eleven amusement parks, six outdoor water parks, one indoor water park, and five hotels. The Partnership owns and operates Cedar Point; Kings Island; Canada's Wonderland; Dorney Park and Wildwater Kingdom (Dorney Park); Valleyfair; Michigan's Adventure; Kings Dominion; Carowinds; Worlds of Fun; Knott's Berry Farm; California's Great America; Castaway Bay Indoor Waterpark Resort in Sandusky, Ohio; and six separate-gated outdoor water parks. www.cedarfair.com

Chipotle Mexican Grill (CMG NYSE) develops and operates fast-casual, fresh Mexican food restaurants in 33 states throughout the United States, Canada, and London, England. The Company operates 1,084 restaurants as of December 2010. The company is guided by the idea of "Food with Integrity." www.chipotle.com

Circuit City Stores (CCTYQ NYSE) was a specialty retailer of consumer electronics, home office products, entertainment software, and related services. The company filed for bankruptcy on November 10, 2008. The company is no longer operating and all assets have been liquidated.

CitiGroup (CIT NYSE) provides a range of financial services to consumers and corporate customers. As of December 2010, Citigroup has more than 200 million customer accounts and does business in more than 160 countries primarily through its two operating units, Citicorp and Citi Holdings. www.citigroup.com

Coca-Cola Company, The (KO NYSE) was established in 1886 and is now the world's largest soft drink company operating in approximately 200 countries and commanding approximately 50% of the global soft-drink market. The firm, which does no bottling, sells about 300 drink brands, including Coca-Cola, Sprite, Barq's, Minute Maid, and Dasani and Evian water. www.cocacola.com

Costco (COST NASDAQ) operates international membership warehouses offering its members products in a range of merchandise categories. It buys the majority of its merchandise directly from manufacturers and routes it to a cross-docking consolidation point (depot) or directly to its warehouses. Many consumable products are offered for sale in case, carton, or multiple-pack quantities. As of December 10, 2011, Costco operates 598 membership warehouses. www.costco.com

Darden Restaurants, Inc. (DRI NYSE) is a dining restaurant company that operates over 1,894 restaurants in the United States and Canada, including Red Lobster, Olive Garden, Bahama Breeze, Smokey Bones Barbeque & Grill, and Three Seasons. www.darden.com

Dell (DELL NASDAQ) has four main operating segments: Large Enterprise, Public, Small & Medium Business, and Consumer. The Company is moving from a consumer focus to an enterprise focus. The Company acquired Perot Systems in 2010 and made additional acquisitions in 2011. www.dell.com

DineEquity, Inc. (DIN NYSE) franchises and owns restaurants under the IHOP and Applebee's brands. As of December 2010, the company owns and operates 309 Applebee's and 11 IHOPs, whereas franchisees operate 1,701 Applebee's and 1,493 IHOP restaurants. www.dineeqeuity.com

Disney Company, The Walt (DIS NYSE) together with its subsidiaries, is a global entertainment company. The business segments of the Company are Media Networks, Parks and Resorts, Studio Entertainment, and Consumer Products. The Media Networks segment consists of a domestic broadcast television network, television production and distribution operations, domestic television stations, cable networks, domestic broadcast radio networks and stations, and Internet and mobile operations. The Studio Entertainment segment produces and acquires live-action and animated motion pictures, direct-to-video programming, musical recordings, and live stage plays. The Consumer Products segment engages with licensees, manufacturers, publishers, and retailers globally to design, develop, publish, promote, and sell a range of products based on Disney characters. www.corporate.disney.go.com

eBay (EBAY NASDAQ) provides online marketplaces for the sale of goods and services, as well as other online commerce or ecommerce platforms, online payment services, and online communications offerings to a diverse community of individuals and businesses. The Company has three business segments: Marketplaces, Payments, and Communications. Its Marketplaces segment provides the infrastructure to enable global online commerce through a variety of platforms, including the traditional eBay.com platform and eBay's other online platforms. eBay's Payments segment comprises its online payment solutions PayPal and Bill Me Later. The Communications segment consists of Skype Technologies S.A., which enables voice over Internet protocol (VoIP) calls between Skype users and provides connectivity to traditional fixed-line and mobile telephones. www.ebay.com

Ford Motor Company (F NYSE) is a producer of cars and trucks. Ford operates in two sectors: Automotive and Financial Services. During 2010, the Company sold 5.5 million vehicles world wide. Recently, the company sold off or discontinued many operating segments such as: Mercury, Volvo, Aston Martin, Mazda, Jaguar, and Land Rover. www.ford.com

Freeport McMoRan Copper & Gold Inc. (FCX NYSE) through its wholly owned subsidiary, Phelps Dodge Corporation (Phelps Dodge), is a copper, gold, and molybdenum mining company. As of December 2010, consolidated recoverable proven and probable reserves totaled 120.5 billion pounds of copper, 35.5 million ounces of gold, 3.39 billion pounds of molybdenum, 325 million ounces of silver, and 0.75 billion pounds of cobalt. www.fcx.com

Gap Inc., The (GPS NYSE) is a global retailer focusing on apparel and accessories. The Company has a line of brands including: Gap, Old Navy, Banana Republic, Piperlime, and Athleta. The Company operates stores in the United States, Canada, the United Kingdom, France, Ireland, Japan, China and Italy. www.gap.com

General Electric Company (GE NYSE) is one of the top players in a vast array of markets including: aircraft engines, locomotives and other transportation equipment, appliances (kitchen and laundry equipment), lighting, electric distribution and control equipment, generators and turbines, nuclear reactors, medical imaging equipment, and plastics. Its financial arm accounts for nearly half of the company's revenues, making GE one of the largest financial services companies in the U.S. Other operations include the NBC television network. www.ge.com

General Mills (GIS NYSE) is a supplier of branded and unbranded food products to the foodservice and commercial baking industries. General Mills manufactures its products in 15 countries and markets them in more than 100 countries. Its joint ventures manufacture and market products in more than 130 countries and republics worldwide. The Company's major product categories in the United States are ready-to-eat cereals; refrigerated yogurt; ready-to-serve soup; dry dinners; shelf stable and frozen vegetables; refrigerated and frozen dough products; dessert and baking mixes; frozen pizza and pizza snacks; grain, fruit and savory snacks; microwave popcorn; and a variety of organic products including soup, granola bars, and cereal. General Mills operates in three operating segments: U.S. Retail; International; and Bakeries and Foodservice. www.generalmills.com

General Motors Corporation (GM NYSE) is engaged primarily in the development, production, and marketing of cars, trucks, and parts. The Company develops, manufactures, and markets vehicles worldwide. The Company's finance and insurance operations are primarily conducted through GM Financial. GM Financial provides a range of financial services. In June 2009, the Company filed for bankruptcy. In November 2010, the Company issued an IPO for $20.1 billion. www.gm.com

Google Inc. (GOOG NASDAQ) maintains an index of websites and its search technology enables people to obtain nearly instant access to relevant information online. Google offers its services and products free of charge and generates revenue primarily by delivering online advertising. www.google.com

Harley-Davidson Inc. (HDI NYSE) produces heavyweight motorcycles, motorcycle parts, and related accessories. It operates in two segments, Motorcycles and Related Products and Financial Services. The Motorcycles and Related Products segment engages in the design, manufacture, and sale of primarily heavyweight, touring, custom, and performance motorcycles, as well as a line of motorcycle parts, accessories, clothing, and collectibles. www.harley-davidson.com

Hewlett-Packard Company (HPQ NYSE) is a provider of computing and imaging solutions for business and home. The company provides enterprise and consumer customers a full range of high-tech products, including personal computers, servers, storage products, printers, software, and computer-related services. www.hp.com

International Business Machines (IBM NYSE) is an information technology (IT) company. IBM also provides business, technology, and consulting services. The Company has five main operating segments: Global Technology Services, Global Business Services, Software, Systems & Technology and Global Financing. www.ibm.com

Intel Corporation (INTC NASDAQ) is the largest chipmaker in the world, currently possessing 80% of the market share. Intel's most notable products include its Pentium and Celeron microprocessors. Intel also makes flash memories and is #1 globally in this market. Dell and HP are the company's largest customers. www.intel.com

J. Crew Group (JCG NYSE) is an integrated multi-channel, multi-brand, specialty retailer. The Company offers complete assortments of women's, men's, and children's apparel and accessories. J.Crew products are distributed through its retail and factory stores, its J.Crew catalog, and the Internet. The Company conducts its business through two primary sales channels: Stores and Direct. www.jcrew.com

J.C. Penney Company Inc. (JCP NYSE) provides merchandise and services to consumers through its department stores and Direct (catalog/Internet). The Company operates 1,106 department stores. The Company markets family apparel, jewelry, shoes, accessories, and home furnishings. In addition, the department stores provide customers with additional services such as salon, optical, portrait photography, and custom decorating. Their brands include jcpenney, Every Day Matters, Okie Dokie, Worthington, east5th, a.n.a, St. John's Bay, she said, The Original Arizona Jean Company, Ambrielle, Decree, Linden Street, Article 365, Stafford, J. Ferrar, jcpenney Home Collection and Studio by jcpenney Home Collection. www.jcpenney.com

Kroger (KR NYSE) is a publicly owned supermarket that operates retail food and drug stores, multi-department stores, jewelry stores, and convenience stores throughout the United States. It manufactures and processes some of the food for sale in its supermarkets. As of January 2011, the Company operated, either directly or through its subsidiaries, 2,460 supermarkets and multi-department stores, 1,014 of which had fuel centers. www.kroger.com

Lenovo Group Limited (LNVGY OTC, HKG) develops, manufactures, and markets technology products and services worldwide. The Company, through its subsidiaries, is engaged in manufacturing and distribution of information technology (IT) products and provision of IT services, property holding and property management, procurement agency, group treasury, supply chain management, intellectual property rights management, and provision of repair services for computer hardware and software systems. www.lenovo.com

McDonald's Corporation (MCD NYSE) is the world's #1 fast-food chain, operating more than 32,000 restaurants in 121 countries worldwide. In addition to the familiar freestanding locations,

McDonald's has mini-restaurants at locations within Wal-Mart and Chevron stores. Much of the company's new growth is in foreign markets that now generate over 60% of sales. www.mcdonalds.com

Microsoft Corporation (MSFT NASDAQ) is the world's #1 software company that develops, manufactures, licenses, and supports a variety of products and services, including its Windows operating systems and Office software suite. The Company sells the Xbox video game console and has expanded into interactive television, and Internet access. It is also targeting services for growth, looking to transform its software applications into web-based services for enterprises and consumers. Microsoft has reached a tentative settlement to end an ongoing antitrust investigation, agreeing to uniformly license its operating systems and allow manufacturers to include competing software with Windows. www.microsoft.com

News Corporation (NWS NASDAQ) is a diversified entertainment company with operations in eight industry segments, including Filmed Entertainment, Television, Cable Network Programming, Direct Broadcast Satellite Television, Magazines and Inserts, Newspapers and Information Services, and Book Publishing. It is engaged in the operation of broadcast television stations and the development, production, and distribution of network and television programming. www.newscorp.com

Nike Inc. (NKE NYSE) is engaged in the design, development, and worldwide marketing of footwear, apparel, equipment, and accessory products. NIKE sells athletic footwear and apparel. It sells its products to retail accounts, through NIKE-owned retail, and through a mix of independent distributors and licensees. Its products include running, training, basketball, soccer, sport-inspired urban shoes, and children's shoes. It also markets shoes designed for aquatic activities, baseball, bicycling, cheerleading, football, golf, lacrosse, outdoor activities, skateboarding, tennis, volleyball, walking, wrestling, and recreational uses. www.nike.com

Oracle Corporation (ORCL NASDAQ) is a leading provider of systems software, offering a variety of business applications that include software for data warehousing, customer relationship management, and supply chain management. Oracle's software runs on a broad range of computers including mainframes, workstations, desktops, laptops, and handheld devices. Oracle also provides consulting, support, and training services. www.oracle.com

PepsiCo, Inc. (PEP NYSE) is the world's #2 soft-drink maker and the world's #1 maker of snacks. Beverages include Pepsi (the #2 soft drink), Mountain Dew, Slice, Tropicana Juices (the world's leading juice manufacturer), Aquafina bottled water, All-Sport, Dole juices, and Lipton tea. PepsiCo also owns Frito-Lay, the world's #1 maker of snacks such as corn chips (Doritos, Fritos) and potato chips (Lay's, Ruffles, WOW!). Its international divisions operate in over 200 countries, with its largest operations in Mexico and the United Kingdom. The Company is organized into four business units: PepsiCo Americas Foods, PepsiCo Americas Beverages, PepsiCo Europe, and PepsiCo Asia, Middle East and Africa. www.pepsico.com

Research in Motion (RIMM NASDAQ) is a designer, manufacturer, and marketer of wireless solutions for the worldwide mobile communications market. Through the development of integrated hardware, software, and services that support multiple wireless network standards, RIM provides platforms and solutions for access to information, including e-mail, phone, short message service (SMS), Internet, and intranet-based applications. RIM's portfolio of products, services, and embedded technologies are used by organizations worldwide and include the BlackBerry wireless solution, the RIM Wireless Handheld product line, software development tools, and software. www.rim.com

Royal Caribbean Cruises Ltd. (RCL NYSE) is the world's second-largest cruise line (behind Carnival) providing cruises to Alaska, the Caribbean, and Europe on 40 different cruise ships. The Company has many brands such as: Royal Caribbean International, Celebrity Cruises, Azamara Club Cruises, Pullmantur, and CDF Croisières de France. The Company had 420 destinations in 2010 and had more than 4.5 million passengers. www.rccl.com

Sears Holdings Corporation (SHLD NASDAQ) is a retailing company that owns Kmart Holding Corporation and Sears, Roebuck and Co. Sears Holdings Corporation has over 2,201 full-line stores and 1,354 specialty retail stores in the United States along with 483 full-line and specialty retail stores in Canada. Its three segments include Kmart, Sears Domestic, and Sears Canada. www.searsholdings.com

Southwest Airlines Co. (LUV NYSE) has expanded its low-cost, no-frills approach to air travel throughout the U.S. to service over 69 cities in 35 states. The Company offers point-to-point transportation rather than using a hub-and-spoke method. This business approach has resulted in 38 profitable years in a row. Southwest currently operates 559 Boeing 737 jets (as of September 30, 2011). www.southwest.com

Starbucks Corporation (SBUX NASDAQ) is the leading specialty coffee retailer with 17,003 coffee shops positioned throughout 50 countries in office buildings, malls, airports, and other locations. In addition to coffee, Starbucks offers coffee beans, pastries, mugs, coffee makers, coffee grinders, and even coffee ice cream. www.starbucks.com

Time Warner (TWX NYSE) operates in three business segments: Cable Television Networks, Filmed Entertainment, and Magazine Publishing. The cable television segment is the largest of the three segments. www.timewarner.com.

The Trump Organization is privately owned by Donald Trump and controls several New York real estate pieces including Trump International Hotel, Trump Tower (26 floors), 40 Wall Street, and 50% of the General Motors Building. Trump also has a 42% stake in Trump Hotels & Casino Resorts, which operate three casinos in Atlantic City and a 50% stake in the Miss USA, Miss Teen USA, and Miss Universe beauty pageants. www.trump.com

Under Armour (UA NYSE) is engaged in the business of developing, marketing, and distributing branded performance apparel, footwear, and accessories for men, women, and youth. The Company's products are sold in North America, the United Kingdom, France, and Germany in approximately 23,000 retail stores. www.underarmour.com

United Airlines Corporation (UAUA NASDAQ) transports persons, property, and mail throughout the United States and abroad. In May 2010, the Company merged with Continental. United is a passenger airline that operates more than 5,800 flights a day to more than 375 destinations in 28 countries and two United States territories. www.united.com

Urban Outfitters (URBN NASDAQ) is a lifestyle specialty retail company that operates under the Urban Outfitters, Anthropologies, Free People, Terrain, Leifsdottir and BHLDN brands. The Company also operates a wholesale segment under the Free People and Leifsdottir brands. In addition to its retail stores, the Company offers its products directly to the consumer through its e-commerce websites. www.urbanoutfittersinc.com

Wal-Mart Stores, Inc. (WMT NYSE) is the largest retailer in the world with over 8,361 stores. Its sales are greater than Sears', Target's, and Kroger's combined. Its stores include Wal-Mart discount stores, Wal-Mart Supercenters (combined discount and grocery stores), and Sam's Club membership-only warehouse stores. Most Wal-Mart stores are in the United States, but international expansion has made it the #1 retailer in Canada and Mexico. Wal-Mart also has operations in South America, Asia, and Europe; those markets were comprised of 4,457 stores in 2011. www.walmartstores.com

Yahoo! Incorporated (YHOO NASDAQ) is a global Internet brand. The Company generates revenues by providing marketing services to advertisers across a majority of Yahoo! Its offerings to users on Yahoo! Properties fall into three categories: Communications and Communities; Search and Marketplaces; and Media. It also offers online properties and services to users. www.yahoo.com

Yum! Brands, Inc. (YUM NYSE) is the largest restaurant operator in terms of number of locations (second to McDonald's in sales) with over 37,000 units in more than 110 countries. Yum consists of three operating segments: the U.S. segment consisting of KFC, Pizza Hut, Taco Bell, Long John Silver's (LJS), and A&W All-American Food Restaurants (A&W); Yum! Restaurants International; and Yum! Restaurants China. www.yum.com

APPENDIX B – RATIOS

Ratios are extremely valuable as analytical tools, but they also have limitations. They can indicate areas of strength and weakness, but do not provide answers. To be most effective, they should be used in combination with other elements of financial analysis. Also, please note that there is not one definitive set of key financial ratios, no uniform definition for all ratios, and no standard which should be met for each ratio. Each situation should be evaluated within the context of the particular firm, industry, and economic environment.

There are five major categories of ratios listed to help analyze a particular aspect of the financial condition. Categories and ratios are described on the following pages.

PROFITABILITY	EFFICIENCY	LIQUIDITY	SOLVENCY	INVESTMENT
Return on Sales (ROS)	Asset Turnover	Current Ratio	Debt Ratio	Price Earnings (P/E)
Return on Assets (ROA)	Accounts Receivable Turnover	Cash Flow Liquidity	Financial Leverage	Dividend Rate per share
Return on Equity (ROE)	Accounts Receivable Days		Times-Interest-Earned	
DuPont Analysis of ROE	Inventory Turnover		Free Cash Flow	
Gross Profit Margin (GP%)	Inventory Days		Cash Flow Adequacy	
Earnings Per Share (EPS)				
Quality of Income				

* Shaded ratios are included in the Capstone Project – Chapter 9

RATIOS	CONCEPTUAL FORMULAS
Profitability Ratios	*Are we generating enough returns on revenues and investments?*
Return on sales (ROS), also known as *Net profit margin*	= Net income / Sales revenue
Return on assets (ROA)	= Net income / Total assets
Return on equity (ROE)	= Net income / Stockholders' equity
DuPont Analysis of ROE	*= ROS x Asset turnover = ROA x Financial leverage = ROE*
ROS	= Net income / Sales revenue
x Asset turnover	= Sales revenue / Total assets
x Financial leverage	= Total assets / Stockholders' equity
Gross profit margin	= Gross profit / Sales revenue
Earnings per share	= (Net income - Preferred dividends) / Average number of common shares outstanding
Quality of income	= Net cash from operating activities / Net income
Efficiency Ratios	*Are we using the firm's resources efficiently?*
Asset turnover	= Sales revenue / Total assets
Accounts receivable turnover	= Sales revenue / Accounts receivable
Accounts receivable days	= 365 / Accounts receivable turnover
Inventory turnover	= Cost of goods sold / Inventory
Inventory days	= 365 / Inventory turnover
Liquidity Ratios	*Are we meeting our current obligations?*
Current ratio	= Current assets / Current liabilities
Cash flow liquidity	= (Cash + Marketable securities + NCOA) / Current liabilities
Solvency Ratios	*Are we handling debt appropriately?*
Debt ratio	= Total liabilities / Total assets
Financial leverage	= Total assets / Stockholders' equity
Times interest earned, also known as *Interest Coverage Ratio*	= Operating income / Interest expense
Free cash flow	= Net cash from operating activities (NCOA) – (Capital expenditures + Dividends paid)
Cash flow adequacy	= Net cash from operating activities / (Capital expenditures + Dividends paid)
Investment Ratios	*How do we appear to our shareholders?*
Price earnings ratio (P/E)	= Market value per share / Earnings per share
Dividends rate per share	= Annual common stock dividends paid / Average number of common shares outstanding

RATIO CATEGORIES

PROFITABILITY measures the ability to generate profits; the overall performance of a firm.

EFFICIENCY measures the efficiency of managing the assets; resources of the firm; cash, accounts receivable, inventory, and property, plant, and equipment.

LIQUIDITY measures a firm's ability to meet cash needs as they arise, within the next 12 months.

SOLVENCY measures the extent of debt relative to equity, if financial leverage is being used effectively, and the ability to cover interest, investing activity, financing activity, and other fixed payment requirements.

INVESTMENT compares the market value per share to other per share amounts and indicates the level of dividend payment.

PROFITABILITY RATIOS

Return on Sales (ROS), also known as **Net Profit Margin**, measures the profitability from each dollar of revenue. It expresses net income as a percentage of revenue, which reflects a firm's ability to translate revenue into profits; control expenses.

ROS	=	$\dfrac{\text{Net income}}{\text{Sales revenue}}$

Return on Assets (ROA) **measures how productively a company uses its assets to generate profits. A high ROA depends on managing asset investments to produce the greatest amount of revenue and controlling expenses to keep net income high. ROA is the most comprehensive measure of profitability since it takes into account both the profitability of each dollar of revenue (ROS) and sales volume (Asset Turnover).   ROS x Asset Turnover = ROA

ROA	=	$\dfrac{\text{Net income}}{\text{Total assets *}}$

*   Average amounts may be used to calculate the formula to better represent the balance in the
         account over the entire year.

**   Alternate formula for ROA = [*Net income before nonrecurring items + Interest expense (net of tax)*]
         / *Average total assets*. This is a more complex formula that incorporates interest expense as the
         return on liabilities to creditors and net income as the return to shareholders. A = L + SE.

The **Return on Equity (ROE)** measures how effectively stockholders' equity is used to produce net income.   ROA x Financial Leverage = ROE

ROE	=	**Net income**
		Stockholders' equity *

The **DuPont Analysis of ROE** divides Return on Equity into components that help to better assess company performance and indicate ways that management can improve ROE. The first two components, **Return on Sales** and **Asset Turnover**, reflect the use of two business strategies: (1) The high-value or product-differentiation strategy relies on the superiority or distinctiveness of the products. This allows charging higher prices and thus earning greater ROS. (2) The low-cost strategy relies on efficient management of assets to produce high Asset Turnover.   (ROS x Asset Turnover = ROA).
Improving ROA also results in increasing ROE. The third component, **Financial Leverage**, is the effective use of debt in a capital structure. ROE increases when ROA is higher than the average cost of debt because the excess return accrues to the benefit of the shareholders. To summarize,

ROS x Asset Turnover = ROA x Financial Leverage = ROE

DuPont Analysis of ROE	=	ROS	x Asset Turnover x Financial Leverage
ROE = ~~Net income~~		**Net income** x ~~Sales revenue~~ x	~~Total assets~~
SE	=	~~Sales revenue~~ ~~Total assets~~	SE

Gross Profit Margin (GP%), also known as **Gross Margin**, compares gross profit to revenue, expressing gross profit as a percentage of sales revenue. It measures how successfully a company buys and sells merchandise at a profit.

GP%	=	**Gross profit**
		Sales revenue

Earnings per Share (EPS) is the amount of net income (loss) earned by each individual common share of stock held by investors.

EPS	=	**Net income - Preferred dividends**
		Average number of common shares outstanding

The **Quality-of-Income** ratio compares cash flows from operating activities to net income. A ratio higher than 1.0 indicates high-quality income because each dollar of net income is supported by one dollar or more of cash. It is cash (not accrual-based net income) that is needed to pay suppliers, employees, etc., to invest in income-producing assets, and to ensure long-term success.

Quality of Income	=	**Net cash from operating activities (NCOA)**
		Net income

*   Average amounts may be used to calculate the formula to better represent the balance in the
          account over the entire year.

EFFICIENCY RATIOS

Asset Turnover measures how productively a company uses its assets to produce revenue. It is a measure of efficiency that leads to greater profitability.

Asset Turnover	=	$\dfrac{\text{Sales revenue}}{\text{Total assets *}}$

Accounts Receivable Turnover indicates how many times average accounts receivable are collected annually. The longer receivables are outstanding, the higher the collection risk and the greater the cost of financing those receivables.

Accounts Receivable Turnover	=	$\dfrac{\text{Sales revenue}}{\text{Accounts receivable *}}$

Accounts Receivable Days indicate the average number of days required to convert receivables into cash. It offers the same information as the accounts receivable turnover ratio, but presents it in a different format.

Accounts Receivable Days	=	$\dfrac{365}{\text{Accounts receivable turnover}}$

Inventory Turnover indicates the number of times a company sells its average inventory level during the year. Inventory is costly in terms of financing and storage, so companies want enough inventory to meet customer demand without stock-outs.

Inventory Turnover	=	$\dfrac{\text{Cost of goods sold}}{\text{Inventory *}}$

Inventory Days indicate the average length of time that inventories are available for sale. It offers the same information as the inventory turnover ratio, but presents it in a different format.

Inventory Days	=	$\dfrac{365}{\text{Inventory turnover}}$

*   Average amounts may be used to calculate the formula to better represent the balance in the account over the entire year.

LIQUIDITY RATIOS

The **Current Ratio** measures the ability to pay current payables as they come due. It compares current assets to current liabilities as current assets are generally used to meet current liability obligations. It is a measure of liquidity, a company's ability to pay amounts due within the next 12 months.

Current Ratio	=	Current assets
		Current liabilities

The **Cash-Flow-Liquidity** ratio compares cash resources to current liabilities. This ratio uses cash and marketable securities (truly liquid current assets) and net cash from operating activities to evaluate whether adequate cash is generated from selling inventory and offering services to pay current liabilities when they come due. Even a profitable business will fail without sufficient cash. It is a cash-basis measure of short-term liquidity.

Cash Flow Liquidity	=	(Cash + Marketable securities + NCOA)
		Current liabilities

INVESTMENT RATIOS

Investors use the **Price Earnings (P/E)** ratio to measure how "expensive" a company's stock is compared to EPS. Regrettably, it does not explain why a stock is expensive or cheap.

P/E Ratio	=	Market price per share
		EPS

The **Dividend Rate** is the amount of dividends paid annually for each common share of stock held by investors.

Dividend Rate	=	Annual common stock dividends paid
		Average number of common shares outstanding

Debt Ratio indicates the percentage of the company financed with debt (liabilities). It is used to measure solvency, a company's ability to pay back long-term debt when due. When the debt ratio is lower, there is less financial risk and stronger solvency.

The **Debt-to-Equity** ratio and the **Financial Leverage** ratio offer the same information as the debt ratio, but present it in a different format, which helps analysts more easily evaluate the trade-offs between risk and return. The following formulas convert the Debt-to-Equity ratio to the Debt Ratio and vice versa.

Debt-to-equity ratio (Total liabilities / Stockholders' equity) = Debt ratio / (1 – Debt Ratio)

Debt ratio = Debt-to-Equity ratio / (1 + Debt-to-Equity ratio)

Debt Ratio	=	$\dfrac{\text{Total liabilities}}{\text{Total assets}}$

Financial Leverage is similar to the debt ratio, in the sense that the more debt a company has, the higher the financial leverage. It measures how debt "boosts" return on assets to increase return on equity.

Financial Leverage	=	$\dfrac{\text{Total assets}}{\text{Stockholders' equity}}$

Times Interest Earned, also referred to as the **Interest Coverage Ratio,** indicates a company's ability to earn (cover) its periodic interest payments.

Times Interest Earned	=	$\dfrac{\text{Operating income}}{\text{Interest expense}}$

Free Cash Flow reflects the amount of cash available for business activities after allowances for investing and financing activity requirements to maintain productive capacity at current levels. Adequate free cash flow allows for growth and financial flexibility.

Free Cash Flow	=	**Net cash from operating activities** **- (Capital expenditures + Dividends paid)**

The **Cash-Flow-Adequacy** ratio evaluates whether net cash from operating activities (NCOA) is adequate to maintain productive capacity at current levels. It presents free cash flow information in a ratio format. This ratio, with modifications in the denominator, is used by credit-rating agencies to identify if there is adequate cash coverage of capital expenditures, dividends, debt, and other annual payments.

Cash Flow Adequacy	=	$\dfrac{\text{Net cash from operating activities (NCOA)}}{\text{(Capital expenditures + Dividends paid)}}$

GLOSSARY

Accounting A system for recording, classifying, and reporting transactions

Accounts Used to classify and record economic events and transactions

Accounts payable Amounts that a corporation must pay to suppliers in the future

Accounts receivable Amounts to be received in the future from customers

Accounts receivable days The average number of days it takes for a company to collect accounts receivable

Accounts receivable turnover ratio Measures how quickly a company collects accounts receivable

Accrual accounting Method of accounting that records transactions when they occur, not necessarily when cash is received or paid

Accumulated depreciation The total amount of depreciation expensed since the assets' date of purchase

Accumulated other comprehensive income (loss) Adjustments to stockholders' equity resulting from three specific types of items that are not recorded on the income statement

Acquisition cost All costs necessary to prepare the asset for use, including the purchase price, delivery, and set-up costs

Additional paid-in capital Amount received in excess of par when stock is issued

AICPA (American Institute of Certified Public Accountants) A professional organization of accountants that prints a Code of Professional Conduct that holds CPAs accountable for serving the public interest

Allowance for bad debts Estimate of uncollectible accounts receivable. Accounts Receivable minus the Allowance for Bad Debts equals Net Accounts Receivable, the amount of receivables estimated as collectible

Allowance for doubtful accounts See allowance for bad debts

Allowance for uncollectibles See allowance for bad debts**Assets** Items of value that a corporation has a right to use. Typical asset accounts include cash, accounts receivable, inventory, equipment, buildings, and land. Assets = Liabilities + Stockholders' Equity

Asset turnover ratio Measures how efficiently the company uses assets to generate revenue

Audits CPAs attest to whether a company's financial statements comply with GAAP

Authorized The maximum number of shares that a corporation is permitted to print.

Available-for-sale securities Investments in stocks not classified as trading securities

Balance sheet One of the four primary financial statements. It provides a snapshot of a company's financial position as of a certain date.

Basic earnings per share Earnings per share calculated based on the actual number of shares outstanding.

Bonds payable Loans with certificates that can be traded among investors

Book value Cost of a long-term asset that a company can still depreciate (expense on the income statement)

Borrowings Loans or other payables due over the long term

Capital assets See property, plant, and equipment

Carrying value See book value.

Cash Physical currency (such as dollar bills, coins, etc.) or bank deposits

Cash and cash equivalents Actual currency, bank accounts, and investments that can be liquidated immediately

Cash-basis accounting Method of accounting that records transactions when cash is received or paid

Cash flow adequacy ratio Evaluates whether cash flow from operating activities is sufficient to cover annual payment requirements

Cash flow liquidity ratio Uses cash and marketable securities (truly liquid current assets) and net cash from operating activities to evaluate whether adequate cash is generated from selling inventory and offering services

Certified Public Accountants (CPAs) Accountants certified by the state to conduct audits

Chart of accounts List of all accounts used by a company

Commitments and contingencies Reminds investors that lawsuits and other events could create new liabilities for the company

Common-size balance sheet Compares all amounts within one year to total assets of that same year

Common-size income statement Compares all amounts within one year to revenue of that same year

Common stock A portion of the ownership of the company. Common stock dividends vary, according to the profitability of the company, and their amounts set by the company's board of directors

Consolidated A financial statement that combines the results of all a company's subsidiaries

Contingent liabilities Potential liabilities from lawsuits and especially for environmental cleanups

Contributed capital Amounts paid-in (contributed) to the company by stockholders to purchase common stock and preferred stock

Cost flow assumption The assumption used to measure cost of sales, the cost of inventory sold to customers during the accounting period. Cost flow assumptions include First-in first-out and Last-in first-out

Cost net yet depreciated See book value

Cost of goods sold See cost of sales

Cost of sales Reports the wholesale costs of inventory sold to customers during the accounting period. Also referred to as cost of goods sold

CPAs (Certified Public Accountants) Accountants certified by the state to conduct audits

Creditor A person to whom money is owed by a debtor

Current assets Assets which are converted into cash, sold, or consumed within the next 12 months

Current liabilities Liabilities due within 12 months

Current portion of borrowings The portion of long-term debt due within the next 12 months

Current ratio Measures the ability to pay current liabilities as they come due. Current assets are usually used to pay current liabilities.

Debt ratio Indicates the percentage of the company financed with debt (liabilities). It is a measure of solvency

Debtor Someone who has the obligation of paying back money owed, a debt

Deferred income tax liabilities Liabilities for tax rules that allow companies to earn income now but pay taxes later

Depreciable base Total amount of depreciation that will be recorded over an asset's life

Depreciation expense The cost allocated to each year of the asset's useful life

Diluted earnings per share Earnings per share calculated based on the number of shares likely to be outstanding under certain circumstances.

Discontinued operations The segment of a business that is closed or sold

Dividend rate Amount of dividends paid annually for each share of stock held by investors

Dividends Distributions of a company's profit paid out to common and/or preferred shareholders

Double-declining balance (DDB) depreciation method An accelerated depreciation method that records more depreciation early in the life of an asset, when it is new, and less depreciation when the asset is old

Earnings Net income

Earnings per share (EPS) Amount of net income (loss) earned by each individual share of stock held by investors

Expenses The costs incurred to produce revenues

Extraordinary items Highly unusual transactions that are considered unusual in nature and infrequent in occurrence

Financial Accounting Standards Board (FASB) An organization that sets most standards for United States GAAP.

Financial leverage ratio Measures how effectively a company uses debt to increase the return to shareholders. The difference between Return on Assets and Return on Equity

Financing activities A section of the statement of cash flows that reports cash transactions involving stockholders and creditors

Finished goods Inventory items completed and ready for sale

First-in, first-out (FIFO) An inventory cost-flow assumption that allocates the cost of units purchased first, the older units, to cost of goods sold

Fixed assets See property, plant, and equipment

Free cash flow ratio Amount of cash available for business activities after allowances for investing and financing activity requirements to maintain productive capacity at current levels

GAAP (Generally Accepted Accounting Principles) Rules that management must follow when preparing financial statements available to investors

Gains These income statement items arise from the sale of long-lived assets or investments. They are computed as the excess of the selling price over the book value of any asset sold

Goodwill Extra value that is recorded when buying another company, representing its reputation, management team, distribution system, customer base, and other intangible value

Gross Total amount

Gross profit Difference between revenues and cost of sales

Gross profit margin (GP%) Also known as gross margin, compares gross profit to revenue, expressing gross profit as a percentage of net revenue

Historical cost See acquisition cost

Income before income tax Income from operations plus or minus nonoperating items

Income from continuing operations before income tax See income before income tax

Income from operations A company's profit from its primary business operations

Income statement One of the four primary financial statements. It reports a company's profitability during an accounting period by adding revenues and gains and subtracting expenses and losses.**Income tax benefit** Benefit that reduces a company's loss as a result of federal, state, or foreign governments issuing tax refunds to the company

Income tax payable Amounts owed for income taxes

Income tax provision See provision for income tax

Initial Public Offering When a company sells stock to the public for the first time as a publicly traded corporation

Intangible assets Include patents, trademarks, and copyrights that have value, but not any physical presence

International Accounting Standards Board (IASB)   The organization that establishes International Financial Reporting Standards

International Financial Reporting Standards (IFRS)   A set of global accounting standards adopted in many countries throughout the world.   These standards are set by the International Accounting Standards Board

Inventories   Merchandise held for sale to customers

Inventory days   The average number of days it takes for a company to sell inventory

Inventory turnover ratio   Indicates the number of times a company sells its average inventory level during the year

Investing activities   A section of the statement of cash flows that reports cash used to purchase and sell property, plant, and equipment and investments in securities offered by other companies

Investments   Purchasing stock, bonds, and other types of securities of other companies

Issue   Selling stock shares to investors in exchange for assets, usually cash

Journal   A book listing the accounts affected by each transaction recorded by a company

Last-in, first-out (LIFO)   An inventory cost-flow assumption that allocates the last (most recent) units purchased to cost of goods sold

Ledger   In an accounting system, a book with one page for each account, keeping track of the balance or amount in each account

Liabilities   Amounts owed to creditors; the amount of debt owed to third parties. Typical liability accounts include accounts payable, wages payable, notes payable, and bonds payable

Limited partnership   A type of business organization that issues limited partnership units rather than stock

Liquidity   Describes a company's ability to pay liabilities as they come due in the next year

Long-term debt   Bank loans that are due over more than one year

Long-term investment   An investment that the company intends to sell after one year

Losses   These income statement items arise from the sale of long-lived assets or investments. They are computed as the shortfall of the selling price less the book value of any asset sold

Mark-to-market   Current or long-term investments reported on the balance sheet at their most recent stock market price

Market value per share   The stock market trading price of the company's common stock

Matching principle   Recording expenses in the period they help generate revenues. A basic principle of accrual accounting

Multistep income statement   Income statement format that lists items in order of importance; revenues and cost of sales, which are deemed most important, are listed at the top. These are followed by operating expenses, nonoperating items, the provision for income tax, and nonrecurring Items.

Net income   The difference between revenues and expenses. Net income is also referred to as profit (loss), earnings, or the bottom line

Net sales   Revenues minus total discounts and other deductions

Noncurrent assets   All assets not listed as current

Noncurrent liabilities   Liabilities due after 12 months

Nonrecurring items   Items that accountants deem unusual and infrequent

Notes to the financial statements   Detailed disclosures reported after the financial statements in the annual report

Operating activities   A section of the statement of cash flows that reports cash transactions related to a company's main business; selling products or services to earn net income

Operating expenses   Costs of generating sales besides cost of sales

Operating income   Gross profit minus operating expenses

Original cost   See acquisition cost

Other comprehensive income (loss)   Additions to or subtractions from net income, consisting primarily of three specific types of items that are not recorded on the income statement.

Par value   Legal value assigned to each share of stock

PCAOB (Public Company Accounting Oversight Board)   Establishes auditing standards and conducts inspections of the public accounting firms that perform audits

Permanent accounts   Balance sheet accounts

Post-retirement benefit liability   Estimate of amount owed for pensions and health-care benefits expected to be paid to workers after they retire

Post-retirement benefits   Pensions and health-care benefits given to workers after they retire

Posting   Copying each of the journal entries to the appropriate ledger account, noting whether the account is debited or credited

PP&E, net   See book value.

Preferred stock   Provides a specific dividend that is paid before any dividends are paid to common stock holders, and which takes precedence over common stock in the event of a liquidation

Price earnings (P/E) ratio   Measure how "expensive" a company's stock is compared to EPS

Principal   Amount due when a loan matures

Productivity   Measures how efficiently you can generate desired outputs from given inputs

Projects in progress   Fixed assets that are being constructed

Property, plant, and equipment   Attractions, buildings, equipment, and land; long-term assets expected to benefit future years

Provision for excess and obsolete inventories   Estimate of the value of inventory no longer saleable, or saleable for less than its historical cost.

Provision for income tax   Income tax expense

Public offering, initial (IPO)   A company who sells stock to the public for the first time as a publicly traded corporation

Publicly traded   Shares bought and sold on stock exchanges

Quality of income ratio   Compares cash flows from operating activities to net income

Raw materials   Materials to be used in the manufacturing process

Realized gains and losses   When a security is actually sold and the proceeds have been realized

Receivables   Monies to be received by the company from customers

Residual value   Estimated value of a long-term asset being depreciated at the end of its estimated useful life

Retained earnings   Net income earned by the company since its incorporation and not yet distributed as dividends

Return on asset (ROA) ratio   Reveals how efficiently assets are used to generate profit (net income)

Return on equity (ROE) ratio   Measures how effectively stockholders' equity is used to produce net income

Return on sales (ROS)   Measures the profitability of each dollar of revenue; how well expenses are kept under control

Revenue recognition principle   Revenues are recorded in the period earned, not necessarily in the period that the company collects the money. A basic principle of accrual accounting.

Revenues   Amounts received from customers for products sold or services provided

Sales   Revenues from the sale of merchandise; common way of referring to sales revenue

Sales revenue   Amounts earned engaging in the primary business activity

Salvage value   See residual value

Scrap value   See residual value

SEC (Securities and Exchange Commission)   Holds legislative authority to set the reporting rules for accounting information of publicly-held corporations

Service revenue   Amounts earned engaging in the primary business activity that involves providing services

Shareholders' equity   See stockholders' equity

Shares authorized   The maximum number of shares that a corporation is permitted to print

Shares outstanding   Total number of shares actually held by investors at a given time, which equals the number of shares issued less the number of shares of treasury stock that were bought back by the company

Short-term investment   An investment intended to be sold within one year

Single-step income statement   Combines all revenues and gains at the top of the income statement and then subtracts all expenses and losses below

Solvency   Describes a company's ability to pay liabilities back long-term debt when due.

Specific identification inventory method   Inventory method used to track when each and every inventory item was purchased and sold

Statement of cash flows   One of the four primary financial statements. It reports cash inflows and cash outflows during an accounting period

Statement of earnings   See income statement

Statement of financial position   See balance sheet

Statement of income   See income statement

Statement of operations   See income statement

Statement of profit and loss   See income statement

Statement of stockholders' equity   One of the four primary financial statements. It provides information about changes in a company's stockholders' equity, including contributed capital and retained earnings. It helps investors understand the structure of a company's ownership.

Stock   Represents a portion of the ownership of a corporation, for example common stock or preferred stock

Stock dividends   Shares of common stock issued that proportionately increase the number of shares outstanding. Sometimes issued in lieu of a cash dividend.

Stock options   Contracts that give their holders the right to buy or sell shares of stock at a certain price

Stock splits   Proportional increases in the number of shares outstanding

Stockholders   Entities owning shares of stock; owners of a corporation; also referred to as shareholders

Stockholders' equity   The portion of assets the owners own free and clear of any liabilities; may also be referred to as shareholders' equity or owners' equity

Straight-line (SL) depreciation method   Depreciates out equally over all periods

Temporary accounts   All income statement accounts and dividends

Times-interest-earned ratio   Measures a company's ability to earn (cover) its periodic interest payments

Trading securities Securities bought and sold with the objective of generating profits on short-term differences in price

Transaction An event that affects the financial position of an enterprise

Treasury stock When corporations buy back shares of stock from investors

Trend analysis An analysis that compares amounts of a more recent year to a base year, the earliest year being studied. The analysis measures the percentage of change from the base year and indicates growth trends for a company. To compute the trend index, divide the amount reported for each account by the amount reported for the base year and multiply by 100

Trial balance Within an accounting system, a list of all accounts in the ledger, with their balances

Unearned royalties Includes prepaid amounts from subscribers and advance sales

Unrealized gains and losses Change in market price during an accounting period

Warranty payable Estimate of amounts that will be owed to customers for product warranties

Work in process Partially completed units of inventory that have entered the assembly line, but have not yet been completed

Write-off Taking bad debt off of a company's books

INDEX